Child Welfare and Rights

This book examines jurisdictional differences in the role of the principle of the welfare interests of the child in common and civil law and focuses on differences within these two legal traditions.

By identifying and analysing the functions of the principle both in the public and private sector of family law, the book compares and contrasts different jurisdictions and assesses their capacity to implement children's welfare interests and rights. Covering a variety of topics including child abuse and neglect, state care, adoption and reproductive rights and family breakdown, the book demonstrates how welfare interests and rights can be balanced to create a coherent framework for family law.

In addition to providing an up-to-date digest of cases and legislation, the book will be of interest to researchers in the field of child welfare and family law.

Kerry O'Halloran, a professionally qualified lawyer, social worker and academic, has recently retired from 13 years as Adjunct Professor to the Australian Centre for Philanthropy and Nonprofit Studies at QUT, Brisbane. In Northern Ireland, he served on the Social Care Tribunal and on a HSS Trust Adoption Panel, advised the Irish government on law reform matters and served in a consultancy capacity to government bodies such as Courts Services (Northern Ireland) and to the Open University in England. Previously employed as Assistant Director (Research) at the Centre for Voluntary Action, University of Ulster in Northern Ireland, his 30 books and many other publications include *Conscientious Objection* (Springer, 2022), *The Politics of Adoption, 4th ed* (Springer, 2021), *Adoption Law and Human Rights: International Perspectives* (Routledge, 2018), *Religion, Charity and Human Rights* (CUP, 2014) and *Child Care and Protection: the Law & Practice in Northern Ireland* (Thompson Reuters, 2003).

Children and the Law

The Principle of the Welfare of the Child
A History
Kerry O'Halloran

Children & the Law
Shaping the Modern Welfare Principle in the British Isles
Kerry O'Halloran

Children, the Law and the Welfare Principle
Perspectives from North America
Kerry O'Halloran

Children, the Law and the Welfare Principle
Perspectives from Australia & New Zealand
Kerry O'Halloran

Children, the Law and the Welfare Principle
Civil Law Perspectives from France and Germany
Kerry O'Halloran

Children, the Law and the Welfare Principle
European Judicial Perspectives
Kerry O'Halloran

Child Welfare and Rights
Differences in Common Law and Civil Law Perspectives
Kerry O'Halloran

For more information about this series, please visit: https://www.routledge.com/Children-and-the-Law/book-series/CHILDLAW

Child Welfare and Rights

Differences in Common Law and Civil Law Perspectives

Kerry O'Halloran

Routledge
Taylor & Francis Group
LONDON AND NEW YORK

First published 2025
by Routledge
4 Park Square, Milton Park, Abingdon, Oxon OX14 4RN

and by Routledge
605 Third Avenue, New York, NY 10158

Routledge is an imprint of the Taylor & Francis Group, an informa business

British Library Cataloguing-in-Publication Data
A catalogue record for this book is available from the British Library

Library of Congress Cataloging-in-Publication Data
Names: O'Halloran, Kerry, author.
Title: Child welfare and rights : differences in common law and civil law perspectives / Kerry O'Halloran.
Description: Abingdon, Oxon [UK] ; New York, NY : Routledge, 2024. | Series: Children and the law | Includes bibliographical references and index.
Identifiers: LCCN 2024015578 (print) | LCCN 2024015579 (ebook) | ISBN 9781032216928 (hardback) | ISBN 9781032216935 (paperback) | ISBN 9781003269595 (ebook)
Subjects: LCSH: Children's rights. | Children—Legal status, laws, etc. | Child welfare | Common law. | Civil law.
Classification: LCC K639 .O35 2024 (print) | LCC K639 (ebook) | DDC 342.08/772—dc23/eng/20240409
LC record available at https://lccn.loc.gov/2024015578
LC ebook record available at https://lccn.loc.gov/2024015579

ISBN: 978-1-032-21692-8 (hbk)
ISBN: 978-1-032-21693-5 (pbk)
ISBN: 978-1-003-26959-5 (ebk)

DOI: 10.4324/9781003269595

Typeset in Times New Roman
by Apex CoVantage, LLC

To Elizabeth with love and thanks for your patience

Contents

Introduction

In this, the seventh and penultimate book of the series,[1] the focus is on characteristic jurisdictional differences in the role of the welfare principle and the recognition given to rights in the law relating to children in the six common law and two civil law nations that have been the subject of this enquiry. In the light of the data derived from the eight jurisdictional[2] profiles – on how the balance between the public and private sectors of family law has changed – it considers the implications arising for children's welfare/rights and the extent to which this reflects differences in the common law and civil law traditions.

Like its predecessors, this book continues to examine the central theme of the welfare principle. However, the concern is now less with the content and application of the principle and more with its changing role. Drawing from the jurisdictional material, it sifts and analyses the evidence that the additional leverage acquired by the principle – in some instances being transformed from welfare to rights – has fundamentally altered the balance in the nexus of state-family-child relationships. This alignment is itself a relatively recent development. For most of the 18th, 19th and 20th centuries, that balance would have been viewed as confined to state and family (the latter meaning parents or, for most of that period, the patriarchal head of the household) and as heavily weighted in favour of the state. From the mid-20th century, as the role of the state shrank, the 'family' became less marital and more impermanent, and a human rights 'ideology' fragmented collective entities into independent rights-bearing units, so also did the interests of children begin to emerge as separate and distinct from those of their parents. As with so many other areas impacted by human rights, this reductionist dynamic switched the legal focus from the whole to its parts, generating something resembling a competition for

1 O'Halloran, K., *The Principle of the Welfare of the Child: A History*, Routledge, Abingdon, Oxon, England 2022; *Children & the Law: Shaping the Modern Welfare Principle in the British Isles*, Routledge, 2022; *Children, the Law and the Welfare Principle: Perspectives from North America*, Routledge, 2023; *Children, the Law and the Welfare Principle: Perspectives from Australia and New Zealand*, Routledge, 2023; *Children, the Law and the Welfare Principle: Civil Law Perspectives from France and Germany*, Routledge, 2024; and *Children, the Law and the Welfare Principle: European Judicial Perspectives*, Routledge, 2024.

2 The UK, Ireland, the U.S. and Canada, Australia, New Zealand, France and Germany.

DOI: 10.4324/9781003269595-1

equality among those parts. In this instance, the switch has been from a coherent integrated body of family law to a reconfiguration of the interests of children with those of parents and state: a configuration that varies according to legal and cultural context. While recognition is now given to the distinctive interests of a child, the weighting accorded to their rights or their welfare depends upon whether the context is framed by criminal or civil law and in the latter instance, whether the issue is predominately public or private in nature. The blurring of the boundaries between the latter two categories is itself an evolving feature of current changes to family law and one which is considered in the next and final book in this series.

Initially, a child was recognised in law solely as the bearer of 'welfare interests' which most often required attention as a consequence of having suffered collateral damage due to family dysfunction. Confirmation of and protection for those interests then led to children being accommodated in the facilities of church and state and in due course to representation and political lobbying on behalf of those interests by voluntary organisations.[3] When brought to the attention of judicial or other authorities, in any of a range of public or private family law proceedings, a child's welfare interests were treated cursorily, mainly as indicating an entitlement to protection. This approach began changing in the post-WWII period when the contribution of developmental child psychology injected an awareness of the significance a child's individuality – their emotional attachments, experiences and particular needs – and with it came a corresponding necessity to treat him or her as the subject rather than the object of proceedings.[4] Further change came with the trickle-down effects of civil rights, human rights and basic principles of justice transmitted through international treaties, conventions and protocols. Equality, non-discrimination and rights to identity, privacy, health, education, etc., inevitably came to be applied – if slowly and with equivocation – to children and to clarify, redefine and, in some instances, confer rights in regard to their relationships with others. These developments would have been enough to transform the *locus standi* of children in relation to their parents and others, but it was the relatively sudden collapse of the marital family unit – ongoing since the latter part of the 20th century – that accelerated fundamental change.

As marital status became increasingly dispensable, accompanied by disrupted and serial parenting arrangements, the resulting volume of family law disputes threatened to both overwhelm the legal system and to jeopardise the welfare interests of the very many children affected by parental decision-making. The state response – as in so many other areas of established public service provision – was to privatise the problem. A rising tide of family litigation, coinciding with depleted state resources, caused the state to retreat from the family by redrawing public-private

3 In the UK, such organisations as the Infant Life Protection Society, the Children's Friendly Society, Barnardos and the National Society for the Prevention of Cruelty to Children.

4 Such as the following: Bettelheim, B., *Love Is Not Enough*, Macmillan, New York, 1950; Bowlby, J., *Attachment and Loss*, Basic Books, New York, 1969; Piaget, J., *The Psychology of the Child*, Basic Books, New York, 1972; Goldstein, J., Freud, A. and Solnit, A., *Beyond the Best Interests of the Child*, Free Press, New York, 1974; and Mnookin, R.H., *In the Interest of Children*, W.H. Freeman and Company, New York, 1985.

family law boundaries, capping the finances for resourcing judicial arbitration of family disputes and diverting much of the latter from the courts to mediatory agencies. Family law in general would leave parents to make their own private parenting arrangements which would be of public interest only if they gave rise to evidence of possible adverse consequences for the welfare of any children involved. The centre of gravity in family law switched from parents to their children. Child care and protection, rather than marital family issues, became the state's priority.

The main outcomes of this state retreat from private to public family law matters can be seen in a rise in the legal salience accorded to children's interests – some being given the additional legal weighting of 'paramountcy', others transformed from a concern for welfare to respect for rights – and the resulting structural change to family law. Firstly, the vulnerability of children to harm by parental decision-making led to recognition of certain rights: those that are positive, such as to physical integrity, family life and to maintain contact with their parents and siblings, and those more negative, including not to be neglected or abused. Secondly, the disaggregation (for some but not all purposes) of a child's legal interests from those of their parents required structural changes to family law, the recognition of party status for children in certain proceedings and the consequent acknowledgment that the state-family balance would (again, for some but not all purposes) need to be adjusted to allow for separate representation to be given to the interests of children. These changes were aided and abetted by international law, not least by the provisions of UN CROC and rulings of the ECtHR.

The purpose of this series has been to examine changes in the role of the principle of the welfare interests of the child in the law relating to children: identify the legal indices of child welfare and child rights; compare and contrast how these are distributed in the laws of sampled countries; use that information to consider how, why and to what effect some countries are changing the balance struck in the relationships between the interests of state, family and child; and consider the implications arising for family law. This book examines the nature and extent of jurisdictional differences in the laws governing the welfare interests and rights of children. In so doing, it prepares the ground for the final book which looks beyond the indices of welfare and rights to consider how the changes from the first to the second are affecting family law as a whole. It is an exercise that proceeds on the basis that as all eight countries subscribe to much the same law governing the welfare interests/rights of the child (all but the U.S. being signatories to UN CROC, the U.S. and Canada being, naturally, non-signatories to the ECHR, but all eight subscribing to a raft of other relevant international instruments), a comparative analysis of their functioning, benchmarked against the same set of principles, is reasonable. This follows the well-established relativist approach that accepts a high degree of congruity subsists among the northwestern Atlantic nations in their acceptance of international human rights law.[5]

5 See, for example, *Rae v. SA* (2022) EWHC 3095 (Admin) in which the court affirmed that ECHR standards can apply to non-contracting states.

Constructed in five parts, the book looks for such patterns as may be found in the themes and their jurisdictional differences as identified in its six predecessors by considering in broad terms how the relationship between parents and the welfare/rights of children has changed in recent years and what this has meant for the consensual/coercive balance in state interventionism. Then it examines jurisdictional differences: firstly, in the context of public family law, then in its private counterpart, leaving to the next and final book a consideration of the nature and extent of the impact made by the ever-growing range of public-private, or hybrid, proceedings on family law coherence. It reflects on the extent to which jurisdictional differences may be attributable to deeply embedded differences between the common law and civil law traditions.

Part I – 'Family, the law and the welfare rights of children' – begins the book in one chapter and in general terms by laying the foundations for the more particular comparative analysis of how the welfare interests and rights of children are interpreted and balanced in the family law of the eight jurisdictions. Chapter 1 – *Family, the law and social context* – examines the modern family. It asks what is now understood to be 'a family', who the constituent parties are and what exactly defines 'family life' for the purposes of contemporary family law.

Part II – 'Children's welfare interests and rights in a public family law context – civil and criminal' – is in three chapters, each focusing on a function of the welfare principle and each differentiating between the common and civil law traditions as regards the functioning of that principle. Chapter 2 – *Prevention: children and families in need* – considers the extent to which the state has a duty to prevent harm to children and to support vulnerable families: the consensual threshold for state intervention. Chapter 3 – *Protection: child abuse and neglect* – deals with what is now the heartland of public family law 'child protection': the coercive threshold for state intervention. Chapter 4 – *Control: juvenile justice and state care* – addresses the issues that arise for the welfare and rights of children following their entry into the state welfare and justice systems.

Part III – 'Children's welfare interests and rights in a private family law context' – is in four chapters. Chapter 5 – *Reproductive rights* – this is the most rapidly evolving area of law, fraught with moral and legal complications, that is in the process of becoming regulated but again very unevenly. Chapter 6 – *Founding families and family life* – starts by examining these two basic constructs that underpin so much of ECtHR rulings on state-family-child relationships and constitute the contemporary foundations of private family law. Chapter 7 – *Adoption* – this area of private family law has changed greatly in recent years but with considerable jurisdictional variation. Chapter 8 – *Family breakdown and parenting arrangements* – is concerned with what is the most important area of private family law for the welfare interests of children: the steady increase in family breakdown, marital and non-marital, which brings a corresponding increase in parental disputes regarding care arrangements for their children.

Part IV – 'Coherence – balancing welfare interests and rights' – is in one chapter. Chapter 9 – *Themes: comparative jurisdictional analysis; common law and civil law differences* – reflects on the material in this and the previous books in the series to draw some tentative conclusions regarding themes and patterns affecting the changing balance between children's welfare interests and rights and considers how these changes are affecting family law coherence.

Finally – the Conclusion – closes the book by summarising the main emerging jurisdictional differences and speculating on their possible significance for the future. It leaves a consideration of the impact of a growing volume of hybrid, or mixed private and public proceedings, on family law as a whole to the final book.

Part I

Family, the law and the welfare rights of children

1 Family, the law and social context

Introduction

The social construct 'family' is of central importance to the law governing children. It is also key to the balance struck between child welfare interests and rights, to the relationship between the state and the health and wellbeing of children and to family law as a body of jurisprudence. It has, however, been exposed to seminal changes in recent years: changes that have seen traditional aspects of private family law[1] slip into the public domain, while some from both have blended to create a new hybrid public-private sector. Any assessment of how, why and to what effect the law relating to children has shifted from an emphasis on protecting welfare interests to asserting rights and any attempt to weigh the resulting implications for family law must start from a basis of appreciating the nature and significance of changes affecting the family.

This opening chapter of the penultimate book in the series begins, therefore, by examining 'the family' and the nature and effect of those changes. This, necessarily, also requires an examination of the context, specifically the family law framework. The systems for the application of that law and its role and functions in relation to the family are clearly crucial. In conducting such an examination, this chapter returns to some basic concepts and constructs identified in Book 1 in order to review the significance of the changes and their consequences for the law relating to children and to the balance of public and private provisions that constitute the body of family law.

The family

The two civil and six common law jurisdictions studied in this series all have their origins in Judeo Christianity, meaning that for centuries, they have shared and been shaped by the same set of beliefs and values and have developed not dissimilar cultures. Central to that culture, for millennia, have been the twin constructs of Christianity and the marital family.[2]

1 See, Rawls, J., *Justice as Fairness*, Harvard University Press, Cambridge, 2001.
2 See, further, O'Halloran, K., *Children & the Law: Shaping the Modern Welfare Principle in the British Isles*, Routledge, 2022, Chapter 3.

DOI: 10.4324/9781003269595-3

Christianity, the state and the family

The symbiotic relationship between Christianity and the marital family was such that when the former began to lose its place as the main pillar of western society, so, too, did the latter. The social mores that had legitimated the marital family for countless generations, and proscribed or at least socially marginalised all other family forms, began to give way in the mid-20th century. As Christianity began to fade, many more religions came to share the same space, and the irreligious proportion of the population steadily expanded.

Moral imperatives and the family: a joint enterprise of church and state

Moral imperatives were always prominent in the law relating to the family: generally as regards marriage and procreation but particularly so in relation to sexuality; their importance to both church and state was underpinned by transgressions – such as blasphemy or heresy – being labelled as a 'sin' by one and punished as a criminal offence by the other. For centuries, the legal status of marriage, founded on the monogamous commitment of heterosexual spouses, was upheld by church and state as an inviolable building block for constructing a sound Christian society. Christian principles established certain 'moral imperatives' that came to inform the law relating to the family and continued to provide the grounds for sustaining such traditional religious beliefs as that marriage was to be monogamous, heterosexual and for life. As Lord Finlay LC commented in *Bowman v. Secular Society Ltd.*, when reflecting on previous centuries of caselaw:[3]

> It has been repeatedly laid down by the Courts that Christianity is part of the law of the land, and it is the fact that our civil polity is to a large extent based upon the Christian religion. This is notably so with regard to the law of marriage and the law affecting the family.[4]

This morality imprinted on the common law nations – and also on their civil law counterparts – a shared understanding of marriage and family. It was not only embedded in the body of family law but was infused throughout the language, the culture and the institutional infrastructure of schools, workplaces and health and social care systems. It deeply affected all citizens – whether or not they were religious.[5] It was an ethos within which children remained legally subject to, and for most purposes assimilated within, the social and legal status of their parents.

3 (1917) AC 406 (H.L.).

4 Ibid, citing: *Briggs v. Hartley* (1850) 19 L. J. (Ch.) 416; *Cowan v. Milbourn* (1867) L. R. 2 Ex. 230; *De Costa v. De Paz* (1754) 2 Swanst, 487; and *In re Bedford Charity* (1819) 2 Swanst. 470, 527.

5 Laws LJ acknowledged as much in *McFarlane v. Relate Avon Ltd.* (2010) IRLR 872; 29 BHRC 249 when he observed that 'the Judaeo-Christian tradition, stretching over many centuries, has no doubt exerted a profound influence upon the judgment of lawmakers as to the objective merits of this or that social policy' at para 23.

Marriage and family

Up until the middle of the 20th century, the distinctively Christian indices defining marriage and the marital family included the following: the sanctity of marriage to the exclusion of non-marital sex, any children thereof and unmarried partnerships; the criminalisation of abortion, homosexuality and suicide; and the rejection of a Darwinian approach to the meaning of 'life'. Both church and state viewed the marital bond as of fundamental importance. It bound the spouses in an exclusive mutually supportive union for procreative purposes, granted legal rights to maintenance and property and provided the only context in which sexual relations and the children born thereof could be legitimate; the families and relatives of the spouses in a kinship network; and the marital family to the state as a unit that conformed to the latter's laws, thereby fulfilling a deep civic contract between family and society. Especially in a hierarchical society – where lineage, class and the orderly devolution of family estates have always been important – marriage was a key social institution. It was primarily a public rather than a private bond, and for many centuries, they were similarly regarded and policed by church and state.

Secularism and the family

By the end of that century, church and state had been largely separated and the family had ceased to be the strategic fulcrum that had enabled both to ensure the inter-generational transmission of Christian beliefs and associated values. Apart from traditional rituals, marriage and family life became secularised. By then, the state in all liberal democracies was championing social diversity and the philosophy of pluralism – a pragmatic response, perhaps, to the many migrants from minority ethnic groups who now required state recognition for their cultural identities.

This was also a period in which civil rights and the ever-extending reach of human rights jurisprudence was questioning the second-class citizenship of socially marginalised groups. While the Indigenous populations in the CANZUS nations presented, and continue to present, the most stark evidence of being discriminated against by being denied the legal status and associated rights of other citizens,[6] recognition and redress came more quickly in respect of gender disparity and for those suffering inequality of treatment due, for example, to disability, age or ethnicity. It was a context which prepared the ground for recognition of the inferior status of children and of the need to distinguish – and at times separate – a child's interests from those of their parents.[7]

6 See, further, O'Halloran, K., *Children, the Law and the Welfare Principle: Perspectives from North America*, Routledge, 2023, Chapter 8 and *Children, the Law and the Welfare Principle: Perspectives from Australia and New Zealand*, Routledge, 2023, Chapters 9 and 10.

7 See, for example, Piaget, J., *The Moral Judgment of the Child*, Kegan Paul, Trench, Trubner and Co., London, 1932; Kohlberg, L., *The Philosophy of Moral Development*, Harper and Row, New York, 1981.

The 'family' in a post-Christian era

Change impacted the marital 'family' and its twin traditional social institution, 'religion', at much the same time and in much the same way. From being of central significance to society for millennia, both have morphed into different forms in the space of the last few generations, have been heavily influenced by cultural context in that process and have shed such former key immutable characteristics as male leadership, lifelong commitment and the unanimity of social endorsement. The loss or fading significance of the two institutions that bridged the state/citizen gap is unmistakable and has certainly undermined social cohesion, though whether this is the cause or effect of current national identity issues, political populism and uncertainty regarding the balance between the interests of state, child and family is open to debate.

Family forms

The contemporary diversity and mutation of family forms provide a striking contrast with the legally and religiously prescribed 'marital family' that was the ubiquitous norm until the latter part of the 20th century. The causes of the diversity are many, but probable key generators of change would include greater longevity, falling fertility rates, more relationship permissiveness, expensive housing, both parents working and de-gendered parenting. This would seem to have resulted in fewer independent nuclear family units and many more vertical (inter-generational, grandparents, etc.) and horizontal (same generation, cousins, etc.) households. There are also many same-sex married and unmarried couples and an increasing number of single parents. The most striking change, however, is the mutation in family forms, where families are reconstituted sometimes repeatedly as adults change partners and children are exposed to serial in-house or distant parenting arrangements.

While in fact 'family' continues to be largely represented by the nuclear marital family of 2.4 children, a variety of other forms now exist alongside, and these are growing to constitute a sizeable proportion of total households.[8] Included among those many different forms are relatives, such as grandparents caring for children; foster parents and adopters; and children born through surrogacy arrangements and their commissioning parents.[9]

By way of contrast, it might be added that the nuclear family is not, and has never been, the norm in some communities – such as in the Indigenous communities of the CANZUS nations – where the extended family circle can include aunts, uncles and grandparents, who share child rearing responsibilities. Even in Ireland, vestiges of its traditional clan system linger to give a broader sense of 'family' and an awareness of where any one unit fits within the network of

8 See, further, O'Halloran, K., *Children, the Law and the Welfare Principle: European Judicial Perspectives*, Routledge, 2024.

9 Ibid.

blood relations. Cultural diaspora – accelerated by the migrant 'crisis' that began in 2015 – has also played a part by enlarging ethnic groups and consolidating their cultural norms as regards family life, within western society (see, further, Chapter 9).

Definitional matters

Contemporary families and family life are not as they once were. The basic concept and its constituent parts have been transformed.

Definition of 'parent'

Developments in the medical science associated with reproductive techniques is such that establishing who is or is not a parent in relation to a particular child has now become, in some instances, quite complicated.

Determining the legal status of 'mother' is not as straightforward as formerly.[10] The outcome of a recent cases in the UK[11] was a Court of Appeal ruling that motherhood is defined by the role a person plays in the biological process of conception, pregnancy and birth regardless of whether that person is legally considered to be a man or a woman. As McFarlane P then acknowledged, 'it is now medically and legally possible for an individual, whose gender is recognised in law as male, to become pregnant and give birth to their child'.[12] The result being that a trans person (FTM) had to be registered as the 'mother' of his child. Surrogacy caselaw, in particular, has done much to elucidate and warn of the risks inherent in relying on the traditional maxim *mater semper certa est* (the mother is always certain), as, in many cases, she will have no genetic link with the child.[13] Indeed, that link may well be primarily with an anonymous sperm donor. It has been pointed out that in such cases, the child may have up to five 'parents' (the commissioning couple, surrogate and partner and donor).

Determining the legal status of 'father' is also not without its problems. While the law struggles to hold onto its conviction regarding the certainty of maternity, it is having to concede that paternity and fatherhood may well be separable. Given the number of sperm donors, any one of whom may genetically but anonymously contribute to dozens of births, the potential for that contribution to be transformed into parental responsibility with associated legal accountability is virtually nil.

10 See, for example, Deery, C., 'Male Mothers: The Law's Struggle to Capture the Modern Family', *The Oxford University Undergraduate Law Journal*, No. X (2021), at: www.law.ox.ac.uk/sites/default/files/migrated/public_law_3.pdf

11 See: *R (TT) v. Registrar General for England and Wales (AIRE Centre intervening)* (2019) EWHC 2384 (Fam) (2020) Fam 45; *R (McConnell and YY) v. Registrar General* (2020) EWCA Civ 559 (2020) 2 All ER 813; and *R (McConnell and YY) v. Registrar General* UKSC 2020/0092.

12 Ibid, EWHC, at para 279.

13 See, further, Welstead, M., 'Every Child Should Have a Mother', *Fam Law,* Vol. 1099 (2020), p. 1102.

The centuries-long judicial pursuit of the 'ill-intentioned begetter of children' – or unmarried father – in order that his paternity be publicly established and his parental responsibilities privately confirmed has been turned on its head: such a person may now claim to be performing a public service. For the many same-sex couples wishing to create family life, such developments in medical science are an immeasurable benefit, but they are clearly compromising for the child wanting to exercise their rights to an authentic identity and parental contact.

Definition of 'child'

An anomalous aspect of family law is the absence of any hard-and-fast rules as to the definition of something as basic as who qualifies as a 'child'. Leaving aside the contentious arguments revolving around the status of embryos and foetuses, which are a polarising aspect of the culture wars in some countries, there are many more mundane areas of uncertainty.

Examples of the lack of consistency in determining who is or is not 'a child' for the purpose of legal proceedings are present in all jurisdictions. In most countries and for most purposes, a child is someone who has not attained their 18th birthday, and this definition is embedded in the UN CROC, Article 1. However, in New Zealand, for example, a 'child' is defined as such until he or she reaches 20 years of age, and in Canada, a minor is so defined until the age of 19. In England and Wales under the 1989 Act, such a person must be below the age of 16 years for the purposes of a s 8 order,[14] below 17 in respect of a care or supervision order[15] and is otherwise taken to mean a person below the age of 18 years. In both France and Germany, there is no age criterion for adoption: 'simple' adoptions are available to persons of any age (though children, under 18, are now restricted to plenary adoptions in Germany). Children in the latter country – aged 13 years of age or younger – cannot be held criminally liable and cannot be prosecuted as a juvenile offender if less than 18 years of age, though in France, a child aged 10 may be tried in a criminal court and from the age of 13 will be treated in law as an adult and as such may be jailed. A Canadian child becomes criminally liable for his or her behaviour at 12 years of age, while in the U.S., it is mostly at age 7, though for federal crimes liability is at age 11. In Germany, youth offenders will be treated as juveniles until they reach 21 years of age, so an offender aged between 18 and 20 will fall within the remit of the juvenile justice rather than the adult justice system, which is a significant extension of the definition and protection assigned to the status of 'child'. By way of contrast, both the Canadian and the U.S. juvenile justice systems define those more than 18 years of age and accused of grave offences as being outside their jurisdiction, though there can be wide variation as to how this is interpreted at state and provincial levels.

14 See, s 9(6).
15 See, s 31(3).

Definition of 'family life'

'Family life', as defined by the ECtHR, is the mutual enjoyment by parent and child of each other's company.[16] Article 8 of the ECHR, reinforced by Article 7 of the EU Charter of Fundamental Rights, requires respect for a person's private and family life, their home and correspondence.[17] Such respect[18] presupposes the existence of a family[19] or at the very least the potential relationship between, for example, a child born[20] to unmarried parents and his or her birth father,[21] or the relationship that arises from a genuine marriage, even if family life has not yet been fully established,[22] or the relationship that arises from a lawful and genuine adoption.[23] In fact, the Court has extended its recognition to encompass arrangements that were illegal at the outset but endured for ten years.[24]

As Kilkelly[25] has pointed out, the ECtHR has found 'family life' to be present in the nexus of a parent-and-child relationship, 'in all but very exceptional cases regardless of the parents' marital status,[26] the family's living arrangements,[27] or their apparent lack of commitment to their children'.[28] Adding that 'family life may exist between children and their grandparents,[29] between siblings,[30] between an uncle and his nephew,[31] and between parents and children born into second

16 See, *W., B. and R. v. the United Kingdom*, Application No. 121 (1987); *Olsson v. Sweden*, Application No. 10465/83, Series A No. 130, 11 EHRR 259; *Eriksson v. Sweden*, Application No. 156 (1989); *Margareta and Roger Andersson v. Sweden*, Application No. 226-A (1992); *McMichael v. the United Kingdom*, Application No. 307-B (1995); *Johansen v. Norway* (1996) 23 EHRR 33; *Bronda v. Italy*, 9 June 1998, *Reports* 1998-IV; and *Buscemi v. Italy*, Application No. 29569/95, ECHR 1999-VI.

17 See, further, O'Halloran, K., *Children, the Law and the Welfare Principle: European Judicial Perspectives*, Routledge, 2024.

18 See, *V.D. and Others v. Russia*, Application No. 72931/10 (2019).

19 See, *Marckx v. Belgium*, *op cit*.

20 An unborn child would not qualify: *Paton v. The United Kingdom*, Application No. 8416/78 (1981).

21 See, *Nylund v. Finland* (dec.), Application No. 27110/95 (1999).

22 See, *Abdulaziz, Cabales and Balkandali v. the United Kingdom*, Application Nos. 9214/80; 9473/81; 9474/81 (1985).

23 See, *Pini and Others v. Romania*, Application Nos. 78028/01 and 78030/01 (2004).

24 See, *Wagner and J.M.W.L. v. Luxembourg*, Application No. 76240/01 (2007).

25 See, Kilkelly, U., 'Child and Family Law', in Kilkelly (ed.), *ECHR and Irish Law*, Jordans, 2004, p. 112.

26 See, *Marckx v. Belgium ibid* (unmarried mother and her child); *Johnston v. Ireland*, No. 9697/92, Series A No. 12 (1987) 9 EHRR 203 (unmarried parents and their child).

27 See, *Berrehab v. Netherlands*, No. 10730/84, Series A No. 138 (1988) 11 EHRR 322.

28 See, *C v. Belgium*, Application No. 21794/93 (1996) and *Ahmut v. Netherlands*, Application No. 21702/93 (1996). See, also, *Söderbäck v. Sweden*, Application No. 24484/94 (1998). However, purely genetic relationships – such as the relationship between a sperm donor and the child born as a result – are unlikely to constitute family life. See, *G v. Netherlands*, Application No. 16944/90 (1993).

29 See, *Marckx v. Belgium*, *op cit*, at para 45.

30 See, *Olsson v. Sweden*, Application No.10465/83, Series A No. 130, 11 EHRR 259. See also *Boughanemi v. France*, Application No. 22070/93, Reports 1996-II, No. 8, p. 593, 22 EHRR 228.

31 See, *Boyle v. UK*, Application No. 16580/90, Comm Rep, 9.2.93.

relationships'.[32] It may also be found in the relationship between an unmarried father and his child,[33] adopters and child,[34] foster parent and child,[35] same-sex relationships and child[36] and in the relationship between commissioning parents and a child born through surrogacy arrangements.[37]

The law: legal system and public services

The identity of a society is to be found in its culture, values and all other attributes that give it a sense of distinctiveness, cohesion and continuity. It is this that allows its members to share a common experience of 'belonging' and distinguishes their society from all others.

Acquiring a sense of identity, as in the case of the western democracies presently studied, is usually by gradual and complex developmental progression, though for those communities that live within but apart from their host society – especially the Indigenous people in the CANZUS nations – that identity is perhaps more an inherited amalgam of custom, practice and beliefs. This series has disclosed the not-insignificant finding that the pluralism and diversity characteristic of western society brings with it identity issues – most apparent in the cultural tensions between Indigenous people and their host society – in terms of balancing the identities of marginalised ethnic groups with that of society as a whole. The welfare interests/rights of children in such groups can be compromised by the resulting culture clash between the values of the traditional patriarchal family life, characteristic of many ethnic groups (that might feature such practices as FGM, physical chastisement and the mandatory wearing of identity apparel) and national child welfare law.

Law

Law reinforces a society's identity. It plays a crucial role in legitimising the particular institutions, bodies, officials and processes that bind the constituent elements of a society and enable it to function as a coherent entity. It supports and sustains social cohesion by asserting and protecting a nation's culture and associated emblems, icons, language and traditions, by providing for the inter-generational transmission of its culture through the education system, by reinforcing its values and principles in social and family legislation, by policing its boundaries and by setting the terms for negotiation with other societies. It can also do so by virtue of

32 See, *Jolie & Lebrun v. Belgium*, Application No. 11418/85, Dec. 14.5.86, DR 47, p. 243.

33 *Johansen v. Norway* (1996) 23 EHRR 33 and *Rieme v. Sweden* (1993) 16 EHRR 155.

34 *Zait v. Romania*, Application No. 44958/05 (2015).

35 *Moretti and Benedetti v. Italy*, Application No. 16318/07 (2010).

36 *X, Y & Z v. UK*, Application No. 21830/93 (1997) and *Gas and Dubois v. France*, Application No. 2595/07 (2010).

37 *Mennesson v. France*, Application No. 65192/11 (2014).

its integrative effect. Law both authorises and operates within a system that exists to give effect to its functions.

Social order and continuity

It falls to the law to ensure the orderly working of the various institutions that comprise the social infrastructure and to regulate the mechanisms necessary for their continuance. The law establishes and maintains order by enforcing values-compliant conduct, by authorising judicial and other forums to arbitrate and mediate disputes and by establishing the related rules, processes and procedures.

Every society, however established, has a vested interest in ensuring its own continuity. The absence of grounds for a shared belief in continuity is inherently destabilising. For those self-contained communities that exist within society – Indigenous people, ethno-religious groupings of migrants, extreme religious adherents, etc. – the struggle to maintain their cultural identity, while simultaneously subscribing to that of the host society, can be profoundly challenging.

Maintaining social cohesion and providing for continuity requires the law to project its functions to some degree into the future. This it does by prescribing rules and procedures, by imposing related penalties and by adhering to custom and precedent. Together, these increase the probability of values-compliant conduct and the predictability of conformity in social functioning. Rules operate to give society clearly understood common parameters for present conduct and a basis for confidence that such conduct will be similarly provided for in the future.

Institutions

Society aims to secure continuity partly through its institutional infrastructure: the legislature promulgates laws which require a range of government agencies to give effect to them, and the courts, tribunals, commissions, boards, registrars, etc., are equipped with the powers necessary to deal with any breaches. In this way, the legal system serves to perpetuate society's established structures and policies in an ordered and coherent fashion while remaining open and responsive to change.

Principles

The capacity of law to provide social continuity is greatly facilitated by the role of principles, whether benchmarked by established precedent and proclaimed by statute as in the common law or as prescribed and codified in civil law. Principles have a most important role to play in guiding the application of law and in providing the underpinning necessary to extend that application beyond prescribed circumstances and so allow for continuity in legal practice. This is particularly the case with 'grundnorms', or overarching norms which command wide acceptance and are powerful enough to govern other principles, as posited by Kelsen (e.g. the 'paramountcy principle' in family law).[38] The moral content of a principle may justify its use in relation to a certain set of circumstances, but its validity as a component of law comes from repeated judicial endorsement, through the doctrine of precedent, and by institutional acceptance. Principles inject an added dimension to the law, lifting it beyond being merely a technical response to a particular set of circumstances and setting standards for future conduct.

Precedents

An important means of facilitating continuity of principle and practice is through the doctrine of precedent, whereby justification for a contemporary decision can be found in a similar one taken earlier. This entrenched aspect of the common law has an extensive history in the related jurisdictions and has played a crucial role in building very similar bodies of family law jurisprudence (and other areas of law) throughout the common law world. Extending the welfare/rights of children, in particular by giving recognition to the paramountcy principle, has been expedited by the transfer of established precedents and thereby made a significant contribution to the current high level of congruity in the law relating to children, at least among the common law nations.

Human rights law

The signature hallmark of human rights lies in the fact that they are vested uniformly in each human being – adult and child – and bring an entitlement: to exercise any such right in the context of relationships either with other human beings or with the state and to appeal to supra-national authorities to have that entitlement enforced should the state fail in its legal obligation to respect such rights. By the turn of the century, a multilayered international framework of laws was in place providing for equity, equality and respect for the fundamental human rights of all citizen, which have ever since been binding upon the nations currently being studied, as upon many others, and are very largely replicated in their domestic laws.

Rights/welfare interests of the child

The emphatic individualism of human rights law has done much to disaggregate the various sets of interests that constitute 'the family' and, in particular, to develop the law relating to welfare/rights of the child.[39]

The importance to the parties concerned of the relationships that constitute a family was recognised long ago by the ECtHR in a series of rulings that emphasised 'the mutual enjoyment by parent and child of each other's company constitutes a

38 See, for example, Hans Kelsen, *Pure Theory of Law*, The Lawbook Exchange Ltd., New Jersey, 2009.

39 See, further, O'Halloran, K., *Children, the Law and the Welfare Principle: Perspectives from Europe; France and Germany*, Routledge, 2023 at Chapter 3.

fundamental element of family life'.[40] The Court has also ruled that the state has a duty, once put on notice of a need for supportive intervention, to ensure the provision of such services as may be necessary to protect children and maintain family unity.[41] However, this protective approach towards the family has been counterbalanced by rulings from at least the 1980s, which establish the caveat that in any context where there is conflict between the rights and interests of the child and those of a parent which can only be resolved to the detriment of one of them, the interests of the child must prevail.[42] While continuing its recognition of welfare interests and acknowledging a blending of some such interests with those of parents, the law was also recognising that both sets of interests could in some circumstances be separated.

Legal system

A legal system[43] comprises a body of law drawn from a particular tradition (such as the common law or civil law) and from different sources (national legislation, international treaties and conventions), together with the institutions authorised to implement that law and the formal processes, procedures, forums and officials for applying it. For all societies – including the modern democracies studied in this miniseries – the legal systems have been created and operate to have an integrative effect: ordering the relationships between government and the governed, validating and policing the institutional framework, balancing and adjudicating between different sets of interests and structuring that society's internal and external relationships for the present and foreseeable future. More simply, 'a modern legal system is thus understood as a distinct set of mechanisms of government, employing rationally developed doctrine, created, interpreted and applied by state agencies'.[44] However, all those modern democracies are now characterised by social diversity, espouse a policy of pluralism and contain substantial ethnic cultural groups, not all of whom wholly subscribe to the same set of social mores. The alienation of Indigenous communities in the CANZUS nations has long represented the non-integrative effect of a national legal system.

Set of mechanisms

For the purposes of the nations surveyed in this series, the set of government mechanisms giving effect to the law relating to children and their families is formed by

40 See, for example, *K. and T. v. Finland,* Application No. 25702/94 (2001), at para 151.

41 See, for example, in *Z. and Others v. the United Kingdom,* Application No. 29392/93 (2001) and *Wallová and Walla v. the Czech Republic,* Application No. 23848/04 (2006).

42 See, for example, *Hendricks v. The Netherlands* (1982) 5 EHRR 223 and *Kroon v. The Netherlands* (1994) Series A No. 297 – C, 19 EHRR 263.

43 See, further, Hart, H.L.A., *The Concept of Law* (2nd ed.), Clarendon Law Series, Oxford University Press, Oxford, 1994, pp. 100–123.

44 Cotterrell, R., *The Sociology of Law: An Introduction*, Butterworths, London, 1984, pp. 48, 49.

an institutional framework that includes the judiciary, the child protection agencies, juvenile justice agencies, etc. For these component parts to operate as a system, however, there has to be uniformity, clarity and consistency of role in the institutions involved and a level of co-ordination, but in practice, there is considerable jurisdictional variation because, as Parsons has noted, a characteristic of developed western nations is the 'relative independence of the judiciary from both executive and legislative organs of the State'.[45] Such independence makes the legal system susceptible to a lack of cohesion that varies in accordance with the level of judicial involvement in it, with corresponding jurisdictional variation in the law as it relates to children and their families. In fact, a lack of cohesion in the legal system is likely, perhaps even more likely, when the judiciary are not so independent. Parson's observation, while largely true, is subject to the caveat implied in 'relative'.

As illustrated by recent decisions of the USSC, it is apparent that the impartiality of politically appointed judiciary on political issues can be at least suspect: ultimately, their divisiveness on politically loaded issues may reflect that of those who appointed them, thereby amplifying system instability. When the judiciary are institutionally insulated from politics, as in France, and instead of being empowered to do no more than officiate and adjudicate proceedings are intimately engaged in input and output processes, then the legal system would seem more stable. For example, the role of the *juge des enfants* with child offenders and those in need of protection in France when contrasted with that of white Caucasian judiciary and child protection social workers in Indigenous communities illustrates the importance of an independent legal system not only functioning efficiently but also of it being acceptable and accessible to the local community.

Doctrines

Internal consistency for a legal system is provided by the body of law it draws from, by the standards, principles and unifying concepts that guide its administration and by the custom and practice of the professionals that operate within it. The concepts of 'parental responsibility' of 'attachment', 'permanency planning', 'good-enough parenting' and 'significant harm' are among those which offer a doctrinal basis for achieving and maintaining such consistency in the system's relation to children and families. As with the application of a legal system to any other subject area, consistency is greatly enhanced by the manner in which law is mediated through the knowledge and experience of a specifically trained cohort of professionals. As regards the legal system as it relates to children, although each country has such a cohort, the extent to which they are sensitive to and intervene in a culturally appropriate manner with the more marginalised communities – for example, Indigenous people, Muslims and evangelical Christians – varies considerably. Not all have members of that cohort who belong to or are otherwise acceptable to those communities.

45 Parsons, T., *Structure and Process in Modern Societies*, The Free Press, New York, 1960, p. 144.

The core doctrine for present purposes is the importance that the legal system in all countries is required to place on protecting the welfare interests of children.

Legal functions

Law relates to any subject through the particular set of functions intended to give effect to its purpose, which are then assigned as duties to designated entities. Protection, for example, the most basic function of the law in relation to children, is held to be vested in the parents of a child, and the law has identified indices – health, physical and mental wellbeing, education, etc. – for benchmarking whether or not that function is being appropriately addressed. Agencies – in this case primarily state child welfare bodies – are required and empowered to generally monitor standards of functional effectiveness and to intervene by legally specified consensual or coercive methods to restore standards or retrieve the child when parental protection fails. Institutional mechanisms, such as those mentioned earlier, then come into play. Other legal functions are similarly identified and assigned to various agencies to be administered, regulated and otherwise given effect in accordance with specified standards and guided by related doctrines.

Public services

By the turn of the century, in the nations studied as elsewhere in the developed western world, the contraction of public service provision led to much uncertainty as to what in such circumstances might be an appropriate public-private balance to be struck between the state and other for-profit and not-for-profit agencies that would be compatible with the principles of liberal democracy. There had been a marked shift from a position that the state should own and maintain national resources, institutional infrastructure, etc., to one that it should, to some degree, settle for controlling service provision and access to services and for monitoring delivery standards by regulatory legislation and inspectoral bodies. Personal responsibility – the 'user pays' philosophy – has largely and rather suddenly displaced public taxes as the basis for funding a growing proportion of health and social care services. The policy presumption that public benefit provision is wholly the responsibility of government has long gone.

Reduced public service

The steady contraction of state responsibility for provision or delivery of public services and the devolving – or franchising out – of that responsibility to private business, charities, other non-government organisations or varying combinations of such bodies has been driven by the need to ease the costs of public service provision while ostensibly also broadening consumer choice and raising standards by forcing competition upon service providers. The pressure to reduce government spending has led to a retraction of state provision not only in health, education and social care but also across many sectors regarded until recently as the heartland of public services. The move towards privatisation of social utilities has enabled the state to leave the market to provide, at a price, services such as water, sanitation, transport, phones, housing, prisons, electricity, gas, etc., and is now similarly shedding responsibility for nursing home care, residential and day care for children, the disabled and the elderly. A proliferation of private finance initiatives has resulted in responsibility for the future provision of such services being devolved to or now being shared with charities, other not-for-profit bodies and commercial organisations. In particular, the sharing of service provision responsibilities with well-established children's charities – Barnardos, Save the Children, NSPCC, UNICEF, etc. – whose running costs are subsidised by tax exemptions, donor contributions and volunteer input, has served to reduce government costs and deflect accountability for service shortfall.

Effects of public service reduction

All modern democracies are now wrestling with the implications arising from privatising the delivery of essential services and working through the consequent considerable challenges for sustaining civil society. Paradoxically, the delegation of service delivery responsibility has led to increased centralisation, in terms of government strategic management and in terms of reducing the authority and resources available at local level.[46]

The shift from needs-based universal access to essential services delivered at a local level by public benefit-driven providers to targeted provision by independent organisations with transport and other cost margin concerns cannot have worked to the advantage of everyone. For those already poor, the reduction in the volume of services available, together with the introduction of profit margins for some providers, has made their vulnerable position more precarious. For the culturally marginalised – Indigenous people and other ethnic groups – the problems of accessing services became exacerbated, particularly when providers were not local and not part of or attuned to the cultural norms of prospective recipients. The consequences of an inadequate safety net of public service provision have been too obvious in all eight countries surveyed in this series. Whether measured in terms of infant mortality rates in the U.S. and France, teen suicides in New Zealand or abandoned infants in the Indigenous communities of Canada, the effects of not having access to adequate and appropriate public services will inevitably increase the numbers of children entering state child care and justice systems.

Family law

Family law offers one framework for safeguarding or promoting the welfare/rights of children, but there are a myriad of others, including the vast range of prohibitions

46 See, for example, Foster, C. and Plowden, J., *The State Under Stress*, Oxford Union Press, Oxford, 1996, for an assessment of the strategic significance of government policy at this time.

loosely categorised as health and safety. There is also a swathe of law which impacts children indirectly by granting benefits or imposing restrictions on their parents and on third parties such as employers. Then there is the safety net of public services, perhaps best categorised as administrative law, which applies to government social policy affecting levels, range and access to services that contribute much to offsetting childhood poverty and determining quality of life for the socially disadvantaged.

Family law in all the jurisdictions studied was rooted in Christian morality: the 'family' in effect was defined by marriage, sexual relations and any resulting children were thereby 'legitimated', property and succession rights were secured, while all relationships and related issues outside that definition were denied equivalent legal protection. In all the Judeo Christian jurisdictions, much the same archives are to be found, holding layers of similar statutes accreted over the centuries, saturated with assumptions of morality specific to Christian culture and religious heritage, which strive to regulate the marital family, its boundaries and social status.

Family law has since become an uncertain entity. Traditionally understood as referring to matters confined to the making, managing and breaking up of family units, it is now greatly expanded by issues relating to the following: the preliminary stage of forming a family through such means as IVF and surrogacy or of denying it through access to abortion; by the complications arising from the various configurations of adults and children that now qualify as constituting family life; by issues of sexual orientation, gender identity and gender transitioning; by rights associated with the ending of life with medical assistance; and by the possible contingencies involved in deferring family life through the storage of eggs and embryos.

Law relating to children

Criminal law, civil law, health and safety and a variety of international instruments may all have either a direct bearing on some aspect of children's lives, welfare interests and rights or do so indirectly by affecting the caring capacity of their parents: indeed, the extent to which the welfare/rights of parent and child are separable, particularly as regards very young children, is itself debatable. The functional emphasis in such law varies somewhat from country to country. A primary objective of this series has been to examine the jurisdictional variation in emphasis given to the functions of the law as they relate to children and their methods of application, to identify any significant jurisdictional differentiation between those functions when aligned with rights as opposed to alignment with welfare interests, to explore the extent to which any such jurisdictional differences may correlate with national social policy objectives and to assess the implications arising for family law. Parts II, III and IV of this book endeavour to draw some, albeit tentative, conclusions regarding these matters.

Family law proceedings

Family law – once a discrete and neatly compartmentalised area of law constructed around readily understood concepts and principles – has in recent years lost a good deal of its coherence. Its parameters have become uncertain and varied in the countries studied.

Public and private

Initially a body of private law, family law was traditionally comprised of civil proceedings: marriage, divorce and separation; parental disputes regarding child custody, contact and maintenance; and ancillary proceedings relating to property and personal protection. It is now organised around a basic binary distinction between public and private, which remains very largely civil in nature but includes some criminal matters. As illustrated by contemporary UK law, there are often two sets of proceedings relating to children: family proceedings, in which their welfare is given a paramount weighting, and criminal proceedings, where the welfare principle is balanced against considerations of justice and public policy. Moreover, and more generally, family law is in the process of developing an adjacent set of hybrid public-private proceedings. As mentioned earlier, this follows, or is perhaps being driven by, a reorientation of family law from a central concern for the spousal relationship to the welfare/rights of their children.

Legal principles: child related

Family law is underpinned by certain core principles, some but not all of which transect the public-private divide and lend a degree of consistency and coherence to this body of law.

Consent

There are virtually no statutory provisions that provide a child – someone under the age of 18 years – with a right to give or withhold a legal consent. Nevertheless, it is generally accepted that the consent of a child aged 16 or older should be sought on any decision affecting him or her and that consent will be legally binding.[47] However, there are a number of seemingly anomalous sets of circumstances in which a child's consent is in law both necessary and valid. For example, the consent of a child aged 12 or more is mandatory for their adoption in 11 Member States of the EU, though not in the UK nor in the U.S. A child of any age in Germany may give a valid legal consent to being taken into state care while most if not all countries have established an age at which a child can give a valid consent to a sexual relationship (see, further, Chapter 2).

Paramountcy

This principle, with its origins in the wardship jurisdiction of England and Wales, was initially applied to govern judicial determination of all issues affecting a child's upbringing and administration of his or her property. It requires the welfare

47 Established in the UK by the ruling in *Gillick v. West Norfolk and Wisbech Area Health Authority* (1986) 1 AC 112, HL and thereafter largely followed in most common law jurisdictions.

interests of a child to be given priority over all other considerations in certain – but largely vague – circumstances. In recent years, it has been asserted by the ECtHR, though the UN CRC has expressed regret:

> the right of the child to have his or her best interests taken as a primary consideration is still not reflected in all legislative and policy matters and judicial decisions affecting children, especially in the area of alternative care, child welfare, immigration, asylum and refugee status, criminal justice, and in the armed forces.[48]

Parental responsibilities

In many of the jurisdictions studied, parental responsibilities have replaced the concepts of 'parental rights' and 'parental duties', which for centuries formed the basic constructs of family law. It has been defined as encompassing all the rights, duties, powers, responsibilities and authority that, by law, a parent of a child has in relation to that child and their property.[49] In so doing, it has altered the previous 'all-or-nothing' perception – that had continued to cloud the functions of care and custody orders – and substituted a legal bond between parent and child that endures beyond the making of any public or private family law order (excepting adoption). More than one person may bear parental responsibility in respect of the same child at the same time. The mother does not lose parental responsibility merely because the father has it or because he later acquires it nor do either or both parents lose it should the child be admitted or committed to state care.

The change signalled a profound difference of approach from a proprietal frame of reference to one which implied that parental use of authority was valid only if employed for the benefit of the child. This reframed concept is now enabled to play a more consistent role in both public and private family law.

Consanguinity

The 'blood tie', or biological link between birth parent and child, is a factor that plays a variable role in private family law. In some jurisdictions, it attracts a positive presumption for custody, in others, it does not and, in either case, this may change. This culturally sensitive variable is of greatest weight and is most consistently upheld in relation to the care/custody arrangements for Indigenous children. Indeed, it is and has probably always been the foundation of Indigenous sociocultural life. The natural and key relationship nexus is that of the clan formed by the nuclear family and all those with some degree of blood relationship to the core familial unit.

48 See, the UN Committee on the Rights of the Child, *Concluding Observations: United Kingdom Of Great Britain And Northern Ireland*, United Nations (2016) at para 25.

49 See, further, Lowe, N.V., 'The Allocation of Parental Rights and Responsibilities: The Position in England and Wales', *Family Law Quarterly*, Vol. 39 (2005), pp. 267, 268.

Currently, ECtHR caselaw would seem to establish the blood-link as a factor of some legal weight in differentiating between the rival claims of birth parents and others – whether in a same-sex context, a child care and protection context or otherwise – and increasingly so in relation to surrogacy disputes. The ruling in the English case – *Re G (Children)*[50] – which was something of a milestone in UK jurisprudence, may prove to have wider implications in terms of elucidating the *ratio decideni* applicable in such disputes. Baroness Hale then argued that the birth parent could not be viewed as being on the same footing in relation to the children as the other 'parent' because she was 'both their biological and their psychological parent . . . in the overall welfare judgment that must count for something in the vast majority of cases'. This resurgence of judicial interest in the 'blood tie' as the rationale for preferring first party to third party care arrangements for a child resonates with earlier decisions.[51] In keeping with ECtHR caselaw, this approach would seem to establish the blood-link – or genetic link – as a significant factor particularly when it comes to differentiating between the rival claims of those involved in surrogacy disputes.

Legal functions; child related

Legal functions relating to children have evolved over time and would seem to be on the cusp of becoming either increasingly elaborate or greatly simplified as a consequence of the growing salience given to the welfare/rights of children relative to all other considerations.[52] The jurisdictional differences in the weighting given to each of the legal functions identified later, relative to others, is a matter examined in Parts II, III and IV of this book.

Protection

Beginning with 'care and protection', a dual function deemed to be inherently vested in the child's parents, this core private family law function has two public law dimensions.

The private law function imposes a mandatory requirement that protection be provided for the health and wellbeing of a child, and security be ensured for any property that he or she might be entitled to, for the duration of the child's upbringing. This duty rests, in the first instance, jointly upon both birth parents, reinforced by a statutory public law obligation on the state to monitor and support the parents and prevent them from any action or inaction that would harm the wellbeing of their child. The public law function also extended state protection outside the family to address exploitive forms of employment, relationships of a contractual or

50 (2006) UKHL 43 (2006) FLR 629.

51 See, for example, *Re W (A Minor) (Residence Order)* (1993) 2 FLR 625; *Re B (Adoption: Child's Welfare)* (1995) 1 FLR 895; and *Re M (Child's Upbringing)* (1996) 2 FLR 441.

52 See, also, O'Halloran, K., *The Principle of the Welfare of the Child: A History*, Routledge, 2022, at chapter 8.

sexual nature, the availability of alcohol, drugs, cars, cigarettes and fireworks and many other such sources of potential harm.

In circumstances of parental death, abandonment or abuse of a child, their duties might pass to an appointed guardian, or by default in the absence of any other arrangement, it would devolve as a public law duty to the state. This most fundamental function of the law relating to children has been upgraded in many countries by the paramountcy principle to permit it to prevail over all other considerations – including any wishes or rights of the child. Recognised as a right, a key jurisdictional difference is whether it is permitted to prevail, in any circumstances, over the parental right to withhold consent to the state-sanctioned adoption of their child.

Prevention

This positive legal function gives effect to a modern interpretation of the welfare principle in a public family law context by imposing an obligation, on those in a position to do so, to take the necessary steps to prevent a child from suffering foreseeable harm. Much depends on the specification of 'harm' and the preventative steps to be taken, whether the obligation rests universally on all as part of general health and safety regulations or on particular identified entities and whether this is stated as an obligation or as a strict duty.

Some elements of this function are specific as regards the nature of the preventable harm, the duty to intervene and upon whom it rests. So in relation to administering corporal punishment and in reporting instances of child neglect or abuse, the law is often explicit in identifying the persons and the mandatory action they are required to take or refrain from taking. It requires action to avoid any further deterioration in the circumstances of a particular child or children such as might result in a breach of the welfare threshold. This legal function is, of course, most likely to be effective when stated as a statutory duty, but even then – as starkly illustrated by female genital mutilation (FGM) – it needs to be accompanied by cultural sensitivity and by appropriate enforcement mechanisms if it is to be effective. As a public law function, it neither authorises nor seeks to achieve anything further than the maintenance of the basic welfare threshold, is predicated on the principle that welfare is best assured by parental care and is intended to prompt action that will avoid any need for coercive state intervention.

Promotion

This relatively modern additional legal function raises the threshold of the law's concern for children from its most basic starting point of securing protection to the more aspirational objective of maximising opportunities for their further development.

'Promotion' is a legal function that belongs to private family law. As it only comes into play when the decision to be made is intended to achieve more than the mere maintenance of the welfare threshold, it is very largely outside the brief of public authorities entrusted with policing that threshold. Instead, it is much more likely to be a factor in judicial deliberations regarding the competing claims of parents in disputes relating to parental responsibilities and contact. In general, despite the scattered statutory references in national child care legislation to the effect that the relevant authorities are required to promote the welfare of children, these tend to be devoid of any specific functional content.

Support

In all modern democracies, such as the eight profiled in the present series, the coercive, or mandatory legal requirements imposed by statute, tends to be offset by supportive or enabling provisions. This public family law function emanates from the traditional role of the state – now often embedded in constitutional provisions – to exercise a duty of care towards families, possibly a remnant of the joint church and state patronage of that unit as the key to securing community allegiance. As all eight jurisdictions accommodate both significant levels of poverty and shrinking levels of universal public service provision, the effectiveness of this legal function in strengthening the coping capacity of socially disadvantaged families is clearly important. Moreover, it is often the support provided to parents, but also of indirect benefit to children, that can be most effective in the long term, including pre- and post-birth health visitor input, welfare benefits, suitable housing, employment opportunities, etc.

This being 'soft' law, however, such enabling statutory provisions are often expressed in general and discretionary terms and can be inadequately resourced. An important point of jurisdictional difference lies in the degree of state commitment to effective service provision for vulnerable families and their children (see, further, Chapter 2).

Control

This legal function is essentially negative, is rooted in private family law and owes its origins to the doctrine of parental rights. As such, it acknowledges that the recipient of parental care has a corresponding duty to the provider, not to obstruct or make impossible by wilful behaviour, the provision of such care. The responsibility to exercise control, so as to ensure that the behaviour of a child or young person does not breach socially acceptable norms, is in law distributed with some uncertainty between child, parent and state. The basis for that distribution determines whether the control exercised serves a private or public family law function.

While it continues to be a matter for the civil jurisdiction of the courts, the control function also represents a public law interest in the protection of third parties from the unreasonable or delinquent behaviour of children and young persons inadequately supervised by their parents. In fact, it can come into play along a spectrum of behaviour that at one end attracts a private family law function as it deals with civil issues arising from lack of parental control (such as non-school attendance), while at the other, the response is a public law function, as the behaviour is criminal (such as theft or grievous bodily harm) and arises from deliberate anti-social animus. The jurisdictions studied varied as to where on that spectrum the line was drawn to separate private and public legal functions (see, further, Chapter 5).

Removal of parental rights/responsibilities

While a parent may lose – or, in some countries, voluntarily relinquish – their legal responsibilities to care for a child, the grounds for state removal of those rights are essentially set by the criminal law.

Care

The state, as carer of last resort, may step into the shoes of parents – in circumstances of the latter's death, absence, incapacity or conviction for child abuse – and be judicially vested with full responsibility for their child. While in that eventuality, 'care' is clearly being deployed as the ultimate public family law function, it may also serve an important role as a family support service. Respite care may be provided on a temporary basis by the state at parental request to alleviate family stress. Arguably, the care then provided is of a hybrid public-private variety as although a form of state provision, it is in effect subject to parental decisions. The extent to which the state in fact permits such a service to be utilised and terminated at parental request, on a 'no-strings attached' basis, is open to considerable jurisdictional variation, reflecting a corresponding variation in state interpretation of respite care as representing a public or private family law function.

Family law and changes in child-related legal functions

The working hypothesis running through this series has been that national differences in the way law relates to children – any differences within and between nations regarding matters treated as welfare interests or rights – will be apparent in the corresponding difference in emphasis given to particular legal functions. Any such jurisdictional variation will also be reflected in the distribution of legal functions between the private, public and hybrid sectors of family law.

Private family law

It would seem probable that the nations maintaining the strongest links with their traditional patriarchal culture and associated values would also have laws relating to children which lean more towards private than public family law provisions. When faced with parental disputes in divorce proceedings or in relation to custody and contact, the courts are perhaps likely to favour arrangements that are equitable between the parties and in which the child's views will be sought and taken into account but would not be determinative. They would be more likely to stress the legal functions of protection of a child's welfare interests and control of anti-social behaviour: the primary axis being between state and parents with little scope for state recognition and respect for any rights of their children. The preventative function – particularly respite care – would tend to be interpreted as a service response to the needs of parents rather than to the welfare interests of their child. Such nations are otherwise less likely to license state intervention into family affairs whether on a consensual or on a coercive basis.

Public family law: civil jurisdiction

Some nations would seem to have become accustomed to a higher level of state intrusion into family matters than others: the threshold for intervention being set not simply by harm to a child but extended to include preventative, promotional and support functions. The primary axis is between state and the welfare if not the rights of children; family support and preventative or promotional functions are being viewed as methods for channelling assistance to safeguard the welfare interests of children. The laws in such nations may well be less tolerant of parental conduct that violates their child's welfare interests and more likely to result in the removal of all parental rights. Much the same orientation is apparent in relation to parenting disputes, in which context, there may well be an emphasis on recognition of a child's right to enjoy 'family life' and to have contact with their parents. It may be the case that where a child is to be the subject of a private family law order – such as adoption and guardianship – this would be conditional upon his or her consent.

Public family law: criminal jurisdiction

Juvenile justice quite often provides the most interesting context for considering how the legal functions relating to children are balanced. The various configurations of ages, welfare or justice criteria and penalty tariffs – alongside such other factors as preventative strategies and recidivism rates – can reveal a lot about the relationship between state, family and children. It is, however, the context in which control is the primary legal function, where the concept of children's rights has least traction and where even their welfare interests are liable to cursory treatment. There is a tendency in all jurisdictions studied for a hardening of a justice rather than a welfare-oriented approach with a stronger emphasis on accountability and some form of restitution.

Hybrid public-private family law

A feature of modern family law – perhaps particularly as regards the law relating to children – is the blending of legal functions to form a new middle ground that is neither wholly private nor public. For example, contact arrangements for children – whether in respect of those in state care, in custody or the subjects of post-divorce parental disputes – are now routinely determined in accordance with much the same welfare/rights indicators. So, also, in relation to the welfare interests of children born as a result of commercial surrogacy, abducted by a parent or adopted from the state care system. Prevention, promotion and support, have become established focal points that attract both government funding and voluntary organisation involvement in the delivery of mediatory services that may be accessed by those in need either of their own volition or, in some cases, as directed by the Court (see, further, Chapter 9).

Conclusion

The law relating to children, its recognition of and differentiation between their welfare interests and their rights, is ultimately determined by the political balance struck between the aforementioned individual legal functions, as interpreted and applied by the different components of the national legal system, and subject to the supra-national rulings of bodies such as the ECtHR, the CJEU and the UN CRC. This introductory chapter has sought to sketch the broad outline of the remit and divisions of family law, identify its governing principles and consider the main functions of that part of the law as it relates to children.

Part II

Children's welfare interests and rights in a public family law context – civil and criminal

2 Prevention

Children and families in need

Introduction

The purpose of this chapter is to conduct a comparative evaluation of how the legal function of 'prevention' is given effect across the eight jurisdictions studied, assess its relative significance as a component of the welfare principle and consider any implications for family law. As the only relevant international instrument (in terms of setting out benchmarks for children's rights) is the UN Convention on the Rights of the Child, as very largely assimilated within the ECHR and given effect through the rulings of the UN CRC, the CJEU and the ECtHR (largely the latter), it would seem reasonable to measure the relative progress of jurisdictions against those rulings.

Concepts and the law

The legislative intent underpinning the concepts of 'prevention', 'support' and 'promotion' is that together, they should constitute the threshold for consensual state intervention with vulnerable families indicating the assistance necessary to ensure the standard of parental care stays above the threshold for coercive intervention. The consensual intervention threshold represents a legislative intent to focus professional concern and agency resources on putting in place the supports necessary to forestall possible future coercive intervention in the affairs of a family on child protection grounds. This approach is one that envisages the provision of general support services, drawn from such statutory agencies as are relevant to a family's particular circumstances, to maintain that family's private responsibility for safeguarding and promoting the welfare of its child or children. It is an approach firmly established in international and domestic law, both of which stress the importance of preventative service provision.

Concepts

'Prevention', 'support' and 'promotion' are soft law concepts that are not always realisable. In practice, they may fail to function as express duties – legally enforceable aspects of a child's right to protection – and instead be treated as aspects of a discretionary state power.

DOI: 10.4324/9781003269595-5

Prevention

As mentioned in the first book, this positive legal function gives effect to a modern interpretation of the welfare principle in a public family law context by imposing an obligation, on those in a position to do so, to take the necessary steps to prevent a child from suffering foreseeable harm. As a public law function, it neither authorises nor seeks to achieve anything further than the maintenance of the basic welfare threshold and is predicated on the principle that the welfare of a child is best assured by parental care. However, only when stated as a statutory duty requiring specified action does the concept of prevention acquire functionality. Most usually – but not always – this takes the form of a duty resting on particular government bodies to provide specified services to families in need, accompanied by dedicated ring-fenced funding. In practice, there is considerable jurisdictional variation in such functionality.

Identifying families and children in need

The state duty to provide services designed to prevent the welfare interests of children being impaired begins with the requirement that the appropriate authorities identify children in need, or at risk of becoming so, rather than wait for requests for assistance. This necessitates adopting proactive measures to locate vulnerable families, assess their needs and determine appropriate services. In practice, state authorities often turn to those charities and organisations in the not-for-profit sector that have for generations worked with designated disadvantaged groups – e.g. Barnardos and the NSPCC with children, MENCAP with the mentally impaired, etc. – and fund them to act as their agents in fulfilling the delegated statutory duty.

Service provision

Functionality requires the delivery of appropriate and sufficient services. Again, legislative specificity is important; details regarding the type of services, the prospective service delivery mechanism and the entitlement criteria clarify the precise nature of the legal duty. At this stage, if the service response is to alleviate the need, thereby contributing to the child's right to protection, then delivery must be sensitive and appropriately responsive to the recipient's particular circumstances to ensure the services are accessible and utilised.

Support

Similar to 'promotion', this concept is also an adjunct to 'prevention' and one which all too often is of spurious functionality. Much turns on whether support services are specified, are culturally appropriate, are adequate, available on demand and their delivery is imposed as a duty rather than a discretionary power on a government body, and not left to the vagaries of providers in the not-for-profit sector.

Promotion

As mentioned in the previous book, this concept is one that does not always translate into a binding legal duty on the relevant government authorities or on anyone else. Although often stated as a legal objective, in the absence of accompanying specified goals, it may well remain aspirational.

Public-private family law

Essentially, because it only comes into play when the choice to be made is intended to achieve more than the mere maintenance of the welfare threshold, this function belongs to private rather than public law. There is little scope for it to play a role in the decisions of government bodies – other than in health services for young children and adoptions from state care – and virtually none in respect of child offenders. It is much more likely to be a factor in judicial deliberations regarding the competing claims of parents in disputes relating to parental responsibilities and contact.

International law

The history of international law requiring state intervention with families to prevent harm to children dates back to at least the statement of principles in the Geneva Declaration of the Rights of the Child 1924 as consolidated in the 1959 Declaration. Subsequently, the International Covenant on Economic, Social and Cultural Rights (ICESCR) 1966 asserts in Article 12 the right to 'adequate food, clothing and housing', while the Preamble to the European Convention on the Exercise of Children's Rights 1996 states its purpose as being to promote the rights and 'best interests' of children, and Article 11 of the European Social Charter 1996 requires states to ensure that children receive the care, assistance, education and training they need.

Currently, the provisions of both UN CROC and the ECHR impose duties on the state to provide preventative services to known vulnerable families.[1] Other international instruments, such as UNDRIP, also do so.

UN CROC

The Preamble declares:

> that the family, as the fundamental group of society and the natural environment for the growth and well-being of all its members and particularly children, should be afforded the necessary protection and assistance so that it can fully assume its responsibilities within the community.

This is underpinned by Articles 18 and 20, which reinforce the principle that the state should give priority to measures that keep children in their families and culture

1 See, O'Halloran, K., *Children, the Law and the Welfare Principle: European Judicial Perspectives*, Routledge, 2024.

of origin. They stress that while parents have the primary responsibility for the upbringing and development of their children, the state must 'render appropriate assistance to parents and legal guardians in the performance of their child-rearing responsibilities' and should establish 'social programmes to provide necessary support for the child and for those who have the care of the child, as well as for other forms of prevention'. It is further reinforced by the United Nations Guidelines which advises that in accordance with the predominant opinion of experts, alternative care for young children, especially those under the age of 3 years, should be provided in family-based settings.[2] Adding that 'where such arrangements are not possible or are not in the best interests of the child, efforts should be made to find a permanent family placement within a reasonable period'.[3] These statements of principle, favouring state support to preserve the care of a child within his or her family of origin – or, failing that, to require the state to find an alternative family placement for such a child – are counterbalanced by principles that distinguish the separate interests of children. For example, the Preamble also states:

> the child, for a full and harmonious development, should grow up in a family environment, in an atmosphere of happiness, love and understanding.

It is a statement that falls short of declaring that a child has a right to a family.

Article 27, emphasising social inclusion, adds that states must 'recognize the right of every child to a standard of living adequate for the child's physical, mental, spiritual, moral and social development', and while this is the primary responsibility of parent(s) or others:

> States Parties, in accordance with national conditions and within their means, shall take appropriate measures to assist parents and others responsible for the child to implement this right and shall in case of need provide material assistance and support programmes, particularly with regard to nutrition, clothing and housing.

Children with a disability

Article 23 is directed more specifically towards provision for children with a disability. It declares that states must 'recognize that a mentally or physically disabled child should enjoy a full and decent life, in conditions which ensure dignity, promote self-reliance and facilitate the child's active participation in the community'. In particular, they should do the following:

> ensure that the disabled child has effective access to and receives education, training, health care services, rehabilitation services, preparation for

2 The United Nations Guidelines for the Alternative Care of Children 2009, at para 22.
3 Ibid, at para 44.

> employment and recreation opportunities in a manner conducive to the child's achieving the fullest possible social integration and individual development, including his or her cultural and spiritual development.

Minority groups

Article 30 requires state assistance for ethnic, religious or linguistic minorities and for Indigenous people. It declares:

> a child belonging to such a minority or who is Indigenous shall not be denied the right, in community with other members of his or her group, to enjoy his or her own culture, to profess and practise his or her own religion, or to use his or her own language.

The ECHR

Article 8 of the ECHR – the right to respect for family life – requires state intervention to prevent family breakdown and the consequent separation of children from their parents. The related rulings of the ECtHR have focused on two benchmarks for giving effect to this requirement: that state intervention is prompt (a child once identified as in need should be offered swift remedial state assistance) and that assistance should be such as is most likely to keep the child at home and in the care of his or her parents.

Comparative jurisdictional analysis of state intervention: prevention

The U.S. is not a party to UN CROC, and of course, neither the U.S. nor Canada are parties to the ECHR (though both are signatory states to UNDRIP). Nonetheless, their domestic laws – particularly judicial rulings on constitutional matters – are sufficiently proximate to permit comparative analysis with their European counterparts on child welfare/rights.

Established international standards

Both UN CROC, Articles 18 and 19, and the ECHR, primarily Article 8, impose duties on the state to provide preventative services to vulnerable families. Assurances of additional protection from socio-economic hardship can be found in other international instruments such as the European Social Charter and of the EU Charter of Fundamental Rights, Article 34 (1), which states that the 'Union recognises and respects the entitlement to social security benefits and social services'. The ECtHR has warned:

> the authorities' role in the social welfare field is, precisely, to help persons in difficulty, to provide them with guidance in their contact with the welfare

> authorities and to advise them, *inter alia*, on how to overcome their difficulties. In the case of vulnerable persons, the authorities must show particular vigilance and afford increased protection.[4]

Once put on notice of families and children in need, these international provisions require such consensual state intervention as is necessary to ensure the standard of parental care prevents any necessity for coercive intervention. So, for example, in *Iliya Petrov v. Bulgaria*,[5] when a 12-year-old boy was seriously injured in an unlocked electricity substation, where children and young people were known to meet, the state was found to be culpable because, although it knew about the safety problems, it had failed to ensure that the premises were secured. Again, in *Z. and Others v. the United Kingdom*,[6] the applicants were successful in their claim that the local authority had failed to take adequate protective measures in respect of the severe neglect and abuse which they were known to be suffering due to their ill-treatment as children by their parents and because they had no access to a court or effective remedy. The comment offered by the ECtHR, in *Kutzner v. Germany*,[7] that it was 'questionable whether the domestic administrative and judicial authorities [had] given sufficient consideration to additional measures of support as an alternative to what is by far the most extreme measure, namely separating the children from their parents'[8] could have been made in many such cases.

The ECtHR has often ruled that a child has a legal right to preventative state intervention,[9] and its rulings over many decades provide a useful means of gauging the nature and extent of jurisdictional differences in state preventative intervention.

Preventative policy initiatives

Public policy determines the balance to be struck between state intervention in family matters on consensual as opposed to coercive grounds. The different jurisdictional responses to a number of preventative child welfare measures – clearly intended to ameliorate risk to the welfare interests of children – reflect the corresponding public policies of the nations concerned.

Mandatory reporting

The duty to report instances of child abuse or neglect – or reasonable suspicions thereof – is mandatory in the U.S., Canada, Australia and France and is universally

4 See, *S.S. v. Slovenia* at para 84. The Court cited in support its judgments *S.H. v. Italy*, Application No. 52557/14 (2015) and *Akinnibosun v. Italy*, Application No. 9056/14 (2015).

5 Application No. 19202/03 (2012).

6 Application No. 29392/93 (2001).

7 (2002) 35 EHRR 25.

8 Ibid at para 75.

9 See, for example, *Soares de Melo v. Portugal*, Application No. 72850/14 (2016); *Saviny v. Ukraine*, Application No. 39948/06 (2008); *Wallová and Walla v. the Czech Republic*, Application No. 23848/04 (2006); and *Olsson v. Sweden*, Application No. 10465/83 (1988).

applicable.[10] There is no general UK mandatory requirement in the UK, Germany or in New Zealand that members of the public report to the appropriate authorities any instance of child abuse or neglect that comes to their attention, though there is such a duty on UK local authority staff,[11] on German child care workers (public and private) and a similar limited reporting requirement rests on all staff in Irish public services.[12]

Safe havens

Some countries – but not Australia, New Zealand, Ireland nor the UK – retain the practice of having designated facilities where a parent can safely, anonymously and legally abandon their child. In the U.S., every state has introduced safe haven laws and facilities. Canada has no comparable laws, but this has not stopped the introduction of such facilities in Edmonton, Alberta, and in three hospitals. In Germany, the practice is illegal but continues to be tolerated by the state, while in France, it was officially prohibited in 1904 but made irrelevant by the *accouchement sous X* procedure which continues to be the legally accepted means, whereby a mother may anonymously relinquish her child.

Prohibition of physical chastisement

The traditional parental right to administer reasonable physical chastisement almost certainly falls within the definition of 'degrading treatment or punishment' to which Article 37 of UN CROC states that no child should be made subject. Nonetheless, this continues to be legal in England and Wales,[13] the U.S.,[14] Australia[15] and Canada[16] but is prohibited in Ireland,[17] Germany,[18] France[19] and New Zealand.[20]

Raising age of criminal responsibility

The lower the age of criminal responsibility, the more children will be eligible to be admitted to the justice system, and the higher the age, the more of those with

10 The Child Protection Act 1998, s 10.
11 The Children Act 1989, s 47.
12 The Children First Act 2015.
13 The Children Act 2004, s 58.
14 The Child Abuse Prevention and Treatment Act (CAPTA) 2003 (amended by the CAPTA Reauthorization Act 2021).
15 The Criminal Code Act 1924, s 50.
16 The Criminal Code, s 43, and *Canadian Foundation for Children, Youth and the Law v. Canada (Attorney General)* (2004) 1 SCR 76, 2004 SCC 4.
17 Affirmed in the Children Act 2004, s 58, but repealed in 2015.
18 The Civil Code, Article 1631.
19 The Civil Code, Article 371–1.
20 The Crimes (Substituted Section 59) Amendment Act 2007.

problematic behaviour will be directed towards treatment rather than punishment options. The UN CRC have recommended that criminal responsibility be set at 14 years of age.

While Germany is compliant with the CRC recommendation, Australia – where it is fixed at 10 years of age – is not. It is also low in both the UK[21] (10 in England and Northern Ireland and 12 in Scotland) and Ireland (12 years with exceptions for those aged 10 or 11 charged with murder, manslaughter, rape or aggravated sexual assault).[22] In the U.S., it is not federally determined, other than for federal crimes for which the threshold is 11 years of age, but otherwise, it varies across the states and is set at 7 years of age in 35 states. In Canada, also, criminal responsibility starts at 12 years of age.[23] In France, there is no specific age; liability for criminal behaviour will depend on the judge's assessment of a child's maturity and capacity for discernment.

Raising the age of consent

Again, the lower the age at which a child can give or withhold their consent to decisions affecting their welfare, the more children will be held accountable for the consequences of those decisions. Both Ireland and the UK share a similar reluctance to enact legislative provisions that specifically require a child's consent to a decision affecting his or her welfare. Raising that age threshold could be viewed as a protective measure designed to shield children from personal liability; though, equally, this may be seen as patronising. Arguably – like the age of criminal responsibility – there is a lot to be said for correlating age thresholds with the gravity/complexity of the subject matter.

Contemporary preventative practices

As with the following jurisdiction specific chapters, the identification of jurisdictional characteristics – coupled with a comparative analysis of jurisdictional differences – in the law relating to the welfare interests of children, is best examined by benchmarking such indices against the common standards set by the UN CROC, mainly Articles 18, 19 and 27 as illustrated in the rulings of the ECtHR.

Right to life

UN CROC, Article 6, declares both that 'every child has the inherent right to life' and the responsibility of states to 'ensure to the maximum extent possible the

21 Set at 10 years of age by the Children and Young Persons *Act* 1933 (as amended), s 50. See, for example, comments of the UN Committee on the Rights of the Child, *Concluding Observations: United Kingdom Of Great Britain And Northern Ireland*, United Nations, 2008, at para 78. Note that in Sweden, Finland and Norway, the age of criminal responsibility is set at 15 years.

22 In 2016, The CRC reiterated its previous concern (CRC/C/IRL/CO/2, para 66) regarding the lowering of the age of criminal responsibility to 10 years for serious crimes (at para 71).

23 The Criminal Code, s 13.

survival and development of the child'. This right was clearly violated in *Nencheva and Others v. Bulgaria*[24] when the ECtHR found the state had failed to prevent the deaths of 15 children from cold and hunger in a state facility during the winter months of 1997. It was also violated in *Re A* (*conjoined twins*)[25] which concerned a moral and legal dilemma as to whether it was permissible to surgically sever conjoined twins, an operation which would inevitably result in the death of the weaker child while giving the other the only chance she would have to live a 'normal' life. The twins' parents opposed the surgery, and it was the doctors who brought the case into court, asking whether separation of the twins would be a more ethical alternative to both children living predictably short and likely difficult lives. The Court ultimately decided that the parents' views could not be determinative and authorised the operation which had the predicted outcome. Advances in medical science have brought many such intractable cases to court where one child's Article 6 right can only prevail at the cost of that of another child and/or the human rights of the parents.

Right to be cared for by birth parents

As was stated in an English court 'so long as a parent adequately cares for his or her children (i.e. is fit), there will normally be no reason for the State to inject itself into the private realm of the family to further question the ability of the parent to make the best decisions concerning the rearing of that parent's child'.[26]

The common law jurisdictions

In the U.S. and Ireland, unlike the UK, there is a presumptive right of a child to be cared for by their birth parents. This right is constitutionally protected and well established.[27] Should parental care – for whatever reason – fall below acceptable standards, then UN CROC, Article 3, requires the state to 'ensure the child such protection and care as is necessary for his or her well-being' while 'taking into account the rights and duties of his or her parents' and 'shall take all appropriate legislative and administrative measures'.[28] Article 3(3) requires States Parties

24 Application No.48609/06 (2013).

25 (2001) 2 WLR 480.

26 See, *Re W (A Child)* (2016) EWCA Civ 793, at pp. 68, 69. An approach asserted earlier by Templeman LJ 'the best person to bring up a child is the natural parent' in *Re KD (A Minor Ward) (Termination of Access)* (1988) 1 AC 806 and by Hedley J 'children are best brought up within natural families' in *Re L (Care: Threshold Criteria)* (2007) 1 FLR 1050.

27 For the U.S., see, for example, *Troxel v. Granville*, 530 U.S. 57 (2000). For Ireland, see, the Child Care Act 1991, s 3, 'it is generally in the best interests of a child to be brought up in his own family'.

28 See, for example, *Child and Family Agency v. IB and HB (placement in care – parental capacity assessment)* (2019) IEDC 1 when instead of granting an application for care orders, the court directed that the children should have a phased return to their parents' care under the authority of a supervision order. The judge explained that she 'does not believe that such an order would secure the welfare of RB or CB and/or is a necessary and/or proportionate interference with family life in this case'.

to ensure that 'the institutions, services and facilities responsible for the care or protection of children shall conform with the standards established by competent authorities'. In England, Pauffley J drew attention to the importance of the mother-baby bond in *Re: NL*[29] when he asserted that 'there is, after all, an elemental as well as a physiological need to keep mothers and new born babies together wherever possible, so long as the child will not be endangered'. Accordingly, as was previously stated in *Re B*,[30] the Court must consider that a child's welfare includes the interest of that child in being brought up by his or her family of origin and must, therefore, assess the possibility of that family meeting the child's needs with appropriate support services from the state.

In both the UK and Ireland, there is a shortage of adequate placements for troubled teenagers – secure accommodation and facilities for adolescents with mental health issues – but the situation is worse in Ireland, where the authorities often look to England and Wales for placements which is clearly not conducive to promoting the welfare of the children concerned and may well violate their rights.

Article 18 requires States Parties to assist parents and legal guardians in the upbringing and development of their children. It is reinforced by Article 18(2) which requires the development of appropriate services for the care of children and by Article 19(2) which adds that such services should include 'effective procedures for the establishment of social programmes to provide necessary support for the child and for those who have the care of the child'. Article 27 adds that states are required to recognise the right of every child to a standard of living adequate for that child's physical, mental, spiritual, moral and social development. In this context, the CRC have expressed concern that poverty is a factor in the care admissions in England and Wales.[31] This might go some way to explaining the recent change in policy established by Templeman LJ and others that 'the best person to bring up a child is the natural parent'. Instead, the current judicial approach, as expressed by Vincent J is that there can be no right or presumption that a child should be brought up by their natural family.[32]

In relation to Ireland, the Committee was also 'deeply concerned about the significant increase in the number of children living in consistent poverty, including reports that such poverty disproportionately affects children from Traveller, Roma and refugee backgrounds, as well as those who live in single-parent households'.[33] In the U.S., the Urban Institute estimates that currently, 24 million children use welfare every month, and at 41%, they constitute the biggest percentage of all

29 (2014) EWHC 270 at [53].

30 (2013) UKSC 33, paras 26–28.

31 See, UN Committee on the Rights of the Child, *Concluding Observations: United Kingdom Of Great Britain And Northern Ireland*, United Nations 2016, at para 52.

32 *Re E-R (A Child)* 2015 EWCA Civ 405, per Vincent J.

33 UN Committee on the Rights of the Child, Concluding Observations of the Committee on the combined third and fourth periodic reports of Ireland, 2016, at para 59.

welfare beneficiaries. The corresponding situation in Canada is much the same. It has recently been argued:[34]

> Child poverty in Canada still remains a 'national disgrace'. Recent data show that 1 in 5 children live in poverty. For Indigenous children, the rate is 1 in 2. Children with disabilities are twice as likely to live in households relying on public assistance.

The fact that two of the leading developed democratic nations continue to have serious, apparently systemic, problems of child poverty, closely linked to high rates of children admitted to child welfare and youth justice systems, is, of course, deeply troubling.

In England and Wales, the legislation helpfully differentiates between the authorities preventative and protective duties, even if the distinction is becoming blurred in practice as government cutbacks lead to a diverting of resources from one to the other. As regards the former, the duties begin with the requirement in Schedule 2 of the 1989 Act that local authorities take reasonable steps to identify the extent to which there are children in need within its area. The Act then imposes a general duty upon local authorities in England 'to safeguard and promote the welfare of children within their area who are in need' and states nine separate and quite specific preventative duties which are mostly permissive, but only a few are mandatory. Much the same duty, in almost the same wording, is imposed on their Irish counterparts.[35] Interestingly, in that jurisdiction, there is judicial authority that a recent constitutional amendment has significantly lowered the bar for state intervention in circumstances where parental failure endangers a child's safety and welfare.[36]

Both Australia and New Zealand have policies that permit state investment in culturally accessible support services for vulnerable Indigenous and Māori families. In New Zealand, there are various statutory provisions of a preventative nature intended to support vulnerable families and children in need: under the *Oranga Tamariki* Act 1989, the Children's Act 2014 and the Children's Action Plan. In Australia, the issue of 'Action Plans' every three years by the Department of Social Services place a strong emphasis on the need for prevention and early intervention in order to reduce the likelihood of children entering the child protection system. Both countries provide voluntary respite care for children in state facilities where this is necessary to relieve families in stressful circumstances, and both rely heavily on charities and voluntary organisations to provide family support services.

34 See, Press Release: Canadian Coalition for the Rights of Children, et al. (May 16, 2022) at: https://rightsofchildren.ca/childrens-rights-in-canada/press-release-on-the-eve-of-canadas-appearance-at-the-un-crc/

35 The Child Care Act 1991, s 3(2)(a).

36 See, *In the Matter of JJ* (2021) IESC 1, per McKechnie J.

In the U.S., the Trump Administration targeted new laws and resources on service provision intended to support families and children in need and reduce the level of foster care admissions, which would seem to be very much in keeping with UN CROC principles. In Canada, on the other hand, the authorities have for some years been in breach of Articles 18 and 19 as regards providing funds and support for Indigenous children.[37] Criticism from international bodies such as the UN CRC resulted in the Jordan's Principle and other federal initiatives to address the long-running Canadian service shortfall to the children in greatest need. In both, state intervention to assist vulnerable families has traditionally been a weakly resourced public service, but the scale of Canada's failure is not just greater than that of the U.S.; it's greater than most developed countries.

The civil law jurisdictions

In both France and Germany, state investment in support services for families with pre-school children is high but would seem more so in France. As the Court commented in *Kutzner v. Germany*,[38] it was 'questionable whether the domestic administrative and judicial authorities [had] given sufficient consideration to additional measures of support as an alternative to what is by far the most extreme measure, namely separating the children from their parents'.[39] The law in both requires service provision appropriate to prevent vulnerable families failing to provide for the care and protection of their children; the former differs from the latter – and from the UK and other countries – by empowering the Court (the *juge des enfants*) to order support for parents in the form of specific services.[40] The principle of subsidiarity requires the state in both to respect and support parents in the upbringing of their children, which is their prerogative right and duty.[41] In Germany, this is accompanied by a stronger implication of state supervision of parents to ensure that the standards of care owed to their children are not breached.

Consensual intervention to avoid need for coercive state care

The ECtHR has emphasised, in several cases, that before a state resorts to coercive intervention in cases of parental neglect, it must first show that every reasonable effort has been made to alleviate the situation by appropriate preventative service provision.[42]

37 See, *Canada (Human Rights Commission) v. Canada (Attorney General)* 2012 FC 445.

38 (2002) 35 EHRR 25.

39 Ibid at para 75.

40 Judicial case management in France would seem very different from the position of their counterparts in the UK, where, as has been pointed out, 'if a local authority doggedly resists taking the steps which are appropriate to the case of children at risk of significant harm it appears the court is powerless' (*Nottinghamshire County Council v. P [No. 2]* [1993] 2 FLR 134, *per* Sir Stephen Brown P, at p. 148).

41 See, for France, the Civil Code, Articles 371–2, and for Germany, the Basic Law, Article 6(2).

42 See, for example, *K. and T. v. Finland,* Application No. 25702/94 (2001).

Preventative intervention failure in a common law context

In England and Wales, the Children Act 1989 requires local authorities to take reasonable steps to protect children from abuse and neglect and 'so far as is consistent with that duty, to promote the upbringing of such children by their families',[43] reduce the need to bring children into care and to expose them to other proceedings.[44] However, in several instances,[45] the authorities were found to have breached Articles 3 (prohibition of inhuman or degrading treatment) and 13 (right to an effective remedy) when – despite receiving reports of child abuse or of being in possession of information that should have alerted them to the risk of such abuse – they failed to intervene. In Ireland, also, there is evidence of a similar failure of preventative intervention. In *PT and AHT v. Wicklow County Council,*[46] the applicants sought to require a public body to provide services for a child at real and immediate risk of sleeping rough, but the application was dismissed; the High Court found that there was no mandatory obligation on the Council to house such children.

In the U.S., the USSC in *DeShaney v. Winnebago County Social Services*[47] took the view that nonintervention was explicable and excusable, as intervening officials are often charged with 'improperly intruding into the parent-child relationship'. In Canada, there would seem to be much truth in the observation:

> Canadian child protection systems as they are currently structured are funded to respond to reports of child maltreatment, or risk of maltreatment, but are generally not well funded to take action in areas of social service that would prevent maltreatment from happening in the first place.[48]

The fact that children in out-of-home care are over-represented in the Australian criminal justice system has caused the UN CRC to blame the ineffectiveness and/or insufficiency of early preventative state intervention.[49] In response, 'Action Plans' are now issued every three years which place a strong emphasis on the need for prevention and early intervention, though the evidence from the reports generated by *National Agreement on Closing the Gap* show that significant objectives are not being met. Preventative intervention in New Zealand, to be effective, would have to improve its capacity to address rates of domestic violence which are reported to be

43 Children Act 1989, s 17(1).

44 Children Act 1989, Sched 2, paras 4 and 7.

45 *Z and Others v. the United Kingdom*, Application No.29392/95 (2001), *TP and KM v. UK* (2001) 2 FLR 549 and *E and Others v. the United Kingdom*, Application No. 33218/96 (2002). See, also, *O'Keeffe v. Ireland* [GC], *op cit.*

46 (2017) IEHC 623.

47 489 U.S. 189 (1989).

48 Gough, P., et al., 'An Overview of the Child Welfare Systems in Canada', *International Journal of Child Health and Human Development*, Vol. 2, No. 3-Special Issue, pp. 357–372, at p. 357.

49 CRC/c/AUS/CO/4, *Concluding Observations: Australia*, 2012, at para 19.

the highest in the developed world[50] and where rates of child abuse and neglect are high relative to other developed nations.[51] Given that during the period 2004–2019 an estimated 1 in every 8 New Zealand homicide victims was a child and that the country has one of the world's highest rate of teenage suicides, there has to be some misgivings about the effectiveness of preventative intervention in that country.[52]

Preventative intervention failure in a civil law context

In France, although there is a strong traditional policy of state support to maintain family unity, the ECtHR has found the French state to be culpable for failing to effect prompt intervention resulting in preventable harm.[53] For example, in *Association Innocence en Danger v. France and Association Enfance et Partage v. France*,[54] it was severely censored for not providing unaccompanied migrant minors with access to health care services and in *Affaire A.L, c. France*,[55] when protracted proceedings were found to have compromised the welfare interests of the child who was only 4 months old when contested proceedings began but was 6 1/2 years old when they concluded. In Germany, while much the same policy of state support for family unity prevails, this would seem to be accompanied by state deference towards family autonomy which may be responsible for a somewhat hesitant approach to preventative intervention,[56] indicating that the preventative intervention role of the *Jugendamt* is failing some children.[57]

Prevention in an Indigenous context

The record of state intervention on child welfare grounds in the Indigenous families of the CANZUS nations would seem to have been pretty much one of consistent failure. This is perhaps particularly true as regards preventative intervention in respect of which the generally applicable provisions of the UN Convention on the Rights of the Child (UN CROC) are reinforced by those of the UN Declaration on

50 See, Stephen, E., 'Child Protection' (2020), at: https://talkingtroublenz.org/wp-content/uploads/2020/12/Emily-Stephen-SLT-child-protection.pdf

51 See, Gilbert, R., et al., 'Child Maltreatment: Variation in Trends and Policies in Six Developed Countries', *Lancet* (2011), at: https://scholar.google.com/scholar_lookup?hl=en&publication_year=2011&author=R+Gilbert&author=J+Fluke&author=M+O%27Donnell&author=A+Gonzalez-Izquierdo&author=M+Brownell&author=P+Gulliver&title=Child+maltreatment%3A+variation+in+trends+and+policies+in+six+developed+countries

52 See further, for example, at: www.theguardian.com/world/2018/mar/08/study-one-in-four-new-zealand-children-reported-welfare-agencies

53 Note, however, that France launched a Global Action Plan 2015–2017 for the protection of children.

54 Application No. 15343/15 (2020).

55 Application No. 13344/20 (2022).

56 See, 'Eight-year-old Child Reportedly Locked Up for Life in Germany', *The Brussels Times* (22 April 2023), at: www.brusselstimes.com/318698/eight-year-old-child-reportedly-locked-up-for-life-in-germany

57 As required under Book VIII of the Social Code, ss 8a and 42.

the Rights of Indigenous Peoples (UNDRIP) and other international instruments.[58] The First Nations and the American Indians, the Indigenous citizens of Canada and the U.S., respectively, together with their counterparts, the Indigenous People and the Māori in Australia and New Zealand, respectively, have all experienced serious disadvantage relative to their non-Indigenous fellow citizens,[59] and this has not been significantly alleviated by preventative state intervention.

Early state intervention on child welfare grounds

The early experience of the Indigenous people in the CANZUS nations was of government policies of assimilation or integration that targeted children. This ostensibly child welfare–driven form of state intervention – purposefully directed towards separating children from their birth families – originated with the residential schools, continued with adoption and was followed by child protection laws. That history causes contemporary state preventative intervention to be treated with suspicion by the Indigenous communities, resulting in its conspicuous failure in all jurisdictions studied. An outcome not helped by the intransigent reluctance of governments in all CANZUS nations to endorse international instruments – such as UNDRIP – designed to specifically protect their Indigenous communities.[60]

Consensual intervention to avoid need for coercive state care

There is evidence that in Canada, the management of state preventative services has been such as to achieve the opposite of its intended outcomes: it has increased the numbers of Indigenous children being admitted to the care system.[61] In 2016, the Canadian Human Rights Tribunal found that the federal government's funding formula failed to consider 'the actual service needs of First Nations children and families', creates 'incentives to remove children from their homes and communities' and that 'too many children living in First Nations communities are being

58 Including the International Covenant on Civil and Political Rights (ICCPR) 1966, Articles 1, 24, 26, 27; the International Covenant on Economic, Social and Cultural Rights (ICESCR) 1966, Articles 2, 10, 14, 15; the International Convention on the Elimination of all forms of Racial Discrimination (ICERD) 1965, Articles 1, 2 and 5; the International Labour Organisation's Convention (ILO); and the Children's Rights and Business Principles: Good Practices Per Principle (UN Global Compact, 2012–2015).

59 See, further, O'Halloran, K., *Children, the Law and the Welfare Principle: Perspectives from North America*, Routledge, 2023, at Chapter 8 and *Children, the Law and the Welfare Principle: Perspectives from Australia & New Zealand,* Routledge, 2023, at chapters 9 and 10.

60 The United Nations Declaration on the Rights of Indigenous Peoples (UNDRIP) was adopted by the General Assembly on 13 September 2007 by a majority of 144 states in favour, 4 votes against (Australia, Canada, New Zealand and the United States). Eventually, the U.S. and New Zealand endorsed it in December 2010, with Canada following in September 2021. Australia announced its support for UNDRIP in 2009 but has yet to formally adopt it.

61 The 'Jordan's Principle' was formulated to strengthen preventative child welfare services to Indigenous children (named after Jordan River Anderson, a 5-year-old Indigenous child who died while federal and provincial governments argued over which should pay for his medical treatment).

taken from their families and placed in care'.[62] It concluded that a consequence of the inequity in service provision was that First Nations children were being prematurely and disproportionately removed from their homes and placed in care in violation of their best interests. These findings were echoed by research projects in the U.S., where the Indian Child Welfare Act 1978 (ICWA) had been introduced with the explicit objective of reducing the disproportionate numbers of AI/AN children entering the public child welfare system and explicitly mandated intensive service provision for vulnerable families to prevent child abuse and neglect and keep children safely in their homes. Carter's research findings in 2009 were typical of many others: 'neglect was the child maltreatment type most associated with the disproportionate placement of American Indian/Alaskan Native children into out-of-home care', indeed that they were 'four times more likely to be removed from their families because of physical neglect' and that neglect was a direct consequence of inadequate state preventative service provision.[63] Access to Title IV-E funding, in order to provide subsidised guardianship for relative caregivers, enabling them to assist or replace failing parental care, was a crucial mechanism for channelling preventative state intervention, but many tribes could not directly access it. This, as noted in a Pew report,[64] resulted in large numbers of AI/AN children under tribal jurisdiction not having the same access to child welfare resources as other children and the consequent disproportionate rate of tribal children being admitted to the public child welfare system.

The historical record and contemporary experience of state intervention on child welfare grounds in respect of the Indigenous communities in Australia and the Māori in New Zealand is no better than that of their North American counterparts. The evolving policy, its main guiding principles, the pattern of separating children from their birth families and communities, the related laws and associated legislative intent – regarding the welfare interests of Indigenous and Māori children – unfolded in Australia and New Zealand much the same as it did in North America and elsewhere. Māori and their children, however, very largely escaped the assimilationist policy inflicted upon their Indigenous counterparts in Australia and other CANZUS nations. Contemporary legislation imposes explicit preventative intervention duties on relevant government agencies. In New Zealand, the *Oranga Tamariki* Act 1989, s 13(2)(e), requires that 'assistance and support should be provided, unless it is impracticable or unreasonable to do so, to assist families, *whānau, hapū, iwi*, and family groups where: (i) there is a risk that a child or young person may be removed from their care' followed by extensive, if generalised,

62 *First Nations Child and Family Caring Society of Canada et al v. Attorney General of Canada (for the Minister of Indian and Northern Affairs Canada)*, 2016 CHRT 16.

63 See, Carter, V., 'Prediction of Placement into Out-of-home Care for American Indian/Alalskan Natives Compared to Non-Indians', *Children and Youth Services Review* (2009), pp. 1–7 at pp. 2 and 5.

64 See, Pew Charitable Trust Report, 'Time for Reform: A Matter of Justice for American Indian and Alaskan Native Children', 2007, at: www.pewtrusts.org/-/media/legacy/uploadedfiles/wwwpewtrustsorg/reports/foster_care_reform/nicwareportpdf.pdf

provisions regarding services and issues of cultural compliance. In Australia, the absence of federal care and protection legislation leaves state preventative duties and services to be determined by each state and territory. Though as they all subscribe to the principle in s 60CA of the Family Law Act 1975 that the welfare interests of the child must be treated as the matter of paramount importance, this might suggest a particularly high level of preventative intervention. In fact, there are very strong contra-indicators.

In New Zealand, indicators of failed preventative state intervention include the fact that Māori babies are at least five times more likely to die of Sudden Infant Death Syndrome than non-Māori.[65] Despite Māori comprising only 16.5% of the population, their children constituted 63% of those coming before the courts in 2021[66] and 68% of the 4,800 children in state care in 2022,[67] and the suicide rate for Māori children and adolescents is the second highest in the OECD.[68] In Australia, equivalent indicators would include an infant mortality rate twice that of non-Indigenous children[69] and an of out-of-home care rate for Indigenous children estimated in 2022 to be 10.5 times greater than that for others.[70]

For many years, there has been gross over-representation of Indigenous,[71] Māori,[72] First Nations and AI/AN children in their respective national child welfare and youth justice systems and much evidence to show that most of those admitted are there not because of harm wilfully inflicted by or to them but because of neglect due to environmental factors that in theory should be amenable to state preventative intervention. This gross over-representation inevitably testifies to the extent and persistence of state failure to provide appropriate, sufficient and culturally accessible preventative services to those communities. One aspect of that failure is the difficulty in finding and approving foster parents or kinship carers from culturally compatible backgrounds who would be willing and able to offer respite care, and in other ways engage in preventative work, with such children and their

65 See, Rutter, C. and Walker, S., 'Infant Mortality Inequities for Māori in New Zealand: A Tale of Three Policies', International *Journal for Equity in Health*, Vol. 20, No. 10 (2021), at: https://doi.org/10.1186/s12939-020-01340-y

66 See, further, at: https://youthcourt.govt.nz/youth-justice/youth-justice-statistics/

67 See, further, at: www.orangatamariki.govt.nz/about-us/performance-and-monitoring/quarterly-report/care-and-protection-statistics/

68 See, UNICEF, Report Card (2021), at: www.unicef.org.nz/stories/new-report-card-shows-that-new-zealand-is-failing-its-children

69 See, further, the Australian Institute of Health and Welfare at: www.indigenoushpf.gov.au/measures/1-20-infant-child-mortality

70 See, further, at: www.familymatters.org.au/wp-content/uploads/2022/11/20221123-Family-Matters-Report-2022-1.pdf

71 See, further, at: www.aihw.gov.au/reports/child-protection/child-protection-australia-2020-21/contents/children-receiving-child-protection-services/aboriginal-and-torres-strait-islander-children-in-the-child-protection-system

72 See, further, at: www.rnz.co.nz/news/national/393208/oranga-tamariki-stats-increase-in-maori-children-taken

families. This is a significant gap, as – given the history – there is naturally a great reluctance to allow, or accept, non-culturally compliant placements.[73]

Discrimination

The Canadian Human Rights Tribunal found, in 2016, that the federal government's provision of child welfare services to First Nations children and families on-reserve had been 'wilfully and recklessly discriminatory'.[74] The provisions were flawed and inequitable, specifically, that the on-reserve child welfare system received up to 38% less funding than elsewhere. In *Daniels v. Canada (Indian Affairs and Northern Development)*,[75] a landmark ruling that established a state duty to rebalance provision for Indigenous children, it was held that 'failure to ensure comparable funding for on- and off-reserve services can be considered racial or ethnic discrimination'. In the recent U.S. case of *Haaland v. Brackeen,*[76] there were also strong elements of racial discrimination. The USSC ruling, upholding the constitutionality of the Indian Child Welfare Act (ICWA), found that the Act – requiring placements (for the purposes of foster care or adoption) to be culturally compatible whenever possible – was an important and justifiable measure that afforded much needed protection for tribal sovereignty, cultural integrity and the welfare interests of Native American children. This decision will have a profound influence on state preventative intervention in the affairs of AI/AN tribes, families and their children for the foreseeable future.

The UN CRC has expressed concern at what it viewed as 'the serious and widespread discrimination faced by Aboriginal and Torres Strait Islander children, including in terms of provision of and accessibility to basic services'. It strongly recommended that the state 'take urgent measures to address disparities in access to services by Aboriginal and Torres Strait Islander children and their families'.[77] Similar allegations of discriminatory intervention have been made regarding the role of Oranga Tamariki with Māori children and the disproportionate 'uplift' of such children into the care system.[78]

Prevention in a criminal context

In the UK, the preventative duty requiring local authorities to take reasonable steps to reduce the need to bring criminal proceedings against children and to encourage

73 See, for example, Choate, P. and Tortorelli, C., 'Attachment Theory: A Barrier for Indigenous Children Involved with Child Protection', *International Journal of Environmental Research and Public Health*, Vol. 19, No. 14 (2022), at: www.ncbi.nlm.nih.gov/pmc/articles/PMC9319150/

74 See, further, at: www.theguardian.com/global-development/2021/sep/29/canada-indigenous-children-first-nations-trudeau

75 (2016) S.C.R. 425 (Can.).

76 21–376 *Haaland v. Brackeen* (15 June 2023).

77 CRC/c/AUS/CO/4, *Concluding Observations: Australia*, 2012, at para 29.

78 See, for example, the Pulitzer Centre at: https://pulitzercenter.org/stories/maori-new-zealand-are-reimagining-child-protection

them not to commit criminal offences[79] was extended to specifically require them to set up at least one 'youth offending team' in its area and to make available youth justice services.[80] There does not appear to be an explicit comparable statutory duty on equivalent Irish authorities. In the U.S., the established approach is more punitive than prevention oriented. Federal legislation provides funding streams for state crime prevention schemes, but the IACHR, in its 2018 report, details at length the many ways in which the juvenile justice system is currently failing youth who commit offences and has 'highlighted the need to prioritise prevention policies'.[81] In Canada, the Youth Criminal Justice Act 2003 introduced an emphasis on prevention with a focus on encouraging and supporting local community initiatives that, for example, help youth learn new social skills and channel their energies into positive activities; ensure that youths are educated and trained for constructive careers that contribute to their communities; ensure that youths receive good nutrition, housing, and health care; and protect children from physical, emotional or sexual abuse.

In France, legislation in 2002 introduced preventative measures including 'educational sanctions' for children aged 10–18, such as attendance at training courses, while the Law of 5 March 2007 on the prevention of delinquency, primarily targeting young offenders, assigned more responsibility to civic authorities, specifically mayors, to develop preventative strategies that might reduce levels of delinquency. In Germany, children (under 14 years), juveniles (14–17) and young adults (18–20) all have the right to support and education and to be protected in their personal development by the child and youth welfare agencies. Youth services are established at the local community level, where priority is given to private nonprofit organisations.

Preventative measures in New Zealand would seem to have considerably reduced the rate of juvenile offending in recent years, though Māori offenders continue to be over-represented.[82] Much of the drop in offending by children in New Zealand has been because fewer children are becoming offenders in the first place due to effective targeting of high-risk child offenders. These themes are replicated in Australia, where a range of diversionary options are available in respect of children in trouble with the law. Legal action taken by police may include non-court actions (such as warnings, formal cautions, referral to a family group conference, counselling or infringement notices), while the Court may decide to divert the young person from further involvement in the system (for example, by referral to other services or to a specialist programme).

Child offenders from Indigenous communities

There is a general consensus among the CANZUS nations that their present justice systems are failing the youth of their Indigenous communities.

79 Children Act 1989, Sched 2, para 7.

80 Crime and Disorder Act 1998, s 39 and ss 38–41, respectively.

81 See, the Inter-American Commission on Human Rights, 'Children and Adolescents in the United States' Adult Criminal Justice System', *op cit* at p. 75.

82 Ibid.

The U.S. and Canada

In Canada, the objectives of Youth Criminal Justice Act 2003 include preventing crime by addressing the circumstances underlying a young person's offending behaviour, rehabilitating of young persons who commit offences and facilitating their reintegration back into society and ensuring that a young person is subject to meaningful consequences for his or her offences in order to promote the long-term protection of the public. It supports crime prevention by providing for the referral of young persons to programmes or agencies in the community to address the circumstances underlying their offending behaviour. However, the statistical trends since the introduction of the 2003 legislation reveal the extent of its failure to fulfill a preventative function: in 2017/2018, while representing 8% of the Canadian population, Indigenous youth accounted for 48% of admissions to custody in nine jurisdictions as opposed to 37% in 2014/2015.[83] As the Department of Justice has acknowledged: 'Indigenous youth are over-represented at all stages of the criminal justice system'.[84]

The previous depiction of failed Canadian state preventative intervention in a criminal context is mirrored by similar facts in the U.S., where Indigenous communities receive a disproportionately low level of public service provision which means that tribal authorities do not have the resources, staff or the infrastructure to implement effective prevention. Inadequate resources for juvenile justice have long been a challenge for tribal communities, resulting in insufficient training of law enforcement and other justice personnel and a shortage of programmes to combat juvenile delinquency through appropriate prevention strategies. As has been said,[85] American Indian and Alaska Native (AI/AN) young people are almost twice as likely to be petitioned to state court for skipping school, violating liquor laws and engaging in other behaviours that are only illegal because of their age (often known as status offences). Once involved with the state court system, they are less likely to be placed on probation and experience higher rates of detention and residential placements.

Not only are AI/AN youth disproportionately represented in the juvenile justice system (with one 2008 study finding that tribal youth comprise 60% of the juvenile justice population) but they are also often held in long-term facilities far away from their tribal lands.[86]

Australia and New Zealand

The single most obvious shared jurisdictional characteristic of the law as it relates to child offenders in Australia and New Zealand is that preventative state

83 See, further, at: www.publicsafety.gc.ca/cnt/rsrcs/pblctns/ststclsnpsht-yth/index-en.aspx?wbdisable=true

84 See, Department of Justice, 'Indigenous Youth Roundtables', at: www.justice.gc.ca/eng/cj-jp/yj-jj/tools-outils/iyr-trja.html#ftnref1

85 See, Coalition for Juvenile Justice, *op cit*, at p. 1.

86 See, further, at: https//youth.gov/youth-topics/american-indian-alaska-native-youth/juvenile-justice

intervention on behalf of Indigenous and Māori children is conspicuously and consistently failing. As Judge Walker has pointed out '66% of those appearing in the Youth Court are Māori (14% of the population)'.[87] In Australia, it has been estimated that although only 5.8% of children are Indigenous, almost half (49%) of those being supervised by the Youth Justice Service on an average day in 2020–2021 were so identified.[88] The embedded and systemic nature of that failure is demonstrated by the fact that not only are children from those communities grossly over-represented in their respective justice systems but a high proportion will also have transferred from child welfare and will progress through to the adult criminal system.[89] Moreover, preventative intervention fails those who first come to the attention of the criminal courts: more than 1 in 3 Indigenous children – as opposed to 1 in 7 others – under supervision in 2020–2021 were repeat offenders, which suggests that recidivism is more than twice as big a problem for Indigenous as for non-Indigenous children. In Australia, unlike New Zealand, an important contributing factor to the numbers of children in the justice system is the low age threshold for entry: a recent Australian Institute of Health and Welfare report showed that 15.5% of Indigenous children in detention on an average day were aged 14 or under; the current 10-year age of criminal responsibility clearly forces more children into that system than would the age of 14 as recommended by the UN CRC.[90]

Comparative jurisdictional analysis of state intervention: support

In a family law context, the legal function of 'prevention' only acquires traction if it is made the subject of duties in respect of specified support services, the delivery of which is assigned to a named agency accountable for using them to achieve stated aims and objectives. Specificity of support services is of central importance.

Support services

Traditionally, the basic support services have been centred on the provision of 'necessaries', meaning food, clothing and shelter or the funds to acquire them. Respite care in state facilities, usually just for children, to relieve parents under stress due to illness or bereavement, etc., was a standard support service in most jurisdictions.

87 Judge John Walker, 'Barriers to Engagement', address to the Justice for Young People Conference, Adelaide, Australia (7 November 2018), at: www.districtcourts.govt.nz/youth-court/publications/barriers-to-engagement-enabling-full-participation-in-the-justice-system-for-young-people/

88 See, further, at: www.aihw.gov.au/reports/youth-justice/youth-justice-in-australia-2020-21/contents/summary

89 See, for example, *Care to Custody: Incarceration Rates Research Report* (2022), at: www.abuseincare.org.nz/our-progress/library/v/500/care-to-custody-incarceration-rates-research-report

90 See, CRC/c/AUS/CO/4, *Concluding Observations: Australia*, 2012, at para 43.

Common law jurisdictions

In England and Wales, under the 1989 Act, the two main sets of specific support services relate to day care and accommodation, both of which are made legislatively available. But although a claimant may satisfy the threshold criteria and be designated a 'child in need', he or she may be refused the service, as a local authority has a discretion in permitting service access. Also, while there is a strict duty to ensure the availability of pre-school child care services, many are financially inaccessible.[91] Support services specific to preventing the admission of a child to state care include provision of assistance which may be a cash grant, a loan or a grant of 'necessities'; such family centres as it considers appropriate within its area; such resources as may be necessary to reduce the need to bring proceedings in respect of children, encourage them not to commit criminal offences and avoid the need to place them in secure accommodation; and resources to prevent children within their area suffering ill-treatment or neglect. Sched 2(9) places a duty on a local authority to provide an explicit programme of services to support children in need. However, court rulings have established that this 'duty' is in fact discretionary: the Court has no power to direct a local authority to recognise a child as being in need within the definition of s 17 for the purposes of ensuring a service entitlement.[92]

In Ireland, the Child Care Act 1991, s 3(3), states a general duty to 'provide child care and family support services' followed by specific duties relating to voluntary care admission, accommodation for homeless children, provision of an adoption service and arrangements for working with voluntary organisations. Unlike in the UK, the preventative duties are stated in general terms, the methods for giving effect to them (with the exception of references to adoption, pre-school services, etc.) being largely left to agency discretion.[93] There is a similar lack of specificity in the Canadian legislation for support services.

In the U.S., by the turn of the century, preventative state intervention to assist vulnerable families had become defined as a public health matter, centred on the Maternal, Infant, and Early Childhood Home Visiting programme, and was being delivered across most states.[94] The introduction in 2019 of the Family First legislation allowed federal funds, provided by way of Title IV-E of the Social Security Act, to give vulnerable families the support necessary to prevent their children entering the public care system.[95] These funds are now directed by states – that have federally approved family assistance plans – towards the provision of preventative

91 See, CRC/C/GBR/CO/5: *Concluding observations on the sixth periodic report of the United Kingdom of Great Britain and Northern Ireland* (2016), at para 50.

92 See, *Re J (Specific Issue Order: Leave to Apply)* (1995) 1 FLR 699 and *R v. Cambridge District Health Authority ex parte B (No. 2)* (1995) 1 FLR 1055.

93 There is an absence of specified relevant services such as home help, parent training, or in-home creative child play and development progammes.

94 See, Information Gateway, at: www. childwelfare.gov/topics/preventing/prevention-programs/homevisit/homevisitprog/

95 Family First Prevention Services Act 2018, TITLE VII – Subtitle A – Investing in Prevention and Supporting Families, s 50702.

services that enable children to stay with their parents or relatives, and there has been a widespread take-up across the country.[96] Preventative intervention takes the form of home visiting by nurses and social workers, parent education programmes, parent support groups, family resource centres and other services. The 'Strengthening Families National Network', providing programmes and services in more than 20 states and specifically targeted towards supporting families and preventing child abuse and neglect, must be conducive to improving the welfare interests of many children.

The Canadian preventative services would seem to be less well developed than that of their U.S. neighbours, and in general, state intervention is oriented more towards protection than prevention. Responsibility for Canadian preventative service provision – the low level of which has been criticised by UNICEF[97] – rests on the provinces and territories (except for First Nations provision which is largely federally funded), and each gives effect to its duties through the national network of Children's Aid Societies. One measure of the relative ineffectiveness of this provision was the slow official response over many years regarding large numbers of missing young First Nations women and girls.[98]

In New Zealand, an interesting aspect of preventative service provision is that 'a child' maintains that status until aged 20, which presumably extends the right of families to state support accordingly. Under the *Oranga Tamariki* Act 1989, the Children's Act 2014, the Children (Children's Services) Order 2016 and the Children's Action Plan, there are various provisions of a preventative nature intended to support vulnerable families and children in need, and they specify related service provision. In Australia, the lack of adequate state investment in family support services was a matter of concern to the UN CRC:

> further reiterates its previous recommendations to the State Party that it take measures to strengthen the current programmes of family support, inter alia, by targeting the most vulnerable families, in order to reduce the number of children placed in out-of-home care.[99]

It urged 'the State party to prioritize early intervention approaches, including at the antenatal period, to provide support to families in situations of heightened vulnerability and prevent or mitigate abuse and neglect of children and violence in the home'.[100] Partly in response to such concerns, the families and children

96 See, further, at: www.ncsl.org/research/human-services/family-first-prevention-services-act-ffpsa.aspx#:~:text=The%20Family%20First%20Prevention%20Services%20Act%20also%20seeks%20to%20curtail,for%20more%20than%20two%20weeks.

97 See, 'UNICEF Child Well-Being Index: Canada Ranked 17th Out of 29 Wealthy Nations', *Huffington Post* (10 October 2013), at: www.huffingtonpost.ca/2013/04/10/unicef-child-well-being-canada_n_3050119.html

98 See, the report *Reclaiming Power and Place,* published by the National Inquiry into Missing and Murdered Indigenous Women and Girls, Ottawa, 2019.

99 CRC/c/AUS/CO/4, *Concluding Observations: Australia*, 2012, at para 19.52.

100 Ibid, at para 56.

branch of the Department of Social Services now administers a number of federal programmes and services, including the Child Support Scheme and the Early Years Strategy.[101]

Civil law jurisdictions

In France, the *juge des enfants* is empowered to order support for parents in the form of *assistance éducative* measures (*aide éducative en milieu ouvert*) when the health, the safety or the morality of a minor is in danger or when the conditions of his/her 'education' are gravely compromised.[102] This is markedly different from the corresponding position in UK, where the ruling in *Liverpool*[103] established that the Court has no such power in relation to a local authority's discretion to carry out its statutory defined service provision role as it sees fit. The laws of 1986 and 1989 require social workers and psychologists to provide assistance such as managing conflicts between parents and children, overseeing housekeeping budgets, school attendance, etc. Interestingly, in circumstances where parental neglect is due to or associated with mismanagement of social benefits, then French law provides that the *juge des enfants* may appoint a *tuteur* to administer those benefits. Much the same family support policy prevails in Germany, where support services such as assistance for expectant mothers and those with new-born children are mandated under the provisions of the Social Code[104] and the Act on Cooperation and Information on Child Protection,[105] while services for vulnerable families with health issues and services are available either at counselling centres for children, adolescents and parents or in the form of home visiting services.[106] All services are preventative and non-invasive in nature, but all service providers must report any parental neglect, failure to cope, dependency issues, etc., they cannot cope with to the Youth Welfare Office, thus implementing the policy priority of keeping families together before addressing parenting deficits and triggering child protection intervention procedures. Constitutional principles require any intervention in the context of children at risk to prioritise the provision of support services – such as day care centres and therapeutic services – to avoid child removal.[107] Furthermore, early access to families, even before the birth of a child, was introduced in 2012[108] to install a primary preventive system of help and support for vulnerable families.

101 See, further, at: www.dss.gov.au/families-and-children/programs-services
102 The Civil Code, Article 375.
103 *A v. Liverpool City Council* (1982) FLR 222.
104 Book VIII of the Social Code, s 16.
105 Section 2 (1).
106 Book VIII of the Social Code, s 17, 18 and 52a; Act on Cooperation and Information on Child Protection, s. 2.
107 Galm, B. and Derr, R. *Combating Child Abuse and Neglect: Child Protection in Germany – National Report*, Deutsches Jugendinstitut e.V., 2011, at: www.dji.de/fileadmin/user_upload/bibs/DAPHNEGermanReportLayoutFIN.pdf
108 Act on Cooperation and Information on Child Protection, s. 2.

Respite care: common law jurisdictions

State provision of regulated respite care for children – in foster homes, kinship placements or residential facilities – is an expensive service but one much valued in all countries, particularly by single parents and in circumstances where a family is affected by illness, incapacity or death.

In the UK, a child voluntarily admitted to state care nonetheless acquires the status of a 'looked-after child' and may be allowed to 'drift in care' either because the parent/s are unable/unwilling to resume responsibility or are considered not ready to do so by the local authority.[109] Such a respite care arrangement may be transformed over time into one that gives foster parents a claim to consider adoption.[110] In sharp contrast, the singular characteristic of Irish public family law is that most children in state care are admitted with the voluntary agreement of their parents, most usually for reasons of respite, though this can become extended.[111] This service, indicative of a consensual and supportive state-family relationship, requires the state authorities to take into its care any child requiring care and protection but not 'against the wishes of a parent' *nor* to maintain him or her in its care 'if that parent or any such person wishes to resume care'.[112]

In the U.S., Title IV-E funds[113] can now be directed by states – that have federally approved family assistance plans – towards the provision of preventative services that enable 'candidates for foster care' to stay with their parents or relatives.[114] This federally funded respite care programme has had a widespread take-up rate across the country. Respite care is also available in Canada, but accessing such services and coping with the associated lengthy time delays are acknowledged to be issues for Canadian families in need.

In all Australian states and territories, there is general provision of accommodation on a voluntary basis, in circumstances where families are in need of respite care for their child or children, and has been a much valued service in Australia but in some states is only available if judicially sanctioned.[115] In New Zealand, parents or others with care responsibility can transfer that responsibility to the *Oranga Tamariki* by voluntary agreement; this may, for example, be to relieve stress in a

109 Under the Children Act 1989, s 20(8), discharge from respite care is subject to the authority being satisfied that this would not be exposing the child to a risk of significant harm

110 See, for example, *Williams & Anor v. London Borough of Hackney* (2018) UKSC 37.

111 Around 55% of admissions to state care in Ireland take place pursuant to voluntary care agreements. See, further, O'Mahony, C., Burns, K. and Brennan, R., 'Voluntary Care in Ireland Study (2018–21)', at: www.ucc.ie/en/appsoc/resconf/res/voluntarycareinirelandstudy2018-2021/

112 The Child Care Act 1991, s 4.

113 Family First Prevention Services Act 2018, TITLE VII – Subtitle A – Investing in Prevention and Supporting Families, s 50702.

114 See, further, at: www.ncsl.org/research/human-services/family-first-prevention-services-act-ffpsa.aspx#:~:text=The%20Family%20First%20Prevention%20Services%20Act%20also%20seeks%20to%20curtail,for%20more%20than%20two%20weeks.

115 In Victoria, this can be facilitated by the issue of an interim accommodation order.

family by providing carer respite. The consent of the child concerned, if 12 years of age or more, is mandatory if the respite is for an extended period.[116]

Respite care: civil law jurisdictions

There is a strong legal presumption in both France and Germany that a child should remain in his/her family and that the latter should receive such state support as may be necessary to overcome the material and moral difficulties it encounters. That support may include the voluntary placement of a child in state care on a temporary basis for family respite reasons. In France, when such respite care is required, the parents must apply to a court for the exercise of parental authority to be delegated to the *Aide Sociale á 1 Enfance* (ASE), the state child protection service, for that purpose, which is a serious constraint on parental access to an ostensibly consensually available state family support service.

Support services in an Indigenous context

In Canada, the Jordan's Principle was formulated in 2007 to eliminate service inequities and delays in provision for First Nations children, and it established a procedure to bridge the jurisdictional gap between federal and provincial governments.[117] Since then, Bill C-92 – an act respecting First Nations, Inuit and Métis children, youth and families – became law, with effect from January 2020, recognising the right of Indigenous people to self-governance of their child welfare systems, with resources provided by the federal government.[118] However, constant problems caused the UN CRC, in its May 2022 report, to question government support services for First Nations children.[119] In the U.S., only 60 tribes – a fraction of the total of 574 – currently operate child support programmes, providing services to Native American families consistent with tribal values and cultures.

In Australia, the extent of neglect among the Indigenous communities is apparent across a range of social indicators – such as overcrowding, unemployment and in the limited access to services[120]- and has caused the UN CRC to express concern at what it viewed as 'the serious and widespread discrimination faced by Aboriginal and Torres Strait Islander children, including in terms of provision of and accessibility to basic services'. It strongly recommended that the state 'take

116 The *Oranga Tamariki* Act 1989, ss 139 and 140.

117 See, further, the Jordan's Principle Working Group, 'Without denial, delay, or disruption: Ensuring First Nation children's access to equitable services through Jordan's Principle' (2015), at: www.afn.ca/uploads/files/jordans_principle-report.pdf

118 See, further, O'Halloran, K., *Children, the Law and the Welfare Principle: Perspectives from North America*, Routledge, 2023, at chapter 8.

119 See, further, at: www.ohchr.org/en/press-releases/2022/06/un-child-rights-committee-issues-findings-cambodia-canada-chile-croatia-cuba

120 See, further, Scott, D., *Understanding Child Neglect,* 2014, at: https://aifs.gov.au/resources/policy-and-practice-papers/understanding-child-neglect

urgent measures to address disparities in access to services by Aboriginal and Torres Strait Islander children and their families'.[121] These international concerns echo those expressed in the *Little Children are Sacred* report[122] and the Warrki Jarrinjaku report[123] which attributed some of the causes of low service availability and take-up to the fact that the majority of service programmes were designed by non-Indigenous people and staffed from outside the community, and the outcomes were judged from a mainstream (non-Indigenous) perspective.

In New Zealand, the *Oranga Tamariki* Act 1989, s 5(1)I(i), states that the primary responsibility for ensuring the welfare of a child lies with their family, while s 13(2)(b)(i), states that agency service provision should be such as to 'strengthen and support the child's or young person's family'. Despite legislator's good intentions, however, there has long been public consternation regarding the fact that state removal of children from their families has been found to be many times more necessary for Māori – who constitute 65% of those in care but only 16.5% of the population – than for others. This persistent gross over-representation was the subject of a review by the Children's Commissioner, the 2020 report of which found that Māori children were five times more likely to be taken into care than other children. The Human Rights Commission has noted what has been termed the entrenched institutional racism in *Oranga Tamariki*: a perception that mirrors criticisms made of Canadian child welfare agencies and is evidenced by similar facts.[124] Again, it is alleged that a cultural clash is responsible: Caucasian child welfare staff do not seem to always respect the practice of allowing extended family members to share child care responsibilities with birth parents.

Culture specific placements

American Indian children are at least three times more likely to be placed in foster care than children in the general population:[125] in Alaska, for example, Indigenous children make up 18% of the child population but 55% of the children in foster care; while in Canada, the 2016 National Household Survey indicated that Indigenous children aged 0–14 years were placed in foster care at 13.1 times the rate of others.[126] However, there has long been a critical lack of Indigenous foster carers

121 CRC/c/AUS/CO/4, *Concluding Observations: Australia*, 2012, at para 29.

122 See, further, Wild, R. and Anderson, P., *Little Children are Sacred, Report of the Northern Territory Board of Inquiry into the Protection of Aboriginal Children from Sexual Abuse*, Board of Inquiry into the Protection of Aboriginal Children from Sexual Abuse, Darwin, NT, 2007.

123 Warrki Jarrinjaku, ACRS Project Team, *Warrki Jarrinjaku Jintangkamanu Purananjaku: Aboriginal Child Rearing and Associated Research*, Department of Family and Community Services, Canberra, 2002.

124 See, further, at: www.theguardian.com/world/2021/jan/22/new-zealand-child-welfare-head-resigns-amid-furore-over-maori-baby-separations-oranga-tamariki

125 See, Center for the Study of Social Policy, Annie E. Casey Foundation, & Alliance for Racial Equity in Child Welfare, 2011.

126 See, Fallon, B., Lefebvre, R., Trocmé, N., et al., 'Denouncing the Continued Overrepresentation of First Nations Children in Canadian Child Welfare' (2019), at: https://cwrp.ca/sites/default/

and prospective adopters. Across North America, the shortfall in the availability of culturally compliant foster care and adoption placements for Indigenous children results in a constant stream of legal cases initiated by complainants objecting to or defending cross-cultural placements.[127]

Support services in a disability context

The welfare interests/rights of children with a disability are framed in an international legislative context primarily by UN CROC, Article 8 of the ECHR, as interpreted in ECtHR caselaw and the United Nations Convention on the Rights of Persons with Disabilities.

Common law jurisdictions

In England and Wales, such a child is defined as 'in need' which requires a local authority to undertake a needs assessment in respect of family and child and is then specifically required to provide appropriate social care support services. In Ireland, concern has been expressed regarding the lack of adequate respite services available for specifically for children in care with disabilities.[128] In the U.S., the Individuals with Disabilities Education Act (IDEA) 2004 states that all children with disabilities are entitled to a free appropriate public education to meet their unique needs and prepare them for further education, employment and independent living. Parts C and D of the Act provide guidance concerning the funding, services and national activities to be undertaken to improve the education of children with disabilities. Canadian services would seem to be less well developed.

In Australia, at the turn of the century, it was estimated that about 296,400 children, or 7.6% of those aged 0–14 years, had a disability: of which most – 144,100 (or 3.7%) – had a physical/diverse disability. The next most common group was intellectual/learning disability (143,000 children or 3.7%).[129] State service provision to such children and their families includes a range of income support benefits, such as respite care, therapy and early child intervention, aids and equipment services, housing and crisis accommodation services and child protection. Most carers receive the carer allowance as their main 'disability-related' support payment, with some also receiving the carer payment. Commonwealth State/Territory Disability

files/publications/FNCIS-2019%20-%20Denouncing%20the%20Continued%20Overrepresentation%20of%20First%20Nations%20Children%20in%20Canadian%20Child%20Welfare%20-%20Final_1%20%282%29.pdf

127 See, for example, for the U.S., *Brackeen v. Bernhardt*, No. 18–11479 (5th Cir.2019); and for Canada, *Racine v. Woods* (1983) 2 SCR 173.

128 Ombudsman for Children's Office, *Molly Two Years On: Have Tusla and the HSE Delivered on Commitments to Children with a Disability in the Care of the State?* (2020), at p. 5, at: www.oco.ie/app/uploads/2020/01/Molly-Two-Years-On.pdf.

129 Madden, R., 'Children with Disabilities in Australia', *Australian Institute of Health and Welfare*, AIHW cat. no. DIS 38, Canberra (2004).

Agreement (CSTDA)–funded support services are a primary source of official support while community-based support – including services such as therapy, early childhood intervention and behaviour/specialist intervention – were the most common, followed by respite services. Notably, in 2002, 81% of children with disabilities attending government schools and 91% of children with disabilities attending non-government schools attended mainstream rather than special schools. As in Germany, this indicator of an inclusive policy must benefit the welfare interests of children with a disability.

In New Zealand, the 2013 Disability Survey estimated that there were around 95,000 disabled children up to the age of 14 (or 11% of all children in this age group) which, compared to Australia, seems very high.[130] Interestingly, as in Australia, the survey defines a child with a disability as one aged between 0–14 years. Recent research indicates that children with a disability are much more likely to suffer from the effects of poverty: 30% of the disabled children in New Zealand lived in one-parent households, 86% of the disabled children who lived in households earning less than $30,000 a year were in one-parent households and the unemployment rate of primary carers of disabled children was 17%.[131] It notes that a key factor in the prevailing poverty is the low disability-related allowance: in the United Kingdom, for example, the median payment rate is almost three times higher than the New Zealand equivalent. This is exacerbated by the fact that relevant services are only partially government funded. It would seem that children with a disability are more likely to spend their childhood in relative poverty and that their welfare interests will be correspondingly negatively impacted.

Civil law jurisdictions

In France, the CRC in its 2016 report drew attention to 'the persistent discrimination against children with disabilities, especially children with multiple disabilities, in their access to education, regarding equality with others, including during recreation, extracurricular activities, in school facilities, and vocational training'. It expressed regret:

> the law provides for a system of special units within mainstream schools for children as young as three; that some children with disabilities are

130 See, Stats New Zealand, at: www.google.co.uk/search?q=Statistics+New+Zealand%2C+2014d&sca_esv=570700320&sxsrf=AM9HkKmNRo3dui__1Fq_bsUyt98wdrQLLA%3A1696437679591&source=hp&ei=r5UdZafDIYjMgAbOvqOYBQ&iflsig=AO6bgOgAAAAAZR2jv5UUk2o7U7OLBup-UB5M2rrV7TTV&ved=0ahUKEwjn1pfq6tyBAxUIJsAKHU7fCFMQ4dUDCAs&uact=5&oq=Statistics+New+Zealand%2C+2014d&gs_lp=Egdnd3Mtd2l6Ih1TdGF0aXN0aWNzIE5ldyBaZWFsYW5kLCAyMDE0ZDIFECEYoAFIlg1QAFgAcAB4AJABAJgBfqABfqoBAzAuMbgBA8gBAPgBAvgBAQ&sclient=gws-wiz

131 See, Murray, S., 'Breaking the Link between Disability and Child and Whanau Poverty', *Policy Quarterly,* Vol. 14, No. 4 (2018), at: www.victoria.ac.nz/__data/assets/pdf_file/0003/1713621/Murray.pdf

> institutionalised, some are still in segregated schools, and others drop out of school as a result of a lack of accommodation and support.

It urged the authorities to 'effectively adopt a human rights- based approach to disability without delay' and 'to take immediate measures to ensure that the rights of children with autism, especially their right to inclusive education, are respected'.[132] As regards Germany, the CRC in its 2022 report[133] recommended that Germany 'streamline all support for children with disabilities into one body, such as child and youth support services, with a view to ensuring that all children with disabilities have equal access to benefits under Book VIII of the Social Code'.[134] In response, the practice of segregation has been ended by introducing a rule that children with and without disabilities are to be cared for together in child day care and other Youth Welfare facilities. Also, special consultants for parents and/or handicapped children have been introduced.[135]

Support services in a criminal context

Prevention of further offences is the declared primary aim of the justice system as it relates to children in England and Wales. Nonetheless, the fact that the age of criminal responsibility is set at 10 years of age is itself a considerable obstacle to any prevention policy and one that has attracted criticism from the CRC in 2016 and again in 2019.[136] Both the Children Act 1989 (Sched 2, para 7) and the Crime and Disorder Act 1998 (ss 38–41) require local authorities to engage in preventative intervention to reduce the need to bring criminal proceedings against children, but in the current era of tight budgetary controls, it is unlikely that the necessary public funds can be channelled in that direction. In Ireland, the Irish Youth Justice Service has declared that a primary policy objective is focused on 'diverting children from crime and the criminal justice system'. In keeping with trends elsewhere, youth crime in Ireland reduced significantly in the 2000s, decreasing by one-third from a peak of 27,853 incidents reported in 2007 to 18,567 in 2019.[137] In the current *Youth Justice Strategy 2021–2027,*[138] there is an emphasis on expanding the 'Diversion Programme', while increased use of family group conferences and community-based programmes responding to youth crime, social exclusion, early school

132 Ibid, at para 57, citing General Comment No. 9 (2006).

133 CRC/C/DEU/CO/5–6.

134 Ibid, at para 29(a).

135 See, the Social Code, Book VIII, s. 10a.

136 See, the UN Committee on the Rights of the Child, *Concluding Observations: United Kingdom of Great Britain And Northern Ireland*, United Nations, 2016, at paras 41(b) and 21, respectively. Also, see, Committee against Torture concluding observations on the sixth periodic report of the United Kingdom of Great Britain and Northern Ireland (2019) at para 23.

137 See, Reddy, J., *The Youth Justice System in Ireland: A Review (revised),* Research Evidence into Policy, Programmes and Practice (REPPP) Project, University of Limerick (2022), at: www.drugsandalcohol.ie/37979/1/Review_of_Irish_youth_justice-2022.pdf

138 See, further, at: www.gov.ie/en/publication/3670e-youth-justice-strategy-2021-2027/

leaving and youth unemployment have made an impact in recent years, and restorative justice interventions provide alternatives to detention and residential care.

In France, the fact that a child may be tried in a criminal court from the age of 10 and will be treated in law as an adult from the age of 13 clearly does more to draw children into the justice system than to facilitate preventative intervention. However, the effectiveness of the latter can be seen in the fact that educative measures are imposed more frequently than imprisonment. It is also apparent in the recourse in recent years to restorative justice which, as an alternative to criminal proceedings, offers a more welfare-oriented approach to offending, allowing a child to avoid being burdened by a criminal record. In Germany, children (under 14 years), juveniles (14–17) and young adults (18–20) all have the right to support and education and to be protected in their personal development by the child and youth welfare agencies. The legal system as it relates to child offenders has been praised for being 'particularly instructive' because it 'responds to crimes committed by young people in ways that are age appropriate, centre on rehabilitation, and resort to incarceration only in limited circumstances and when absolutely necessary'.[139] Both the Criminal Code and the Juvenile Justice Act 1953[140] continue to emphasise the welfare approach to children who offend by diversion, educational and restorative justice measures. The fact that youths are treated as juveniles until they reach 21 years of age significantly extends the period when they may claim an entitlement to supportive rather than punitive measures. The CRC, in its 2022 report, recommends that the federal government 'continues to actively promote, in all *Länder*, the application of non-judicial measures, such as diversion, mediation and counselling, and, wherever possible, the use of non-custodial measures for children, such as probation or community service'.[141]

In the U.S., levels of youth violence and crime are among the highest in the developed world, making it a leading cause of injury and death for young Americans aged 15 to 24 years and strongly indicating that preventative intervention strategies lack effectiveness. Children of African American descent remain disproportionately represented in the criminal justice system: constituting 16% of the total youth population in the U.S. but 28% of all youths arrested, 35% of youths transferred to adult courts and 58% of youths sentenced to confinement in adult prisons.[142] This must say something about ineffective prevention – or racial bias – in relation to supportive intervention with that particular group. Preventative

139 See, Fair and Just Prosecution Report, 'Lessons Learned from Germany: Promoting Developmentally Appropriate and Rehabilitative Youth and Young Adult Justice' (2022), at: https://fairandjust-prosecution.org/wp-content/uploads/2022/06/FJP-Germany-Youth-Justice-Brief.pdf

140 Amended in 1974 and most recently in 2008.

141 CRC/C/DEU/CO/5–6, at para 42. See, also, the CRC general comment No. 24 (2019) on children's rights in the child justice system.

142 See, Hartney, C. and Silva, F., 'Justice for Some: Differential Treatment of Youth of Color in the Justice System', National Council on Crime and Delinquency (publishers), 2007, at: https://search.issuelab.org/resource/and-justice-for-some-differential-treatment-of-youth-of-color-in-the-justice-system.html

intervention is not helped by the low age of criminal responsibility – set at seven years of age in 35 states – which clearly draws a higher proportion of child offenders into the justice system than would be the case in any other developed nation. The IACHR, in its 2018 report, details at length the many ways in which the juvenile justice system is currently failing youth who commit offences and has 'highlighted the need to prioritise prevention policies'.[143] In Canada, during 2020–2021, the number of youths in custody decreased by more than one-quarter, the largest decline in almost two decades,[144] though Indigenous children continue to be over-represented.[145] The Youth Criminal Justice Act 2003 introduced a new emphasis on prevention. Prevention programmes now focus on encouraging and supporting local community initiatives that, for example, help youth learn new social skills and channel their energies into positive activities; ensure that youths are educated and trained for constructive careers that contribute to their communities; ensure that youths receive good nutrition, housing and health care; and protect children from physical, emotional or sexual abuse.

In Australia, as has been pointed out,[146] for most of the 20th century, juvenile justice services were provided by state departments responsible for community and family welfare where, under that inclusive umbrella, young offenders would have had access to social services, housing services and welfare agencies more generally, which permitted community support packages and facilitated preventative intervention. However, since the turn of the century, there has been a trend to relocate these services within departments responsible for justice and adult corrections which has brought with it a firmer focus on personal accountability and reparation, leaving less scope for a supportive role. A particular aspect of the failure of preventative intervention is revealed by the consistent over-representation of Indigenouus children in the criminal justice system, a matter which has repeatedly attracted criticism from international bodies, most recently by the UN Committee Against Torture in 2022.[147] Nonetheless, the numbers of children entering the juvenile justice system have fallen over the five years from 2016–2017 to 2020–2021, so perhaps prevention is in fact working. New Zealand has seen a similar drop over recent years since the introduction of the *Oranga Tamariki* Act 1989 and an ostensibly welfare-oriented approach to child offenders that accentuated diversionary measures which retained the child in their family and community. Preventative policies in that country are based on the view that early identification and application of effective interventions that target high-risk child offenders present an opportunity to steer the children onto a more positive path, thereby preventing

143 See, the Inter-American Commission on Human Rights, 'Children and Adolescents in the United States' Adult Criminal Justice System', *op cit* at p. 75.

144 See, further, at: https://www150.statcan.gc.ca/n1/daily-quotidien/220420/dq220420c-eng.htm

145 See, further, at: www.justice.gc.ca/eng/rp-pr/jr/jf-pf/2019/may01.html

146 See, Cunneen, C., 'Youth Justice in Australia', *Oxford Academic* (2014), at: https://academic.oup.com/edited-volume/41333/chapter/352357407

147 See, further, at: www.ohchr.org/en/press-releases/2022/11/un-committee-against-torture-publishes-findings-australia-chad-el-salvador

many future crimes and reducing the number of victims.[148] However, the fact that rates of recidivism are high – within four years of being apprehended in 2009, two-thirds of children had re-offended – must represent a failure of effective preventative intervention.

Comparative jurisdictional analysis of state intervention: promotion

Arguably, 'promotion' has an inherently spurious quality that is not amenable to much in the way of analysis. Unless given effect by specific affirmative action duties, it can only too readily lapse into aspirational policies.

State promotion services

In England and Wales, the term 'promotion' is used fairly ubiquitously in child-related legislation. For example, the 1989 Act imposes a general duty upon local authorities 'to safeguard and promote the welfare of children within their area who are in need' (s 17[1]) and, 'so far as is consistent with that duty, to promote the upbringing of such children by their families' and, in relation to any child who is 'looked after', to safeguard and promote the welfare of that child (s 22[3]). In addition, the Children and Families Act 2014 reformed the service provision for vulnerable children and promoted 'fostering for adoption' in which approved adopters are allowed to foster children during the wait for formal court approval, and it strengthened the Children's Commissioner's role from simply representing the views and interests of children to focusing on promoting and protecting the rights of children. Moreover, the Children and Social Work Act 2017, s 1(2), requires the authorities to 'promote their physical and mental health and well-being'. In Ireland, the authorities have the somewhat similar statutory duty 'to promote the welfare of children who are not receiving adequate care and protection'.[149] To some extent, these provisions are given effect by working in collaboration with voluntary and community organisations to provide local sports as well as recreational and other such programmes to engage young people. In contrast to the lack of any specificity in such vaguely worded duties, government promotional initiatives have included the removal of any discretion to impose physical chastisement on pupils in schools, together with new protocols governing bullying and the introduction of lunch clubs and afterschool supervised activities.

In the U.S., federal service provision duties intended to safeguard children's welfare interests are usually specified in legislation as, for example, in the Family First legislation, while Title IV-E Prevention Services Clearinghouse consists of a continuously updated comprehensive list of evaluated and tested prevention

148 See, Ministry of Social Development, 'Child and Youth Offending Patterns – Research Reports', at p. 4. See further, at: www.msd.govt.nz/about-msd-and-our-work/publications-resources/research/child-and-youth-offending-patterns/index.html

149 The Child Care Act 1991, Part II, as amended by the Child and Family Agency Act 2013, s 3.

services and programmes.[150] Service provision aimed at promoting children's welfare interests, rather than preventing their impairment, is hard to identify but would probably include grant aiding voluntary community-based family support organisations, financial and other support for adopters and the new federally subsidised services to youth who have aged out of foster care. In Canada, it would seem that the mandating of state intervention in family matters is more oriented towards child protection than towards promoting the welfare of children and families in need.

In Australia, the federal government's national 'Early Years Strategy', published in 2022, is an illustration of federal leadership to promote the welfare interests of children. In New Zealand, it is unlikely that there is the luxury of being able to divert resources towards the promotion of child welfare. The acute problems associated with having one of the worst rates of child abuse in the developed world, the highest rates of domestic violence and one of the world's highest rates of teenage suicides probably absorbs all available government funding and professional expertise.

Arguably, in the civil law countries of France and Germany, the approach adopted is fundamentally different from that of their common law counterparts. Both countries would seem to share a patriarchal attitude towards the family unit, one which instead of focusing on breaches of the child welfare threshold emphasises the integrity of the family unit as a whole. Maintaining the parent-child bond is all important, as Eglin puts it in a remark that might apply equally to Germany 'the French system close to a defence of the birth family and parents' rights ideology . . . the whole system is constructed so as to promote the upbringing of the child by his/her parents'.[151] The *assistance éducative*[152] intervention aims to invest the resources necessary to reinforce parental coping capacity and avoid future child protection measures; the notion is not that of providing more, over and above a statutorily defined package of services in exceptional circumstances but, in all instances, of providing such services as the *juge des enfants* directs as being appropriate. Similarly in Germany, if there is any separate promotional function, it lies in the policy of keeping families together before addressing parenting deficits and triggering child protection intervention procedures. Due to the constitutional principle of proportionality, any intervention in the context of children at risk must prioritise the provision of the necessary public support – such as day care centres and therapeutic services – required to avoid child removal.[153]

150 See, further, at: www.childwelfare.gov/topics/systemwide/laws-policies/federal/family-first/

151 See, Eglin, M., 'Judicial Child Protection in France and England: A Comparative Approach' (June 2001), at: www.afmjf.fr/Judicial-child-protection-in.html

152 The ordinance of 23 December 1958 created the modern concept of *assistance éducative* (assistance in upbringing).

153 Galm, B. and Derr, R. *Combating Child Abuse and Neglect: Child Protection in Germany – National Report*, Deutsches Jugendinstitut e.V., 2011, at: www.dji.de/fileadmin/user_upload/bibs/DAPHNEGermanReportLayoutFIN.pdf

Affirmative action

'Promotion' in a public family law context is at times interpreted to permit 'affirmative action', meaning the targeting of extra resources towards groups that are considered to be particularly socially disadvantaged through preferential quotas, etc.

So, for example, in the UK, the Equality Act 2010, s 158, provides specific opportunities for state affirmative action if it is a proportionate means of addressing the disadvantages of a group with shared protected characteristics[154] or subject to discrimination[155] and if it serves to encourage a more proportionate take-up in activities or services by members of such a protected group. It is only lawful if the statutory criteria are met; it must be 'reasonably thought' that one of the conditions applies, such as disadvantage or disproportionately low participation. An example might be the practice in the U.S and the UK of state bonuses payable to adoption agencies that exceed certain agreed targets for the adoption placements of children in public care. In the U.S., a school voucher scheme was introduced that allowed state funding to be made available to enable parents in poor areas with failing public schools to pay for tuition at private schools and thereby get a better education for their children. This 'levelling-up' initiative, used by many parents to send their children to religious schools, was examined by the Court to assess whether this amounted to the state indirectly channelling funds in a discriminatory way to preference religious schools. The Court thought not. The fact that in practice, most parents used their vouchers to transfer to religious schools was incidental: they were entitled to make that choice; it did not mean that government was funneling public dollars to religious institutions. The Court found it important that whether any particular secular or religious private school received voucher funds depended on the decision of the individual student and his or her parents or guardians and not on the government.[156]

Affirmative action may well be justified by a particular set of circumstances, but it is also necessarily discriminatory – those who benefit will do so at the cost of others – and has been open to criticism for that reason.[157]

Promotion services in an Indigenous context

Given the gross and consistent over-representation of the CANZUS Indigenous children in their national child welfare and criminal justice systems, it could be argued that 'promotional' intervention is largely a misnomer: state intervention is failing at such a rudimentary level in safeguarding the welfare interests

154 The 'protected characteristics' being age, disability, gender reassignment, marriage and civil partnership, pregnancy and maternity, race, religion or belief, sex and sexual orientation.

155 See, *R (Kaur and Shah) v. Ealing LBC* (2008) EWHC 2062 (Admin).

156 *Zelman v. Simmons-Harris,* 536 U.S. 639 (2002).

157 See, for example, Laycock, D., 'The Broader Case for Affirmative Action: Desegregation, Academic Excellence, and Future Leadership', *Tulane Law Review*, Vol. 78, No. 6 (2021), at: www.tulanelawreview.org/pub/volume78/issue6/the-broader-case-for-affirmative-action

of Indigenous children, present intervention strategies cannot achieve and maintain a basic welfare threshold and there is little capacity to engage in promotional activities.

However, some state initiatives could be interpreted as intended to promote the welfare interests of children. The *Closing the Gap* campaign, launched in 2018 by the Australian Human Rights Commission, might be viewed in that light. It is intended to address the inequity between Indigenous and non-Indigenous communities in terms of health and social care services and outcomes.[158] The statutory requirement in all CANZUS nations that preference be given to culturally compatible out-of-home placements might also be defined as promotional. In Canada, the courts found that state intervention, far from promoting the welfare interests of First Nation children, had been negatively discriminating against them for many years.[159] Bill C-92, which promises Indigenous people the right to self-governance of their child welfare systems, with resources provided by the federal government, could be seen as promotional. In the U.S., the AI/AN tribes, unlike their counterparts in other CANZUS nations, have constitutional recognition as sovereign entities. Providing access to Title IV-E funding, in order to subsidise guardianship for relative caregivers, enabling them to assist or replace failing parental care, was a crucial mechanism for channelling preventative state intervention and could perhaps be viewed as promoting the welfare interests of children.

State respect for Indigenous culture

In the U.S., state recognition of AI/AN culture in a child welfare context came with the introduction of the Indian Child Welfare Act in 1978. Possibly, the fairly recent respect for Indigenous culture in Australia could be viewed as promotional: there has been a widespread introduction of state-funded programmes to support Indigenous customs, practices, languages, music, art, values and world-views and to give recognition to the cultural significance of Indigenous myths. Māori cultural identity has also been affirmed more recently by the state in practices such as inclusion in national ceremonies, in environmental and planning legislation, in the performance of *hikitapu* or spiritual cleansing rituals in overseas embassies and in the increasing use of *karakia* (prayers) to commence court proceedings or public meetings. Respect for culture is included in the requirement in the *Oranga Tamariki* Act 1989 that the provision of any support or services 'should recognise and promote *mana tamaiti (tamariki)* and the *whakapapa* of the child or young person

158 This initiative was launched because of the perceived failure of the federal government's 2008 'Close the Gap Statement of Intent' to make much progress. See, further, at: https://humanrights.gov.au/our-work/aboriginal-and-torres-strait-islander-social-justice/projects/close-gap-indigenous-health

159 *First Nations Child and Family Caring Society of Canada and the Assembly of First Nations v. Attorney General of Canada*, 2016 CHRT 2 (2016) 2 C.N.L.R. 270.

and relevant *whanaungatanga* rights and responsibilities of their family, *whānau, hapū, iwi*, and family group'.

Promotion services in a disability context

There is little evidence that children with a disability are the subject of state intervention designed to promote their welfare interests, that is, to do more than provide support as detailed earlier. In the UK, however, it could be argued that the specialist multidisciplinary disability teams (consisting of social workers, nurses and occupational therapists) working closely with psychologists, housing departments and voluntary organisations do bring an extra dimension of wraparound care that might be termed promotional.

Promotion services in a criminal context

It seems improbable that promoting – rather than safeguarding – a child's welfare interests is a viable proposition in a criminal context. While all developed nations have legislation requiring the relevant authorities to engage in preventative work, once offences are committed, then welfare interests must be balanced against the interests of justice: personal accountability, reparation and social rehabilitation are likely to weigh heavier in the balance than any concern to promote the welfare interests of an offender.

Conclusion

The best gauge of the success of a nation's preventative child care policies is the crude but telling statistics of the children it fails and who must then be admitted to state care. Applying that measure provides clear evidence in relation to the nature and extent of jurisdictional differences regarding the role of the preventative function. The evidence in this chapter strongly suggests that while all six common law and the two civil law jurisdictions fail to satisfy the preventative legislative intent of their domestic statutes and the UN CROC requirements in Articles 18 and 19, none fail quite so convincingly as New Zealand.

The commitment to engage in preventative state intervention in order to support family coping capacity and protect children from harm is clearly stated in the *Oranga Tamariki* Act 1989, the Children's Act 2014, the Children (Children's Services) Order 2016 and the Children's Action Plan which also specifies the services to be made available. Article 27 of UN CROC, adding to Articles 18 and 19, declares that states must 'recognize the right of every child to a standard of living adequate for the child's physical, mental, spiritual, moral and social development' and 'shall take appropriate measures to assist parents and others responsible for the child to implement this right and shall in case of need provide material assistance and support programmes, particularly with regard to nutrition, clothing and housing'. However, while there can be little doubt regarding the fact and nature of New

Zealand's commitment to preventative service provision, there is every reason to conclude that it has wholly failed to meet that commitment. Indicators of failure would include rates of domestic violence which are reported to be the highest in the developed world[160] rates of child abuse and neglect which are high relative to other developed nations[161] and the fact that it has one of the world's highest rate of teenage suicides.[162] Further evidence would suggest that the scale of failure has been even worse in relation to the Māori, who have experienced serious disadvantage relative to their non-Indigenous fellow citizens.[163] Indicators of failed preventative state intervention would include the fact that Māori babies are at least five times more likely to die of Sudden Infant Death Syndrome than non-Māori.[164] Despite Māori comprising only 16.5% of the population, their children constituted 63% of those coming before the courts in 2021[165] and 68% of the 4,800 children in state care in 2022,[166] while the suicide rate for Māori children and adolescents is the second highest in the OECD.[167]

The scale of the failure in New Zealand may be unusual, but it is representative of a general state failure to provide the services necessary to prevent harm to the welfare interests of children.

160 See, Stephen, E., 'Child Protection' (2020), at: https://talkingtroublenz.org/wp-content/uploads/2020/12/Emily-Stephen-SLT-child-protection.pdf

161 See, Gilbert, R., et al., 'Child Maltreatment: Variation in Trends and Policies in Six Developed Countries', *Lancet* (2011) at: https://scholar.google.com/scholar_lookup?hl=en&publication_year=2011&author=R+Gilbert&author=J+Fluke&author=M+O%27Donnell&author=A+Gonzalez-Izquierdo&author=M+Brownell&author=P+Gulliver&title=Child+maltreatment%3A+variation+in+trends+and+policies+in+six+developed+countries

162 See, further, for example, at: www.theguardian.com/world/2018/mar/08/study-one-in-four-new-zealand-children-reported-welfare-agencies

163 See, further, O'Halloran, K., *Children, the Law and the Welfare Principle: Perspectives from North America*, Routledge, 2023, at Chapter 8 and *Children, the Law and the Welfare Principle: Perspectives from Australia & New Zealand*, Routledge, 2023, chapters 9 and 10.

164 See, Rutter, C. and Walker, S., 'Infant Mortality Inequities for Māori in New Zealand: A Tale of Three Policies', International *Journal for Equity in Health*, Vol. 20, No. 10 (2021), at: https://doi.org/10.1186/s12939-020-01340-y

165 See, further, at: https://youthcourt.govt.nz/youth-justice/youth-justice-statistics/

166 See, further, at: www.orangatamariki.govt.nz/about-us/performance-and-monitoring/quarterly-report/care-and-protection-statistics/

167 See, UNICEF, Report Card (2021), at: www.unicef.org.nz/stories/new-report-card-shows-that-new-zealand-is-failing-its-children

3 Protection

Child abuse and neglect

Introduction

The expertise of professionals, such as those in the fields of psychiatry and developmental psychology, together with the everyday experiences of parents, have long ago established that childhood is not, has never been and should not be totally risk free. However, if it is to make a positive contribution for those on the road to adulthood, it would be best if the risk level could be loosely correlated with age and ability.

Contemporary social life, presenting all the usual risks for children and risk management dilemmas for their parents, has been made more complicated in recent years by a raft of new challenges unknown to previous generations. The domination of social media platforms in which the grooming of children for nefarious and often clearly criminal purposes can merge into the more insidious modelling of social influencers – manipulating children into pornography, addictive games, violent videos, expensive hobbies, etc. – and lead to public-private issues regarding risk-taking. Vaping, phone sexting, unaccompanied travel or unsupervised internet access, adventurous sports – including the many and varied attempts to acquire celebrity status for being the youngest/disabled child to establish a new world record for a particular feat of skill or endurance – these and many other activities may or may not present opportunities for children but will certainly compound existing risk management problems for their parents while also raising issues as to the appropriate distribution of responsibilities between parents and state. Added to which are the complexities associated with negotiating the fraught minefield of sexual orientation, gender identity and gender transitioning that currently trouble many children. Drawing lines between a child's privacy rights and the responsibilities of state and/or parents to ensure an age-appropriate level of child protection – without intruding more than necessary – has become a pressing concern for modern society.

This chapter examines the legal function of child protection, the risk management issues and the balancing of responsibility between state and parents in relation to incidences of child abuse and neglect. Like its predecessor, it begins with a brief examination of key concepts. It then outlines the relevant legal framework before conducting a comparative analysis of the role of this legal function across

DOI: 10.4324/9781003269595-6

the eight jurisdictions studied. It concludes by assessing its relative significance in relation to the welfare principle and considers any implications arising for family law.

Concepts and the law

The legislative intent underpinning the concepts of 'care' and 'protection', 'neglect' and 'abuse' is that together they should constitute the threshold for coercive state intervention by identifying the circumstances of failed family care requiring child protection measures. A breach, or threatened breach, of that threshold both justifies and requires prompt state intervention to safeguard the welfare of any children involved. The concern to protect children, in circumstances of abuse or neglect at the hands of their parents or third parties, represents the earliest expression of the welfare principle and continues to be the most basic function of the law relating to children. As it grows in salience relative to other family law proceedings – becoming a focus for specialist professional, judicial and agency expertise – it increasingly seems set on forging a developmental path quite separate from that of any other rationale for involvement in the lives of parents and their children.

Concepts

'Care' and 'protection' represent the sharp end of state engagement with vulnerable families: ameliorative intervention – or working in partnership with parents – having failed and children being judged to be at risk of harm, these concepts signify that standards of parental care are now such that the state must step in to protect the children. The coercive intervention threshold is intended to identify those situations and families requiring particular agencies and professionals to intervene and thereafter act on the presumption that safeguarding the welfare of a child has become a matter of public concern. It leaves no room for equivocation: whether the breach in standards is due to parental absence, illness, physical incapacity or mental incapacity; whether due to wilfulness or negligence; and whether or not parental care has previously been exemplary. Intention, motivation and attitude regarding the consequences are beside the point. The effect, or the prospective effect, on the welfare interests of a child is the only legal issue.

Child protection

The protective function, being the first and most basic recognition of a child's status before the law, establishes a baseline for state responsibility in relation the best interests of a child. The functions of 'prevention', 'support' and 'promotion' – addressed in the previous chapter – are refinements that came later, are of secondary importance and essentially serve as accessories to this fundamental right. A child has a legal right to state protection that is both prompt and effective. In practice, meeting both criteria can be problematic: intervention that is too precipitate or unduly delayed can defeat the purpose of securing protection for the child with minimal disruption to his or her family life. Proportionality is probably the key legal principle in this context: while intervention must be prompt and effective, it must also be no more than is necessary to secure appropriate and sufficient protection.

Child protection is necessarily a multi-professional and inter-agency matter, requiring at the very least the involvement of doctors, social workers and judiciary. Teachers, health visitors, police, psychiatrists, psychologists and others may also become involved.

Neglect

The right to 'a standard of living adequate for the child's physical, mental, spiritual, moral and social development' is every child's most basic entitlement.[1] The liability of a parent, a person with parental responsibility or someone with *loco parentis* standing, for any harm which befalls a child as a consequence of their failure to afford him or her an adequate standard of care or protection is well established.[2]

In order to justify removal of children on grounds of parental neglect, the relevant authorities must first show that every reasonable effort had been made to alleviate its effects by appropriate service provision. In *Wallová and Walla v. the Czech Republic*,[3] for example, the care orders were ultimately only lifted when the parents' economic and housing situation improved. The ECtHR found that had this been provided earlier, there would have been no need to remove the children. Consequently, the applicants' Article 8 rights had been violated. Again, where two young children were removed from their unemployed mother – a drug addict facing criminal charges – this was found to be unjustified. In the absence of any concrete evidence that she had left her children unattended, had not provided care for them or had neglected them in any way that might have endangered their health or life and there being no indication that the authorities had attempted any lesser form of intervention, the ECtHR found that her Article 8 rights had been breached.[4]

Fault

Neglect can be grounded equally on fault or default: wilfulness is never a determining factor; it is the actual or prospective consequences for the child, not the intentions of the carer, that matters. The standard of child care required is judged objectively in the sense that the measure applied is that of a hypothetical average caring parent, i.e. no allowance can be made for the fact that the actual parent is too young, inexperienced, disabled or distressed to cope any better. The standard applied is also subjective in the sense that the level of care expected from such a

1 Ibid, Article 27(1).

2 See, for example, *R v. Senior* (1989) 1 QB 283, where Russell LJ described neglect as 'the omission of such steps as a reasonable parent would take' (at p. 291).

3 Application No. 23848/04 (2006).

4 *Y.I. v. Russia*, Application No. 68868/14 (2020).

parent is that actually required to meet the particular needs of the child in question, i.e. the fact that the level of care provided would be adequate for an average child is irrelevant if the child in question requires care of a higher standard due perhaps to a disability. However, while such a shortfall in standards indicates that a child is at risk, it does not follow that the state should necessarily remove that child; an onus rests on the state to first demonstrate that all reasonable measures have been taken to offset the shortfall through relevant support services before resorting to such a drastic interference in family life.

Neglect in state care

Where the neglect is incurred in a state institution or facility – such as a foster home – the state is directly liable, as it has a strict duty to ensure the protection of children it has placed there. The ECtHR found a dereliction of this state duty in a home for the physically and mentally disabled where 15 children and young adults died of neglect.[5] As evidenced by the long litany of national public enquiries into the child abuse suffered by countless children in many facilities, owned, funded or regulated by the state across several continents, the state has too often proven to be an ineffectual guardian of the children entrusted to its care.

Abuse

Child abuse is a crime and one that can take many forms: physical or mental violence, injury, neglect or negligent treatment, maltreatment or exploitation; exposure to domestic violence; and sexual abuse. It can happen in different settings such as in school, at home or on the street but also online through the use of mobile phones or other electronic devices. One incident may be sufficient to meet the definition but so also will a culture of systemic abuse consisting of multiple incidents, involving a number of children over many years. It may involve the production and sharing of child sexual abuse material but also grooming, online harassment, victimisation and cyberbullying.[6] Most perpetrators are either members of the child's family or extended family or close family friends. Systemic abuse by 'strangers' often occurs in contexts where those in a *loco parentis* relationship with children cultivate a culture of abuse. This has been evident from the number of enquiries

5 *Nencheva and Others v. Bulgaria*, Application No. 48609/06 (2013). Note that Article 16 of the United Nations Convention on the Rights of Persons with Disabilities requires States Parties to take specific measures to protect children with disabilities from abuse and exploitation.

6 Note: the directive on combating child sexual abuse which obliges Member States' authorities to remove web pages containing or disseminating child sexual abuse material, both when hosted within their territory and outside it (2011/93/EU, 2011); the e-Commerce Directive which determines the existing liability rules for online intermediaries, Article 3, allows for the notice and takedown mechanisms for illegal content (2011/93/EU of 2011); and the temporary derogation from certain provisions of Directive 2002/58/EC permitting the processing of personal and other data for the purpose of combating online child sexual abuse (PE/38/2021/REV/1, 2021).

centred on children's homes, other residential care units, foster homes, etc. Paedophilia, or child sexual abuse, has taken root in facilities variously established to provide accommodation, organised games, outdoor pursuits or religious activities.

The state's duties in relation to abuse include preventive measures, protection, assistance to victims and a duty to prosecute offenders. The ECtHR has examined the states' duties in relation to a wide range of acts constituting child abuse, mainly through proceedings under articles 2, 3 and 8 of the ECHR.

Physical

This is the most frequently recorded form of abuse. The legal issues are most often relatively straightforward, as evidence, in the form of injuries and testimonies from victim and perpetrator, is readily available. Sometimes it may be possible to establish the fact that a child has been harmed but impossible to establish which of the child's carers was the perpetrator. This most usually occurs where both parents in effect indemnify each other from blame for injuries caused to their child, a significant factor in explaining the low success rate of criminal prosecutions against parent perpetrators. In such cases, it is open to the Court to conclude either – in accordance with the *res ipsa loquitor* doctrine (the thing speaks for itself) – that the facts are such that no innocent explanation is viable or that the doctrine of 'common enterprise' prevents either from denying liability for the likely consequences of actions plainly within the awareness of both. While they may escape liability as perpetrator, he, she or both will nonetheless be culpable due to their failure to protect the child.

Physical chastisement inflicted by a well-intentioned parent, or someone acting on his or her behalf, for the purposes of disciplining a child is prohibited in many but not all European countries. The issue as to if and when parents, or third parties acting in *loco parentis*, have a right to administer such chastisement arose for consideration in the ECHR[7] in a case where a 7-year-old boy had been punished by his headmaster. The Court decided, by a majority verdict of 5:4, that the punishment had not been so severe as to constitute a breach of Article 3. It also decided, unanimously, that the punishment had not adversely affected the child's physical or moral integrity to a degree that would have constituted a breach of Article 8. The headmaster was found to have been acting within the scope of his *loco parentis* responsibilities as, subsequently, was a childminder[8] who admitted smacking a child in her care but with parental permission. However, in *A v. UK*,[9] the ECtHR decided that a stepfather[10] who had beaten a 9-year-old boy on more than one

7 See, *Costello – Roberts v. United Kingdom* (1994) ELR 1, ECHR. Note, also, Article 37 of the UN Convention on the Rights of the Child.

8 See, *London Borough of Sutton v. Davies (No. 2)* (1995) 1 All ER 65.

9 (1998) 2 FLR 959.

10 (1999) 27 EHRR 611.

occasion, causing bruising on his legs and bottom, had inflicted excessive punishment which breached Article 3.

Emotional

Like neglect, emotional abuse has more often been viewed as a sin of omission than commission. Unlike neglect, it has only gained legal recognition as a form of abuse, requiring coercive state intervention to protect a child's welfare interests, comparatively recently. This is largely because of its association with domestic violence. Increasingly, child psychiatrists, psychologists and others working with troubled children have noted that, if exposed to the volatile turbulence of a dysfunctional parental relationship, children will become emotionally distressed and this may justify removing them from parental care. Whether resulting from deprivation (e.g. the 'silent treatment') or deliberation (e.g. threatening or manipulative behaviour), emotional abuse, like all other forms of child abuse, is a consequence of the misuse by adults of their authoritative role in relation to children.

Emotional abuse of a child can derive from parental incapacity due to the latter's physical or learning disability; by definition, such a person will have less capacity in some areas and may not be able to provide the range of parenting skills required by the particular needs of their child. There have been a number of cases where the courts have, albeit reluctantly, concluded that the quality of parenting provided by a person with learning disability is such as to stunt the emotional development of their child. The fact that such a parent is entirely without fault is beside the point, as the Court will judge the quality of care by objectively measuring it against the needs of the particular child and the standards required from a competent parent (i.e. one not suffering from such a disability). Occasionally, the same remorseless logic may apply in circumstances where effective parenting is constrained by severe physical disability, though the ECtHR is quite clear that in such circumstances, social service provision should then be made available to supplement the parental deficit.

Sexual

Child sexual abuse in its many forms can take place in as many settings, including home, schools, care institutions and churches, as well as online. While the protective duties of articles 3 and 8 of the ECHR are very relevant, so also is Article 13 of the Convention and the Lanzarote Convention, the EU Directive on combating child sexual abuse and the interim regulation adopted in 2021 on the processing of personal and other data for the purpose of combating such abuse.

So, for example, *O'Keefe v. Ireland*,[11] which was not untypical of many other such cases in that country at around that time, concerned the question of the responsibility of the state for the sexual abuse of a schoolgirl, aged 9, by a lay teacher

11 Application No. 35810/09 (2014).

in an Irish National School in 1973. The teacher was eventually charged with 386 criminal offences of sexual abuse involving a total of 21 pupils. The Irish courts dismissed the claims of direct negligence against the state and determined that the state could not be held vicariously responsible for the sexual assaults. The ECtHR disagreed. It found that it was an inherent obligation of a government to protect children from ill-treatment, especially in a primary education context. That obligation had not been met when the Irish state, which had to have been aware of the sexual abuse of children by adults prior to the 1970s because, among other things, it had instigated the prosecution of many such cases at a significant rate. The Court held that there had been violations of articles 3 and 13.

International law

The relevant European legal framework is comprised of the European Convention on Human Rights (ECHR), the Brussels II bis Regulation, in conjunction with the EU Charter of Fundamental Rights, in particular Article 24, together with UN CROC. The law is applied in accordance with procedures, grounds and outcomes that have been examined for decades largely by the ECtHR but also to a degree by decisions of the CJEU and rulings of the UN CRC.[12]

United Nations Convention on the Rights of the Child 1989 (UN CROC)

Although it has no enforcement mechanism, this Convention is the most important international legal instrument for the protection of children's rights and welfare interests because it has the greatest number of nation state signatories and has been assimilated into the domestic law of many countries and because the ECtHR frequently takes judicial notice of particular provisions which it references in its rulings.

Article 3

Article 3 states the most important principle in the Convention. It requires that in all actions concerning children, whether undertaken by public or private social welfare institutions, courts of law, administrative authorities or legislative bodies, the best interests of the child shall be the primary – but not the paramount – consideration.

Article 9

Article 9 requires the state to ensure that a child shall not be separated from his or her parents against their will, except when competent authorities subject to judicial

12 See, further, O'Halloran, K., *Children, the Law and the Welfare Principle: European Judicial Perspectives,* Routledge, 2024, at Chapter 1.

review determine in accordance with applicable law and procedures that such separation is necessary for the best interests of the child. So any separation, short or long term, requires specific legal justification.

Article 19

Article 19 requires the state to take appropriate legislative, administrative, social and educational measures to protect a child from all forms of physical or mental violence, injury or abuse, neglect or negligent treatment, maltreatment or exploitation, including sexual abuse, while in the care of parent, legal guardian or other person. The UN Committee on the Rights of the Child has issued an important number of general comments and recommendations interpreting states' obligations.[13]

European Convention on Human Rights 1950 (ECHR)

The threshold justifying state intervention in family affairs on child protection grounds is loosely governed by articles 2, 3, 8 and 13 of the ECHR requiring, respectively, respect for human life, prohibition of inhuman or degrading treatment, respect for private and family life and the right to an effective remedy.

Article 2

The guarantee in this article that everyone's life shall be protected by law has been explored by the ECtHR in relation to children in cases in which the latter's welfare interests and rights have played a central role.[14] For example, in *Kontrovà v. Slovakia*,[15] the complaint of a mother who had warned the police about her husband's violence, but they had failed to intervene and prevent his subsequent killing of their two children, was upheld by the ECtHR. It found that there had been a breach of Article 2, as the police had failed to protect the children's right to life.

Article 3

This Article prohibits 'cruel and degrading treatment'. So, for example, chastising a child by administering corporal punishment – whether by teachers,[16] police

13 Including General Comment No. 13 which describes measures to protect children against all forms of violence and No. 8 which calls on states to take appropriate measures against all forms of corporal punishment.

14 The right to life also finds protection in UN CROC: every child has a right to life – regardless of her health conditions. Children with special medical needs should be protected and cared for; a truly humane society will care for its weakest members. This is why international law calls for 'appropriate legal protection, [for children] before as well as after birth'.

15 Application No. 7510/04 (2007).

16 See, *Campbell and Cosans v. the United Kingdom*, Application Nos. 7511/76 and 7743/76 (1982) and *Costello-Roberts v. the United Kingdom*, Application No. 13134/87 (1993).

officers[17] or by a stepfather[18] – has been found to constitute a violation of Article 3. The ECtHR has found that long-term neglect by parents,[19] repeated sexual abuse by school teachers,[20] rape[21] and physical chastisement[22] all fall within the definition of this term. While the ECtHR in *X. and Others v. Bulgaria*[23] stressed that Article 3 has to be interpreted in the light of other applicable international instruments, in particular, the Lanzarote Convention, with regards to investigation and procedural requirements.

Article 8

This requires respect for a person's private and family life and declares that a public authority shall not interfere with the right to respect for family life. In order to determine whether an interference by the authorities with the applicants' private and family life was necessary in a democratic society and a fair balance struck between the different interests involved, the ECtHR examines whether the interference was in accordance with the law, pursued a legitimate aim or aims and was proportionate to the aim(s) pursued.[24]

Under Article 8, in a child protection context, the Court has been largely concerned about the impact of abuse on the physical or psychological integrity of the victim and on their right to respect for family life: in *R.B. v. Estonia,*[25] it concluded that there had been significant flaws in the domestic authorities' procedural response to the 4-year-old applicant's allegation of sexual abuse by her father – which had not sufficiently taken into account her particular vulnerability and corresponding needs as a young child – thereby breaching the respondent state's positive obligations under Article 8 and, indeed, under Article 3.

Article 13

This Article provides a right to an effective remedy. In *D.P. and J.C. v. the United Kingdom,*[26] for example, it was found to have been violated in respect of two children who had been sexually abused by their stepfather from the

17 *Tyrer v. the United Kingdom*, Application No. 5856/72 (1987).
18 *A. v. the United Kingdom,* Application No. 25599/94 (1998).
19 *Z and Others v. the United Kingdom* [GC], Application No. 29392/95 (2001).
20 *O'Keeffe v. Ireland* [GC], Application No. 35810/09 (2014).
21 *M.C. v. Bulgaria*, Application No. 39272/98 (2003); M.G.C. *v. Romania*, Application No. 61495/11 (2016), para 58.
22 *M.C. v. Bulgaria*, Application No. 39272/98 (2003), para 150; *O'Keeffe v. Ireland* [GC], *op cit* at para 146.
23 Application No. 22457/16 (2021).
24 See, further, European Court of Human Rights, 'Guide on Article 8 of the Convention – Right to Respect for Private and Family Life' (2022), at: www.echr.coe.int/documents/d/echr/guide_art_8_eng
25 Application No. 22597/16 (2021).
26 Application No. 38719/97 (2002).

ages of 8 and 10. They claimed they informed the local authority of the abuse but that the authorities failed to protect them and both suffered from long-term depression and trauma. The Court found that there had been no effective remedy or access to compensation available to the children concerning their allegations.

Other

The many additional international instruments with a bearing on child protection include the following: the European Social Charter (revised in 1996) that provides for the protection of general social rights and requires states to take all appropriate and necessary measures to ensure that children receive the care, assistance, education and training they need and are protected from negligence, violence or exploitation; the International Covenant on Economic, Social and Cultural Rights (ICESCR) 1966 that requires special measures of protection to be taken on behalf of all children and young persons without any discrimination and that they should be 'protected from economic and social exploitation'; the International Covenant on Civil and Political Rights (ICCPR) 1966 and its periodic review process requiring signatory states to submit a review of progress on human rights issues; the European Convention on the Exercise of Children's Rights 1996 which declares the child's right to be informed and to express his or her views in legal proceedings and their right to representation; the Optional Protocols; the 'Lanzarote Convention' 2007, requiring states to criminalise certain forms of sexual abuse against children, to take measures to prevent sexual violence, to protect child victims, to prosecute perpetrators and to protect children against sexual abuse in the digital environment; the 'Istanbul Convention' 2014, which aims to provide protection for women against all forms of violence; and the EU Strategy on the Rights of the Child.[27]

Comparative jurisdictional analysis of state intervention: protection

As with the analysis of 'prevention' in the previous chapter, the legal function of 'protection' – its interpretation and role – is best understood by benchmarking the function against relevant rulings of the ECtHR, drawn from its consideration of cases arising in all 46 Council of Europe member countries[28] and with universal application to them. This provides a baseline for identifying and broadly considering relative national differences in the application of this legal function. It paves the way for the more focused comparative analysis of the extent to which each of the six common law and two civil law jurisdictions gives effect to the rights of the child as declared in UN CROC.

27 EU, *The EU Strategy on the Rights of the Child 2021–2024*, European Commission, 2021.
28 Russia, the 47th member, having been expelled following its invasion of Ukraine.

Established international standards

Under Article 3 of the ECHR, state authorities are required to conduct effective investigations into allegations of child abuse, while both Article 8 and UN CROC impose the additional requirement that state intervention, to ensure adequate protection for any child deemed to be at risk of harm, is conducted expeditiously.

Delay

In *P.M. v. Bulgaria,*[29] for example, the applicant complained that, following her report of being raped at the age of 13, the Bulgarian authorities took more than 15 years to complete the ensuing investigation and she had no remedies against their reluctance to prosecute her aggressors. The ECtHR held that there had been a violation of Article 3. In *M.C. v. Bulgaria,*[30] it found a breach of Article 13 due to the authorities' ineffective investigation into a 14-year-old girl's allegation of rape where she was unable to show evidence of her physical opposition to the attack.

Ineffective

Delay and ineffectualness featured in *C.A.S. and C.S. v. Romania*[31] and were also prominent factors in *X. and Others v. Bulgaria*[32] which concerned allegations by three Bulgarian children that they were sexually abused in an orphanage in Bulgaria prior to their adoption in Italy. In *Kontrová v. Slovakia,*[33] the Court criticised the tardiness and ineffectualness of state intervention when, despite having given advance notice of his intentions, the husband shot dead himself and his two children. When the advance notice is not of physical violence but of harassment – as where a school pupil complained, to no avail, of repeated insulting behaviour from his teacher – the ECtHR came to a similar conclusion.[34]

Contemporary jurisdictional comparison: prompt and effective intervention

Having broadly outlined the range of child protection issues arising before the ECtHR, this section focuses on those that are specific to the eight selected jurisdictions. The objective being to identify those that constitute differentiating jurisdictional characteristics and to gauge their relative significance. As with earlier books

29 Application No. 49669/07 (2012). See, also, *C.A.S. and C.S. v. Romania,* Application No. 26692/05 (2012), where the investigation of the reported repeated rape of a 7-year-old boy took five years to complete.

30 Application No. 39272/98 (2003).

31 Application No. 26692/05 (2012). See, also, *E v. United Kingdom,* Application No. 33218/96 (2002).

32 Application No. 22457/16 (2021).

33 Application No. 7510/04 (2007).

34 *F.O. v. Croatia,* Application No. 29555/13 (2021).

in this series, the UN CROC provisions are used where feasible as common reference points to aid comparative jurisdictional analysis.

UN CROC: Article 3(1) – 'ensure the child such protection and care as is necessary for his or her well-being'; and Article 6 – 'every child has the inherent right to life'.

Common law jurisdictions

In several UK cases,[35] the authorities were found to have breached the earlier articles 3 and 13 of the ECHR when – despite receiving reports of child abuse or of being in possession of information that should have alerted them to the risk of such abuse – they failed to promptly institute protective measures.[36] This was the case in *E v. United Kingdom*,[37] when the ECtHR found that the authorities 'should have been aware that the children remained at potential risk' and had 'failed to take steps which would have enabled them to discover the exact extent of the problem and, potentially, to prevent further abuse taking place',[38] which was held to have violated Article 3. The emphasis on attempts to police standards of child protection in this jurisdiction, perhaps to the detriment of preventative intervention, is reflected in judicial warnings that there can be no right or presumption that a child be brought up by their natural family[39] and that there must be hard evidence of risk because 'the threshold conditions are there to protect both the child and his family from unwarranted interference by the state'.[40] There is some evidence that the threshold for protective intervention has been raised in this jurisdiction[41] as illustrated by the redirecting of resources – such as family centres, respite care foster parents, home helps, etc. – initially designated for preventative intervention towards child protection.[42] In this context, it is of some significance to note the ruling in *Liverpool*[43] which established the principle that the Court had no reviewing

35 *Z and Others v. the United Kingdom*, Application No. 29392/95 (2001), *TP and KM v. UK* (2001) 2 FLR 549 and *E and Others v. the United Kingdom*, Application No. 33218/96 (2002). See, also, *O'Keeffe v. Ireland* [GC], *op cit*.

36 Note that the Ministry of Justice launched a review of this presumption in 2020 to assess whether the right balance is being struck between the risk of harm to a child and their right to have a relationship with both parents.

37 Application No. 33218/96 (2002).

38 Ibid at [96] to [97].

39 *Re E-R (A Child)* 2015 EWCA Civ 405, per Vincent J.

40 *In the matter of J (children)* (2013) UKSC 9, *per* Lady Hale at para 44.

41 See, for example, Fortin, J., *Children's Rights and the Developing Law*, Butterworths, 1998, pp. 383–387, who argues that the ruling in *Re H and R (Minors) (Sexual Abuse: Standard of Proof)* (1996) 1 ALL ER 1 has raised the threshold of proof by requiring a somewhat higher standard of evidence in sexual abuse cases.

42 See, for example, Eekelaar, J. and Dingwall, R., *The Reform of Child Care Law: A Practical Guide to the Children Act 1989*, Routledge, 1990, at p. 129.

43 *A v. Liverpool City Council* (1982) FLR 222.

power over the exercise of a local authority's discretionary decisions in carrying out its statutory role: the two remits are quite separate; the judiciary may not challenge the local authority's distribution of its resources. In Ireland, traditional family values – constitutionally entrenched – have tended to have the opposite effect with the judiciary taking the view that coercive intervention was only justified in circumstances where there was an immediate threat to the child's life, an immediate threat of serious injury or an immediate threat to the child's capacity to function as a human person.[44] This has changed since the ECtHR rebuke in *O'Keefe v. Ireland*[45] that such a threshold was inadequate: the mere risk of abuse, rather than its actuality, triggered a duty to intervene; and not to do so violated Article 3 of the ECHR. The Irish judicial view now is that Article 42A has lowered the bar to permit,[46] and indeed to require, state protective intervention at an early stage.[47]

In Australia, the near doubling of care and protection orders issued over the period 2000–2017 may be partly due to an increase in notifications to the authorities in compliance with the mandatory duty to report child abuse or neglect in relation to all children. The reverse might be the case in New Zealand which has one of the highest abortion rates in the world relative to the size of its population, where the OECD[48] reports that rates of child abuse and neglect are high relative to other developed nations, and the UNICEF[49] comments that this country has one of the worst rates of child abuse in the developed world. As in France,[50] this may in part be attributable to the particularly high rates of domestic violence to which children in those countries are exposed, resulting in a consistent failure to provide sufficient and effective protective state intervention.

Other forms of what might be interpreted as systemic forms of state failure to implement effective child protection strategies can be seen in indices such as comparative infant mortality rates. The fact that these are so high in countries such as the U.S., New Zealand and France relative to countries such as the UK and Germany must reflect the respective social policy commitments of the countries concerned. Similarly, so with other indicators of national concern for child protection strategies such as mandatory reporting of child abuse, age of criminal responsibility and provision for 'baby hatches'. Again, the markedly low use of family-based

44 *North Western Health Board v. HW* (2001) 3 IR 622. Also, see, *MQ v. Gleeson* (1998) 4 IR 95.

45 Application No. 35810/09 (2014).

46 See, for example, *TR v. Child and Family Agency* (2017) IEHC 595.

47 See, *In the Matter of JJ* (2021) IESC 1.

48 See, Gilbert, R., et al., 'Child Maltreatment: Variation in Trends and Policies in Six Developed Countries', *Lancet* (2011) at: https://scholar.google.com/scholar_lookup?hl=en&publication_year=2011&author=R+Gilbert&author=J+Fluke&author=M+O%27Donnell&author=A+Gonzalez-Izquierdo&author=M+Brownell&author=P+Gulliver&title=Child+maltreatment%3A+variation+in+trends+and+policies+in+six+developed+countries

49 Of the 41 developed countries included in the 2020 UNICEF Innocenti Report Card, New Zealand ranks 35th overall for child wellbeing.

50 The CRC noted in May 2023 that 'a child died every five days within their homes in France'. See, further, at: www.ohchr.org/en/news/2023/05/experts-committee-rights-child-praise-france-outreach-patrols-supporting-families

care for children in need of out-of-home placements in France and Germany – where recourse is had to residential care rather than to foster parents and adopters – is a shared jurisdictional characteristic at variance with internationally accepted good practice and one that has been a matter of concern to the CRC.[51]

It is probable that the child protection threshold in the U.S. is set quite low and that, as Vreeland alleges, parental poverty, rather than parental neglect or abuse, triggers coercive state intervention.[52] This 'criminalization of child welfare law' she claims 'is having a dramatic effect on the rights of children within the family'.[53] In Canada, there is no uniform nationwide interpretation of what constitutes 'abuse' or 'neglect' which results in a varying thresholds for coercive state intervention, but overall, judging from the annual numbers of children admitted to the public care system, it would seem that Canadian thresholds are not only lower than in the U.S. but are lower than most other developed nations.

Civil law jurisdictions

Higher thresholds would appear to prevail in France and Germany. In France, *Association Innocence en Danger v. France and Association Enfance et Partage v. France*[54] concerned a complaint from two French child protection associations that, despite a 'report of suspected ill-treatment' being sent by a headteacher in 2008, the French authorities had failed to protect a child from parental abuse which eventually caused her death. The ECtHR found that the measures taken by the authorities between the time of the report and the child's death had been insufficient, and therefore, there had been a violation of Article 3. So, also, in *Affaire A.L, c. France*,[55] in which the protracted proceedings regarding a child – who was only 4 months old when contested proceedings began but was 6 1/2 years old when they concluded – were found to have been wholly prejudicial to the claimant and to the welfare interests of the child. In Germany, the combined effect of articles 2(1) and 6(2) of the Basic Law is to place an obligation on the state to ensure that children and adolescents will receive adequate and safe parental care. There would appear to be a strong sense of family matters being private, coupled with a low tolerance for prying and reporting neighbours to the authorities – again, a probable historical legacy from the Nazi era – which may account for the much-publicised case of the stepfather who had been sexually abusing his stepdaughter for 20 years from when she was 13 years of age and who had borne him eight children. More recently, media reports in November 2022 revealed that an 8-year-old girl had been kept locked up in her grandparents' house for almost her entire life – never attending school nor dental checkups nor any other health/social care services. She had no

51 See: for France, CRC/C/FRA/CO/5, at para 53; for Germany, CRC/C/DEU/CO/5–6, at para 26(a).

52 Vreeland, A.B., 'The Criminalization of Child Welfare in New York City: Sparing the Child or Spoiling the Family?', *Fordham Urban Law Journal*, Vol. 27, No. 3 (2000), pp. 1053–1103.

53 Ibid, at p. 1054.

54 Application No. 15343/15 (2020).

55 Application No. 13344/20 (2022).

friends and was never seen playing with other children. In brief, she had no social interaction of any form.[56]

Jurisdictional comparison: parent-child contact

Contact arrangements are relatively easily managed when birth parents and foster carers are living in the same urban area and are respectfully attuned to any cultural differences but can be problematic when – in either case – they're not.

UN CROC: Article 9(3) – 'respect the right of the child who is separated from one or both parents to maintain personal relations and direct contact with both parents'.

Without the regularity of face-to-face contact, and regardless of whether the separation is a consequence of public or private proceedings, the parent-child relationship is likely to fade and thereby violate the child's Article 9(3) rights.

Common law jurisdictions

The contact rights of UK children in care can be subject to the policy favouring concurrent planning, whereby a care plan provides for the possibility of adoption by foster parents, resulting in restrictions being imposed on birth parent-child contact. So, for example, in *H v. UK*,[57] the parent complained of the 'deplorable delay' of approximately two years in court proceedings concerning her contact application in relation to her child in local authority care. By the time the matter was brought before the Court, almost three and a half years had elapsed since she had last seen her child, who was by then well settled with prospective adopters. In Ireland, where there is no tradition of non-consensual adoption from care, official policy requires children to be placed, where possible, in foster care convenient to their family homes so as to facilitate ongoing parental contact. This is achieved by prioritising kinship foster care.

In the U.S. and Canada, as most domestic adoptions are in respect of older children, there is a corresponding likelihood that they will have formed attachments crucial to their welfare interests which the Court will want to protect when making an adoption order. It would seem probable that there will be a stronger willingness to do so in the U.S. than in Canada, as the latter is less prepared to accommodate 'openness'. However, given the preponderance of step and kinship adoptions in both jurisdictions the probability is that the courts in both are well used to attaching contact conditions to adoption orders. Much the same applies to Australia and New Zealand. In both countries, kinship placements, step-parent adoptions and 'open'

56 See, 'Eight-year-old Child Reportedly Locked Up for Life in Germany', *The Brussels Times* (22 April 2023), at: www.brusselstimes.com/318698/eight-year-old-child-reportedly-locked-up-for-life-in-germany

57 (1988) 10 EHRR 95.

adoptions have traditionally accounted for a large proportion of 'out-of-home' care arrangements and, as they all facilitate ongoing child and birth parent contact then, to that extent, both countries are more Article 9(3) compliant than others.

Civil law jurisdictions

In Germany, a child is vested with a legal right of contact with his or her parent.[58] In France, the contact right is clearly assigned to the parent rather than their child.[59] In both countries, kinship placements, step-parent adoptions and 'open' adoptions have traditionally accounted for a large proportion of 'out-of-home' care arrangements and, as they all facilitate ongoing child and birth parent contact then, to that extent, both countries are more Article 9(3) compliant than others. Moreover, this is also more likely due to the fact that adoptees now tend to be older with established relationships to parents that may well be judicially construed as important for their future welfare and by the heavier onus on the state authorities in both countries to work towards the rehabilitation of children to birth parent care.

Jurisdictional comparison: rehabilitation of child to parental care

The state's protective responsibilities are not limited to the duty to remove children suffering significant harm – or at risk of doing so – and to safeguard their welfare in an approved out-of-home placement. The ECtHR has repeatedly stressed that from the moment of placement, state authorities are required to work towards returning the child to their family home. The protection function extends to completing the cycle of state intervention by rehabilitating the child to safe care in the family home.

UN CROC: Article 8 – 'States Parties undertake to respect the right of the child to preserve his or her identity, including . . . family relations' and, where necessary, 'to provide appropriate assistance and protection, with a view to re-establishing speedily his or her identity'; and Articles 9 and 10 – 'Right of the child not to be separated from his or her parents'.

Common law jurisdictions

As in the UK and such other countries as the U.S. and Canada, these rights are challenged when the issue arises as to whether rehabilitation with birth parents should be pursued in respect of a child compulsorily admitted to the public child welfare system. Under the provisions of UN CROC, the authorities are required, from point of admission, to work towards returning a child to his or her family of origin, but for reasons such as lack of resources, hostile birth parents, the distances

58 The Civil Code, s 1626(3).
59 The Civil Code, Article 375–7 para 2.

involved and a 'play safe' strategy where there are child protection risk factors, it may be that steps towards rehabilitation are not immediately taken. Alternatively, from point of admission, it may be decided to place the child in a concurrent placement, with a view to a possible future adoption by the foster parent. In either case, the passing of time works in favour of the day-to-day carers and against the birth parents. Concurrent placements as practiced in the UK do not always go to plan, and some children, having been removed from their parents on grounds of child protection, are neither rehabilitated nor adopted.[60]

Rehabilitation programmes are resource intensive, often requiring residential placement for parent and child in an intensive assessment/training facility and/or day centre programmes. These are not always available when needed – and are more readily availed of in urban environments – nor can the stability of an initial foster placement be guaranteed. Disruption and drift in care can easily become the default reality resulting in disrupted or long-term separation from parental care, which would appear to be the outcome of most out-of-home placements in both countries, despite state obligations to the contrary under articles 9 and 10.

Civil law jurisdictions

This right has proven problematic in the context of transnational child abductions by parents, as illustrated in some particularly protracted German cases.[61] In addition, it might be noted that the availability of simple adoptions for children in France – but not in Germany – increases the probability that in France, there will be continued contact with parents and other members of the adoptee's birth family; it also, of course, constitutes an important point of jurisdictional difference between the two countries.

Protection in an Indigenous context

A considerable body of international law, some Indigenous specific (such as UNDRIP) but mostly of a general application which includes the Indigenous (such as the ECHR and UN CROC) exists to afford protection to Indigenous children. Moreover, in the main, the body of contemporary domestic law relating to Indigenous communities and the welfare of their children is the same as it is for their non-Indigenous counterparts, allowing for certain culture-specific provisions.

60 See, for example, *A and S (Children) v. Lancashire CC* (2012) EWHC 1689 (Fam), where two brothers were taken into care, aged just 3 and 6 months old, after their mother abandoned them but no adoptive placement was ever found and the boys were passed from one foster carer to another over the course of the next 14 years. Also, see, *M & T v. Medway County Council* (2015), where the court awarded damages to the mother and child following their lengthy separation which had wholly prejudiced any likelihood of family rehabilitation.

61 See, for example, the 2022 decision of the *Bundesverfassungsgericht* (BVerfG) in respect of a 9-year-old German child abducted from his father in Spain when aged 1 and retained in Germany throughout the proceedings.

All of which serves only to highlight the gross over-representation of the former, relative to the latter, in the national child welfare and juvenile justice systems. Despite international and national legislative efforts to create a level playing field, the resulting disparity provides the single most damning piece of evidence of state failure to provide effective protective state intervention on behalf of the welfare interests and rights of Indigenous children.

UN CROC: Article 2 – 'States Parties shall respect and ensure the rights set forth in the present Convention to each child within their jurisdiction without discrimination of any kind, irrespective of . . . ethnic or social origin' and Article 30 – 'a child . . . who is Indigenous shall not be denied the right, in community with other members of his or her group, to enjoy his or her own culture, to profess and practise his or her own religion, or to use his or her own language'.

Historical legacy of coercive state intervention

The CANZUS nations share the experience of their Indigenous children being targeted by the state – primarily through the use of residential schools and forced adoptions – that has left their communities deeply traumatised and apprehensive of any form of contemporary intervention declared to be for the protection of their children. This now inhibits state authorities from interventions which might rekindle memories of earlier brutalisation.

Contemporary state intervention

State caution in its intervention in matters relating to the welfare interests of Indigenous children is evident in provisions such as those in the U.S. which require a court order for the removal of parental rights to be accompanied by immediate notification of relevant tribal authorities so that they may consider whether an appropriate tribal placement is available and suitable for the needs of that particular child[62] and in New Zealand which warn:

> a child or young person should be removed from the care of the member or members of the child's or young person's family, *whānau, hapū, iwi*, or family group who are the child's or young person's usual caregivers only if there is a serious risk of harm to the child or young person.[63]

Nevertheless, state coercive intervention would seem to be many times more necessary for Indigenous children in all CANZUS nations – for example, despite Māori comprising only 16.5% of the population, their children constituted 63% of

62 See, the Indian Child Welfare Act (ICWA) 1978.
63 See, the *Oranga Tamariki* Act 1989, s 13(2)(g).

those coming before the courts in 2021[64] and 68% of the 4,800 children in state care in 2022[65] – than for their non-Indigenous counterparts. Indeed, as mentioned in the previous chapter, the New Zealand state is clearly failing to protect its children: rates of child abuse and neglect are high relative to other developed nations,[66] and it has one of the world's highest rate of teenage suicides.[67] Moreover, a strong correlation has been found to exist between levels of poverty, state assessments of parental neglect and resulting admissions to the care system – a correlation that is strongest in the Indigenous communities.[68] Unquestionably, the Indigenous communities in all CANZUS nations are disproportionately affected by poverty, and the evidence indicates a direct correlation between that and the over-representation of their children in the child welfare and juvenile justice systems.

Despite its over-representation in annual statistics, research suggests that there is considerable underreporting of Indigenous child abuse[69] due to factors such as fear, mistrust and loss of confidence in the police, the justice system, government agencies and the media; fear of racism; fear that the child may be removed from the community; community silence and denial; social and cultural pressure from other members of the family or community not to report; and a lack of understanding about what constitutes family violence, shared parenting and child sexual abuse specifically.[70] Current efforts to ensure that the staff of intervening state agencies are drawn from the Indigenous communities, or have at least developed relevant 'cultural competency' skills, would seem to be showing some signs of success in terms of building trust between state authorities and Indigenous communities. In the U.S., this is reinforced by measures that confer responsibility for court proceedings and child protection on tribal authorities and by government funding that enables tribal delivery of tribal services – such as foster care and adoption – to tribal members. The concept of 'tribal sovereignty' – applicable, if to an uncertain

64 See, further, at: https://youthcourt.govt.nz/youth-justice/youth-justice-statistics/

65 See, further, at: www.orangatamariki.govt.nz/about-us/performance-and-monitoring/quarterly-report/care-and-protection-statistics/

66 See, Gilbert, R., et al., 'Child Maltreatment: Variation in Trends and Policies in Six Developed Countries', *Lancet* (2011), at: https://scholar.google.com/scholar_lookup?hl=en&publication_year=2011&author=R+Gilbert&author=J+Fluke&author=M+O%27Donnell&author=A+Gonzalez-Izquierdo&author=M+Brownell&author=P+Gulliver&title=Child+maltreatment%3A+variation+in+trends+and+policies+in+six+developed+countries

67 See, further, at: https://kidspot.co.nz/health/new-zealands-appalling-youth-suicide-rate/

68 See, further, O'Halloran, K., *Children, the Law and the Welfare Principle: Perspectives from the U.S. and Canada* and *Children, the Law and the Welfare Principle: Perspectives from Australia and New Zealand,* Routledge, 2022 and 2023.

69 See, for example, Prentice, K., Blair, B. and O'Mullan, C., 'Sexual and Family Violence: Overcoming Barriers to Service Access for Aboriginal and Torres Strait Islander Clients', *Australian Social Work*, Vol. 70, No. 2 (2017), pp. 241–252; and Willis, M., 'Non-disclosure of Violence in Australian Indigenous communities', in *Trends and Issues in Crime and Criminal Justice,* No. 405, Australian Institute of Criminology, 2011.

70 See, O'Halloran, K., *Children, the Law and the Welfare Principle: Perspectives from the U.S. and Canada* and *Children, the Law and the Welfare Principle: Perspectives from Australia and New Zealand,* Routledge, 2022 and 2023.

degree, in the U.S., Canada and New Zealand – is facilitating the integration of statutory child protection provisions into Indigenous culture.

Discrimination

The scale of the over-representation of Indigenous children in the child welfare and criminal justice systems of the CANZUS nations cannot be satisfactorily explained other than by the action of discriminatory biases at work in the catchment environment and in the workings of those systems. While the fact and consequences of such systemic forms of discrimination are readily recognized, it is the more subtle forms that are less easily detected and which may do more damage in the long-term. In an educational context, for example, it is the editing out of historical information and the reshaping of narratives to present the 'civilising' influence of the host nation in a more favourable light that can be demeaning for the Indigenous and constitute indirect discrimination.

Conclusion

Now, as always, the legal function of 'protection' forms the bedrock of the law governing the rights and welfare interests of children in all jurisdictions. However, although that law is becoming more complicated, as it seemingly struggles to encompass the growing spectrum of harm that children may now be exposed to, there must be some doubt as to its effectiveness. Leaving aside the questions that may be raised regarding the legal veracity of terms such as 'promotion', the statistical data referenced in this chapter indicates a scale of state failure to protect children that is truly worrying, particularly so in relation to Indigenous children.

It is hard to avoid the fact that this crude snapshot of state failure is one that pictures the relative failings of the protective function as deployed by and within those nations that are among the richest on this planet. To take one example, the infant mortality rate – possibly the most basic measure of state child protection – and one customarily used to assess the relative progress of developing nations. Any state's claim to be genuinely concerned about child protection would need to have a credible response to the UN CROC, Article 6, injunction to ensure that 'every child has the inherent right to life'. As the record earlier shows, these eight nations are not meeting that challenge, particularly as regards Indigenous children. That the U.S. should in 2022 have a rate of 5.60 infant deaths per 1,000 live births,[71] 3% higher than the rate in 2021 (5.44) – meaning an estimated 20,538 U.S. infant deaths in 2022, an increase from the 19,928 deaths in 2021 – is shocking.[72]

71 See, further, at: https://worldpopulationreview.com/country-rankings/infant-mortality-rate-by-country#:~:text=Infant%20mortality%20in%20the%20United%20States&text=The%20mortality%20rate%20in%20the,%2C%20and%20Australia%20(3.14).

72 This rate placed the U.S. at 51st globally, alongside Croatia, significantly higher than in dozens of other developed countries such as Sweden (2.15), Japan (1.82) and Australia (3.14).

4 Control

Juvenile justice and state care

Introduction

While originally a matter of private family law and for the civil jurisdiction of the courts, 'control' also represents a public law interest in the protection of third parties from the unreasonable behaviour of children and young persons who reject the supervision of parents or of those in *loco parentis*, or who commit criminal offences. This public law dimension, a natural corollary to the parental duties of care and protection, has grown to become a significant and contentious area for modern social policy.

This chapter concludes the introductory assessment of the three main legal functions relating to the welfare of the child by focusing on 'control'. Like its two predecessors – prevention and protection – the chapter begins with a brief examination of key concepts and an outline of the relevant legal framework. It then divides into two parts, each dealing with an area of most concern for present purposes: juvenile crime and state care. Before conducting a comparative analysis of the role of this legal function across the eight jurisdictions studied. It concludes by assessing its relative significance in relation to the welfare principle and considers any implications arising for family law.

Control, concepts and international law

This area of family law is prone to public policy swings that alternate between prioritising welfare or justice concerns. These oscillations vary from time to time and from country to country. Currently, in most developed nations, there would seem to be an emphasis on establishing a child's responsibility and accountability for criminal conduct or for a breach of educational requirements and for the responsibility of a parent or third party for any failure in their legal duty to that child. This central focus is offset to a varying degree by a concern to protect the welfare interests of a child, to provide for his or her social rehabilitation and to protect the public from the risk of a repetition of such harmful behaviour.

Concepts

The responsibility to ensure that the behaviour of a child or young person does not breach socially acceptable norms is in law distributed with some uncertainty

DOI: 10.4324/9781003269595-7

between child, parent and state. Once such a breach has occurred, then the role to be played by the welfare principle will depend very much on whether the issues of liability for the consequences, and for imposing measures to ensure future restraint, arise for judicial determination in civil or in criminal proceedings. In either case, the basic concepts are much the same, but primarily in the latter, the extent to which judicial disposal is influenced by considerations of justice and punishment, or mitigated by those of education, treatment/training and rehabilitation, provides a significant indicator of jurisdictional differences in the role of the welfare principle.

Culpability

From the outset, the law relating to the welfare interests of children was closely circumscribed by the rights of others: unlike its long-delayed and still equivocal approach to recognising the autonomous rights of a child, the law never had any difficulty in recognising his or her personal accountability for a breach of duty. As far as the common law was concerned, where it was found that the *actus reus* (or physical act) of a child was accompanied by the appropriate *mens rea* (or malicious intent), then unless exempted by the *doli incapax* rule (a late introduction that established a legal presumption that a child below a specified age was held not to have the requisite *mens rea* to commit a crime), he or she would be accountable in the criminal law for their actions.

Civil law

In civil law, responsibility for the consequences of a child's behaviour was traditionally held to rest solely with the parent but is now best viewed as shared between child and parent, the proportional distribution varying in accordance with the age and understanding of the child as per the *Gillick* test.[1] The role of the principle in relation to the control function broadly follows that of the other 'prevention' and 'protection' functions (see, further, chapters 3 and 4). The threshold of coercive and mandatory intervention by specified authorities is legislatively set in prescriptive terms. The grounds underpinning the threshold are objectified. What matters is that the behaviour is uncontrolled; the fact that a parent is too ill or otherwise too incapacitated to exercise adequate control is beside the point. Judicial determination provides adjudication on the issues but is discretionary in relation to disposal: the options being essentially of a treatment and rehabilitative nature in all developed jurisdictions; the choice made, while generally governed by considerations for the welfare interests of the child concerned, varies to some degree on a jurisdictional basis.

Criminal law

While the civil law denied a child the right to give a valid consent to contract, etc., the criminal law held him or her wholly accountable for consenting to such activities as robbery.

1 *Gillick v. West Norfolk & Wisbeck Area Health Authority* (1986) AC 112.

In most contemporary developed nations, the law relating to juvenile offenders now maintains a primary focus on children's deeds rather than their needs (following an earlier reverse prioritisation): a distinction reinforced by related proceedings now being mainly located within a separate body of legislation dealing with criminal justice matters. The thresholds for state intervention on such matters tend to be coercive, mandatory and legislatively explicit, while the judicial role is adjudicatory. Disposal options are heavily influenced by considerations of justice and public protection, they are preset in accordance with a 'tariff' which matches orders available with crimes on a proportionality basis and they most usually have a definite punishment and deterrent orientation. There is considerable jurisdictional variation, however, in the part played by discretion – from the point of initial contact with the police until the point of judicial disposal – and the extent to which this is guided by considerations for the welfare of the child concerned, for their social rehabilitation rather than their punishment, is an important aspect of jurisdictional difference in relation to the role of the welfare principle. A particularly important aspect of judicial discretion is the latitude available to transect the broadly separate and alternative 'care' and 'offence' contexts enabling the criminal behaviour of a child to be defined as indicating a need for a welfare rather than for a punishment-oriented disposal option.

Culpability: parent and child

The 2023 Crumbley case in the U.S. cannot be overlooked in a book such as this.[2] It necessarily raises questions about the balance to be struck between the functions of control and those of prevention and protection when assessing the welfare interests of a child, the right of a 15-year-old child to make and be accountable for autonomous decisions and the extent to which parents can be held accountable for the actions of a child of that age.

The conviction of the mother on four counts of involuntary manslaughter, following the mass school shooting carried out by her 15-year-old son – previously convicted and sentenced – may well turn out to be a landmark case (depending on the outcome of any appeal lodged). While very much a 'fact sensitive case' – with a verdict delivered by a jury in a local court – it nonetheless marks a point of departure in a long history of such shootings featuring children who kill other children, often in school settings and most often in the U.S.[3] Before this verdict, prosecutions for similar school shootings would seem to have been restricted to the child shooter, accountability would have extended to include anyone who knowingly sold the gun to an underage person and to any accomplice/s (also anyone implicated under the 'common enterprise rule')[4] but in the absence of evidence of gross negligence would not stretch to include a parent. The verdict clearly does not

2 See, further, at: https://edition.cnn.com/2024/02/06/us/jennifer-crumbley-oxford-shooting-trial/index.html

3 The son, 15-year-old Ethan, killed four students and wounded six students and a teacher at an Oxford, Michigan, high school in 2021, where he was a pupil, with a handgun bought for him by his parents as a Christmas present.

4 See, further, at: www.supremecourt.uk/docs/joint-enterprise-debate-pack.pdf

detract from the culpability of the 15-year-old child (who had received parental instruction on using the gun on a firing range), but it does open up questions about the nexus of liability: school staff who were in a position of *loco parentis*; police, who may intervene too late or ineffectually; gun shop staff; firing range officials and such others with a public safety responsibility who might have been expected to be alert to the risks of children with guns; and any relatives, friends or neighbours who might have had concerns about the particular child.

Should the conviction stand, it may establish a principle of contributory negligence to be applied to gauge the liability of anyone considered to have a risk management responsibility in respect of a child's behaviour. Arguably, such a principle would have a potentially wide application: not only as regards a child's potential for criminal acts but also in relation to those who permit or sponsor activities that expose a child or children to risk (e.g. the innumerable entrants in charity sponsored contests to be the youngest child ever to engage in some particular physically demanding sport, antivax teenagers, etc.). Any such calibration relating to the distribution of responsibility between a child and others would need to start with an evaluation of that particular child's capacity for autonomy: their age, together with his or her level of maturity/discernment and skill in relation to the type of activity, and the degree of risk it entails to that child and/or to others.

Justice

Justice and welfare, the two competing frames of reference governing the response of the law to the problems presented by children whose behaviour is both out of parental control and criminal, are – as noted earlier – prone to being balanced and rebalanced in accordance with the social policy prevailing in a particular country at any point in time.

Due process

It seems probable that the now generally embedded national benchmarks of 'due process' emanated from the civil rights movement in the U.S. which brought with it an awareness of a need to recognise and protect the rights of individuals in the justice system. Due process implies a requirement that all persons are served with notice of proceedings affecting them and that legal representation is provided to those (such as children) whose interests are being determined. It also implies that any delay in proceedings relating to children is prejudicial to their interests. Time is clearly an important factor: timely professional involvement, appropriate representation, prompt decision-making and expeditious legal proceedings all contribute in giving effect to due process.[5] As the USSC has noted:

> inconsistent approaches taken by the lower courts in determining when, if ever, the failure of a state or local governmental entity or its agents to provide

5 See, for example, *DeShaney v. Winnebago County Department of Social Services*, 489 U.S. 189 (1989).

an individual with adequate protective services, constitutes a violation of the individual's due process rights.[6,7]

Punishment

Traditionally, children found guilty of criminal activity were treated by the legal system as adults and flogged, imprisoned, transported overseas or hanged in accordance with the prevailing statutory tariff for such offences.[8] Only relatively recently, in a development reminiscent of other government initiatives to privatise matters and facilities previously regarded as being in the public domain, has legislation broadened liability to also hold parents accountable for the activities of their children.

Diversion

Article 17 of the European Social Charter states the principle that, wherever possible, diversion from judicial proceedings diversion (such as by way of settlement, conditional termination or withdrawal of criminal proceedings) should be the preferred response to child offenders.

Detention

This is defined as any form of placement in an institution by decision of a judicial or administrative authority, from which the juvenile is not permitted to leave at will.[9] This may take the form of committal to a residential training or treatment centre or a period of confinement in 'secure accommodation'.

Secure accommodation

There has probably always been a form of 'secure accommodation' within specially designated residential provision for children and young persons who have been convicted of a criminal offence but are considered to be a danger to themselves or others or are likely to abscond if placed in other settings and also for those who are not guilty of criminal offences but are in state care for reasons of child protection and have behavioural or mental health issues. While it is accepted that the imposition of extreme controls on the liberty of children severely constrains their welfare interests, and as such may breach Article 5 of the ECHR, these measures are viewed as compatible with the welfare principle and a proportionate response in certain circumstances. The use of restraints must not, however, breach UN CRC,

6 Ibid.

7 Ibid.

8 As noted in Morris, A., and Giller, H., *Understanding Juvenile Justice*, Croom Helm, London, 1987, on one day in 1814, five children aged between 8 and 12 were hanged in England for petty larceny.

9 See, Council of Europe, Committee of Ministers, Recommendation CM/Rec (2008) 11 on the European Rules for juvenile offenders subject to sanctions or measures (2008), Rule 21.5.

Article 37(c), which provides that 'every child deprived of liberty shall be treated with humanity and respect for the inherent dignity of the human person, and in a manner which takes into account the needs of persons of his or her age'.

Rehabilitation

This concept refers to both the successful reunification of a child in the public care system with his or her family of origin and the socialisation of a child offender who rejects criminal activity in favour of normal peer pursuits.

UN CROC, Article 9, requires States Parties to 'ensure that a child shall not be separated from his or her parents against their will . . . except when . . . such separation is necessary for the child's best interests'. This right comes into play when the issue arises as to whether rehabilitation with birth parents should be pursued in respect of a child compulsorily admitted to the public child welfare system. Under the provisions of UN CROC, the authorities are required, from point of admission, to work towards returning a child to his or her family of origin, as, except in rare circumstances, this is viewed as being in their best interests. However, for various reasons, it may be that steps towards rehabilitation are not immediately taken. Alternatively, from point of admission, it may be decided to place the child in a concurrent placement. In either case, the passing of time works in favour of the day-to-day carers and against the birth parents. Drift in care can easily become the default reality.

A school of thought suggests that programmes designed to facilitate the integration of child offenders into normative activities for their peer group – through education, sport, relationship counselling, job training, etc. – are warranted both because they address the personal and environmental issues that are the root causes of much delinquency and because such strategies stand the best chance of preventing re-offending.[10] A multi-agency, coordinated approach to engage individual child offenders and their particular profile of needs – offering support and a route to social rehabilitation rather than applying a uniform tariff of punishments – is held to be more effective for offenders and for society. Similarly, the psycho-social preparation that enables a child in care to return safely to their family offers the best chance for all concerned to recover their self-respect and get on with their lives.

The extent to which both juvenile justice and child welfare systems can be differentiated on the basis of their investments in social rehabilitation provides one measure of jurisdictional leanings towards promoting the welfare principle in a control context.

Restorative justice

This concept is anchored on the twin aims of holding a perpetrator personally accountable for their offence and ameliorating the harm inflicted upon their victim.

10 See, for example, Elsea, K.K., 'The Juvenile Crime Debate: Rehabilitation, Punishment or Prevention', *Kansas Journal of Law & Public Policy*, Vol. 5 (1995–1996), p. 135, at: https://heinonline.org/HOL/LandingPage?handle=hein.journals/kjpp5&div=14&id=&page=

Again, the part it plays – or does not play – in a juvenile justice system is an indicator of jurisdictional leanings towards welfare rather than punishment considerations. Restorative justice is held to be more effective than traditional retributive justice because it substitutes a direct and personal mutual exchange between offender and victim for the anonymity of a tariff of crime and punishment, thereby promoting a healing process for both parties.[11]

Restorative justice has been defined as follows:

> a process through which parties with a stake in a specific offence collectively resolve how to deal with the aftermath of the offence and its implications for the future. It can take the form of victim-offender mediation either through direct contact between the offender and victim or indirect communication involving third parties. It can also involve restitution or reparation where this is agreed between offenders and their victims.[12]

Further, that this form of intervention can be an 'effective and proportionate responses to low level offending where the public interest does not require a formal criminal justice disposal'. It may take place at any stage of the criminal justice process including after conviction and can also form an integral part of any sentencing disposal. This approach emphasises the importance of restorative justice 'especially with children and young people' and one that is 'more widely used with youth offenders'.[13]

International law

The relevant European legal framework governing the legal function of 'control' as it relates to the role of the welfare principle, in the twin contexts of child welfare and juvenile justice, is largely the same as that governing the functions of 'prevention' and 'protection' and outlined in the preceding two chapters.[14]

European Convention on Human Rights 1950 (ECHR)

Control issues may arise under Article 5, which deals with deprivation of liberty, and under Article 6, the 'right to a fair trial', which includes the right to be informed promptly about the charges in a language she/he understands (Article 6 (3) a); the right to have adequate time and facilities for the preparation of her/his defence (Article 6 (3) b); the right to have legal assistance of her/his own choosing (Article 6 (3) c); the right to examine or have witnesses examined (Article 6 (3) d); and the

11 See, further, 2014, Boyes-Watson, C., 'The Value of Citizen Participation in Restorative/Community Justice: Lessons from Vermont', *Criminology and Public Policy*, Vol. 3 (2004), pp. 687–692.

12 See, further, the Crown Prosecution Service (England and Wales), at: www.cps.gov.uk/legal-guidance/restorative-justice

13 Ibid.

14 See, also, O'Halloran, K., *Children, the Law and the Welfare Principle: European Judicial Perspectives*, Routledge, 2024, at Chapter 9.

right to have the free assistance of an interpreter (Article 6 (3) e). Also more generally relevant are rights to no delay, to an independent adjudicating forum and, more broadly, in respect of principles such as 'equality of arms', right to remain silent, presumption of innocence and 'proportionality'.

The ECtHR has developed an interpretation of Article 6 to identify specific requirements for ensuring children's effective participation in court hearings. So 'effective participation' may be taken to include the child's presence during the hearing, holding of *in-camera* hearings, limiting trial publicity, ensuring that the child understands what is at stake and reducing the formality of court processes. Another aspect of effective participation is the child's right to be heard and the CRC have drawn attention to the need for this right to be exercised.[15] In *T and V v. United Kingdom*,[16] which concerned two 10-year-old boys, the ECtHR found that they had been denied any meaningful opportunity to participate, as they were tried in an adult court and subjected to most of the rigours of a criminal trial, thereby violating their Article 6 rights.

United Nations Convention on the Rights of the Child 1989 (UN CROC)

Article 37 of UN CROC recognises the distinct legal status of children by requiring states to ensure the separation of juvenile and adult detainees, to keep deprivation of liberty to a minimum and to ensure that every child deprived of his or her liberty has prompt access to legal and other appropriate assistance, as well as the right to challenge the legality of that deprivation before a court or other competent, independent and impartial authority and to a prompt decision on any such action.[17] Article 39 requires the promotion of rehabilitation for offenders in the community. Article 40 acknowledges that every child alleged, accused of or recognised as having infringed penal law is entitled to be treated fairly and in a manner that takes into account his/her age. It states that the key objective of juvenile justice is to reintegrate children into society. It recognises children's right to a fair trial and declares that children have some additional entitlements, including the right to be assisted by parents, the right to appeal and the right to have their privacy fully protected at all stages of the proceedings.

United Nations Standard Minimum Rules for the Administration of Juvenile Justice 1985 (Beijing Rules)

The rules state, as an opening principle, that 'Member States shall seek, in conformity with their respective general interests, to further the well-being of the juvenile and her or his family'. They provide basic guidelines regarding standards of treatment for children in any juvenile justice system and have since been extended ad developed.

15 United Nations, Committee on the Rights of the Child (CRC) (2009), *General Comment No. 12 (2009) on the right of the child to be heard*, CRC/C/GC/12, 1 July 2009.

16 Ibid.

17 Note, also, EU, European Parliament and Council of the European Union: Directive 2013/48/EU on the Right of Access to a Lawyer (2013); and Directive 2016/800/EU on Procedural Safeguards (2016).

Other

The European Social Charter and the European Rules on Juveniles Subject to Sanctions and Measures and the CoE 'Guidelines on child-friendly justice' are also very relevant.[18] Article 17 of the former states the principle that, wherever possible, diversion from judicial proceedings (such as by way of settlement, conditional termination or withdrawal of criminal proceedings) should be the preferred response to child offenders. Diversion options should be available from as early as possible after contact with the justice system, before a trial commences and throughout the proceedings. The principle applies to an even greater degree when children are below the age of criminal responsibility.

Article 24 of the EU Charter of Fundamental Rights requires that due weight be given to the child's best interests in cases where children are the subject of any of the provisions of the directives. The CRC General Comment No. 10 is also relevant, as it states that deprivation of liberty must be used as a measure of last resort and for the shortest appropriate period of time and stresses the need to embed the best interests of the child in the juvenile justice system.[19] The Lanzarote Convention adds that the effective participation of children in proceedings must be 'treated as a priority and carried out without any unjustified delay', advice that is reiterated in General Comment No. 10. In addition, the Procedural Safeguards Directive in reference to criminally suspected or accused children includes the right to effective participation, including in the individual assessment, as well as the right to legal representation,[20] while the Access to a Lawyer Directive includes references to children in its preamble and in Article 5 (2)–(4) requires that where a child is deprived of liberty, he or she should have immediate access to a lawyer. This is further reinforced by Article 47 of the Charter which states the right to an effective remedy and to fair trial, while also establishing requirements of particular relevance for children, such as a fair and public hearing within a reasonable time, the right to be defended, represented and advised and the right to legal aid.

(A) Juvenile justice

The Beijing Rules[21] are self-described as broad fundamental perspectives which 'aim at promoting juvenile welfare to the greatest possible extent, which will

18 Also see: the UN guidelines for the prevention of juvenile delinquency 1994 (Riyadh Guidelines); the UN Rules for the Protection of Juveniles Deprived of their Liberty 1990 (Havana Rules); and the UN CRC General Comment No. 10 on children and juvenile justice 2007 and No. 24 on Children's rights in juvenile justice 2007.

19 United Nations, Committee on the Rights of the Child, *General Comment No. 10* (2007) on children's rights in juvenile justice, CRC/C/GC/07 (2007).

20 See, EU, European Parliament and Council of the European Union, Directive (EU) 2016/800 on procedural safeguards for children suspected or accused in criminal proceedings, OJ 2016 L 132/1.

21 The UN Standard Minimum Rules for the Administration of Juvenile Justice 1985. See, further, at: www.ohchr.org/en/instruments-mechanisms/instruments/united-nations-standard-minimum-rules-administration-juvenile

minimize the necessity of intervention by the juvenile justice system, and in turn, will reduce the harm that may be caused by any intervention'.[22] It is customary when referring to welfare interests in this context to draw attention to the four Ds of juvenile justice – diversion, decriminalisation, deinstitutionalisation and due process – which are held to have contributed much to shifting the emphasis from punishment to rehabilitation.[23]

Control in a juvenile justice context: established international standards

The 1989 Convention[24] and the Beijing Rules[25] emphasise policies of diversion and the reintegration of children into society as more appropriate responses to youth crime than control and punishment. However, the evidence points to this being counter to the contemporary policies in most of the countries currently being studied.

Constraints on state use of the control function

State authorities faced with placing a child in detention are prohibited from doing so – under the terms of Article 40 (1) of UN CROC – without first giving consideration to alternatives to protect their best interests and to further his or her reintegration. Under Article 40(4), such alternatives might include 'care, guidance and supervision orders; counselling; probation; foster care; education and vocational training programmes'. Only where these are not feasible should detention be considered and then only for the shortest period of time and under appropriate substantive and procedural guarantees.[26]

Access to a lawyer

The ECtHR considers access to a lawyer to be a fundamental element of the right to a fair trial.[27] In addition, Article 37 of UN CROC states that every child deprived of his or her liberty shall have the right to prompt access to legal and other appropriate assistance, as well as the right to challenge the legality of that deprivation before a court or other competent, independent and impartial authority and to a prompt

22 Ibid.

23 See, for example, Young S., Greer B. and Church R., 'Juvenile Delinquency, Welfare, Justice and Therapeutic Interventions: A Global Perspective', *BJPsych Bulletin,* Vol. 41, No. 1 (2017), pp. 21–29.

24 See, Article 40(3)(b) of the UN Convention on the Rights of the Child 1989.

25 See, Rules 11.1–11.4 of the previously cited UN Standard Minimum Rules 1985.

26 See, EU Procedural Safeguards (2016), *op cit.*

27 *Salduz v. Turkey* [GC], Application No. 36391/02 (2008), at para 51; *Ibrahim and Others v. the United Kingdom* [GC], Application Nos. 50541/08 et al. (2016); and *Beuze v. Belgium*, Application No. 71409/10 (2018).

decision on any such action.[28] The importance of providing access to a lawyer for a child in custody was stressed in ECtHR rulings in *Salduz v. Turkey*[29] and *Panovits v. Cyprus,*[30] both of which concerned 17-year-old children, and in *Blokhin v. Russia,*[31] where the child was only 12 years old.

Delay

The ECtHR has ruled that due diligence must be exercised in bringing children to trial within a reasonable time,[32] while the Concluding Observations of the Committee on the Rights of the Child, Turkey, 2001, also states that juvenile offenders should be dealt with without delay.[33]

Involvement in decision-making

The parties to proceedings must be placed in a position where they have equal knowledge of and be permitted to comment on evidence held by the other.[34] What is considered under the ECHR, Article 8, is whether 'the parents have been involved in the decision-making process [. . .] to a degree sufficient to provide them with [a] requisite protection of their interests'.[35]

So, for example, in *Case Soares de Melo v. Portugal,*[36] among the many noted violations of Article 8, the ECtHR listed 'the decision-making process that led to the placement of children in institutions for their adoption, which was not conducted fairly saw the lack of effective involvement of the applicant'.[37] Again, in *Buchberger v. Austria,*[38] the ECtHR found that Article 8 rights had been breached by the failure of a local authority to sufficiently involve the claimant in its decision-making process. Where a mentally ill claimant was not provided with legal representation, during a decision-making process that concluded with her children being taken into state care, then again, there had been a violation of her Article 8 rights.[39]

28 Note, also, EU, European Parliament and Council of the European Union: Directive 2013/48/EU on the Right of Access to a Lawyer (2013); and Directive 2016/800/EU on Procedural Safeguards (2016).

29 Application No. 36391/02 (2008).

30 Application No. 4268/04 (2008).

31 Application No. 47152/06 (2010).

32 *Kuptsov and Kuptsova v. Russia*, Application No. 6110/03 (2011), at para 91.

33 See, further, at: https://www.refworld.org/policy/polrec/crc/2001/en/29965

34 See *P, C and S v. United Kingdom, op cit.*

35 *W. v. the United Kingdom*, Application No. 9749/82 (1988), at para 64.

36 Application No. 72850/14 (2017).

37 Ibid, at para 123.

38 Application No. 32899/96 (2001).

39 *B. v. Romania (No.2)*, Application No. 1285/03 (2013).

Detention

Detention is defined as any form of placement in an institution by decision of a judicial or administrative authority, from which the juvenile is not permitted to leave at will.[40] The ECHR limits legal detention to the six circumstances listed under Article 5(1) (a) to (f) of which the following apply to children: (a) detention after conviction by a competent court; (c) pre-trial detention; or (d) detention for the purpose of educational supervision, in particular. The latter two have given rise to specific duties for state authorities.

The ECtHR has determined that detention comprises three elements: the objective element of confinement in a restricted space for a non-negligible period of time, the subjective element that the person has not validly consented to that confinement and the detention being imputable to the state.[41] The CRC General Comment No. 24 encourages states parties to 'fix an age limit below which children may not legally be deprived of their liberty, such as 16 years of age' and adds that 'no child should be deprived of liberty, unless there are genuine public safety or public health concerns'. Article 37(b) of UN CROC adds that the deprivation of liberty, in the case of children, 'shall be used only as a measure of last resort and for the shortest appropriate period of time'.

Article 5 of the ECHR states that no one shall be deprived of their liberty except in specified cases and in accordance with specified procedures. Among the excepted circumstances are those governed by Art 5(1)(d) 'the detention of a minor by lawful order for the purpose of educational supervision'. This term has a broad meaning, covering many aspects of the exercise by a public body of parental rights for the benefit and protection of the person concerned.[42] In recent years, it has often been applied to the circumstances surrounding state confinement of unaccompanied migrant minors: the ECtHR has ruled against France on 11 occasions in relation to the confinement of children in detention centres.

ECtHR decisions require state authorities to pay particular attention to a child's age when balancing the relevant arguments for and against pre-trial detention.[43] In *Güveç v. Turkey*,[44] for example, which concerned a 15-year-old boy detained by the State Security Court in a prison for adults for five years, the Court noted that his detention contravened several international instruments, including Article 37 (c) of UN CROC. The Court maintains that detention should be used as a measure of last resort, for the shortest possible period,[45] after all other alternatives have been ruled out.

40 See, Council of Europe, Committee of Ministers, Recommendation CM/Rec (2008) 11 on the European Rules for juvenile offenders subject to sanctions or measures (2008), Rule 21.5.

41 See, *Storck v. Germany*, Application No. 61603/00 (2005).

42 See, *P & S v. Poland*, Application No. 57375/08 (2012) at para 147 and *D.G. v. Ireland*, Application No. 39474/98 (2002) at para 80.

43 *Dinç and Çakır v. Turkey*, Application No. 66066/09 (2013), at para 63; and *Güveç v. Turkey*, Application No. 70337/01 (2009), at para 108.

44 Application No. 70337/01 (2009).

45 *Korneykova v. Ukraine*, Application No. 39884/05 (2012), at paras 43–44. See also, *Selçuk v. Turkey*, Application No. 21768/02 (2006), at paras 35–36; and *J.M. v. Denmark*, Application No. 34421/09 (2012) at, para 63.

Conditions in detention

The Procedural Safeguards Directive states that children in detention should be entitled to receive appropriate education, guidance, training and medical care and to be kept separate from adults.[46] A lack of adequate medical care in detention could raise issues under Article 3 or 5 of the ECHR as could a lack of available cell space, lighting and recreational activities.[47]

In a number of cases,[48] the ECtHR has found that the placement of a juvenile in detention, by judicial or regulatory authorities, as a means of containing the juvenile's disruptive behaviour was unaccompanied by any evidence of supervised education and, therefore, breached the detainee's Article 5(1)(d) rights. So, for example, in *Blokhin v. Russia*,[49] a 12-year-old suffering from attention deficit hyperactivity disorder was arrested and ordered to be detained in a temporary detention centre for juvenile offenders for 30 days to 'correct his behaviour' and prevent his committing further acts of delinquency. The ECtHR did not see how any meaningful educational supervision, to change a child's behaviour and offer appropriate treatment and rehabilitation, could be provided in such a facility within such a time period and ruled that the applicant's Article 5 rights had been violated. This is arguably an important ruling – differentiating between the use of detention as a punishment, as a form of protection for others and as an opportunity to provide a detainee with therapy/training – that has implications for those responding to problematic child behaviour in many different settings.

The ECtHR has repeatedly held that persons in detention must be protected from death, abuse or ill-treatment caused by other inmates or by the authorities themselves. *Çoşelav v. Turkey*,[50] for example, concerned the suicide of a 16-year-old in prison, who had previously unsuccessfully attempted to commit suicide on several occasions. The Court concluded that there had been a violation of Article 2 of the ECHR, as the authorities had failed to take reasonable measures to prevent the risk of suicide.

Victim protection

While justice requires criminal proceedings to be instigated against an alleged offender, the justice system has become increasingly aware that, in this context, the control function may need to be constrained to the degree necessary to ensure protection for victims. This issue has been recognised in Article 39 of UN CROC, and in 2011, the CRC drew attention to it.[51] Additionally, it has also been addressed by Article 31 of the Lanzarote Convention, while the UN has adopted the *Guidelines*

46 *Nart v. Turkey*, Application No. 20817/04 (2008).

47 *Kuptsov and Kuptsova v. Russia*, Application No. 6110/03 (2011), at para 70.

48 For example, *D.G. v. Ireland, op cit.*

49 Application No. 47152/06 (2016). See, also, *D.G. v. Ireland*, Application No. 39474/98 (2002).

50 Application No. 1413/07 (2012).

51 UN CRC, General Comment No. 13 (2011).

on justice in matters involving child victims and witnesses of crime[52] which call for child victims and witnesses to be treated in a 'child-sensitive manner', which 'denotes an approach that balances the child's right to protection and that takes into account the child's individual needs and views'.[53]

The ECtHR has ruled that the state has a duty to protect victims' interests, including victims who participate as witnesses in criminal proceedings: their interests under ECHR provisions, such as those protected by Articles 2 and 8, must be balanced against the interests of the defence.[54] In child sexual abuse cases, special measures may need to be taken for the purpose of protecting the child victims[55] which did not happen in *G.U. v. Turkey,*[56] when an adolescent child claimed that she had been raped by her 62-year-old stepfather. Her complaint to the ECtHR included the fact that she was obliged to give evidence in open court and hear the report by the Institute of Forensic Medicine, suggesting that she might have consented to the acts. Much the same approach faced the 14-year-old girl in *I.C. v. Romania,*[57] whose allegations of rape were met with a criminal justice system that was more inclined to believe the men involved in the abuse, rather than her.

Control in a juvenile justice context: jurisdictional comparison

The threshold for state intervention in the family on grounds that a child has, or is alleged to have, committed a criminal offence clearly indicates the balance struck between the interests of justice and welfare in a country at a particular point in time. A breach of that threshold authorises use of the control function to remove the child offender from his or her family of origin and begin the process of their admission to the juvenile justice system. In general, the welfare/justice balance in the common law jurisdictions has oscillated from one extreme to the other over the decades, a trend which has perhaps excluded the U.S., where there has been a more consistent public protection and personal accountability approach.

Control function and welfare considerations in the common law jurisdictions

The 'control function' – more so than 'prevention' and 'protection'– varies in scope and weighting in accordance with whether the social policy governing child offenders favours a justice or welfare approach. The availability of measures such as diversion programmes vary accordingly.

52 UN Economic and Social Council, Resolution 2005/20, *Guidelines on justice in matters involving child victims and witnesses of crime*, 22 July 2005.

53 Ibid, para 9 (d). See, also, the EU, European Parliament and Council of the European Union, Directive 2012/29/EU (2012) (the 'Victim's Rights Directive').

54 *Doorson v. the Netherlands*, Application No. 20524/92 (1996).

55 See, for example, *Kovač v. Croatia*, Application No. 503/05 (2007) and *S.N. v. Sweden*, Application No. 34209/96 (2002).

56 Application No. 16143/10 (2016).

57 Application No. 36934/08 (2016).

England, Wales and Ireland

In England and Wales, government policy in relation to children in the criminal justice system is currently oriented less towards their welfare interests and more towards controlling delinquency and protecting the general public. In part, this is given effect by involving the parent in rehabilitation measures: s 1(2A) of the 1989 Act requires a court, when determining any question with respect to the upbringing of a child, to presume that the involvement of a parent in the life of their child will further the latter's welfare, unless there is evidence to the contrary. However, under the 1933 Act, s 44, the Court is required to have no more than a cursory 'regard to the welfare of the child'. The mere fact that the age of criminal responsibility is set at 10 years of age in itself draws attention to a policy emphasis on protecting the interests of the general public rather than the welfare of offending children. In Ireland, the equivalent age is 12 years with corresponding advantages in terms of affording protection to younger children from the consequences of criminal convictions. Additional protection is to be found in the Probation of Offenders Act 1907 which allows the Court a discretion – in circumstances where the facts have been proven but there are mitigating factors and the offender is remorseful – to issue mild control measures such as a probation order, supervision order or a community service order.

The U.S. and Canada

Juvenile justice policy in the U.S. is more firmly control driven with a focus on considerations of accountability, punishment[58] and public protection: children as young as 13 may be tried as adults in federal courts when accused of felonies such as murder, attempted murder and bank robbery; and 'a significant number of children are being consistently treated as adults in the U.S. criminal justice system'.[59] The practice in both the U.S. and Canada of transferring some juveniles to be tried in adult courts is clearly not Convention compliant. Moreover, the fact that children of African American descent are disproportionately represented in the number of children processed by the legal system suggests that control strategies are targeting them more than others: African American youths are twice as likely as their Caucasian counterparts to be arrested,[60] and a similar marked disparity can be seen in the treatment of Hispanic and Caucasian youths.[61] The U.S. policy emphasis on control and accountability is illustrated by the fact that the death penalty may be

58 The Inter-American Commission on Human Rights, 'Children and Adolescents in the United States' Adult Criminal Justice System' (2018), p. 9. See, further, at: www.oas.org/en/iachr/reports/pdfs/Children-USA.pdf at p. 61.

59 Ibid.

60 National Center for Juvenile Justice, Juvenile Arrest Rates by Offense, Sex, and Race (1980–2011), February 2014.

61 Note that the Youth Criminal Justice Act, s 38(2)(b), requires regional parity of sentencing for similar crimes.

pronounced in respect of those who were minors when they committed particular crimes.[62]

In Canada, the Youth Criminal Justice Act 2003 sought to balance a focus on accountability, through meaningful consequences, with rehabilitation and reintegration. It emphasised out-of-court and non-custodial options for nonviolent youth. Essentially, however, policy considerations are not unlike those that prevail in the U.S. As the Canadian Department of Justice has explained, 'the purpose of youth sentences is to hold young people accountable by imposing sanctions that have meaningful consequences for them and that promote their rehabilitation and reintegration into society, thereby contributing to the long-term protection of the public'.[63] Moreover, in the U.S., although 'due process' should provide a level of protection equivalent to the requirement in Article 40 of UN CROC that every child offender be justly treated – and a juvenile accused of an offence does have a constitutional right to be advised and represented by an attorney[64] – there is no guarantee that this will happen. Rules such as 'three strikes and you're out' and 'common enterprise' when applied to juvenile offenders may well constrain welfare considerations for children in the U.S. more so than for their counterparts elsewhere. In Canada, the Department of Justice, through its Legal Aid Program, provides funding to the provinces for the delivery of criminal legal aid services to young persons facing criminal proceedings. In practice, most youths charged with an indictable offence will qualify for the legal aid necessary for attorney representation, but most facing a possible summary conviction will not.

Australia and New Zealand

In Australia, the introduction of similar policies 'represent a move to seeing young people as more akin to adult offenders and a shift from focusing on the special needs of young people to emphasizing their responsibility for offending behaviour'.[65] This was despite evidence from the Children and Young People's Commissioner that such children are often more in need of protection than of control as 'a high proportion of young people in the youth justice system have mental health conditions, cognitive disabilities, problematic drug or alcohol use, or a background of childhood trauma'.[66] The commissioner's report goes on to argue for an easing of the control function and for preference to be given to welfare considerations: 'the best approach, both for the young people involved and for long term community safety, is diversion out of the justice system to appropriate community support and

62 A total of 38 states permit the use of the death penalty of which 23 authorise its use in respect of those who were juveniles when they committed the crime.

63 See, further, at: www.justice.gc.ca/eng/cj-jp/yj-jj/tools-outils/sheets-feuillets/syp-dpaa.html

64 *In re Gault*, 387 U.S. 1 (1967).

65 See, Cunneen, C., 'Youth Justice in Australia', *Oxford Academic* (2014), at: https://academic.oup.com/edited-volume/41333/chapter/352357407

66 See, Roy, A., McGill, B. and Fenn, L., *Children & Young People with Complex Needs in the ACT Youth Justice System*, published by the ACT Children & Young People Commissioner, 2016.

therapeutic intervention'.[67] However, the protective function is given some recognition through the considerable range of diversionary options available: action taken by police may include non-court actions (such as warnings, formal cautions, referral to a family group conference, counselling or infringement notices), while the Court may decide to divert the young person from further involvement in the system (for example, by referral to other services or to a specialist programmes). In New Zealand, the juvenile justice system had adopted an ostensibly welfare-oriented approach to child offenders until the introduction of the *Oranga Tamariki* Act 1989 which brought with it a change of emphasis towards control, accountability and rehabilitation. Age parameters both constrain and promote the role of welfare in relation to the criminal liability of children in this jurisdiction: on the one hand, a child becomes criminally responsible for their actions at the early age of ten; but on the other, he or she continues to be legally defined as a 'minor' until the age of 20.[68] Judicial discretion also plays an important part in mitigating the effect of the control function: under s 280a of the Crimes Act 1961, the judge may direct that a case be transferred from the criminal justice system to the welfare system; while under s 282 of the *Oranga Tamariki* Act, those appearing before the Court most often receive an absolute discharge, usually because he or she has admitted their offending and successfully completed the set of interventions and programmes (such as drug and alcohol counselling, community work, reparations and curfews as agreed at their family group conference).

Control function and welfare considerations in the civil law jurisdictions

The two civil law countries – France and Germany – provide an interesting contrast to the earlier policies pursued by their common law counterparts. In both, rehabilitation programmes seem to be more firmly entrenched in law and attract a more positive policy commitment than in the common law countries.

France

In France, the basic principle that educative measures – or welfare services – must take precedence over punishment has endured through many decades of youth justice reforms and continues to have priority over the control function. However, in practice, this principle does not sit well alongside the repeated concerns expressed by the ECtHR in relation to the confinement of children in detention centres. It is estimated that since the first ruling against France in 2012 for inhuman and degrading treatment, until 2023, more than 35,000 children have been locked up in detention centres.[69]

67 Ibid, at p. 5.
68 See, the age of Majority Act 1970, s 4.
69 See, further, at: www.statewatch.org/news/2023/may/detention-of-children-european-court-of-human-rights-rules-against-france-11-times/

The *juges des enfants*, exercising both civil and criminal jurisdictions, have long been vested with authority to direct the provision of such educative measures as is deemed appropriate, and in practice, these are imposed more frequently than imprisonment.[70] This flexible welfare orientation is supplemented by an increased recourse to restorative justice:

> constitutes any measure allowing a victim along with the perpetrator of the offence to participate actively in the resolution of the difficulties resulting from the offence, and in particular in reparation for the harms of any kind resulting from its commission.[71]

This optional alternative to criminal proceedings offers a more welfare-oriented approach to offending by protecting a child from being burdened by a criminal record. The overall welfare-oriented approach has been counterbalanced somewhat following the introduction of the Perben Law of 2002 which emphasised control, accountability and consequences for deviant behaviour and initiated new penalties for those aged 13–18.

Germany

In Germany, as in France, juvenile justice policy continues to emphasise the welfare dimension – with its diversional, educational and restorative justice measures – rather than give priority to the control objective as has steadily become the case in most other developed nations. The lower end of the sanctions tariff for juvenile offenders is firmly focused on the educative and disciplinary measures necessary to effect successful social rehabilitation.[72] These include the requirement that the offender accept certain forms of educative assistance – socio-educational input – or residential accommodation with backup support from social workers. These measures are not punitive or controlling but aim to promote the juvenile's upbringing in an educative manner. However, in 2021, it did introduce legislation to focus inter-agency collaboration on combating sexualised violence against children and to significantly increase the sentencing range for child sexual abuse and child pornography offences in the German Criminal Code, for which it attracted praise from the CRC.[73] Overall, German policies have been welcomed for 'responding to crimes committed by young people in ways that are age appropriate, centre on rehabilitation, and resort to incarceration only in limited circumstances

70 The criminal and civil jurisdictions being authorised by the 1945 Ordinance and articles 375 ff. of the French Civil Code, respectively.

71 *Gouvernement de la République française*, 2020, Article 10–1. See, also, Circular of March 15, 2017 (*Ministère de la justice*, 2017).

72 See, Jörg-Martin Jehle, *Criminal Justice in Germany* (7th ed.), the Federal Ministry of Justice and Consumer Protection, 2019, p. 41.

73 See, Experts of the Committee on the Rights of the Child Praise Germany for Prosecuting International Perpetrators of Sexual Abuse against Children. See, further, at: www.ohchr.org/en/press-releases/2022/09/experts-committee-rights-child-praise-germany-prosecuting-international

and when absolutely necessary'.[74] As the CRC mentioned in its 2022 report, rather than emphasise the control function, it recommended that the federal government 'continues to actively promote, in all *Länder*, the application of non-judicial measures, such as diversion, mediation and counselling, and, wherever possible, the use of non-custodial measures for children, such as probation or community service'.[75]

Jurisdictional comparison: age of criminal responsibility

The age until which a child may be excused liability for criminal conduct is clearly a matter of some importance for their welfare interests, which the CRC has recognised by encouraging states to raise the age of criminal responsibility to 'at least 14 years'.[76] The age threshold also provides a reasonable indicator of where on a spectrum – from an emphasis on the legal function of protecting those interests to the function of controlling behaviour – lies the juvenile justice policy of the nations currently being studied. It bluntly reveals whether or not there is a willingness to extend either protection or accountability to more children of prepuberty age.

The common law jurisdictions

It should, perhaps, come as no surprise that the U.S. comfortably holds its position at the control end of such a spectrum. The fact that the age of criminal responsibility is mostly set at 7 years of age in 35 states indicates that policy objectives are primarily directed towards child accountability: a finding reinforced by this being the only nation that retains the death penalty for those who were children when they committed certain crimes.

Positioned in the middle of the welfare/control spectrum, the UK, Australia and New Zealand have set the age of criminal responsibility at 10 years; in Ireland, it is 12. In Canada, where the control emphasis in juvenile justice policy is not dissimilar to that of the U.S., this is ameliorated to some degree by the age of criminal responsibility being federally set at 12. The control bias in Australia is exacerbated by the low age of criminal responsibility – set at 10 years of age – which has been challenged by the Law Council of Australia[77] and at Australia's last Universal Periodic Review in 2021 when 31 countries recommended that it be raised, and as was then noted, 'the fact that children as young as 10 are being locked up in jails

74 See, Fair and Just Prosecution Report, 'Lessons Learned from Germany: Promoting Developmentally Appropriate and Rehabilitative Youth and Young Adult Justice' (2022), at: https://fairandjust-prosecution.org/wp-content/uploads/2022/06/FJP-Germany-Youth-Justice-Brief.pdf

75 CRC/C/DEU/CO/5–6, at para 42. See, also, the CRC general comment No. 24 (2019) on children's rights in the child justice system.

76 Ibid.

77 See, Law Council of Australia, 'Minimum age of Criminal Responsibility' (2019), at: www.lawcouncil.asn.au/files/pdf/policy-statement/AMA%20and%20LCA%20Policy%20Statement%20on%20Minimum%20Age%20of%20Criminal%20Responsibility.pdf?21fb2a76-c61f-ea11-9403-005056be13b5

across the country is clearly an issue of significant international concern'.[78] In New Zealand, the policy focus on control has been facilitated by the similar retention of 10 years as the age of criminal responsibility which, in both countries, serves to draw more children into the juvenile justice system.

The civil law jurisdictions

At the other end of the spectrum, the civil law countries of France and Germany would seem – on the face of it – to offer a distinctly more welfare oriented juvenile justice policy than their common law counterparts. In France, the rejection of any fixed age for determining criminal responsibility allows accountability to be established by the *juge des enfants* who determines whether or not the child concerned has attained a sufficient degree of discernment to be held criminally liable for his or her actions, an approach supplemented by a presumption favouring the application of educative rather than punitive measures. However, with the flexibility of judicial discretion comes uncertainty, and this does not always work in favour of welfare interests: from the age of 10, for example, a child may be tried in a criminal court and from the age of 13 may be treated in law as an adult and imprisoned. Germany shares with France a policy emphasis that leans towards welfare rather than control, and this approach is supplemented by the fact that children aged 13 years of age or younger cannot be held criminally liable and none younger than 18 can be prosecuted as adults.[79] Further, since 1953, for the purposes of differentiating between degrees of venality in youths and adults, the former have been treated as juveniles until they reach 21 years of age. This stretching of the age group of those entitled to a more rehabilitative than punitive outcome in criminal proceedings means that those aged between 18 and 20 fall within the remit of the juvenile justice rather than the adult justice system which is strongly indicative of a policy that favours promoting the welfare rather than tightening the control of children in trouble with the law.

(B) State care

'Control', as explained in the first book of this series, is – in the context of child welfare – an essentially negative legal function, rooted in private family law, with its origins traceable to the doctrine of parental rights.[80] As such, it acknowledges that the recipient of care provided by a parent – or by someone or somebody in *loco parentis* – has a corresponding duty to the provider, not to obstruct or make impossible by willful behaviour, the provision of such care. Differentiating between

78 See, remarks of Hugh de Kretser, Executive Director, Human Rights Law Centre, as reported at: www.hrlc.org.au/news/2021/1/20/un-review-highlights-need-for-aust-to-raise-the-age-criminal-responsibility

79 Note – under s 828 of the Civil Code – a child aged 7 or older can be held civilly liable for damage he or she has caused.

80 See, O'Halloran, K., *The Principle of the Welfare of the Child: A History*, Routledge, 2022, at Chapter 8.

behaviour, in terms of its relative appropriateness to civil or criminal proceedings, varies according to prevailing social values and falls to be determined by the social policy of the government of the day. Where a court determines that such behaviour, while not criminal, is no longer manageable within the family home, then it may make a care order committing the child to state care, most probably with a care plan for placement in a foster home or in a small specialised residential facility.

International law

The main international instruments that establish the standards applicable to state use of the 'control' function in the context of children in the public care system are the European Convention on Human Rights 1950 (ECHR), the United Nations Convention on the Rights of the Child 1989 (UN CROC), the United Nations Guidelines for the Alternative Care of Children followed in 2019 by the Resolution on the Rights of the Child and the European Social Charter 2009 (Article 17). The Handbook on European Law Relating to the Rights of the Child[81] notes the range of European and international law governing the rights of the child in alternative care arrangements[82] and also the CJEU ruling that the Brussels IIa Regulation applies to decisions to place a child in alternative care. The European Rules on Juveniles Subject to Sanctions and Measures and the CoE 'Guidelines on child-friendly justice' are also very relevant[83] (for information on these and other relevant instruments, see previous sections and at chapters 3 and 4).[84]

According to the United Nations Guidelines, removing a child from the care of the family should be seen as a measure of last resort and should, whenever feasible, be temporary and for the shortest possible duration (para 14). The Guidelines direct States to ensure that children grow up in their families where possible; that alternative forms of care provide a supportive, protective care environment; and that children living in residential care who have a family network receive support to reintegrate into those families in safety. Decisions regarding children in alternative care should have due regard for the importance of ensuring they have a stable home that meets their

81 See, further, Council of Europe (2022), at: www.echr.coe.int/documents/handbook_rights_child_eng.pdf

82 Ibid. Listing the following: Council of Europe, Committee of Ministers (2011), Recommendation CM/Rec(2011)12 on children's rights and social services friendly to children and families, 16 November 2011; Council of Europe, Committee of Ministers (2005), Recommendation Rec(2005)5 on the rights of children living in residential institutions, 16 March 2005; Council of Europe, Committee of Ministers (2010), Recommendation CM/Rec(2010)2 on deinstitutionalisation and community living of children with disabilities, 3 February 2010; Council of Europe, *Children and Young People in Care*, CoE, Strasbourg, 2009.

83 Also see: the UN Guidelines for the Prevention of Juvenile Delinquency 1994 (Riyadh Guidelines); the UN Rules for the Protection of Juveniles Deprived of their Liberty 1990 (Havana Rules); and the UN CRC General Comment No. 10 on children and juvenile justice 2007 and No. 24 on Children's rights in juvenile justice 2007.

84 Also, see, O'Halloran, K., *Children, the Law and the Welfare Principle: Perspectives from European Judiciary*, Routledge, 2024, at Chapter 9.

basic need for a safe and continuous attachment to their caregivers, with permanency generally being a key goal (para 12). In 2021, four new EU policy initiatives were launched to accelerate deinstitutionalisation: the EU Action Plan on the European Pillar of Social Rights,[85] the EU Strategy on the Rights of the Child, the European Child Guarantee[86] and the European Strategy for the Rights of People with Disabilities.[87]

Children temporarily or permanently deprived of their family environment, or in whose best interests cannot be allowed to remain in that environment, are entitled under the UN CROC to special government protection and assistance (Article 20[1]).

Control in a public child care context: established international standards

The United Nations Guidelines have considerable influence in this context. Adopted by the UN Human Rights Council in 2009, the Guidelines were intended to enhance implementation of UN CROC 'regarding the protection and well-being of children deprived of parental care or who are at risk of being so' (para 3). They start from the general principle that efforts should primarily be directed towards enabling children to remain in or return to the care of their parents.

Alternative care arrangements

Alternative care – or 'out-of-home care' – can include 'foster placement . . . adoption or, if necessary, placement in suitable institutions for the care of children'.[88]

Having had a child admitted or committed into state care, the first and most critical exercise of control by the authorities is to secure him or her in the placement most appropriate for facilitating the agreed care plan. International law would now seem to have established that a child in state care has a right to 'family life'. This should in the first instance be given effect by returning him or her to parental care. Failing that, it should be given effect through kinship care. And if both those options are unavailable, then foster care is to be preferred to residential care. Adoption, because it violates the child's right to maintain links with their family of origin, should be pursued only in exceptional circumstances.

Residential care

This, the traditional form of 'out-of-home care', faded in the mid-20th century following many official enquiries and substantiated findings of abusive treatment in such facilities. Most developed nations have long since substituted care in family

85 See, further, at: https://ec.europa.eu/info/strategy/priorities-2019-2024/economy- works-people/jobs-growth-and-investment/european-pillar-social-rights/european-pillar-social-rights-action-plan_ en

86 See, further, at: https://ec.europa.eu/info/policies/justice-and-fundamental-rights/rights-child/eu-strategy-rights-child- and-european-child-guarantee_en.

87 See, further, Union of equality: Strategy for the rights of persons with disabilities 2021–2030 (European Commission).

88 See, UN CROC, Article 20(3).

settings and reserve the use of small residential units for children with special health or social care needs.[89] Not all have done so, however. The civil law countries – France and Germany – continue to place a large proportion of their respective child care populations in residential facilities: France, for instance, has 28 children's villages consisting of family-like units which are often used for sibling groups; while in Germany, the proportion of children similarly accommodated is rarely less than 60% of its child care population. Such small family group homes, with trained residential staff, are also much used in countries such as Finland which raises the question: Is foster care mostly a common law phenomenon, and has its wholesale displacement of residential care been a change for the good?

The influence of the ECtHR in establishing parameters for using the control function in relation to the welfare interests of children in the public care system can be seen, for example, in *Koniarska v. United Kingdom*[90] and in domestic court actions that have relied on ECHR provisions to successfully challenge the widespread unlawful restraint of children in secure training centres.[91]

Foster care

Almost all children now entering state care in the common law nations are placed with foster parents. The ECtHR has recognised that foster parents and child fall within the meaning of 'family life' and that such units warrant protection.[92] For example, *V.D. and Others v. Russia*[93] concerned a foster mother who complained that having cared for a disabled child for the first nine years of his life, the birth mother was denying her access following his return to his family of origin. Her complaint, on behalf of herself and her other foster children, was that their rights under Article 8 were violated due to both the decision to return the child to his parents as well as the denial of contact rights between them. The Court took the view that there were circumstances that justified the first decision which complied with domestic law, but it also considered that family life had been established between the foster mother, the other foster children and the disabled child. Accordingly, it found that the denial of contact between those parties constituted a breach of the Article 8 rights of foster mother and foster children.

Kinship care

Most developed nations now look first to the relatives of a child as the preferred placement for a child admitted or committed to state care. Such kinship placements,

89 See, 'The Harm of Institutionalisation', in ChildPact, *Putting Child Protection and Family Care at the Heart of EU External Action* (2017), at: https://codeofgoodpractice.com/wp-content/uploads/2019/05/Lumos-Putting-Child-Protection-and-Family-care-at-the-heart-of-EU-External-Action.pdf

90 (2000) 30 EHRR CD 139.

91 Ibid.

92 See, for example, *Moretti and Benedetti v. Italy*, Application No. 16318/07 (2010) and *Kopf and Liberda v. Austria,* Application No. 1598/06 (2012).

93 Application No. 72931/10 (2019).

often paid and managed as part of the state foster care service, enable a child to retain a close sense of their identity – personal and cultural – while maintaining important family relationships.

For example, *M.L. v. Norway*[94] concerned a claim by the applicant mother that the authorities' refusal to place her second child with her mother and stepfather – registered foster parents – who were already caring for her first child, a half-brother of the second, constituted a breach of her rights under Articles 6 and 8 of the ECHR. However, the authorities had reasonable grounds for not placing the second child with the first, mainly to do with the particular needs of the former and the risk of competing needs between the two, and the fact that the child was well settled in his foster home, where he was forming attachments to his carers. The ECtHR found that the authorities had given full consideration to the merits of a kinship placement, had conducted an appropriate balancing exercise and had been justified in concluding that the merits of such a placement were outweighed by other concerns.

A distinct trend in recent caselaw – perhaps growing in strength – is that of ECtHR rulings rejecting a proposed change of status from foster parent to adopter but nonetheless consolidating foster parent care while denying the competing claims of birth parents.[95] This would seem attributable to the Court's view that only the most unusual circumstances will justify such a draconian exercise of the control function that permanently severs the legal relationship between birth parents and child: a non-consensual adoption order not only irrevocably terminates that relationship but also has a long-term compromising effect on the child's right to an uncompromised identity.

Cultural identity

An aspect of the Article 8 right to private and family life is a requirement that state authorities show respect for the cultural identity of the children for whom it assumes responsibility. In *Jansen v. Norway*,[96] for example, the applicant was a member of the Roma community. Her daughter had been taken into emergency foster care at a secret address when she was about a year old, and the applicant was allowed only one hour of supervised contact per week because of the risk that the child might be abducted. The contacts were then further reduced to four visits per year before being suspended altogether because the High Court considered that there was a risk of abduction during contact sessions and a risk that the foster family's address and identity could become known to the applicant's family. The ECtHR considered that the potential negative long-term consequences for the daughter of losing her Roma identity and contact with her mother, and the positive duty to take measures to facilitate family reunification as soon as reasonably

94 Application No. 43701/14 (2017).
95 See, for example, *S.S. v. Slovenia*, Application No. 40938/16 (2018).
96 Application No. 2822/16 (2018).

feasible, had not been sufficiently weighed in the balancing exercise, resulting in a violation of Article 8 of the ECHR.

Rehabilitation

The capacity of the ECHR to promote the welfare interests of children by constraining state use of the control function in respect of those in the public care system was clearly demonstrated in cases[97] where the ECtHR ruled that the power of authorities in the UK, to coercively assume full parental responsibilities in respect of children consensually placed in care, contravened the Convention. This led directly to the abolition of that domestic power (even if it was replaced, to a degree, by applications for care orders for children voluntarily admitted but deemed to be at risk if discharged into parental care).

From the moment of admission to state care, an obligation rests on the authorities to nurture parent-child contact and work towards ending its control of the child, restoring family unity and withdrawing its coercive intervention in that family.[98] For example, in *W v. United Kingdom,*[99] the ECtHR stressed that '[t]he mutual enjoyment by parent and child of each other's company constitutes a fundamental element of family life. Furthermore, the natural family relationship is not terminated by reason of the fact that the child is taken into public care'.[100] A theme it returned to in *Olsson v. Sweden (No. 1)*[101] when it found that the domestic court's care decision should have been regarded as a temporary measure, to be discontinued as soon as circumstances permitted, given that adoption was not being considered. Measures taken should have been consistent with the ultimate aim of reuniting the natural family.[102]

Contact

Any prospect of family reunification hinges on state authorities first establishing and then maintaining regular and meaningful contact arrangements between the child in its care and his or her family members,[103] as well as others who have a meaningful relationship with that child.[104] For example, as mentioned earlier, in *YC v. United Kingdom,*[105] it warned that 'family ties may only be severed in

97 See, *W, O, B and R v. United Kingdom* (1987) 10 EHRR 29, ECHR and *R v. United Kingdom* (1988) 2 FLR 445.

98 See, for example, *K and T v. Finland* (2000) 2 FLR 79.

99 Application No. 9749/82 (1987).

100 Ibid, at [59] and reiterated in *Olsson v. Sweden (No. 1),* Application No. 10465/83 (1988) at [59]; *Eriksson v. Sweden,* Application No. 11373/85 (1989) at [58]; and *Andersson v. Sweden,* Application No. 12963/87 (1992) at [72].

101 Application No. 10465/83 (1998).

102 Note also, the CoE Family Reunification Directive 2003/86/EC on the right to family reunification.

103 *Haase v. Germany,* Application No. 11057/02 (2004).

104 *Nazarenko v. Russia,* Application No. 39438/13 (2015).

105 (2012) 55 EHRR 967.

very exceptional circumstances and . . . everything must be done to preserve personal relations and, where appropriate, to "rebuild" the family'.[106] In *Johansen v. Norway*,[107] it considered a domestic court decision that a child should be taken into care and placed in a foster placement with a view to adoption, and contact between the child and her applicant mother should be refused. The Court viewed these measures as 'particularly far reaching in that they totally deprived the applicant of her family life with the child and were inconsistent with the aim of reuniting them'. Since 2019, the ECtHR has ruled that in nine cases where the Norwegian authorities had taken children into care, they had exceeded a justifiable exercise of the control function by restricting parental contact to the extent that the Article 8 rights of the parents had been violated.[108]

Control in a public child care context: comparative jurisdictional analysis

The care and protection threshold – in tandem with that for juvenile justice – orchestrates the welfare/justice balance for state intervention in the family, on grounds of concern for children, in a country at any particular point in time. A breach of the former threshold authorises use of the control function to remove the child from his or her family of origin and begin the process of their admission to the public child care system. The fact that this threshold is judged to have been breached more often in some than in other jurisdictions must say something about relative jurisdictional tolerance levels: Why, for example, would Manitoba in 2011 have an admission to care rate ten times that of Western Australia?[109] Further, in 2001, why were 1.1% of Canadian children in state care compared to the following: 0.07% in Germany (in 2004), 0.55% in England (in 2005), 0.66% in the United States (in 2005) and 1.2% in France (in 2003)?[110] A closer examination of these statistics would undoubtedly reveal important information about jurisdictional differences in the interpretation of children's rights and welfare interests, but unfortunately, this would be well beyond the word count limitations of the present book, which should not detract from recognising that different standards are clearly being applied in respect of the

106 Ibid, at para 134.

107 (1996) 23 EHRR 33.

108 See: *Strand Lobben and others v. Norway,* Application No. 37283/13 (2019); *A.S. v. Norway,* Application No. (2019); *Abdi Ibrahim v. Norway,* Application No.15379/16 (2021), *K.O. and V.M. v. Norway,* Application No. 64808/1 (2019); *Hernehult v. Norway,* Application No.14652/16 (2020), *Pedersen and others v. Norway,* Application No. 39710/15 (2020); *R.O. v. Norway,* Application No. 49452/18 (2021), *K.E. and A.K. v. Norway*, Application No. 57678/18 (2021); and *F.Z. v. Norway,* Application No. 64789/17 (2021).

109 See, Brownell, M.D. and Jutte, D.P., 'Administrative Data Linkage as a Tool for Child Maltreatment Research', *Child Abuse & Neglect,* Vol. 37, No. 2 (2013), pp. 120–124.

110 See, Thoburn, J., 'Globalisation and Child Welfare: Some Lessons from a Cross-national Study of Children in Out-of-home Care', *School of Social Work and Psychosocial Studies*, Vol. 228, University of East Anglia (2007).

same thresholds, contrary to the principles articulated in UN CROC and the rulings of the ECtHR (notwithstanding the margin of appreciation rule).

Alternative care arrangements: jurisdictional differences

There are some interesting characteristics that differentiate the jurisdictions as regards their provision for the care of 'out-of-home' children – that is, those admitted or committed to state care.

Family based care

In general, there has been full acceptance of the principle of family-based care as stated in UN CROC and in the rulings of the ECtHR. However, while implementation has become standard practice in all common law nations, it is markedly less so in the civil law countries which, as mentioned earlier, raises the question as to why this should be given that, as research has shown, 'overall, the mean cost of residential care was significantly higher than the mean cost of foster care . . . three times as much'.[111] Are there cultural factors at play that permit the privacy of alternative family care or encourage the anonymity of public residential care?

Foster care

The 'family life is best principle' is to a large extent given effect through foster care placements, and this has become the most widely used placement option: in England and Wales by far, the majority of children subject to care orders are placed in foster care; at least 4 out of every 5 are fostered.[112] In Ireland, foster care is and always has been the preferential placement choice in respect of children who are the subjects of care orders, and the abrupt closure of residential facilities has resulted in almost all such children now being in foster care. In 2020, for example, there were approximately 6,000 children in care, of whom 91% were in foster care, 7% in a residential placement and the remaining 2% in other care placements. Similarly in the U.S., where the foster care system is large, comprising a mix of for-profit, not-for-profit and government providers, caring for some 400,000 children on any given day. Again, in Canada, there is the same mix of providers delivering foster care services for some 60,000 children – known as 'permanent wards' – in 2021, though other forms of care are also utilised. In Australia, in 2022, some 45,400 children were in 'out-of-home care' of whom 90% were in foster care or kinship placements which are government regulated and funded but often delivered by religious organisations, charities and nonprofits. The relevant statistics are

111 See, Browne, K., et al., 'A European Survey of the Number and Characteristics of Children Less Than Three Years Old in Residential Care at Risk of Harm', *Adoption & Fostering,* Vol. 29, No. 4 (2005), pp. 23–33, at p. 29.

112 See, *Fostering Network* at www.fostering.net/

difficult to find for New Zealand, but it would seem a third of the 4,400 children in care in 2023 were in family-based placements.

In the civil law jurisdictions, the proportion of children in state care accommodated with foster families is distinctly low relative to other developed nations. In France, in 2004, 56% of children in care lived with foster families, 36% were in institutions and 4% of the remainder were in other forms of accommodation.[113] In Germany, foster care has never been the primary resource for such children as it has in the UK and most other common law countries. In 2016, for example, of the 147,258 children in the public care system, 69,401 were in foster care, but 77,857 were in residential care, hostels or other forms of assisted living.

Kinship care

The placing of a child with approved members of their extended family – a practice probably initiated in Indigenous communities – has become standard practice over the past decade or two and in many countries is now the placement of choice.

In the U.S., the principle of kinship care is well established, but nonetheless, as of 2023, only 3% of children in the public care system were so placed. This should increase following the Biden Administration's 2023 initiative to ease the transfer from kinship to foster care status. In the UK,[114] when placing a child for adoption, s 22C of the 2002 Act requires the local authority to look first to family members as potential adopters for a child in care. Arguably, this statutory duty implies that such a child has a corresponding right to expect the authority to prioritise a kinship adoption placement. Kinship placements, often the preferred placements for Canadian child welfare agencies, can generate controversy, as was the case in *Nova Scotia (Community Services) v. TG*[115] when a foster parent, hoping to adopt a child placed with them, unsuccessfully challenged the social welfare agency's preference for a kinship placement.

Kinship care has a long history in Ireland having been established a thousand years ago, under the Brehon laws, as a practice within and between a child's extended family or clan and continued under the statutes of 1908 and 1991 and into contemporary times. In Australia in 2018–2019, the proportion of the 44,906 children in out-of-home care who were placed with relatives/kin was 52%. In 2022, of the 45,400 children in 'out-of-home care', some 15,500 were in kinship placements. In common with New Zealand, Australian placement practice has been heavily influenced by the long-established practice of its Indigenous communities: both Māori and Indigenous Australians have traditionally shared care responsibility for their children with the extended family. State placement policy in both

113 See, Annick-Camille Dumaret, 'Adoption and Child Welfare Protection in France', at: https://inserm.hal.science/inserm-00476402/file/inserm-00476402_edited.pdf

114 s 1(2)(f) of the 2002 Act directs the agency/court specifically to have regard to relationships with relatives.

115 2012 NSCA 43 at paras 42, 105, 109.

countries is to now look first to a child's relatives when seeking a placement for an out-of-home child.

In France, in 2007, an estimated 7% of children in care were placed with family members.[116] In Germany, the preferred foster care placement is with a relative.[117] Of the total German foster care population in 2005, approximately 60% of the children were in kinship placements.[118]

Step-parent adoption

For many decades, step-parent adoptions have served the same role in all developed countries: that of restoring legal boundaries for families disrupted by breakdown. The control function is very much at work here: not just by the step-parent asserting parental status and imposing new internal legal boundaries on a nuclear family unit but also by both parents deciding to legally exclude the other birth parent and his or her relatives (see, further, Chapter 9).

Residential care

Residential care – or congregate care – plays a very small part in out-of-home provision for children in the U.S. providing for perhaps 10% of children in the public care system.

In the UK, only a small minority of 'looked-after' children, mostly those with complex health or social care needs, now live in residential children's homes. Control has become a serious issue in many of these facilities prompting the Children's Commissioner to publish a series of reports alleging that this care system is broken and is failing many of the most vulnerable children, in particular, those who are most at risk of falling through gaps in the system and becoming victims of criminal or sexual exploitation.[119] In Ireland, this form of care is tarnished with a well-documented history of abuse by the religious orders that provided government funded accommodation: for single women and their children and for children and youths deemed by the courts to be out of parental control.[120] Consequently, it is now seldom used and – along with Australia – has one of the lowest rates of

116 See, Thoburn, J., 'Globalisation and Child Welfare: Some Lessons from a Cross-National Study of Children in Out-of-Home Care', University of East Anglia Social Work Monographs (2007), at: www.researchgate.net/publication/265357214_Globalisation_and_Child_Welfare_Some_Lessons_from_a_Cross-National_Study_of_Children_in_Out-of-Home_Care

117 See, Kiraly, M. and Humphreys, C., 'It's about the Whole Family: Family Contact for Children in Kinship Care', *Child & Family Social Work*, Vol. 21 (2016).

118 See, Walter, M. and Blandow, J., 'Foster Care in Germany' (2004), at: www.uni-siegen.de/foster-care-research/network_conferences/1st_conference/files/foster_care_germany_-_kindler.pdf

119 See, further, 'The Children No One Knows What to Do with', 'Private Provision in Children's Social Care' and 'Stability Index 2020', at: www.childrenscommissioner.gov.uk/report/the-children-who-no-one-knows-what-to-do-with/

120 The period 1922 to 1998 was an era that included the disgrace of the 'Magdalene laundries'; the proliferation of private nursing homes in which very many babies died, to be buried in

residential care for children in the world, accounting for no more than 7% of the nation's child care population.[121] In New Zealand, although residential institutions are no longer seen as appropriate, in 2017, some 1% of children in out-of-home placements were still being accommodated in state and charitable homes.

In the civil law jurisdictions, France (together with Romania) is estimated to have the highest number of children in the EU under the age of three years in institutional care.[122] As of 2020, some 37% of the French child care population was in some form of residential accommodation and a further 16% were in other non-foster home facilities, such as kinship placements and sheltered apartments. There are also some 28 'children's villages', which are family-like units especially designed for sibling groups. As has been noted 'the German child welfare system is characterized by a high proportion of placements in residential care compared to foster care'.[123] In 2015/2016, for example, 77,645 children and young people were in state care of whom 53,300 children were placed in residential care. Residential care has become the default placement for two-thirds of the child care population, as, for them, family life in a foster home is unavailable due to the difficulties experienced in recruiting foster parents.

Secure accommodation

A small proportion of children in residential facilities are in secure accommodation. In England and Wales, this form of residential care is authorised under the Children Act 1989, s 25, and provided for children and young persons of less than 16 years of age[124] who are likely to abscond if in any other form of accommodation and in which case are then likely to suffer significant harm or may injure themselves or others. In Ireland, a very small proportion of the child care population, between 12 and 17 years of age, are placed in Special Care Centres, under the authority of special care orders, due to behaviour issues which may endanger themselves or others. Because of a chronic lack of appropriate facilities, children are often transferred to facilities elsewhere 'out of the country, out of their communities and away from their families'.[125]

---

unmarked graves; and the sexual abuse of children consigned to the care of religious orders in rural reformatories.

121 See, for example, Whittaker, J.K., et al., *Revitalizing Residential Care for Children and Youth: Cross-National Trends and Challenges*, Oxford University Press, 2022.

122 See, Chou, S., and Browne, K., 'The Relationship between Institutional Care and the International Adoption of Children in Europe', *Adoption & Fostering*, Vol. 32, No. 1 (2008), p. 47,

123 See, Schrödter, M., 'German Residential Care: Doing Extremely Well in Doing the Wrong Thing', Conference paterpresented at 'the international Social Work & Society Academy', Sofia, Bulgaria (August 2014), at: www.researchgate.net/publication/265162609_German_Residential_Care_Doing_Extremely_Well_in_Doing_the_Wrong_Thing

124 Note that in *Re P (Application for Secure Accommodation Order)* (2015) EWHC 2971 (Fam), the court sanctioned such accommodation for a girl aged slightly older than 16.

125 See, Colfer, L. and Coulter, C., 'High Court Oversight of Children's Complex Care Needs' (January 2020), at: https://www.childlawproject.ie/publications/high-court-oversight-of-childrens-complex-care-needs/

In the U.S., the policy generally towards children with problematic behaviour leans more towards containment and public protection rather than therapy. As the IACHR has noted, 'the United States continues to be the one of the few countries in the world to sentence children so severely, in some cases incarcerating them for life without the possibility of parole'.[126] It has been estimated that approximately 35,000 children are being held in solitary confinement in the juvenile system alone.[127] In Canada, secure accommodation is very often a form of 'secure care' providing stabilisation and detoxification for those deemed to be at immediate risk of serious physical or psychological harm.

There is little information on the prevalence and use of this type of facility in Australia, though the 2019 redacted report on the Kath French Secure Care Centre does provide some insight.[128] It describes the service as a 'circuit breaker' offering:

> a planned, short- term intensive trauma informed intervention for children and young people aged 12–17 years of age. In exceptional cases, children under 12 years of age who are at extreme risk and where existing services cannot manage the risk can be admitted.

Secure accommodation in New Zealand has a troubled history which culminated in the 2021 closure of the *Te Oranga* secure care and protection facility, following allegations of staff violence towards the child residents.[129]

In France, the lack of facilities for children who harm themselves and refuse protection has prompted the creation of *centres éducatifs renforcés* (CEF), where highly qualified teams of social workers and psychologists work intensively with young people. They mainly house young offenders. In Germany, if secure accommodation is to be compliant with the right to liberty requirement in Article 5 of the ECHR, then it must meet the *Storck* test.[130] This necessitates that the deprivation of liberty be in a specific restricted space for a not-insignificant period of time, without the consent of the detainee and be authorised by the state or other proper authority. However, there would appear to be a lack of information available on the use of such facilities.

Adoption from state care

This, the most extreme form of control that may be exercised by the state in relation to children in the public care system, has mainly been used in the UK and the U.S., where it is central to contemporary government child care policy. The private adoptions of children in public care being a procedure that crosscuts both

126 The Inter-American Commission on Human Rights, *op cit*, at p. 78.

127 U.S. Department of Justice, Office of Juvenile Justice and Delinquency Prevention, Conditions of Confinement: Findings From the Survey of Youth In Residential Placement 9 (2010).

128 See, further, at: www.parliament.wa.gov.au/publications/tabledpapers.nsf/displaypaper/4014008c6105bef3b1cd062848258593001684f7/$file/tp-4008.pdf

129 See, further, at: www.newsroom.co.nz/oranga-tamariki-closing-care-and-protection-residence

130 *Storck v. Germany* (2006) 43 EHRR 6.

sectors of family law can be construed as 'hybrid proceedings' and is, therefore, not addressed in this book.[131]

Rehabilitation: jurisdictional differences

The safe return of children in state care to their families of origin is a UN CROC principle required to be uniformly implemented by all signatory states, but in practice, there is considerable jurisdictional variance.

Common law jurisdictions

In England and Wales, there is a strong policy to make adoption available to children in the care system when feasible, which may well run counter to a fully committed rehabilitation programme. Nonetheless, an opportunity for rehabilitation can be authorised under s 38(6) of the 1989 Act, which allows the Court to direct assessments in respect of the child's best interests, usually accompanied by an interim care order. Local authorities have developed a practice of initiating a rehabilitation programme designed to return a child to safe parental care while also putting in place a parallel permanent placement plan with the same foster parents.[132] The end result is a much higher proportion of children in foster care being adopted than in most other countries. In Ireland, the absence of any similar policy favouring adoption together with the amendment of s 54 of the Principal Act requiring the authorities to offer support to birth parents who have had their child taken into foster care has had the effect of increasing the chances of family reunification. The judiciary would seem to be supportive of this approach.[133]

In the U.S., federal law requires every child welfare agency to make reasonable efforts to achieve family reunification.[134] As was stressed in *Santosky*, 'when the State moves to destroy weakened familial bonds, it must provide the parents with fundamentally fair procedures'.[135] This sentiment is given effect through a step-by-step programme of goals to be achieved by the latter, within a specified timeframe and with the support of identified resources. However, the sentiment is counterbalanced by a policy that favours making adoption available, so birth parents are under pressure to meet stated goals if their child is to be returned. Moreover, the sentiment favours some more than others: it is asserted that 'in the

131 See, O'Halloran, K., *Child Welfare & Rights: a Contemporary Family Law Analysis*, Routledge, forthcoming.

132 See, for example, Wolfson, R., 'Concurrent Planning: A Route to Earlier Permanence for Young Children', *Seen and Heard*, Vol. 23, No. 2 (2012), pp. 46–58.

133 See, *Health Service Executive v. JG & anor (Care Order – Physical Abuse)* (2013) IEDC 16 and *Child and Family Agency v. IB and HB (placement in care – parental capacity assessment)* (2019) IEDC 1.

134 See, 'Reasonable Efforts to Preserve or Reunify Families and Achieve Permanency for Children' in Information Gateway's State Statutes series at: www.childwelfare.gov/topics/systemwide/laws-policies/statutes/reunify/.

135 *Santosky v. Kramer,* 455 U.S. 745 (1982) at 753–754.

United States, Black children . . . are less likely to experience family reunification following involvement with child welfare services'.[136] In Canada, the courts give serious consideration to the question of whether the home circumstances of a child in care have improved sufficiently to warrant the return of the child to parental care instead of proceeding towards possible adoption.[137] The courts will explore whether the parent has been given an opportunity to parent. Where the statutory agency frustrates contact with the parent and offers no services, this consideration must come into the equation.[138] The agency also has a duty to reassess its position as circumstances warrant over time.[139] Given the absence of any equivalent to U.S. policy and the diligence of judicial oversight of parental rights, it would seem probable that rehabilitation programmes are pursued with more vigour in Canada.

In Australia, in 2020–2021, of the approximately 27,300 children in out-of-home care (excluding those on long-term guardianship or custody orders), nearly 5,400 (20%) were reunified with their families of origin.[140] Here, unlike in the U.S. and the UK, the use of long-term foster care as a permanency planning option is encouraged while there appears to be a clearer and firmer policy which militates against non-consensual and family adoptions. The preferred policy has been to work towards family reunification[141] rather than impose the permanent severance effects of non-consensual adoption: reports indicate that all Australian jurisdictions attempt reunification of children in care with their birth families as the preferred permanency option.[142] In New Zealand, the *Oranga Tamariki* Act 1989, s 13(2)(h), requires that a child or young person in care should be returned to their 'family, *whānau, hapū, iwi*, or family group who are the child's or young person's usual caregivers' wherever that is possible and consistent with the child's or young person's best interests. However, this is not happening. Statistics show that once any child is admitted to state care, there is a strong likelihood that he or she will remain there: the percentage of children and young people in 'return-to-home' placements is low (less than 10%)[143] and is decreasing. Over the four-year period from June 2014

136 See, Boatswain-Kyte, A., et al., 'Impacts of Race on Family Reunification Etc', *Child Abuse & Neglect*, Vol. 125 (2022), at: www.sciencedirect.com/science/article/abs/pii/S0145213422000023

137 See, *Children's Aid Society of Kingston v. F.R.* (1975), 23 R.F.L. 391 (Ont. Prov. Ct. – F.D.).

138 See, *Children and Family Services for York Region v. A.W. and M.M.* (2003) O.J. no. 996 (Sup. Ct.); *CCAS v. P.A.M.* (1998) O.J. No. 3766 (OCJ); *CAS of the United Counties of Stormount, Dundas and Glengarry v. C.K.* (2001) O.J. No. 128 (Sup. Ct.).

139 See *Children's Aid Society of the Niagara Region v. D. (W.)* 2004 CanLII 66347 (ON S.C.) (2004), 1 R.F.L. (6th) 84 (Ont. S.C.J.); *Children's Aid Society of the Niagara Region v. B. (C.)* (2005) O.J. No. 3878 (Ont. S.C.J.); *Children and Family Services of York Region v. E. (P.)* (2003) O.J. No. 4884 (Ont. S.C.J.); and *Children's Aid Society of London and Middlesex v. S. (E.V.F.)* 2004 CanLII 34346 (ON S.C.) (2004), 1 R.F.L. (6th) 68 (Ont. S.C.J.).

140 See, further, at: www.aihw.gov.au/reports/child-protection/child-protection-australia-2020-21/contents/permanency-outcomes/how-many-children-exited-out-of-home-care-to-a-permanency-outcome

141 Note, however, that there is no nationally agreed definition of what constitutes 'family reunification'.

142 See, Chapter 7, Permanent Models of Care at para 7.10.

143 'Return to home' meaning return to a biological parent.

to June 2018, the percentage of children and young people in return-to-home placements decreased from 9% to 8.3%.[144]

Civil law jurisdictions

In France, the firm policy of family reunification, wherever feasible for every child taken into state care, has been established for some time. Article 375–2 of the Civil Code emphasises the importance of using the *assistance éducative* procedure to correct the functioning of the family so that it is better able to protect the child. In Germany, also, there is a legal duty to make appropriate efforts to reunify a family, within a reasonable period following the admission of a child into the care system,[145] while birth parents of a child in foster care have the right to request reunification services at any time.[146] However, in practice, German children will only be returned to the birth parents if the latter can show that they have been able to restore the standards of care expected from those with parental rights: a complete change of life and attitude is required compared to the *status quo ante*. As Wolf has noted, 'in Germany there is substantial criticism of the practice of reuniting children with birth families',[147] and in practice, only in 4%–5% of the cases are birth families reunited.

Control in a public child care context: Indigenous children

The use of state control as a means of subjugating Indigenous communities is a matter of historical record in all the CANZUS nations. In each, the state strategy of assimilation focused on the children, tens of thousands of whom were removed from their families and delivered to religious organisations for placement in residential schools or for enforced adoption. Decades later, the trauma caused by that strategy continues to compromise the government-Indigenous relationship and is evident in the social disadvantages born by the Indigenous communities relative to their fellow citizens.

Current statistical data and related trends reveal that the exercise of state control is consistently much greater in relation to Indigenous than to non-Indigenous children in all CANZUS nations, resulting in their gross over-representation in national child welfare and juvenile justice systems. The contrast between the specific protections offered by international law to Indigenous communities and the reality of their continuing subjugation and powerlessness across many indices of social disadvantage is striking.

144 *Oranga Tamariki*, 'OIA responses, Statistics on Children in Care, Placement Type and Returns Home' (15 November 2018), at: https://www.orangatamariki.govt.nz/official-information-act/oia-responses/children/

145 The Social Code VIII, s 37.

146 The Civil Code, s 1632.

147 See, Wolf, K., 'Promoting the Positive Development of Foster Children: Establishing Research in Germany', *Adoption & Fostering*, Vol. 36, No. 1 (2012), pp. 40–51, at p. 49.

International legal framework

Several international instruments, binding on the CANZUS nations for decades, contain provisions with direct relevance for the control function of the welfare principle, which might have been expected to ameliorate the conditions of Indigenous children. In terms of direct legal intervention in the state/Indigenous people, certain provisions of the ECHR and rulings of the ECtHR are most important, but others are also very relevant.

European Convention for Human Rights (ECHR)

Article 8, right to respect for private and family life – as developed by the ECtHR – has particular implications for the rights and welfare interests of Indigenous children, as does Article 14 on the prohibition of discrimination.

United Nations Convention on the Rights of the Child (UN CROC) 1989

The provisions of this Convention (not yet ratified by the U.S.) with most relevance in this context are as follows: Article 2, on non-discrimination, requiring the state to take all appropriate measures to ensure that a child is protected against all forms of discrimination or punishment; Article 7, on identity, which declares that a child has the right to know and be cared for by his or her parents; Article 18, on parental upbringing, requires the state to ensure the right of parents to have the primary responsibility for the upbringing and development of their child and to provide appropriate assistance to parents in the performance of their child rearing responsibilities; Article 20, culturally congruent placements, requiring the state when considering a foster or adoption placement to have due regard to the child's cultural and linguistic background; and Article 30, to enjoy his or her own culture, to profess and practise his or her own religion or to use his or her own language.

International Covenant on Economic, Social and Cultural Rights (ICESCR) 1966

This Covenant commits signatory states to work towards the granting of economic, social and cultural rights, including the right to health, the right to education and the right to an adequate standard of living. Articles 2, 10, 14 and 15 are particularly relevant.

International Convention on the Elimination of all forms of Racial Discrimination (ICERD) 1965

This Convention commits its members to the elimination of racial discrimination and the promotion of understanding among all races. Articles 1, 2 and 5 are particularly relevant. It encourages legislation to outlaw racial discrimination by the state in the provision of services such as housing and education. Discrimination is judged by its effects as determined by whether an action has an unjustifiable disparate impact upon a group distinguished by race, colour, descent or national or ethnic origin.

The United Nations Declaration on the Rights of Indigenous Peoples (UNDRIP) 2007

This Declaration comprehensively addresses issues such as collective rights, cultural rights and identity, in addition to rights to education, health, employment, land and language among others. It emphasises the right of Indigenous people to maintain and strengthen their own institutions, cultures and traditions. Article 8 is of particular importance for present purposes, as it declares that Indigenous peoples and individuals have the right not to be subjected to forced assimilation or destruction of their culture.

Control in an Indigenous public child care context: established international standards

In an Indigenous context, the legal function of control is most usually associated with issues of land ownership and leases, hunting, fishing, logging, etc. As regards Indigenous children, issues most often arise in relation to their discriminatory treatment.

Discrimination in schools

The ECtHR has heard a number of complaints alleging discriminatory treatment of children in schools, many involving Roma children. One such was *Oršuš and others v. Croatia*[148] which concerned the complaint of 15 Croatian nationals of Roma descent, who claimed they had received an inferior and stigmatising education in their state schools. They had at times attended separate classes, comprised of only Roma pupils, in their respective primary schools where the curriculum taught in the Roma-only classes could be reduced by up to 30% in comparison to the regular curriculum and where the proportion of Roma children in the classes for lower grades allegedly varied from 33% to 75%. The ECtHR held that the separation of Roma children was discriminatory because the means were disproportionate to the legitimate aim of ensuring that Roma children received special attention to improve their command of the Croatian language. A very similar case was *D.H. and Others v. The Czech Republic*[149] which concerned 18 Czech nationals of Roma origin and their placement, as children, in special schools allegedly because of their Roma origins. Ultimately, the Court was not satisfied that the difference in treatment between Roma children and non-Roma children was objectively and reasonably justified and that there existed a reasonable relationship of proportionality

148 Application No. 15766/03 (2008).
149 Application No. 57325/00 (2007).

between the means used and the aim pursued. The relevant legislation as applied at the material time had had a disproportionately prejudicial effect on the Roma community, the applicants as members of that community had necessarily suffered the same discriminatory treatment and this had violated their Article 8 rights.

Cultural identity

An aspect of the Article 8 right to private and family life is the requirement that state authorities show respect for the cultural identity of the children for whom it assumes responsibility. In *Jansen v. Norway*,[150] for example, the applicant was a member of the Roma community. Her daughter had been taken into emergency foster care at a secret address when she was about a year old, and the applicant was allowed one hour of supervised contact per week because of the risk that the child might be abducted. The contacts were then reduced to four visits per year before being suspended altogether because the High Court considered that there was a risk of abduction during contact sessions and a risk that the foster family's address and identity could become known to the applicant's family. The ECtHR considered that the potential negative long-term consequences for the daughter of losing her Roma identity and contact with her mother, and the positive duty to take measures to facilitate family reunification as soon as reasonably feasible, had not been sufficiently weighed in the balancing exercise, resulting in a violation of Article 8 of the ECHR.

More recently, *Abdi Ibrahim v. Norway*[151] concerned the decision of the state authorities to remove the parental rights of a mother from an ethnic minority and allow the adoption of her child by a Christian Caucasian foster family against the mother's wishes: a scenario replayed many times in all CANZUS nations. The mother, a Somali Muslim who had moved to Norway as a single parent with her 1-year-old son, had requested that her child should be cared for by her cousin or a Somali or a Muslim family, but instead, he had been placed with ethnically Norwegian foster parents who were active Christians. The mother did not ask for her son's return, as he had spent three years with his foster parents, but wished to maintain contact with him so as to keep alive his cultural and religious roots. The foster parents, however, were unwilling to accept an open adoption with future contact sessions between the applicant and her son and intended to baptise the adopted child and change his name. Mother-and-son contact arrangements were restricted initially to two hours four times a year, then changed to one hour six times a year. The applicant complained to the ECtHR about the withdrawal of her parental rights and the authorisation for adoption. The Court, referring to Article 20(3) of UN CROC, acknowledged the importance of a child maintaining their original identity. It found that the authorities had failed to take account of the mother's interest in allowing her son to retain at least some ties to his cultural and religious origins. The

150 Application No. 2822/16 (2018).
151 Application No. 15379/16 (2021).

Court considered that it had not been shown that such exceptional circumstances existed as to justify a complete and definitive severance of the ties between the child and the applicant or that the overriding requirement behind that decision had been the child's best interests. Indeed, there had been shortcomings in the overall decision-making process leading to the adoption, which had not given sufficient weight to the mother and child's mutual interest in maintaining ties. It held that the mother's Article 8 rights had been violated.

Control in an Indigenous public child care context: comparative jurisdictional analysis

There is a marked similarity in the *locus standi* of the Indigenous communities in each of the CANZUS nations which is reflected in the cases and statistical data relating to the rights/welfare interests of their children.[152]

State consensual intervention

The adverse effects of the control function have been only too evident in the statistics relating to the health (e.g. infant mortality rates) and education (school attendance rates and qualifications obtained) which are similarly poor in all CANZUS nations and are so relative to comparable statistics for non-Indigenous children. Government-controlled funding and services – intended to promote the welfare interests of children – is failing to do so.

State service provision

The failure of consensual intervention to effect positive change in established negative patterns is most likely due to a number of interlocking factors, including ingrained Indigenous mistrust of government intervention, the long-term effects of poverty, possible racism and together with insufficient and inappropriate service provision perhaps delivered by those lacking cultural competence. In Canada, for example, in *First Nations Child and Family Caring Society of Canada and the Assembly of First Nations v. Attorney General of Canada*,[153] the court found that First Nations children were not receiving the same amount of funding as other children in respect of social services intended to support vulnerable families and maintain family unity. The landmark ruling in *Daniels*[154] revealed systemic underfunding for many years and established a state duty to rebalance provision for Indigenous children.

152 See, further, O'Halloran, K., *Children, the Law and the Welfare Principle: Perspectives from North America*, at Chapter 8 and *Children, the Law and the Welfare Principle: Perspectives from Australia and New Zealand*, at Chapters 8 and 9, Routledge, 2023.

153 2016 CHRT 2 (2016) 2 C.N.L.R. 270.

154 *Daniels v. Canada (Indian Affairs and Northern Development)* (2016) S.C.R. 425 (Can.).

State coercive intervention

The effects of the control function in relation to the welfare and rights of Indigenous children is most apparent in their gross over-representation in the public care and justice systems of the CANZUS nations. The children of the Indigenous,[155] Māori,[156] the First Nations/Inuit of Canada[157] and the American Indians and Alaskan Native (AI/AN)[158] are all entering these systems at a consistently much higher rate than the children of their fellow citizens. Consequently, their life opportunities thereafter are more constrained which, in all probability, correlates with continued poverty and the poor health outcomes associated with their communities.

Cultural identity

In all CANZUS nations, respect for cultural identity has become – politically and judicially – an imperative to be recognised and taken fully into account whenever issues arise regarding the care, protection and custody of Indigenous children.

A significant political initiative being pursued in each of these nations is that of ceding control – if only administrative control – to Indigenous communities. This is proceeding incrementally, at a varying pace and to a varying degree across the nations concerned. It involves legislation and a level of institutional transfer: tribal courts have been established; child care and protection agencies and support services for vulnerable families are being set up to facilitate Indigenous capacity to address Indigenous issues. It remains to be seen whether or not such initiatives will be sufficient to redress the imbalance in the welfare interests/rights of Indigenous relative to non-Indigenous children.

Culturally compliant placements

There is a statutory onus on the authorities of all CANZUS nations – to strive to ensure that state care for every Indigenous child entering the public welfare system is secured in an ethnically appropriate placement. Priority is always to be given first to a member of a child's immediate family, followed by the extended family, then other members of the child's tribe and, finally, to other Indigenous families.

155 See, further, at: www.aihw.gov.au/reports/child-protection/child-protection-australia-2020-21/contents/children-receiving-child-protection-services/aboriginal-and-torres-strait-islander-children-in-the-child-protection-system

156 See, further, at: www.rnz.co.nz/news/national/393208/oranga-tamariki-stats-increase-in-maori-children-taken

157 See, Fallon, B., Lefebvre, R., Trocmé, N., et al., 'Denouncing the Continued Overrepresentation of First Nations Children in Canadian Child Welfare' (2019), at: https://cwrp.ca/sites/default/files/publications/FNCIS-2019%20-%20Denouncing%20the%20Continued%20Overrepresentation%20of%20First%20Nations%20Children%20in%20Canadian%20Child%20Welfare%20-%20Final_1%20%282%29.pdf

158 See, Center for the Study of Social Policy, Annie E. Casey Foundation, & Alliance for Racial Equity in Child Welfare, 2011.

In practice, this has and continues to be a pivotal issue for the Indigenous communities. The numbers of such children entering the public care system, coupled with the severe lack of state-approved Indigenous foster parents, results in many Indigenous children being reared by non-Indigenous foster parents, some of whom, in time, lodge adoption applications. While the placement decision will have been administrative, a forced choice dictated by a lack of culturally compliant placements, the adoption application will bring the matter before a court. At which point, issues may well arise that focus on the right of the child to retain their cultural identity as against the prospective adopters' capacity to further the child's long-term welfare interests. As all CANZUS nations have experienced this dilemma, with attendant court cases, the recent U.S. decision in *Haaland v. Brackeen* (in which three similar cases were also joined) will have widespread implications.[159]

This case originated in 2017 with an application from white foster parents to adopt the 2-year-old Indigenous boy placed in their care at age 10 months. The child's biological parents, registered members of the Navajo and Cherokee nations, contested the application, arguing that the matter was governed by the Indian Child Welfare Act 1978 (ICWA) which requires Indigenous children to be placed with their extended families or communities when possible. Moreover, the Navajo Nation had identified an Indigenous family placement in New Mexico. The judge ruled that the ICWA – the law governing the issue – was a 'race-based statute' because it treated Native children differently and gave the applicants permission to proceed with the adoption. In 2023, the USSC, in a strong 7–2 decision, upheld the appeal against the initial judicial ruling with the result, as Justice Gorsuch explained, that 'In affirming the constitutionality of the Indian Child Welfare Act (ICWA), the Court safeguards the ability of tribal members to raise their children free from interference by state authorities and other outside parties'. In other words, culturally noncompliant placements by authorities – for fostering or adoption purposes – will now be much more difficult to justify.

Contact

Article 9(3) requires States Parties to 'respect the right of the child who is separated from one or both parents to maintain personal relations and direct contact with both parents'. Consequently, in all CANZUS nations, there is an onus on the authorities not just to ensure where possible an ethnically matched placement but also to thereafter facilitate ongoing parent-child relationships by encouraging and providing opportunities for contact and a connectedness between child and their community and culture.

While contact arrangements are relatively easily organised when birth parents and foster carers are living in the same urban area, it can be problematic when they're not, which is often the case with Indigenous children in Alaska, Australia

159 See, further, at: www.supremecourt.gov/opinions/22pdf/21-376_7l48.pdf

and northern Canada, particularly as there is such a shortage of Indigenous foster parents.

Conclusion

State retreat from those family matters judged not to give rise to issues of public interest has been accompanied by a decidedly firmer stand on those where it is put on notice that such issues have arisen. This applies with considerable rigour to circumstances where public agencies have initiated proceedings in respect of standards of care, protection or control which are believed to breach civil or criminal law.

Part III

Children's welfare interests and rights in a private family law context

5 Reproductive rights

Introduction

Reproductive rights, self-evidently, are those that entitle women to elect whether or not to reproduce. They include the right to choose: whether to carry or to terminate an unwanted pregnancy; the preferred method of family planning which may involve contraception, sterilisation and related health services; an appropriate method of founding a family; and the right to be assisted in making such choices through ready access to appropriate information and guidance. Since the adoption of the Convention on the Elimination of All Forms of Discrimination Against Women (CEDAW) and the subsequent upholding of the importance of women's rights in the Beijing Platform for Action in 1995, reproductive rights have been viewed as intrinsically linked with the notion of human rights. The exercise of these rights must, clearly, impact the welfare interests of children.

This chapter, like its predecessors, begins with matters of definition and concepts and by outlining the related national and international legal frameworks. It then considers jurisdictional differences in the law: first by identifying the legal benchmarks established internationally (mainly through reference to ECtHR caselaw) with a bearing on such rights before applying those benchmarks to identify significant jurisdictional characteristics (and areas of commonality and difference) in relation to reproductive rights.

Rights, concepts and the law

A woman's right in relation to procreation – to commencing, terminating or otherwise regulating her conception/pregnancy – probably first surfaced as a legal issue in the 1960s. In the wake of the civil rights movement, it became most forcefully asserted and was ultimately established in the U.S. courts first in relation to contraception[1] and then as regards abortion.[2] The advances in medical science that

1 *Eisenstadt v. Baird*, 405 U.S. 438 (1972).

2 Probably beginning with the USSC ruling in *Griswold v. Connecticut*, 381 U.S. 479 (1965) and continuing with its decisions in *Roe v. Wade*, 410 U.S. 113 (1973) and *Planned Parenthood v. Casey*, 505 U.S. 833 (1992).

DOI: 10.4324/9781003269595-9

allowed procreation to become a matter subject to female choice was a transformative development for society as a whole, for women in general and for the welfare interests of children. Such advances also greatly improved the survival rate for babies born with complex health and social care needs, which brought with it a more intense paediatric focus on what might constitute the welfare of a child, a focus that with increased frequency required forensic analysis in the courts.

Women and the 'bundle of rights'

Reproductive rights are best viewed as a bundle that includes those listed earlier. This bundle, an indicator of a democratic society, has more so than anything else done much to revolutionalise the gender construct of 'woman', reset the social parameters for 'family', 'father' and 'spouse' and has probably contributed significantly to the content and trajectory of the 'culture wars'.

Reproductive rights include, as a preliminary, the right to family planning education, information and services. This is key to a capacity to choose and is central to women's sexual and reproductive health. Arguably, where the state does not allow for safe legal abortion, its core obligation is to at least then provide family planning services that enable women to know their options and be placed in a position where they might make a reasoned choice. Adolescent girls in particular require discrete access to sexual and reproductive health education, information and services.

Legalised abortion is central to family planning. The right to access abortion services increases the probability that a born child is a wanted child, one whose welfare interests are most likely to attract parental protection and promotion. It can also provide a means for protecting the standard of parental care available to children and their family life as presently constituted. Needless to say, abortion is an extremely controversial issue. The ECtHR has stopped short of recognising it as an absolute right and has instead settled for ruling that 'the State is under a positive obligation to create a procedural framework enabling a pregnant woman to effectively exercise her right of access to lawful abortion';[3] though its predecessor, the European Commission in *H. v. Norway*,[4] tentatively advised that 'in certain circumstances' the foetus may enjoy 'a certain protection under Article 2, first sentence'. However, while abortion continues to play its traditional role in family planning, its usage has been much diluted by more effective contraception.[5]

Sterilisation, with its historical connotations of eugenics, is relevant to a contemporary interpretation of reproductive rights for a number of reasons: like abortion, on an ethical/morality level, sterilisation raises the pro-life question as to the

3 *P. and S. v. Poland*, Application No. 57375/08 (2012) at para 99. See, also, A. *B. & C. v. Ireland*, Application No. 25579/05 (2010) and *Tysiac v. Poland*, Application No. 5410/03 (2007).

4 Application No. 17004/90 (1992). See, further, at: www.globalhealthrights.org/wp-content/uploads/2016/12/H.-v.-NORWAY.pdf

5 See, for example, Calkin, S., *Abortion Pills Go Global*, University of California Press, 2023.

extent to which congruency is necessary between personal choice and public policy; or, put another way, like abortion, it raises the issue of whether the denial of an opportunity to be born is compatible with the welfare interests principle.

From the initial medical breakthrough with IVF treatment for infertility in the late 1970s, methods of assisted reproduction have greatly impacted the natural process of procreation. The range of related health services is now quite extensive and includes sterilisation, abortion, contraception, research on embryos, pre-implantation genetic diagnosis and genetic editing. However, the law has been clear that neither an entitlement to marry and to found a family nor to a private and family life nor any other entitlement implies a right to procreation.[6]

Finally, surrogacy, which may be either altruistic or commercial, would seem to be outstripping adoption as the preferred route for creating a family. While the altruistic form has no financial element and is most usually arranged between family members or close friends, the commercial form is essentially a contractual transaction, usually conducted between parties who are strangers to each other and most often involving an intermediary agency. The first is lawful in most countries, and if it gives rise to legal issues, these will be a matter for private family, law while the latter is usually prohibited in most developed nations as a matter of public policy (it is expressly prohibited in 14 of the 35 Member States of the Council of Europe) but not, for example, in the U.S.

Fathers' rights

The corollary to a woman's reproductive rights is the corresponding lack of rights available to the man involved.

Abortion

The legal marginalisation of a putative father was illustrated in *Boso v. Italy*[7] which concerned a husband's opposition to his wife's intended abortion. He claimed that the termination deprived him of his right to be a potential father and the unborn child of its right to life. He also challenged the constitutionality of Italian legislation which provided that women could unilaterally decide whether to have an abortion. His claim that the termination of the pregnancy by his wife violated the right to life under the Convention and also his rights under articles 8 and 12 of the Convention, was dismissed by the ECtHR as being 'manifestly unfounded'. The Court was of the view:

> any interpretation of a potential father's rights under Article 8 of the Convention when the mother intends to have an abortion should above all take into

6 See, for example, the ECtHR ruling in *Sijakova v. The Former Yugoslav Republic of Macedonia*, Application No. 67914/01 (2003).

7 Application No. 50490/99 (2002).

account her rights, as she is the person primarily concerned by the pregnancy and its continuation or termination.

Surrogacy

The maxim *mater semper certa est* (the mother is certain), meaning in this context that she who gave birth to the child is the one recognised in law as the mother, has tended to be the guiding principle in surrogacy disputes: she will retain maternal status unless and until her *locus standi* is legally displaced in favour of the commissioning 'mother'. No such legal certainty attaches to the status of 'father'. If he is married to the surrogate mother, then there is a legal presumption that he is – factually and legally – the child's father. When disputes arise, a commissioning putative father will acquire *locus standi* if he can show that he has established family life with the child. It was in *X, Y & Z v. UK*[8] that the ECtHR for the first time recognised that family life existed between a child and her social, rather than biological, father. It was then held that in determining whether a relationship can be defined as 'family life', certain factors are relevant: whether the couple live together, the length of their relationship and whether they have demonstrated their commitment to each other by having children together or by other means. This approach was taken a step further in *Lebbink v. The Netherlands,*[9] where the ECtHR accepted that cohabitation was not an essential criterion.

Foetus and 'the right to life'

The right to abortion, like other rights, is conditional upon its exercise not infringing the rights of others: the right is not absolute. Traditionally, the 'other' of most concern to the law has been the foetus. While the ECtHR made the important finding that embryos do not have a right to life and, therefore, the authorities are entitled, as required by national law, to destroy them,[10] it has not gone so far with its rulings on the status of a foetus which it considers to be outside the frame of reference for child protection law.

Rights of the foetus

The Preamble to UN CROC states that 'the child . . . needs . . . appropriate legal protection before as well as after birth', and ever since the *Dobbs* decision,[11] it is not unusual – at least in the U.S. – to refer to 'the rights of a foetus'. The legal status of a foetus has long been highly controversial: whether the right to life of a

8 Application No. 21830/93, Reports 1997-II No. 35, p. 619, 24 EHRR 143.
9 Application No. 35582/99, ECtHR, 01.06.2004.
10 *Evans v. the United Kingdom.*
11 *Dobbs v. Jackson Women's Health Organisation*, 19–1392.

pregnant woman or that of her foetus should have priority[12] is a well-established fault line not just in law but also in medicine, philosophy and ethics. There is little in the way of conclusive guidance from international law on this matter, though the European Commission in *H. v. Norway*[13] did tentatively advise that 'in certain circumstances', the foetus may enjoy 'a certain protection under Article 2, first sentence', but in *Vo v. France,*[14] the ECtHR considered it was 'neither desirable, nor even possible' to specify whether the unborn child should be considered 'a person' as protected under Article 2 (see, also, Chapter 7).[15]

In *Roe v. Wade*,[16] the USSC weighed the interest of protecting the foetus against a woman's right to privacy in her decision to undergo abortion. Reaffirming the decisions regarding the right to privacy established in both *Eisenstadt*[17] and *Griswold*,[18] the Supreme Court decided that the right to access abortion falls under the scope of said right and, in effect, trumps any 'right to life' that might be imputed to a foetus. In New Zealand, on the other hand, the law recognises the right of a foetus to protection.

Concepts

Certain concepts lie at the heart of women's sexual and reproductive health.

Private family life

Article 8 of the ECHR, reinforced by Article 7 of the EU Charter of Fundamental Rights, requires respect for a person's private and family life, their home and correspondence. Article 8(2) declares that a public authority shall not interfere with the right to respect for family life, the existence or otherwise of which can be determined as a matter of fact. The importance of this demarcation between the public and private interests in family life has been evident since at least *Marckx v. Belgium*[19] when the ECtHR ruled that the ties between an unmarried mother and daughter constituted 'family life', within the meaning of Article 8, regardless of the mother's marital status, and went on to declare that with such recognition came

12 For example, the Dublin Declaration on Maternal Health signed in 2012 prioritises foetal right to life by noting that 'there is a fundamental difference between abortion, and necessary medical treatments that are carried out to save the life of the mother, even if such treatment results in the loss of life of her unborn child'. However, bodies such as the World Health Organisation and Human Rights Watch prioritise women's reproductive rights over foetal rights

13 Application No. 17004/90 (1992). See, further, at: www.globalhealthrights.org/wp-content/uploads/2016/12/H.-v.-NORWAY.pdf

14 Application No. 53924/00 (2004).

15 By way of contrast, in New Zealand, the courts have ruled that a foetus can come within the legal definition of 'child' and, as such, is entitled to protection.

16 410 U.S. 113 (1973).

17 *Eisenstadt v. Baird,* 405 U.S. 438 (1972).

18 *Griswold v. Connecticut,* 381 U.S. 479 (1965).

19 Application No. 6833/74 (1979).

positive obligations on the state to demonstrate its respect for family life.[20] It has since unequivocally found the right to respect for family and private life in Article 8 to extend to include the right of a couple to create family life through medically assisted procreation.[21]

In *X, Y and Z v. United Kingdom,*[22] it was held that in determining whether a relationship can be defined as 'family life', certain factors are relevant: whether the couple live together, the length of their relationship and whether they have demonstrated their commitment to each other by having children together or by other means. This approach was taken a step further in *Lebbink v. The Netherlands*[23] when the ECtHR accepted that cohabitation was not an essential ingredient. A variety of different family forms have now been legally recognised. As Kilkelly[24] has pointed out, 'family life may exist between children and their grandparents,[25] between siblings,[26] between an uncle and his nephew,[27] and between parents and children born into second relationships'.[28] It will be present in the nexus of a parent-and-child relationship, 'in all but very exceptional cases regardless of the parents' marital status,[29] the family's living arrangements,[30] or their apparent lack of commitment to their children'.[31] The relationships between such others as a child and their adopters, or foster parents, or surrogate parents, or with a same-sex couple may similarly qualify.

The ECtHR equivocated before extending the definition of family life to include the role of an unmarried father.[32] Although this presumption has now been established,[33] it may be rebutted.[34]

20 Ibid, at paras 36–7. See, also, Kilkelly, U., 'Protecting Children's Rights under the ECHR: The Role of Positive Obligations', *NILQ,* Vol. 61, No. 3 (2010), pp. 245–261.

21 *S.H. and Others v. Austria,* Application No. 57813/00 (2011).

22 (1997) 2 FLR 892.

23 Application No. 35582/99, ECtHR, 01.06.2004.

24 See, Kilkelly, U., 'Child and Family Law', in Kilkelly (ed.), *ECHR and Irish Law, op cit,* at p. 113.

25 See, *Marckx v. Belgium, op cit,* at para 45.

26 See, *Olsson v. Sweden,* Application No.10465/83, Series A No. 130, 11 EHRR 259. See also *Boughanemi v. France,* Application No. 22070/93, Reports 1996-II, No. 8, p. 593, 22 EHRR 228.

27 See, *Boyle v. UK,* Application No. 16580/90, Comm Rep, 9.2.93.

28 See, *Jolie & Lebrun v. Belgium,* Application No. 11418/85, Dec. 14.5.86, DR 47, p. 243.

29 See, *Marckx v. Belgium ibid* (unmarried mother and her child); *Johnston v. Ireland,* No. 9697/92, Series A No. 12 (1987) 9 EHRR 203 (unmarried parents and their child).

30 See, *Berrehab v. Netherlands,* No. 10730/84, Series A No. 138 (1988) 11 EHRR 322.

31 See, *C v. Belgium,* Application No. 21794/93 (1996) and *Ahmut v. Netherlands,* Application No. 21702/93 (1996). See, also, *Söderbäck v. Sweden,* Application No. 24484/94 (1998). However, purely genetic relationships – such as the relationship between a sperm donor and the child born as a result – are unlikely to constitute family life. See, *G v. Netherlands,* Application No. 16944/90 (1993).

32 See, *Soderback v. Sweden,* 28th October 1998 ECHR. Also, see, *Johansen v. Norway* (1997) 23 EHRR 33, *Rieme v. Sweden* (1993) 16 EHRR 155 and *Schneider v. Germany,* Application No. 177080/07 (2011).

33 See *Johansen v. Norway* (1996) 23 EHRR 33 and *Rieme v. Sweden* (1993) 16 EHRR 155. Note that in *B. v. United Kingdom* (2000) 1 FLR 1, the court found against an unmarried father without parental responsibility and held that the UK court had been justifiably discriminatory between his standing and that of a married father, as he had no custody rights in respect of the child.

34 *Soderback v. Sweden, op cit.*

Autonomy

The right to autonomy in making health decisions in general, and sexual and reproductive decisions in particular, derives from the fundamental human rights to liberty, dignity, privacy, security of the person and bodily integrity. In this context, it refers to the right of a woman to make decisions concerning her fertility and sexuality free of coercion and violence. The capacity to exercise free choice on such matters is of fundamental importance, and this in turn requires that she be enabled to make an informed choice and to do so confidentially. A corresponding duty to make available the information necessary for an informed choice rests on the relevant service providers, as does the obligation to maintain confidentiality, and this duty requires the provider to treat the recipient as an individual in her own right – the sole client of the health care provider and fully competent to make decisions concerning her own health.

In *R.R. v. Poland*,[35] for example, which concerned a woman pregnant with a foetus suffering from abnormalities who had been denied an abortion, the ECtHR found that 'the decision of a pregnant woman to continue her pregnancy or not belongs to the sphere of private life and autonomy' (see, further, next section).

Equality and non-discrimination

Article 1 of CEDAW defines the term 'discrimination against women' as any distinction, exclusion or restriction made on the basis of sex which has the effect or purpose of impairing or nullifying the recognition, enjoyment or exercise by women – irrespective of their marital status, on the grounds of gender equality – of human rights and fundamental freedoms in the political, economic, social, cultural, civil or any other field.

Cultural and religious attitudes may be prejudicial to women's health – most obviously, as regards female genital mutilation – and may be apparent, for example, in rates of maternal mortality. It may also be revealed, if more obliquely, in the rates of abortions, stillbirths and infant mortality which can be associated with government health policies that fail to recognise the particular vulnerabilities of pregnant women.

Gender equality

Gender equality is not simply a matter of guaranteeing women the same rights as men; it also requires that any additional inequality, attributable to gender specific differences, is recognised and compensated for. Women's rights to equality with men in matters of health and health care encompass both comparable health needs as well as those that are gender specific. Failure to allocate resources or to ensure the provision of services for women's special health needs, in addition to those common to women and men, is discriminatory.

35 Application No. 27617/04 (2011).

International law

The legal basis for reproductive rights has had a troubled history,[36] but the law can now be found in various articles of the Convention on the Elimination of All Forms of Discrimination Against Women 1978 (CEDAW).[37] This is reinforced by rights enumerated in the International Covenant on Civil and Political Rights (ICCPR), including protection for the rights to life, liberty, security of the person and privacy.[38] Article 1 of the Universal Declaration on the Human Genome and Human Rights 1997 highlights the importance of the human genome as 'underlying the fundamental unity of all members of the human family, as well as the recognition of their inherent dignity and diversity. In a symbolic sense, it is the heritage of humanity'. Article 8 of the European Convention on Human Rights (ECHR) is of central importance, as it provides for rights to autonomy and privacy in matters of family life.[39] Also significant is Article 12 of the International Covenant on Economic, Social and Cultural Rights (ICESCR) which guarantees 'the right of everyone to the enjoyment of the highest attainable standard of physical and mental health',[40] while the 'Istanbul Convention' in 2014 aims to provide protection for women against all forms of violence; and the 'Oviedo Convention' opens the door to medical interventions such as genetic editing, provided that 'its aim is not to introduce any modification in the genome of any descendants'.[41]

Convention on the Elimination of All Forms of Discrimination Against Women (CEDAW) 1978

This, the only convention to deal specifically with women's health rights, is naturally of fundamental importance to reproductive rights. However, it is also the international instrument to which signatory states have entered the most reservations, and it has not yet been signed by the U.S.

Article 5(b)

This refers to the interests of children being paramount in relation to the common responsibility of men and women for their children's upbringing and development.

36 See, further, at: www.ohchr.org/documents/publications/nhrihandbook.pdf

37 See, Convention on the Elimination of All Forms of Discrimination Against *Women,* 1978 (CEDAW), Articles 10 and 16.

38 See, the International Covenant on Civil and Political Rights, 1964 (ICCPR).

39 Note, also, the Beijing Declaration in 1995 which stated that 'the explicit recognition and reaffirmation of the right of all women to control all aspects of their health, in particular their own fertility, is basic to their empowerment'.

40 See, the International Covenant on Economic, Social and Cultural Rights, 1964 (ICESCR).

41 The Convention for the Protection of Human Rights and Dignity of the Human Being with regard to the Application of Biology and Medicine, Article 13.

Articles 10(h) and 14(b)

These provide a right of access to educational information and advice on family planning and, in particular, the right of women in rural areas to have access to adequate health care facilities, including information, counselling and services in family planning. Article 11(1)(f) adds a right to health and safety protection in the working environment and specifically refers to 'the safeguarding of the function of reproduction'.

Article 12

This requires States Parties:

> to take all appropriate measures to eliminate discrimination against women in the field of health care in order to ensure, on a basis of equality of men and women, access to health care services, including those related to family planning.

More specifically, it requires that they 'ensure to women appropriate services in connection with pregnancy, confinement and the post-natal period, granting free services where necessary, as well as adequate nutrition during pregnancy and lactation'.

Article 15

This guarantees women's right to equality before the law and to full legal capacity.

Article 16(1)(e)

This requires States Parties to guarantee gender equality by ensuring the following:

> the same rights to decide freely and responsibly on the number and spacing of their children, and to have access to the information, education and means to enable them to exercise these rights.

Article 17

This established the CEDAW Committee which consists of 23 expert members elected by States Parties. Its main function is to monitor implementation of the Convention by considering periodic reports submitted by States Parties on the measures taken to give effect to Convention provisions. It may also make general recommendations based on the examination of reports and information received from the States Parties.

As of December 2021, the Committee had adopted 38 general recommendations of which the following are among the most important: No. 23, on 'Political and Public Life', requiring States parties to take all appropriate measures to eliminate discrimination against women in the political and public life of the country and, in particular, to ensure equality with men in participation of all political processes, and No. 35, on 'Gender based Violence', requiring States Parties to accelerate the elimination of gender-based violence against women and girls.

The European Convention on Human Rights 1950 (ECHR)

The state duty under this convention to ensure women's reproductive rights is loosely governed by articles 2, 3, 8 and 13 of the ECHR requiring, respectively, respect for human life, respect for private and family life and the right to an effective remedy.

Article 3

This Article prohibits 'cruel and degrading treatment'.

Article 8

This requires respect for a person's private and family life. In order to determine whether an interference by the authorities with the applicants' private and family life was necessary in a democratic society and a fair balance struck between the different interests involved, the ECtHR examines whether the interference was in accordance with the law, pursued a legitimate aim or aims and was proportionate to the aim(s) pursued.[42]

Article 13

This Article provides a right to an effective remedy.

The International Covenant on Civil and Political Rights (ICCPR) 1964

The Covenant provides protection for certain fundamental freedoms, including the rights to life, to liberty, to security of the person and to privacy. It also provides for a periodic review process requiring signatory states to submit a review of progress on human rights issues, including measures taken to protect and promote women's reproductive rights.

The United Nations Convention on the Rights of the Child (UN CROC) 1989

Signed by nearly 200 countries, this Convention has now been ratified by all UN Member States except the United States.[43] It lists 42 substantive rights that comprehensively address the needs of children, some of which have a bearing on

42 See, further, European Court of Human Rights, 'Guide on Article 8 of the Convention – Right to Respect for Private and Family Life' (2022), at: www.echr.coe.int/documents/d/echr/guide_art_8_eng

43 The U.S. has signed the Convention but has not yet ratified it. See, O'Connor, D., 'Children's Rights and Youth Justice in the USA', *International Family Law Journal* (2006), p. 183.

reproductive rights. While it has no specifically designated means of enforcement, signatory nations are obliged under Article 44 to provide regular reports to the UN Committee on the Rights of the Child detailing the progress made on meeting the terms of the Treaty[44] and the ECtHR regularly references its provisions when making decisions.

Article 3

This requires that in all actions concerning children, whether undertaken by public or private social welfare institutions, courts of law, administrative authorities or legislative bodies, the best interests of the child shall be the primary consideration.

Article 7

Article 7 recognises the right of a child to know the identity of his or her parents and under Article 7(1) the 'right from birth to a name, the right to acquire a nationality and as far as possible, the right to know and be cared for by his or her parents'.

Article 9

This requires states to ensure that a child shall not be separated from his or her parents against their will.

Article 35

Article 35 requires States Parties to do the following:

> take all appropriate national, bilateral and multilateral measures to prevent the abduction, the sale of or traffic in children for any purpose or in any form.

This provision could, arguably, be interpreted to include commercial surrogacy given the often substantial fees that accompany the surrogacy transaction.

Other

The Fourth World Conference on Women, held in Beijing in 1995, concluded with the Beijing Declaration which stated that 'the explicit recognition and reaffirmation of the right of all women to control all aspects of their health, in particular their own fertility, is basic to their empowerment'. The Council of Europe has disseminated some guidance on women's reproductive health.[45]

44 See, Office of the United Nations High Commissioner for Human Rights, Committee on the Rights of the Child: Monitoring Children's Rights.

45 See, for example, Resolution 1399 (Parliamentary Assembly of the Council of Europe 2004b); Recommendation 1675 (Parliamentary Assembly of the Council of Europe 2004a), concerning

Reproductive rights: established international legal standards

The ECtHR recognises that 'states must in principle be afforded a wide margin of appreciation regarding matters which raise delicate moral and ethical questions on which there is no consensus at European level'.[46] Reproductive rights being a classic example of such matters, it is unsurprising that this principle has exercised the Court considerably, for example, in *A, B and C v. Ireland*[47] (see, further, next section).

Private life

The ECtHR has found that 'private life incorporates not only the right to respect for decisions to become or not to become a parent'[48] but also 'the right of a couple to conceive a child and to make use of medically assisted procreation for that purpose'.[49] Paradoxically, the ECtHR has ruled that there is no legal right to found a family by accessing artificial reproduction treatment.[50]

Family planning information

As illustrated in the many abortion-related ECtHR cases, there is, at the very least, a right to information regarding how to access abortion and other reproductive services.[51] In the U.S., from the early 20th century, a family planning movement and a population control movement emerged, both of which evolved through to the 1960s advocating for improved access to contraception and abortion. Following its rulings in *Griswold v. Connecticut*[52] and *Eisenstadt v. Baird*[53] concerning access to contraception, the USSC then examined access to abortion in *Roe v. Wade*. Reaffirming the decisions regarding the right to privacy established in both *Eisenstadt* and *Griswold*, the USSC decided that the right to access abortion similarly fell under the right to privacy. From the 1960s, the Planned Parenthood Federation of America, which influenced the work of Maria Stopes in England, there was constant collaboration in research and dissemination on both sides of the Atlantic.

---

reproductive rights; and a Report (Parliamentary Assembly of the Council of Europe 2008a) and Resolution 1607 (Parliamentary Assembly of the Council of Europe 2008b) on decriminalising abortion.

46 See, *K. K. and Others v. Denmark*, Application No. 25212/21 (2022), at para 45, citing *Mennesson v. France*, Application No. 65192/11 (2014), at paras 78–79, *Valdís Fjölnisdóttir and Others*, Application No. 71552/17 (2021), at para 70, and *A.M. v. Norway*, Application No. 30254/18 (2022), at para 131.

47 (2010) ECtHR (GC) (No. 25579/05) (16 December 2010).

48 See, *Parrillo v. Italy*, Application No. 46470/11 (2015), at para 153.

49 See, *S, H. and Others v. Austria*, Application No. 57813/00 (2011).

50 See, *X v. Belgium and The Netherlands*, Application No. 6482/147 (1975) 7 DR 75.

51 See, for example, *Tysiac v. Poland*, Application No. 5410/03 (2007).

52 381 U.S. 479.

53 405 U.S. 438 (1972).

Abortion

The ECtHR has stopped short of recognising abortion as an absolute right and instead has settled for ruling that 'the state is under a positive obligation to create a procedural framework enabling a pregnant woman to effectively exercise her right of access to lawful abortion'.[54] The many abortion-related ECtHR cases establish that there is, at the very least, a right to information regarding how to access services.[55] Generally, however, the Court has not found that restrictions on abortion violate Convention rights; violations have only been found where an applicant was denied access to an abortion they should have been entitled to under domestic law. In establishing whether or not a state was justified in refusing access to abortion services, the ECtHR has tended to place considerable weight on the vulnerability of those seeking such services. It was unconvinced, for example, in *Tysiac v. Poland*[56] by the circumstances of an applicant with severe myopia who had been advised by doctors that her pregnancy posed a serious risk to her eyesight. The fact that she had been denied a therapeutic abortion was insufficient for the Court to find that her Article 3 rights had been breached (though an application under Article 8 might have had a different outcome). Where the applicant's situation is clearly grievous, perhaps particularly where she is herself a child, the Court is unequivocal. So in *P and S v. Poland*[57] – one of many cases where access to abortion in Poland has been at issue – the ECtHR found that denying such services to a 14-year-old victim of rape, and her subsequent harassment by anti-abortion activists, amounted to a violation of Article 3. The severity of circumstances test was also evident in *A. B, and C v. Ireland*,[58] when of the three applicants the Court only found in favour of the one in particularly serious circumstances and held that she should have been entitled to a therapeutic abortion under domestic law. Such an entitlement was also found in *R.R. v. Poland*,[59] where a mother carrying a child – thought to be suffering from a severe genetic abnormality – was deliberately denied timely access to the genetic tests, to which she was entitled, by doctors opposed to abortion. Following the birth of her severely ill daughter (with Turner syndrome) the mother brought her complaint to the ECtHR which found violations of articles 3 and 8, noting that the applicant, who was in a very vulnerable position, had been humiliated and 'shabbily' treated. The Court affirmed that 'the decision of a pregnant woman to continue her pregnancy or not belongs to the sphere of private life and autonomy. Consequently, also legislation regulating the interruption of pregnancy touches upon the sphere of private life'.

54 *P. and S. v. Poland*, Application No. 57375/08 (2012) at para 99. See, also, *A, B and C. v. Ireland*, Application No. 25579/05 (2010); *Tysiac v. Poland*, Application No. 5410/03 (2007); and *R.R. v. Poland*, Application No. 27617/04 (2011).

55 See, for example, *Tysiąc v. Poland*, ibid.

56 Application No. 5410/03 (2007).

57 Application No. 57375/08 (2013).

58 Application No. 25579/05 (2010).

59 Application No. 27617/04 (2011).

In recent years, while in general retaining the precedent that a foetus is not a child for the purposes of child care and protection provisions, the courts have nonetheless often been concerned to establish the viability of the foetus and to weigh this against the reasons for seeking an abortion.

Justification for abortion

In establishing whether or not a state was justified in refusing access to abortion services, the ECtHR has tended to place considerable weight on the vulnerability of those seeking such services. It was unconvinced, for example, in *Tysiac v. Poland*[60] by the circumstances of an applicant with severe myopia who had been advised by doctors that her pregnancy posed a serious risk to her eyesight. The fact that she had been denied a therapeutic abortion was insufficient for the Court to find that her Article 3 rights had been breached (though an application under Article 8 might have had a different outcome). The severity of circumstances test was also evident in *A. B, and C v. Ireland*[61] when of the three applicants the Court only found in favour of the one in particularly serious circumstances and held that she should have been entitled to a therapeutic abortion under domestic law. Such an entitlement was also found in *R.R. v. Poland*,[62] where a mother carrying a child – thought to be suffering from a severe genetic abnormality – was deliberately denied timely access to the genetic tests, to which she was entitled, by doctors opposed to abortion. Following the birth of her severely ill daughter (with Turner syndrome), the mother brought her complaint to the ECtHR which found violations of articles 3 and 8, noting that the applicant, who was in a very vulnerable position, had been humiliated and 'shabbily' treated. The Court affirmed that 'the decision of a pregnant woman to continue her pregnancy or not belongs to the sphere of private life and autonomy. Consequently, also legislation regulating the interruption of pregnancy touches upon the sphere of private life'. More recently, in the important case of *A.M. and others v. Poland*,[63] the Court declared the applications inadmissible, unanimously denying 'victim' status to the eight women who had filed an application, thereby refusing to establish a 'right to eugenic abortion' within the ECHR framework. It declined to find the women, some of whom were not even pregnant – or in the case of two of them, were carrying healthy children – to be victims of a law prohibiting abortion due to foetal abnormalities.

There are circumstances in which the issue of whether or not abortion should be available is more clear cut and then the ECtHR is less hesitant. Where, for example, the applicant's situation is clearly grievous, perhaps particularly where she is herself a child, the Court is unequivocal. So in *P and S v. Poland*,[64] – one of many

60 Application No. 5410/03 (2007).
61 Application No. 25579/05 (2010).
62 Application No. 27617/04 (2011).
63 Application No. 4188/21 (2023).
64 Application No. 57375/08 (2013).

cases where access to abortion in Poland has been at issue – the ECtHR found that denying such services to a 14-year-old victim of rape, and her subsequent harassment by anti-abortion activists, amounted to a violation of Article 3.

Constraints on accessing abortion

The ECtHR has consistently refused to hold that there is a 'right to abortion',[65] but it has ruled that 'the state is under a positive obligation to create a procedural framework enabling a pregnant woman to effectively exercise her right of access to lawful abortion'.[66] Generally, however, the Court has not found that restrictions on abortion violate Convention rights; violations have only been found where an applicant was denied access to an abortion they should have been entitled to under domestic law.

Cultural context has been successfully deployed as an argument for permitting a state to avail of the margin of appreciation rule and refuse to legislate for the provision of abortion services. This occurred in *A, B and C v. Ireland*,[67] which considered the rights of a Lithuanian resident in Ireland who had been denied access to abortion. The ECtHR held that a broad margin of appreciation should be accorded to Ireland – sufficient to uphold the refusal decision of the Irish court – because of the 'acute sensitivity of the moral and ethical issues raised by the question of abortion or as to the importance of the public interest at stake'.[68] This was challenged in the dissenting opinion of six judges who considered that such reasoning justified exactly the opposite approach and pointed out the following:[69]

> it is the first time that the Court has disregarded the existence of a European consensus on the basis of 'profound moral views'. Even assuming that these profound moral views are still well embedded in the conscience of the majority of Irish people, to consider that this can override the European consensus, which tends in a completely different direction, is a real and dangerous new departure in the Court's case-law.

There is much to be said for the dissenting argument: leaving aside the consequences of applying the rationale of this decision to, for example, the widely established rights of the LGBT community, it also has an implied potential to disrupt

65 See, for example, *AM and Others v. Poland*, Application No. 3639/21 (2023), *P. and S. v. Poland*, Application No. 57375/08 (2013) and *A.B.C. v. Ireland*, Application No. 25579/05 (2010).

66 *P. and S. v. Poland*, Application No. 57375/08 (2012) at para 99. See, also, A. *B. & C. v. Ireland*, Application No. 25579/05 (2010); *Tysiac v. Poland*, *op cit*; and *R.R. v. Poland*, Application No. 27617/04 (2011).

67 (2010) ECtHR (GC) (No. 25579/05) (16 December 2010).

68 Ibid.

69 Joint dissenting opinion of Judges Rozakis, Tulkiens, Fura, Hirvea, Malinverni, and Poalelungi at para 9.

European consensus on promoting the further development of reproductive medical techniques.

Non-consensual abortion

International courts and regulatory bodies have consistently found this practice to be unlawful. In *S.F.K. v. Russia*,[70] for example, the applicant had made it clear to her parents and the medical staff at the public hospital that she wanted to continue with the five-week pregnancy, but the intervention took place against her will. The Court found that this had been an egregious form of inhuman and degrading treatment which had not only resulted in serious immediate damage to the applicant's health – that is the loss of her unborn child – but had also entailed long-lasting negative physical and psychological effects. It held that there had been a violation of Article 3 and noted the reluctance of the authorities to open a criminal investigation into the applicant's credible claims of forced abortion and their failure to take effective measures against the applicant's parents and the relevant health professionals. Again, in *G.M. and Others v. the Republic of Moldova*,[71] the Court condemned the imposition of abortions and birth control measures on three intellectually disabled women, residents in a neuropsychiatric asylum, after they had been repeatedly raped by one of the doctors in charge. It found that the domestic authorities had failed to carry out an effective investigation into the applicants' allegations of ill-treatment despite it having been reopened on four occasions following their appeals. Moreover, the enquiry had not factored in their vulnerability as intellectually disabled women exposed to sexual abuse in an institutional context. The Court held that there had been a violation of Article 3.

Sterilisation

Given its historical association with eugenics – particularly during the Nazi era – it is unsurprising that sterilisation continues to be a contentious form of medical intervention, even if it has only fairly recently become subject to regulatory provisions in the developed nations.

Non-consensual sterilisation

Non-consensual sterilisation would seem to constitute a refutation of the balance required to be struck in any democratic society between the interests of the state, parents and putative child.

The ECtHR has generally regarded non-consensual sterilisation as 'incompatible with the requirement of respect for human freedom and dignity, one of the

70 Application No. 5578/12 (2022).
71 Application No. 44394 (2022).

fundamental principles on which the Convention is based'.[72] So in a number of Slovakian cases involving non-consensual sterilisation, most often of Roma women, the Court has found the authorities to have been guilty of inhuman or degrading treatment in violation of Article 3.[73] *G.B. and R.B. v. the Republic of Moldova,*[74] for example, concerned a mother who when giving birth had a Caesarean section, during which the obstetrician removed her ovaries and fallopian tubes without obtaining her permission. Since then, she had been in treatment to counteract the effects of early menopause and has had health problems, including depression and osteoporosis. The complaint to the ECtHR focused on the non-consensual sterilisation and the low amount of compensation awarded (607 euros). The Court found that the amount of compensation awarded by the domestic courts was considerably below the minimum level of compensation generally awarded and required sufficient just satisfaction, as the devastating effects on the first applicant had made this a particularly serious interference with her Convention rights. It held that there had been a violation of Article 8.

In 2022, the Court delivered its ruling in *Y.P. v. Russia,*[75] dismissing the applicant's claim that her non-consensual sterilisation had breached her Article 3 rights. This case concerned a sterilisation process carried out on a 28-year-old woman as a consequence of unforeseen complications that had arisen during the course of a Caesarean section procedure while she was unconscious, but after, she had signed a form explicitly excluding her consent for sterilisation. Later, she was told in medical terms what had happened, which she did not understand and only discovered that she had been non-consensually sterilised two years later when, upon facing difficulties conceiving, she visited a gynaecologist. The ECtHR concluded that given her explicit denial of permission to sterilise, and given that there was no imminent threat to her life and that less intrusive methods could have been used, there had been an infringement of Y.P.'s right to respect for her private life in violation of Article 8. However, the Court took the view that although the decision to sterilise YP was disrespectful of her autonomy, as the medical professionals had acted collectively, in good faith and with the best of intentions, their actions did not reach the threshold of severity required to find a breach of Article 3. This decision was not unanimous – two judges dissented – and it has been criticised by others. Arguably, a lack of ill-intent on the part of the medical practitioners is wholly beside the point: the particularly vulnerable position of the pregnant and unconscious woman meant that gender-based implications of violating her reproductive autonomy ought to have been taken much more seriously.[76]

72 See, for example, *V.C. v. Slovakia*, Application No. 18968/07 (2012) and *N.B. v. Slovakia*, Application No. 29518/10 (2012).

73 See, for example, ibid, plus: *K.H. and Others v. Slovakia*, Application No. 32881/04 (2009); and *I.G., M.K. and R.H. v. Slovakia*, Application No. 15966/04 (2012)

74 Application No. 16761/09 (2012).

75 Application No. 43399/13 (2022).

76 See, further, at: https://strasbourgobservers.com/2022/09/30/y-p-v-russia-sterilisation-without-consent-article-3-and-weak-reproductive-rights-at-the-ecthr/

IVF, genetic editing, etc.

The ECtHR has begun to explore – under Article 2 ('right to life') and, most often, under Article 8 ('right to respect for private and family life') – the legal issues that lie at the frontiers of medical science as developments unfold in the field of assisted procreation. It has found that the issue of when the right to life begins lies within a state's margin of appreciation[77] which perhaps explains why there are grounds for criticising the Court for being 'consistently inconsistent in applying the Article 3 threshold to reproductive rights cases'.[78] Unquestionably, however, this is a moral minefield (see, also, Chapter 7). While genetic editing may well be a road towards correcting an individual's inherited health issues and towards the elimination of specific diseases, this must be balanced against protection for 'the right to inherit a genetic pattern which has not been artificially changed'.[79]

The ECtHR, in *Evans v. the United Kingdom*,[80] made the important finding that embryos do not have a right to life, and therefore, the authorities were entitled, as required by national law, to destroy them; indeed, international law prohibits the creation of human embryos for research purposes.[81] The Court has ruled that access to services such as IVF – whether legal[82] or illegal[83] – falls under the scope of Article 8 of the ECHR, as 'an expression of private and family life'.[84]

As regards the use of gamete donation for in vitro fertilisation, the Court found that the Austrian authorities action in denying two female couples access to relevant treatment was justified – given the lack of consensus on the law governing such matters across Europe – and noted that the Austrian legislators were concerned to avoid the possibility that two women could claim to be the biological mother of the same child and that the authorities had not banned individuals from going overseas for such treatment.[85] Subsequently, however, in *Parrillo v. Italy*,[86] the ECtHR seemed to take a less dismissive approach to the legal status of embryos when it ruled for the first time that Article 8 was applicable to the relationship between the applicant and her embryos as they contained part of her genetic material and, therefore, constituted part of her identity. Nonetheless, her complaint that she was unable to donate her embryos conceived through medically assisted reproduction to scientific research was found not to breach Article 8 and was dismissed. This was partly because there was no evidence that her deceased partner would

77 *Evans v. the United Kingdom*, Application No. 6339/05 (2006).

78 See, further, at: https://strasbourgobservers.com/2022/09/30/y-p-v-russia-sterilisation-without-consent-article-3-and-weak-reproductive-rights-at-the-ecthr/

79 See, Council of Europe, Parliamentary Assembly, *Recommendation 934* (1982) at para 4.

80 Ibid.

81 See, Convention for the Protection of Human Rights and Dignity of the Human Being with regard to the Application of Biology and Medicine (the Oviedo convention) 1997.

82 *Dikson v. The United-Kingdom*, Application No. 4436204 (2007), at para 66.

83 *S.H. v. Austria*, Application No. 57813/00 (2011) at para 82.

84 Ibid.

85 *S.H. and Others v. Austria*, Application No. 57813/00 (2011).

86 Application No. 46470/11 (2015).

have similarly wished to make such a donation and also because the Court was of the view that human embryos could not be reduced to 'possessions'.

Genetic editing

The ECtHR has found that access to genetic services, whether legal[87] or illegal,[88] falls under the scope of Article 8 of the ECHR, as 'an expression of private and family life'.[89] The potential advantages of genetic screening and editing were illustrated in *Costa and Pavan v. Italy*[90] which concerned the refusal of authorities to make such services available to a couple who were known carriers of cystic fibrosis and wished to avoid transmitting the disease to their offspring. The ECtHR found that the interference with the applicants' right to respect for their private and family life had been disproportionate. It noted, in particular, the inconsistency in Italian law that denied the couple access to embryo screening but authorised medically assisted termination of pregnancy if the foetus showed symptoms of the same disease. The Court held that there had been a violation of Article 8. Clearly, the prospect of parents, who are carriers of a disease with a high genetic risk for their offspring, being able to avail of medical interventions that could correct or erase it so that their offspring and that of the next generation would avoid that disease and its consequences, must hold out great hope for improving the welfare interests of very many children. As stated, this is a field where ethics and the law are at best uncertain. Such international legal provisions as exist are largely to be found in the Universal Declaration on the Human Genome and Human Rights 1997 and in the Oviedo Convention 1997 which warns that genetic editing can only be allowed on condition that 'its aim is not to introduce any modification in the genome of any descendants' which is precisely what genetic editing would wish to achieve.[91]

Of particular importance has been the discovery, in 2012, of a new gene editing tool –

CRISPR/Cas 9 – which has greatly accelerated the capacity to analyse diseases and produce more effective drugs. While it is already significantly impacting agriculture, by improving the development of crops, its potential use for modifying the human genome by editing out of the DNA sequence material that be liable to cause disease has yet to be fully explored. Experiments with CRISPR gene editing was used to create the world's first gene-edited babies in 2018, generating much controversy about the ethics of 'designer babies'.[92]

87 *Dikson v. The United Kingdom*, Application No. 4436204 (2007) at para 66.

88 *S.H. v. Austria*, Application No. 57813/00 (2011) at para 82.

89 Ibid.

90 Application No. 54270/10 (2012).

91 Article 13 Convention for the Protection of Human Rights and Dignity of the Human Being with regard to the Application of Biology and Medicine (Oviedo Convention),

92 See, further, Spaander, M.M., 'The European Court of Human Rights and the Emergence of Human Germline Genome Editing – The Right to Life and the Right to (Artificial) Procreation', in

Surrogacy

Surrogacy – commercial rather than altruistic – has increased exponentially in recent years[93] and is now rapidly displacing adoption as the preferred means of achieving parenthood, for those who can afford to make that choice and, in particular, for those for whom a genetic link to the child is wanted and possible.

The ECtHR has taken judicial notice of the fact that surrogacy is expressly prohibited in 14 of the 35 Member States of the Council of Europe – other than France – in ten of which it is either prohibited under general provisions or not tolerated, or the question of its lawfulness is uncertain, but is expressly authorised in seven Member States and appears to be tolerated in four others.[94] It, therefore, allows states a wide margin of appreciation when making decisions relating to surrogacy. This was illustrated in *K. K. and Others v. Denmark*[95] when four of seven judges voted for the judgment upholding the rights of children born though commercial surrogacy. The remaining three judges' joint dissenting opinion was that Denmark had not violated any ECHR rights. Emphasising that there is no consensus within the Member States of the Council of Europe on the sensitive matter of commercial surrogacy, the dissenters took the view that there must be a margin of appreciation for states to strike a balance between private and public interests. According to the minority, the judgment 'practically eliminate[s] altogether, in substance, the margin of appreciation' for foreign commercial surrogacy arrangements.[96]

This approach is counterbalanced by a much narrower margin of appreciation when it comes to determining parentage because this involves a key aspect of an individual's identity. The approach of the Court and its primary concern for the welfare interests of the children involved was apparent in its treatment of *Mennesson v. France*,[97] *Labassee v. France*[98] and others (see, further, next section).[99]

Genetic link

Surrogacy, whether altruistic or commercial, can include a genetic link between the child and one of the prospective 'parents'. In such circumstances, the courts tend to lean more favourably towards finding that the unit satisfies the definition of 'family life'.

Slokenberga, S., Minssen, T. and Nordberg, A. (eds.), *Governing, Protecting, and Regulating the Future of Genome Editing*, Brill, 2023, pp. 134–159.

93 See, 'How Many Surrogate Births Per Year?' (2022), at: https://worldcenterofbaby.com/blog/how-many-surrogate-births-per-year-statistics-of-newborn-babies/

94 *K. K. and Others v. Denmark*, ibid, at para 78.

95 Application No. 25212/21 (2022).

96 Ibid, at para 88.

97 Application No. 65192/11 (2014).

98 Application No. 65941/11 (2014).

99 The following cases were similarly concluded: *Foulon and Bouvet v. France*, Application No. 9063/14 (2016); *Laborie v. France*, Application No. 44024/13 (2017); *C and E v. France*, Application Nos. 1462/18 and 17348/18 (2019); and *D v. France*, Application No. 11288/18 (2020).

Reproductive rights: contemporary jurisdictional comparisons

By increasing the proportion of children who are 'wanted', the exercise of reproductive rights correspondingly increases the probability of successful parenting and lowers the threshold of risk of willful harm to the welfare interests of the children concerned. The relevant services are well established and generally readily accessible as part of public service provision in the countries studied.

Medical intervention

In general, access to reproductive medical intervention would seem to be more restricted in France and Germany compared with the common law countries. IVF, for example, is available but on a restricted basis. The policy towards abortion as a public service is similar in both countries, but availability is much more restricted basis than in others, such as the UK, while not reaching the levels of political contention and limited geographical distribution as in the U.S.

Abortion

As of 2023, the ethical and legal confrontations that have come to constitute the U.S. 'culture wars' have been largely confined to that country, but recently, there have been indications that they could be exported to Canada, the UK and perhaps into Europe. On the frontline of these 'wars' is the decades long pro-life/pro-choice confrontation.

Liberal regimes

Canada is one of a small number of countries without a law restricting abortion.[100] It has permitted unrestricted access to abortion services ever since 1988 when the SCC[101] ruled that the abortion law prohibitions were unconstitutional as they infringed upon a woman's right to 'life, liberty and security of person' in violation of s 7 of the Charter of Rights and Freedoms. It is now regulated and treated like any other medical procedure. Moreover, its 'Well Women' organisation has demonstrated global leadership in relation to the evolution and social acceptance of women's reproductive rights in countries such as the UK, South Africa and New Zealand.

Abortion services are readily available – up to 24 weeks – in England and Wales, where the law has long and consistently maintained that the foetus has no legal rights, a view that has been judicially revised to establish that this does not equate to 'nothing'.[102] However, it remains very unclear as to what if anything that

100 However, see *Winnipeg Child and Family Services (Northwest Area) v. G.* (D.F.) (1997) 3 S.C.R. 925.

101 *R. v. Morgentaler* (1988) 1 SCR 30.

102 *St George's Healthcare NHS Trust v. SR v. Collins and Others, ex parte S*; (1998) 2 FCR 685.

residual quotient might be. It might be noted that there are regional differences in the UK laws governing abortion: in Northern Ireland, abortion services were legally prohibited until 2023 when the Westminster government imposed legislation repealing the prohibition and introducing abortion services. In Ireland, reproductive rights are only now beginning to be developed: as of 2021, 9 of the nation's 19 hospitals did not provide abortion procedures.

In Australia, abortion remained illegal until the late 1960s,[103] though is now generally available as a legally sanctioned procedure across the country, subsidised by Medicare. As the foetus has no legal standing,[104] this allows abortion to be regulated as just another public service.

In France, abortion is freely available during the first 12 weeks of pregnancy, and in 2021, the national abortion rate was 15.5 per 1,000 women aged 15–49.[105] The French approach may in part be a reflection of the status of a foetus as determined in *Vo v. France*[106] which concerned the involuntarily termination of a pregnancy due to medical negligence and the assertion by the plaintiff that this constituted the unintentional homicide of her child and should be considered a criminal offence in light of Article 2. Due to the lack of consensus on the nature and status of the embryo, however, the ECtHR decided that it was 'neither desirable, nor even possible' to specify whether the unborn child should be considered 'a person' as protected under Article 2. It did, however, take judicial notice that embryos are beginning to receive some protection in light of the scientific progress in the field of genetic engineering, medically assisted procreation and embryo experimentation.

Restrictive regimes

In the U.S., the culture wars create their deepest and most bitter divisions in the polarised stand-off between pro-choice and pro-life advocates. Following the *Dobbs*[107] decision, constraints are being introduced in many states – such as Arizona – on what had been previously been understood under the rubric of *Roe v. Wade*[108] as a woman's right to choose.[109] It has been estimated that even before

103 Not until the judicial decisions in *Menhennit* (1969) in Victoria and *Levine* (1971) in New South Wales did prosecutions for abortion gradually cease in all states (Tasmania in 2013) and not until the Abortion Law Reform Bill 2019 was it finally decriminalised abortion in NSW.

104 *Attorney-General (QLD) (ex rel Kerr) v. T.* (1983) 1 Qd R 404, 406–407; affirmed on appeal in *Attorney-General (QLD) (ex rel Kerr) v. T.* (1983) 46 ALR 275.

105 In 1955, there were 1,170,143 abortions; 550,127 in 1985; 343,024 in 1995; 341,588 in 2001; 190,363 in 2011; 224,300 in 2018; and 223,000 in 2021 (see, *Institut National des Etudes Demographiques*, 'INED').

106 Application No. 53924/00 (2004).

107 *Dobbs v. Jackson Women's Health Organization*, No. 19–1392, 597 U.S. ___ (2022).

108 410 U.S. 113 (1973), overturned by the ruling in *Dobbs v. Jackson Women's Health Organization, op cit.*

109 Note the federal statute the Unborn Victims of Violence Act 2004 which defines violent assault committed against pregnant women as being a crime against two victims: the woman and the foetus.

the *Dobbs* decision,[110] at least 25 states had enacted laws to protect life between conception and 12 weeks.[111] In Ireland, until relatively recently, access to abortion services was blocked by the fact that a foetus had a constitutional right to protection: 'the unborn' had a right to life equal to that of 'the mother'.[112] Not until a national referendum in 2018 did the law change when a constitutional amendment substituted the former provision recognising the right to life of the unborn, with one that permitted legislation for the termination of pregnancies, which was given effect by the Health (Regulation of Termination of Pregnancy) Act 2018 that provides a restricted right to an abortion.

In New Zealand, although abortion is a controlled public service – unavailable on demand[113] – this has not prevented the country from having one of the highest abortion rates in the world, relative to the size of its population. Further, the courts have ruled that a foetus can come within the legal definition of 'child' and, as such, is entitled to protection[114] and also that the Abortion Advisory Committee has the power to enquire as to how the consultants involved in such procedures approached their decision-making and could revoke their appointments if it found that the consultants' views were incompatible with the tenor of the Act.

In Germany, abortion is illegal except in certain circumstances: if the mandatory counselling has been received; or if the pregnancy is the result of rape, it is permissible for the first 12 weeks; or if the pregnancy creates health risks, then it is legally permissible even after the first 12 weeks. These constraints may well explain why Germany has one of the lowest abortion rates in the western world (about one-third that of the U.S.). In 2020, the German abortion rate was 5.9. abortions per 10,000 women aged 15–44 years.[115]

Family planning, IVF, genetic editing, etc.

Improvements in fertility treatment (AID, GIFT, etc.) have evolved to offer an important and constantly improving route for childless couples and singletons who want the opportunity to become parents. As has been pointed out, 'IVF used to be around 7% successful and now it's around 30%'.[116]

110 Ibid.

111 See, further, at: https://eu.usatoday.com/story/opinion/2023/06/23/dobbs-decision-roe-wade-overturned-states-act-protect-unborn/70346336007/

112 See, the Eighth Amendment of the Constitution.

113 See, *Auckland Medical Aid Trust v. Commissioner of Inland Revenue* (1979) 1 NZLR 382.

114 *In the Matter of Baby P (an unborn child)* (1995) NZFLR 577. This is not dissimilar to the interpretation in Irish law.

115 See, National Library of Medicine, at: www.ncbi.nlm.nih.gov/pmc/articles/PMC9275520/

116 See, further, at: www.theguardian.com/society/2018/nov/03/england-adoption-rates-falling-as-ivf-improves-says-senior-official

Liberal regimes

In the UK, these services are well established and generally readily accessible as part of public service provision. Ireland, in contrast, is currently one of only six out of 43 European countries that have failed to introduce specific legislative provisions to regulate assisted reproduction techniques.[117]

Canada, in sharp contrast to its neighbour, has pioneered reproductive rights and access to related services through its 'Well Women' centres – since spreading to countries such as the UK, South Africa and New Zealand – which have done much to promote women's reproductive rights.

Family planning only became widely available in Australia in 1974 when the Family Planning Association introduced abortion and birth control guidance. The New Zealand Family Planning Association (NZFPA) was founded in 1936 opened its first clinic in 1953 and by the 1970s and 1980s was providing medical, education and counselling services in addition to developing its role in abortion referral.

Since 2021, IVF treatment has been available to heterosexuals, same-sex couples and single women in France. This, in all probability, was due to an equality legislative initiative prompted by the decision in *Charron and Merle-Montet v. France*[118] which concerned the not-untypical endeavour of a same-sex couple to found a family by availing of assisted reproduction services. On being refused by the authorities, on the grounds that French law did not authorise such medical provision for same-sex couples, they took their complaint to the ECtHR. The Court found that the applicants had failed to exhaust domestic remedies as the decision to refuse access to such services had been an individual administrative decision that could – and perhaps would have been – set aside on appeal for abuse of authority before the administrative courts. It, therefore, declared the application inadmissible.

Restrictive regimes

In the U.S., all along the continuum from the availability of contraceptives[119] to abortion services[120] to IVF and now to commercial surrogacy and gene editing, there has been a constant stream of caselaw which has entrenched the associated deep social divisions that now characterise the culture wars in this country. In

117 See, further, at: www.eurekalert.org/pub_releases/2020-02/esoh-emt020320.php

118 Application No. 22612/15 (2018).

119 See, for example, *Griswold v. Connecticut*, 381 U.S. 479 (1965), a state may not prohibit distribution of contraceptive devices to married couples; *Eisenstadt v. Baird*, 405 U.S. 438 (1972), single persons cannot be denied contraceptives; and *Carey v. Population Services International*, 431 U.S. 678 (1977), a statute prohibiting the sale of contraceptives to minors under the age of 16 was unconstitutional.

120 See: *Roe v. Wade,* 410 U.S. 113 (1973), which legalised abortion nationwide as subsequently endorsed in *Planned Parenthood of S.E. Pa. v. Casey*, 112 S. Ct. 2791 (1992); *Planned Parenthood v. Danforth*, 428 U.S. 52 (1976) and *Bellotti v. Baird,* 443 U.S. 622 (1979), state laws requiring teenagers to have parental permission for abortion nullified.

Germany, IVF services are regulated by some of the most restrictive legislation in the western world. This is probably a reaction to its experiences during the Nazi era which witnessed an abuse of technological and genetic control of reproduction.[121]

Surrogacy

Surrogacy is legally differentiated between altruistic and commercial models; the latter now constitutes a rapidly growing facet of medical tourism (see, also, Chapter 7).

Liberal regimes

In the U.S., there are no federal laws governing surrogacy, though most states have legislated for surrogacy contracts and tend to be broadly facilitative towards commercial surrogacy,[122] while almost all allow compensatory payments to birth mothers.[123] In Canada, altruistic surrogacy has generally been legal since 2004, but both altruistic and commercial surrogacy are prohibited in Québec.

In Australia, all states and territories prohibit commercial surrogacy basis but permit its altruistic use and allow reimbursement of some of the surrogate's costs. In New Zealand, where there is an absence of surrogacy specific legislation,[124] altruistic surrogacy is legal, but commercial surrogacy is not. Whether the surrogacy arrangement is concluded within or without the jurisdiction, the commissioning parent/s must adopt the child in order to legitimate their parental status. Increasingly, couples are making surrogacy arrangements overseas and returning home to New Zealand which has given rise to jurisdiction issues.

Restrictive regimes

In England and Wales, the law currently favours surrogate mothers: agreements are unenforceable and create insecurity for commissioning couples by allowing surrogate mothers to choose to keep the child after birth; the courts ensure that surrogacy arrangements are altruistic and that no improper payments have been made; while an amendment to the 1989 Act established a presumption that the involvement of a birth parent in the life of the child concerned would further that child's

121 See, further, Robertson, J.A., 'Reproductive Technology in Germany and the United States: An Essay in Comparative Law and Bioethics', *Columbia Journal of Transnational Law* (2004), pp. 189–227.

122 See, for example, Finkelstein, A., et al., 'Surrogacy Law and Policy in the U.S.', Columbia Law School (2016), at: https://web.law.columbia.edu/sites/default/files/microsites/gender-sexuality/files/columbia_sexuality_and_gender_law_clinic_-_surrogacy_law_and_policy_report_-_june_2016.pdf

123 See, further, at: www.modamily.com/blog/us-surrogacy-laws-by-state

124 Note, however, the relevance of the Human Assisted Reproductive Technology Act 2004, the Adoption Act 1955 and the Status of Children Act 1969.

welfare.[125] As yet there is no specific legislation governing surrogacy in Ireland[126] which has led to the CRC expressing concern that insufficient attention is being given 'to the rights and interests of children born as a result of assisted reproduction technologies'.[127]

In France, surrogacy is not merely unavailable, but since 1991, it has been legally prohibited.[128] A surrogacy contract is null and void, and violations are punished by civil and criminal sanctions. Since 2010, French courts have consistently denied recognition to surrogate contracts and to any right to adopt children born abroad from surrogate mothers. In Germany, to make a human being the subject of a contract is legally impermissible: surrogacy is, therefore, illegal;[129] the mother of a child is the woman who gave birth to that child.[130] It is a criminal offence for health professionals to assist someone in need of such a service.

Conclusion

Advances in medical science have allowed parenting to become more a matter of choice: a choice mostly to be exercised by women. Reproductive rights – mainly birth control and abortion services – have clearly affected the number of unwanted births and, therefore, the number of birth parent/s wishing to voluntarily relinquish babies for adoption. Medical science has also greatly improved the survival rate for babies born with complex health and social care needs resulting in more such children becoming available for adoption.

125 See, *in Re H (A Child) (Surrogacy Breakdown)* (2017) EWCA Civ 1798.

126 See, further, at: www.citizensinformation.ie/en/birth_family_relationships/adoption_and_fostering/surrogacy.html

127 UN Committee on the Rights of the Child, Concluding Observations of the Committee on the combined third and fourth periodic reports of Ireland, 2016, at para 33.

128 Under article 16.5 of the Civil Code, such contracts are null and void. The *Cour de cassation* in 1991 invalidated a decision of lower jurisdictions giving effect to surrogacy by creating a filiation link between the child and the wife of the biological father after the completion of such a contract.

129 The Embryo Protection Act 1991, s 1(1)(7).

130 Civil Code, s 1591.

6 Founding families and family life

Introduction

'Family life', as the ECtHR has often stated, consists of the mutual enjoyment by parent and child of each other's company.[1] Indeed, as always, the welfare interests of a child arise for consideration primarily in a family context but that context has been profoundly restructured in recent years, with inevitable implications for the legal interpretation of 'family life' and for the welfare interests and rights of a child.

This chapter, like its predecessors, begins with a brief examination of key concepts and definitions. It then outlines the relevant international legal framework before identifying a generic list of children's rights in a family context. The main section, focusing on a jurisdictional comparison of 'founding a family' and 'family life', follows. This is in three parts: a baseline of established ECtHR rulings on those subjects, a comparative analysis of the eight jurisdictions in relation to the standards set by the ECtHR and an assessment of the law relating to 'founding a family' and 'family life' in an Indigenous context. It concludes by assessing its relative significance in relation to the welfare principle and considers some of the more important implications arising for family law.[2]

Concepts, rights and the law

For centuries, family law, its central concepts and the rights of the parties had remained clearly defined and firmly governed by religious values. As family law slowly emerged from its religious context, hastened by the civil rights movement

1 See, *W., B. and R. v. the United Kingdom*, 8 July 1987, Series A No. 121; *Olsson v. Sweden (no. 1)*, 24 March 1988, Series A No. 130; *Eriksson v. Sweden*, 22 June 1989, Series A No. 156; *Margareta and Roger Andersson v. Sweden*, 25 February 1992, Series A No. 226-A; *McMichael v. the United Kingdom*, 24 February 1995, Series A No. 307-B; *Johansen v. Norway*, 7 August 1996, *Reports* 1996-III; *Bronda v. Italy*, 9 June 1998, *Reports* 1998-IV; and *Buscemi v. Italy*, Application No. 29569/95, ECHR 1999-VI.

2 See, further, O'Halloran, K., *Children, the Law and the Welfare Principle: European Judicial Perspectives*, Routledge, 2024, at chapter 5.

DOI: 10.4324/9781003269595-10

and secularisation more broadly, so it began to shed established verities and adjust to accommodate new social norms.

Concepts and constructs

The nature of the changes that have impacted family law in the course of the past few decades are not readily discernible from the related language and terminology, but their contemporary interpretation is not what it was.

'Family': definition

As the ECtHR has pointed out:[3]

> the notion of 'the family' . . . is not confined solely to marriage based relationships and may encompass other *de facto* 'family' where the parties are living together outside of marriage. A child born out of such a relationship is *ipso iure* part of that 'family' unit from the moment of his birth and by the very fact of it.

As legal recognition for same-sex partnerships, civil unions and, eventually, for marriage, was introduced in one country after another at the turn of the century, so the notion of 'family' underwent a quiet revolution. As the definition broadened, it introduced protection for ancillary matters relating to birth parent's responsibilities for their children, same-sex parenting arrangements, pensions and testamentary entitlements, etc.

Family life

This elastic concept loosely delineates the boundaries of a relationship that in law is recognised as 'private' and entitled to state support. This has been clear since at least *Marckx v. Belgium*[4] when the ECtHR ruled that the ties between an unmarried mother and daughter constituted 'family life', within the meaning of Article 8, regardless of the mother's marital status, and went on to declare that with such recognition came positive obligations on the state to demonstrate its support and respect for family life.[5]

Parents

The birth parent – or 'natural parent' – and/or the legal guardian of a child vested with parental responsibility, have always had full party status in any legal

3 *Keegan v. Ireland*, Application No. 16969/90 (1994) Series A No. 290, 18 EHRR 342, at para 44.

4 Application No. 6833/74 (1979).

5 Ibid, at paras 36–7. See, also, Kilkelly, U., 'Protecting Children's Rights under the ECHR: The Role of Positive Obligations', *NILQ*, Vol. 61, No. 3 (2010), pp. 245–261.

proceedings relating to the upbringing or welfare interests of that child: the birth mother being inherently vested with such responsibility and the birth father also, if married to the mother, otherwise having to legally acquire it. This responsibility is not confined to legal proceedings: parental involvement is required in any decision-making process affecting their child to a degree sufficient to provide that child with the requisite protection of their interests.[6] Parents, for example, are entitled to be involved in the decision-making process relating to the religious education of their children, and their consent will be required if medical treatment is to be provided by hospital staff to their children.[7]

Paternity

The presumption favouring family life has been extended to include an unmarried father and child,[8] but this can be rebutted, as it was in *Soderback v. Sweden,*[9] where the unmarried applicant father had never cohabited with the mother and only had a tenuous relationship with his daughter whom the mother and her spouse were proposing to adopt.

Maternity

Whether a child is born to a married or unmarried woman, the maxim *mater semper certa est* (the mother is certain) applies, and she in law is automatically vested with parental responsibility for that child. If married, she shares parental responsibility with her spouse and may be divested of it only with his consent or by court order. If unmarried, she may choose to voluntarily relinquish the child for adoption – and in some countries, as a surrogate mother, she may do so by availing of appropriate legal proceedings – or she may instead choose to legally share with the father, but unless and until she takes such legal steps, she retains exclusive parental responsibility for the child.

In the latter half of the 20th century, a constellation of different factors from financial and housing benefits for unmarried mothers – including a range of birth control methods, increased opportunities for employment and ease of access to divorce proceedings – to social acceptance of non-marital and serial cohabitation arrangements, combined to transform the *locus standi* of an unmarried mother and enable her to avoid what had previously been the forced option of adoption.

6 *W v. United Kingdom* (1987) 10 EHRR 29.

7 See, *Glass v. the United Kingdom,* Application No. 61827/00 (2004) and *M.A.K. and R.K. v. the United Kingdom,* Application Nos. 45901/05 and 40146/06 (2010).

8 See *Johansen v. Norway* (1996) 23 EHRR 33 and *Rieme v. Sweden* (1993) 16 EHRR 155. Note that in *B. v. United Kingdom* (2000) 1 FLR 1, the court found against an unmarried father without parental responsibility and held that the UK court had been justifiably discriminatory between his standing and that of a married father, as he had no custody rights in respect of the child.

9 (1999) 1 FLR 250.

Children

The traditional legal presumption that any child born to the parties during the course of their marriage is considered to be part of that family continues in force. In effect, the same presumption extends to a child born of a stable partnership, though in some jurisdictions, this requires the father to be registered as such.

Foetus

Recognition for inclusion in 'family life' requires a child to have been born: the law has been very reluctant to extend recognition and protection to a foetus. In the UK case of *Paton v. BPAS*,[10] for example, the court was clear that 'the foetus cannot [. . .] have any rights of its own at least until it is born and has separate existence from the mother'. Again, in *C. v. S.*,[11] 'the claim crystallises upon the birth, at which date, but not before, the child attains the status of a legal persona, and thereupon can then exercise the legal right'. Such views are, however, open to challenge. As the judges in a Canadian case argued, 'technologies like real-time ultrasound, foetal heart monitors and foetoscopy can clearly show us that the foetus is alive', and thus, the born-alive rule is 'outdated and indefensible'.[12] In New Zealand, the courts have ruled that a foetus can come within the legal definition of 'child' and, as such, is entitled to protection[13] (see, further, Chapter 6).

'Child of the family'

A 'child of the family' is one born to both parties of a marriage or civil partnership or any other child who has been treated by those parties as a child of their family.

The right of every child to maintain contact with both their parents is expressly recognised in Article 24(3) of the EU Charter of Fundamental Rights, Article 4(1) of the CoE Convention on Contact Concerning Children 2003 and in Article 9 of UN CROC, where it is subject to the welfare interests of the child concerned.

Welfare interests

The principle that the welfare interests of a child should be of central importance in any decision affecting their upbringing has long permeated the law relating to children in the jurisdictions currently being considered: family law proceedings routinely require that applications be subject to the 'welfare test'. In the U.S., responsibility for the welfare interests of a child is a matter that lies within the

10 *Paton v. British Pregnancy Advisory Service* (1979) Q.B. 276, per Sir George Baker P, at p. 279. As confirmed in *Re F (in Utero)*, All E.LR. 1988 Feb 4: (1988) 2:193–201.

11 QB 135, 1988.

12 See *Winnipeg Child and Family Services (Northwest Area) v. G.* (D.F.) (1997) 3 S.C.R. 925.

13 See, *In the Matter of Baby P (an unborn child)* (1995) NZFLR 577. This is not dissimilar to the interpretation in Irish law.

rights and responsibilities of parents. The latter are generally taken to be vested with the authority to make decisions – certainly medical decisions – on behalf of their child. The law is much the same in Canada. In both countries, while the consent of a child may not always be strictly necessary in all legal proceedings affecting their interests, the court will be slow to take decisions against the wishes of a discerning child.

However, while it was customary for statute law to refer to 'welfare interests', no attempt was made to define or indicate the meaning of this term. In recent years, this anomaly has been addressed in a minority of jurisdictions by the inclusion of a 'welfare checklist' in relevant legislation to indicate the factors to be taken into account by the judiciary or other bodies when determining issues relating to the upbringing of a child. Otherwise, the matter has been left to judicial discretion and has tended to be interpreted as comprising 'material and financial prospects, education, general surroundings, happiness, stability of home and the like'.[14]

International law

A broad umbrella of international law now affords protection for the welfare interests and rights of children: the European Convention on Human Rights 1950 (ECHR) and the United Nations Convention on the Rights of the Child 1989 (UN CROC) being of central importance; others such as the International Covenant on Civil and Political Rights 1966 (ICCPR), the European Convention on Recognition and Enforcement of Decisions concerning Custody of Children and on Restoration of Custody of Children 1980, the Hague Convention on the Civil Aspects of International Child Abduction 1980 and many more instruments may also have relevance (see, also, Chapter 6).[15]

The ECtHR has found that the private life guarantee provided by Article 8 'incorporates not only the right to respect for decisions to become or not to become a parent'[16] but also 'the right of a couple to conceive a child and to make use of medically assisted procreation for that purpose',[17] and it makes no distinction between families comprised of 'legitimate' or 'illegitimate' children.[18] However, the state has no legal obligation to provide the services that may be necessary for the right to be exercised.

UN CROC, Articles 18 and 19, declare the general duties of signatory states in relation to provision of assistance to families and children. They stress that while parents have the primary responsibility for the upbringing and development of their children, the state must 'render appropriate assistance to parents and legal guardians in the performance of their child-rearing responsibilities' and should establish

14 See, *Re B* (1971) 1 QB 437, per Davies L J at p. 443.

15 See, further, O'Halloran, K., *Children, the Law and the Welfare Principle: European Judicial Perspectives*, Routledge, 2024, at Chapter 1.

16 See, *Parrillo v. Italy,* Application No. 46470/11 (2015), at para 153

17 See, *S, H. and Others v. Austria,* Application No. 57813/00 (2011).

18 *Marckx v. Belgium* (1979) Series A No. 31, 2 EHRR 330, at para 31.

'social programmes to provide necessary support for the child and for those who have the care of the child, as well as for other forms of prevention'.

Article 27 declares:

> States Parties, in accordance with national conditions and within their means, shall take appropriate measures to assist parents and others responsible for the child to implement this right and shall in case of need provide material assistance and support programmes, particularly with regard to nutrition, clothing and housing.

Family life and children's rights

Recognition for the rights of children – as separate and distinct from the rights and responsibilities of their parents – is very much a patchy work in progress. Despite decades of uniform and universal application of ECHR and UN CROC principles by the ECtHR and other bodies, there continues to be considerable jurisdictional variation in terms of the type of issues and the age at which a child is entitled to have an independent and decisive role in their determination.

Parental upbringing

The UK judiciary would now seem to be firmly of the view that a child has no right – nor does any legal presumption require a child – to be brought up by his or her family of origin.[19] In the U.S.,[20] unlike the UK,[21] the presumptive right that a child should be cared for by their birth parents is constitutionally protected and well established, as it is Ireland[22] and similarly in France[23] and Germany,[24] though not specifically so in Canada and not in Australia.[25]

Parental punishment

Children in the UK, Ireland and New Zealand have the right not to suffer parental corporal punishment.

Children in Canada,[26] the U.S.[27] and in Australia have no such right. Parents in those countries have the right to physically chastise their child for behaviour

19 *Re E-R (A Child)* 2015 EWCA Civ 405, per Vincent J.

20 See, for example, *Troxel v. Granville*, 530 U.S. 57 (2000).

21 See, *Re W (A Child)* (2016) EWCA Civ 793.

22 Such a presumption arises from the constitutional guarantees in articles 41 and 42 that the state will protect 'the inalienable and imprescriptible rights of the family' and the 'inalienable right and duty of parents'.

23 See references to the inalienable rights of parents in the French Civil Code, Arts. 371 to 387–6.

24 See, Article 6(2) of the Basic Law.

25 *Rice v. Millar* (1993) FLC 92–807 at 85 and 106.

26 The Criminal Code, s 43. See, *Canadian Foundation for Children, Youth and the Law v. Canada (Attorney General)* (2004) 1 SCR 76, 2004 SCC 4.

27 The Child Abuse Prevention and Treatment Act 2003.

judged to be unacceptable by that parent, subject to the condition that the degree of physical force is 'reasonable'.

Contact with parent

Contact – following parental divorce, separation or the issue of a care order – is an established right of the child in the UK[28] and similarly in Germany.[29] In effect, this is also the case in both Australia[30] and New Zealand, where there is a statutory onus on the authorities to facilitate ongoing connectedness between a child and their community and culture and to facilitate ongoing parent-child relationships, by encouraging and providing opportunities for contact.

Post-adoption contact in Australia is judicially viewed as conducive to furthering the welfare interests of the adoptee and contact arrangements – often formally embedded in the adoption order – have become standard practice. This statutory abridgment of the private rights of adopters, in order to give effect to a public interest in establishing the welfare interests of the child, creates a presumptive right to contact for a child in such circumstances.

Sexual relationships

In England and Wales, a child, aged between 16 and 18 years of age, can give a valid legal consent to a sexual relationship.[31] In the U.S., the age of consent is not federally determined. It varies from state to state – from 16 to 18 years of age – and it varies again according to whether the issue arises in a civil or criminal jurisdiction. In both the U.S. and Canada, the capacity of a child – aged less than 18 – to give a valid consent to sex, to accessing contraceptives or abortion, is determined by a combination of age and maturity; if 16 years of age or older, there would be a presumption of capacity.[32] In Australia and New Zealand, the consent of a child to sexual intercourse and access to contraceptives would be legally valid only if he or she was aged 16 years or older.

Medical treatment

The right of a child aged 14–16 to authorise non-invasive medical treatment, such as dental care, is probably accepted and firmly established in all jurisdictions studied. However, the right of a child aged 16 or younger to refuse treatment of an urgent or life-saving nature will almost certainly be denied.[33]

28 The Adoption and Children Act 2002, s 46(6) and the Children and Families Act 2014, s 9.

29 The Civil Code, s 1626(3).

30 See, for example, *Adoption of RCC and RZA* (2015) NSWSC 813.

31 Sexual Offences Act 2003.

32 *Carey v. Population Services International*, 431 U.S. 678 (1977).

33 See, for example, UK, *Re M (medical treatment: consent)* (1999) 2 F.L.R. 1097 (Fam. Div.).

Gender transitioning

The rising numbers of children undergoing gender transitioning is generating much controversy, some of which concerns the age at which the subjects have the right to consent to irreversible puberty-blocking treatment. In the UK, it would appear unlikely – notwithstanding the *Gillick* ruling – that a child aged 16 or less will be able to independently give such a legally valid consent.[34]

Adoption

In France, where a child is 13 years of age or older, then his or her personal consent is mandatory for their adoption: both plenary[35] and simple.[36] Similarly so in Germany, where the age threshold is 14 or older. In England and Wales and Ireland, a child's consent is not an explicit legal requirement. In some Australian states, the consent of a child aged 12 years or more is a prerequisite for their adoption, while in New Zealand, the consent of a child younger than 20 years of age is not a legal requirement.

Many states in the U.S. accept as legally valid the consent of an underage mother – of any age – to place her child for adoption (see, further, Chapter 8).

Founding families and family life: established international legal standards

Over time, the rulings of the ECtHR and other bodies have established standards for the guidance of domestic courts and authorities when interpreting and applying international law, particularly the provisions of the ECtHR and UN CROC.

Founding a family and family life

The right to found a family was established at an early stage by the Universal Declaration of Human Rights (UDHR), Article 16, and subsequently, by the European Convention on Human Rights (ECHR), Article 12, the second part of which – the right 'to found a family' – was clearly intended to confer legal status on a 'family' and vest the spouses with reciprocal duties, parental obligations, inheritance rights, etc. While neither extended the right to include same-sex relationships, it is clear that this interpretation now complies with international law.

Whether there is a corresponding right not to found a family – by having recourse to abortion – has been a contentious issue (see, further, Chapter 6).

34 *R (on the application of) Quincy Bell and A -v- Tavistock and Portman NHS Trust and others* (2020) EWHC 3274 (Admin).

35 See, Art. 345 of the Civil Code.

36 See Art. 360 *in fine* of the Civil Code: L'adoption simple est permise quel que soit l'âge de l'adopté. Si l'adopté est âgé de plus de treize ans, il doit consentir personnellement à l'adoption. Also, see, Arts 345 and 361.

Medically assisted procreation

Recent advances in medical science have greatly increased its potential impact on procreation and thus to found a family.[37]

Embryos and founding a family

In *Evans v. the United Kingdom*,[38] the ECtHR made the important finding that embryos do not have a right to life, and therefore, the authorities were entitled, as required by national law, to destroy them. In *Parrillo v. Italy*,[39] however, the ECtHR seemed to take a less dismissive approach to the legal status of embryos when it ruled for the first time that Article 8 was applicable to the relationship between the applicant and her embryos, as they contained part of her genetic material and, therefore, constituted part of her identity[40] (see, further, Chapter 6).

Respect for family life

Family life, as the ECtHR has reiterated, is essentially to be found in the parent-child relationship. As Kilkelly[41] has explained, the ECtHR has now established that such a relationship will constitute family life 'in all but very exceptional cases regardless of the parents' marital status,[42] the family's living arrangements,[43] or their apparent lack of commitment to their children'.[44] Moreover, that relationship has come to form a model of care which is transferable to other relationships where the parental role has been assumed by adopters, foster parents, same-sex couples, etc., to which legal protection has been similarly transferred. Whether any such relationships are entitled to respect in the eyes of the law[45] will depend upon whether they constitute a family.[46] At the very least, there needs to be a potential relationship between, for example, a child born[47] to unmarried parents and his

37 See, for example, CRISPR/Cas 9 and its potential to lead to 'designer babies'.

38 Ibid.

39 Application No. 46470/11 (2015).

40 Nonetheless, her complaint that she was unable to donate her embryos conceived through medically assisted reproduction to scientific research was found not to breach Article 8 and was dismissed.

41 See, Kilkelly, U., 'Child and Family Law', in Kilkelly (ed.), *ECHR and Irish Law*, Jordans, 2004, p. 112.

42 See, *Marckx v. Belgium ibid* (unmarried mother and her child); *Johnston v. Ireland*, No. 9697/92, Series A No. 12 (1987) 9 EHRR 203 (unmarried parents and their child).

43 See, *Berrehab v. Netherlands*, No. 10730/84, Series A No. 138 (1988) 11 EHRR 322.

44 See, *C v. Belgium*, Application No. 21794/93 (1996) and *Ahmut v. Netherlands*, Application No. 21702/93 (1996). See, also, *Söderbäck v. Sweden*, Application No. 24484/94 (1998). However, purely genetic relationships – such as the relationship between a sperm donor and the child born as a result – are unlikely to constitute family life. See, *G v. Netherlands*, Application No. 16944/90 (1993).

45 See, *V.D. and Others v. Russia*, Application No. 72931/10 (2019).

46 See, *Marckx v. Belgium*, *op cit.*

47 An unborn child would not qualify: *Paton v. The United Kingdom*, Application No. 8416/78 (1981).

or her birth father;[48] the relationship that arises from a genuine marriage, even if family life has not yet been fully established;[49] or the relationship that arises from a lawful and genuine adoption.[50] The existence of 'family life' will depend upon factors such as whether the couple live together, the length of their relationship and whether they have demonstrated their commitment to each other by having children together or by other means.[51] In *Lebbink v. The Netherlands,*[52] the ECtHR accepted that cohabitation was not essential; other factors may serve to demonstrate the required constancy of relationships such as, in that instance, the father's position as auxiliary guardian and his established pattern of contact with the child.

Parental responsibility for child's upbringing

UN CROC, Article 18, declares that parents 'have the primary responsibility for the upbringing and development of the child. The best interests of the child will be their basic concern'.

In both France and Germany, unlike the UK,[53] there is a relatively strong presumption favouring birth parents – all other factors being equal – as best placed to safeguard the welfare of their child. This is accompanied by legislative provisions requiring the state to provide, where necessary, support services enabling them to do so. For example, Article 19(2) states that such services should include 'effective procedures for the establishment of social programmes to provide necessary support for the child and for those who have the care of the child'.

Child's welfare interests and rights

Being recognised as belonging to a family vests certain rights in a child, as mentioned earlier, including to know the identity of their parents; to parental protection;[54] and for contact with their parent/s, where this is compliant with his or her welfare interests.[55] The significance of the latter condition was evident in two cases. Firstly, in *Levin v. Sweden,*[56] where the ECtHR found that the contact restrictions placed upon the mother were to safeguard the welfare interests of the children who had been neglected while in their mother's care and who showed strong

48 See, *Nylund v. Finland* (dec.), Application No. 27110/95 (1999).

49 See, *Abdulaziz, Cabales and Balkandali v. the United Kingdom*, Application Nos. 9214/80; 9473/81; 9474/81 (1985).

50 See, *Pini and Others v. Romania*, Application Nos. 78028/01 and 78030/01 (2004).

51 *X, Y and Z v. United Kingdom* (1997) 2 FLR 892.

52 Application No. 35582/99, ECtHR (1 June 2004).

53 See, *Re W (A Child)* (2016) EWCA Civ 793.

54 See, *Petrov and X. v. Russia*, Application No. 23608/16 (2018) and *Wunderlich v. Germany*, Application No. 18925/15 (2019).

55 *A.I. v. Italy*, Application No.70896/17 (2021). Also, see Article 24(3) of the Charter of Fundamental Rights 2012 and the UN *Guidelines for the alternative care of children,* UN Doc. A/HRC/11/L.13 (2009).

56 Application No. 35141/06 (2012).

negative reactions following contact with her. The Court found that the interference with the applicant's rights had been 'proportionate to the legitimate aim pursued [the best interests of the children] and within the margin of the domestic authorities'.[57] Secondly, in *R.M.S. v. Spain*[58] which concerned a mother's claim that she had been deprived of all contact with her almost-4-year-old daughter on the basis of her socio-economic status. The Court then stated:

> the role of the social welfare authorities is precisely to help persons in difficulty, . . . to provide them with guidance and to advise them on matters such as the different types of benefits available, the possibility of obtaining social housing and other means of overcoming their difficulties, such as those originally sought by the applicant.

Should the state decide to sever all contact between mother and child, by removing a new-born baby, the reasons put forth by the state must be extraordinarily compelling.[59]

Parental alienation syndrome (PAS)

This term refers to circumstances in which a child has become preoccupied with criticism, deprecation and even the vilification of an absent parent – in cases where this is unjustified. It is a well-established and researched phenomenon – perversely intended to alienate a child from a parent – that can often distort their welfare interests and undermine their right, under Article 9.3 of UN CROC, to a relationship with that parent.

PAS may be considered as 'a step further on from brainwashing'. In addition to the systematic and conscious programming of a child by one parent to denigrate the other, it also includes factors that have been induced in such a way that they arise from within the child itself. A PAS-child sees itself as having a 'loved' and 'hated' parent, the hated parent being the one it doesn't live with, and is convinced this is all its personal conviction. This process of 'casting off' the (for the most part) father is generally irreversible.[60]

Family life: forms

The forms that contemporary family life may take are now many and varied. Although the marital family unit continues to be ubiquitous norm, in addition – as

57 Ibid, at paras 57 and 69.

58 Ibid.

59 *K. and T. v. Finland*, Application No. 25702/94 (2001).

60 *Zander v. the Netherlands*, Application No. 32040/96 (2000) at para 11; citing Gardner, R.A., *The Parental Alienation Syndrome: Past, Present and Future* (paper presented to the International Conference on the Parental Alienation Syndrome [PAS] held in Frankfurt/Main, Germany, October 18–19, 2002), at: http://richardagardner.com/ar22

Kilkelly has pointed out – the ECtHR has recognised[61] that 'family life may exist between children and their grandparents,[62] between siblings,[63] between an uncle and his nephew,[64] and between parents and children born into second relationships'.[65] The law has extended its recognition and protection to family life that takes the form of adopters and child,[66] foster parents and child,[67] migrant parents and child,[68] same-sex relationships and child[69] and surrogate arrangements and child.[70] In *Manuello and Nevi v. Italy,*[71] the Court found that family ties existed between the grandparents and their granddaughter, who had not seen each other for about 12 years, and that the former's right to respect for their family life had been violated by the authorities inaction. Once it is established that family life exists, then the state has a duty to support it.[72] In *Strand Lobben and Others v. Norway*,[73] the ECtHR affirmed that, under Article 8, regard for family unity and for family reunification in the event of separation are inherent considerations in the right to respect for family life.

Non-marital families

Some 40 years ago, in *W.J. & D.P.*,[74] the Commission concluded that heterosexual, unmarried couples living together as husband and wife could be viewed as constituting a family and that such relationships deserve special protection in society. It, therefore, followed that the rights of an unmarried father were entitled to recognition in law. So in *Keagan v. Ireland,*[75] the ECtHR established the principle that where an unmarried father had previously enjoyed a settled cohabiting relationship with a mother who had decided to place their child for adoption, then the father should be informed and consulted because the protection given to 'family life' provided by Article 8 extended to include such a relationship. The difference in treatment of married and unmarried fathers was justified by the ECtHR in *McMichael v. UK*[76] on the basis that it was intended to thereby provide a means of identifying

61 See, Kilkelly, U., 'Child and Family Law', in Kilkelly (ed.), *ECHR and Irish Law*, *op cit*, at p. 113.

62 See, *Marckx v. Belgium*, *op cit*, at para 45.

63 See, *Olsson v. Sweden*, Application No. 10465/83, Series A No. 130, 11 EHRR 259. See also *Boughanemi v. France*, Application No. 22070/93, Reports 1996-II, No. 8, p. 593, 22 EHRR 228.

64 See, *Boyle v. UK*, Application No. 16580/90, Comm Rep, 9.2.93.

65 See, *Jolie & Lebrun v. Belgium*, Application No. 11418/85, Dec. 14.5.86, DR 47, p. 243.

66 See, for example, *Zait v. Romania*, Application No. 44958/05 (2015).

67 See, for example, *Moretti and Benedetti v. Italy,* Application No. 16318/07, ECtHR (2010) and *Kopf and Liberda v. Austria*, Application No. 1598/06 (2012).

68 See, for example, *Sen v. the Netherlands,* Application No. 31465/96 (2001).

69 See, for example, *X, Y & Z v. UK,* Application No. 21830/93, Reports 1997-II No. 35, p. 619, 24 EHRR 143.

70 See, for example, *Mennesson v. France,* Application No. 65192/11 (2014).

71 Application No. 107/10 (2015).

72 *Melo Soares v. Portugal*, Application No. 72850/14 (2017).

73 Application No. 37283/13 (2019).

74 *W.J. & D.P. v. the United Kingdom*, Application No.12513/86 (1987).

75 (1994) 18 EHRR 342.

76 (1995) Fam Law 478. Also, see, *B v. UK* 2000 1 FLR 1.

'meritorious' fathers. However, with its decision in *Elsholz v. Germany,*[77] it found merit in the legal status of unmarried fathers, although extending that recognition to same-sex couples took a while longer.

Same-sex families

In 2010, when the ECtHR came to consider *Schalk and Kopf v. Austria,*[78] it was open to the argument that the Convention was a living instrument which could adjust to meet changes in society, and it took the view that 'a cohabiting same-sex couple living in a stable *de facto* partnership, falls within the notion of "family life", just as the relationship of a different-sex couple in the same situation would'. However, given the lack of consensus in Europe on same-sex marriage, the Court reasoned that in the meantime, rather than be pre-emptive, it should apply the 'margin of appreciation' rule and leave the matter to be determined by individual states. Again, in *Oliari and Others v. Italy,*[79] the ECtHR came to the same conclusion, though it conceded that there was an emerging consensus in Europe and elsewhere,[80] favouring granting legal recognition and protection to stable same-sex relationships. In *Pajić v. Croatia,*[81] the Court explained that although gender identification, sexual orientation and sexual life fell within the scope of 'private life' as understood by Article 8, same-sex relationships could not be construed as 'family life'. Inclusion for same-sex couples did not come until the decision in *Bonnaud and Lecoq v. France,*[82] when the ECtHR determined that such a cohabiting couple living with their children in a stable *de facto* partnership fell within the notion of family life. Subsequently, parity of legal status between family units led by heterosexual and same-sex couples was acknowledged in cases such as *Kozak v. Poland.*[83]

Transgender families

The argument that 'family' as understood by Article 12 of the ECHR referred to the traditional marriage between persons of different genders, to the exclusion of couples where one had undergone a change of gender identity, was initially strongly defended by the ECtHR.[84] Not until *Christine Goodwin* v. *The United*

77 (2000) 2 FLR 486. But, also see, *Sahin v. Germany; Sommerfeld v. Germany; Hoffman v. Germany,* ECHR 11.10.01.

78 Application No. 30141/04 (2010).

79 Application Nos. 18766/11 and 36030/11 (2015).

80 Notably, the decision of the USSC in *Obergefell v. Hodges,* 135 S. Ct. 2584 (2015) established legal recognition for same-sex marriage across all states.

81 Application No. 68453/13 (2016).

82 Application No. 6190/11 (2018).

83 *Kozak* v. *Poland,* Application No. 13102/02 (2010).

84 See, *Rees* v. *The United Kingdom,* Application No. 9532/81 (1986) and *C. and L.M.*, Application No. 14753/89 (1989). Also see *W.W. v. The United Kingdom,* Application No. 11095/84 (1989) and *Sheffield and Horsham v. The United Kingdom,* Application Nos. 22985/93 and 23390/94 (1998).

Kingdom[85] did the ECtHR change tack and declare that biological factors could no longer be determinative of capacity to marry and found a family. The more recently determined cases of *A.H. and Others v. Germany*[86] and *O.H. and G.H. v. Germany*[87] concerned the birth certificate registration of children whose parents had undergone gender transition. In the case of *O.H. and G.H.*, the first applicant was born female. After obtaining legal recognition of gender change, he gave birth to the second applicant, his son, conceived through a sperm donation. On the child's birth certificate, he was recorded as mother. In the case of *A.H. and Others,* the first applicant was born male and obtained legal recognition of gender change to female. The second applicant, her girlfriend, gave birth to the third applicant, their son, who had been conceived with the first applicant's sperm. The first applicant was recorded on the birth certificate as the child's father. The civil registration authorities refused to record the first applicant as father of the second (in *O.H. and G.H.*) and the first applicant as second mother of the third applicant (in *A.H. and Others*) on the ground that the person who gave birth to a child must be recorded as the mother: relying on the maxim *mater semper certa est* (the mother is always certain). The transgender parents were not complaining of a lack of recognition of their gender change in the official documents concerning themselves but of the authorities' refusal to indicate their current gender and forenames in an official document concerning their respective sons. The main question to be addressed in both cases was whether the regulatory framework in place and the decisions taken in that connection in relation to the applicants showed that the state had fulfilled its positive obligations to ensure respect for their private life in accordance with the principles established in *Hämäläinen v. Finland.*[88] These had to be considered together with the relevant factors: the importance of the interest at stake for an applicant and whether 'fundamental values' or 'essential aspects' of private life were in issue, together with the impact on an applicant of a discordance between the social reality and the law, and the impact of the alleged positive obligation on the state, depending on its nature, namely, whether it was narrow and precise or broad and indeterminate. The Court noted that the German authorities had determined that motherhood and fatherhood, as legal categories, were not interchangeable.

Founding families and family life: contemporary jurisdictional comparisons

The legal models currently available for forming and reforming families are much the same in the common law and civil law jurisdictions, as are the legal indicators for establishing family life. In addition to procreation within the orthodox marital

85 Application No. 28957/95 (2002).
86 Application No. 7246/20 (2023).
87 Application Nos. 53568/18 and 54741/18 (2023).
88 Ibid.

family unit, the most common means of founding families are by way of reproductive medical intervention, adoption, foster care and surrogacy. There is considerable jurisdictional variation in recourse to these options.

Medical intervention

Medically assisted procreation has grown in sophistication and effectiveness in the past few decades. This must result in many more couples founding families than was formerly the case.

Assisted procreation

As mentioned earlier, the ECtHR has found that 'private life incorporates not only the right to respect for decisions to become or not to become a parent'[89] but also 'the right of a couple to conceive a child and to make use of medically assisted procreation for that purpose'.[90] As the latter has increased in effectiveness so also have the numbers of people availing of such services: 'IVF used to be around 7% successful and now it's around 30%'.[91]

Infertility treatment

In the U.S., reproductive medicine is a well-established, readily accessible and highly commercialised enterprise. It has been estimated that some 55,000 women in the U.S. give birth to babies conceived through assisted reproductive technologies every year.[92] However, it may well suffer as collateral damage from the anti-abortion laws currently being passed in many states.[93] In Canada also, IVF is readily available, although expensive: four provinces provide publicly funded subsidies. In both countries, the high cost makes IVF treatment inaccessible for many people.

Recent developments (AID, GIFT, etc.) in England and Wales have made this an important and improving route for childless couples who want the opportunity to become parents. In France, the law which had restricted IVF treatment to heterosexuals was extended in 2021 to same-sex couples and single women bringing France into alignment with most other European nations. German ART services, on the other hand, are regulated by some of the most restrictive legislation in the western world.[94]

89 See, *Parrillo v. Italy,* Application No. 46470/11 (2015), at para 153.

90 See, *S. H. and Others v. Austria,* Application No. 57813/00 (2011).

91 See, further, at: www.theguardian.com/society/2018/nov/03/england-adoption-rates-falling-as-ivf-improves-says-senior-official

92 See, further, more than 55,000 women give birth to a baby conceived through assisted reproductive technologies (ART) every year.

93 See, further, at: www.theguardian.com/us-news/2022/may/12/ivf-treatment-us-anti-abortion-laws-bills

94 See, further, Robertson, J.A., 'Reproductive Technology in Germany and the United States: An Essay in Comparative Law and Bioethics', *Columbia Journal of Transnational Law* (2004), pp. 189–227.

In Ireland, donor-assisted human reproduction (DAHR) services are accessed by married couples – including female couples – and by single women but are fraught with legal complications.[95] It's failure to introduce specific legislative provisions to regulate assisted reproduction techniques (1 of 6 out of 43 European countries not to have done so) must adversely affect the number of Irish couples able to found a family by such means.[96] In Australia and in New Zealand, assisted reproduction treatment services are widely available; indeed, it is estimated that approximately 4% of Australian babies are born as a result of IVF.

Use of embryos

Research involving human embryos and stem cells has been at the heart of improved fertility treatment (AID, GIFT, etc.), including donor embryo implantation, but it remains a complex area of ethics and law: much contention surrounds the moral and legal status of a human embryo, and there is much uncertainty in relation to consents and ownership.

In the U.S., the majority of states allow embryo-related research, either by directly permitting it or by the absence of laws that would restrict it. However, it is probable that the states currently passing laws to prohibit or seriously restrict abortion will extend those constraints to laws related to embryo and foetal tissue research. As a result, the U.S. – in the absence of any federal policy or law – is rapidly developing a complicated patchwork of state laws relating to the use of embryos.[97] In the UK, the law would seem to have moved a step closer towards recognition of embryos as having some degree of legal status for the purposes of family law. In *Jennings v. Human Fertilisation and Embryology Authority*,[98] the applicant sought court permission to found a family by using his deceased wife's eggs (she clearly not being in a position to give her consent). The court granted his application for 'a declaration that it is lawful for him to use an embryo created using his sperm and the eggs of his late wife . . . in treatment with a surrogate'. In so doing, it drew upon the ECHR, Article 8, jurisprudence to note regarding the applicant:

> Article 8 right to respect for the decision to become a parent in the genetic sense has been interfered with. The interference with that right is not proportionate on the facts of this case. . . . There are no weighty countervailing factors to justify the significant interference.[99]

95 See, for example, *Roche v. Roche* (2010) 2 IR 321.
96 See, further, at: www.eurekalert.org/pub_releases/2020-02/esoh-emt020320.php
97 See, for example, Matthews, K.R.W. and Morali, D., 'Can We Do That Here? An Analysis of US Federal and State Policies Guiding Human Embryo and Embryoid Research', *Journal of Law and the Biosciences*, Vol. 9, No. 1 (2022), at: www.ncbi.nlm.nih.gov/pmc/articles/PMC9183789/
98 (2022) EWHC 1619 (Fam).
99 Ibid, at para 102.

It is probable that national laws in general are having difficulty in catching up with the advancement of medical research in this area (see, also, Chapter 6).

Methods of founding families

While advances in medical science continue to broaden the ways available for founding a family, these are supplemented by more orthodox methods of doing so.

Adoption

Adoption, traditionally the most archetypal alternative to procreation as a method of founding a family, would seem to have evolved to function as a safety valve for tensions in contemporary western society: its functions have been adapted to relieve pressure in areas where other legal proceedings are insufficient or inappropriate to cope with the needs of nuclear impermanent family units within a more fluid cosmopolitan society. Arguably, the role it currently plays in any such society is a telling indicator of the overall public-private balance being struck in that nation's family law processes (see, further, Chapter 8).

Kinship and step-parent

Adoption in all modern developed nations is now dominated by these two types of applicants, which – in a reversal of its traditional legal role – almost always results in a continuation of established care arrangements within a settled family environment while also facilitating an 'openness' in relationships between the adoptee and his or her birth parents. As marriage becomes less popular and less durable and parenting arrangements more fluid, so an adoption order has come to be regarded as a useful authority for securing the boundaries of a reformed family unit.[100]

Public care system

By the early decades of the 21st century, in keeping with long-established U.S. practice, UK government policy aimed to provide permanent family life for children in the public care system by accelerating the number and pace of non-consensual adoptions. While these were not the only countries to do so, they were the first to prioritise this option for such children, to provide considerable public funds to support adopters and to succeed in using this route to found families for significant numbers of children. This strategy of mainstreaming adoption into child care and protection policy created a new platform for addressing the needs of children failed by their parents and was made possible by embedding the paramountcy principle into child care law. It was an approach that attracted criticism from the CRC

100 See, Utting (1995), who noted that 40% of marriages end in divorce, 20% of families are headed by a lone parent and 8% of dependent children live in step families.

which expressed concern that 'parents have not been provided with adequate family support' and that 'children have reportedly been removed from their biological families owing to the family's economic situation or because a foster family may provide a more beneficial environment for the child'[101] (see, further, Chapter 10).

Children with complex or 'special needs'

Founding a family by way of adoption has radically changed in recent years. In all western societies, the reduction in the number of voluntarily relinquished healthy babies has led to prospective adopters broadening their outlook. This has been matched by a commensurate change in the factors governing the availability of children, particularly babies. Previously, the few children with complex health care or special needs, unwanted or inadequately cared for by their birth parents, would have been consigned to long-term institutional care. Due to the advances made in medical sciences, many more vulnerable children are surviving and may need an intensity of care well beyond the abilities of 'average' parents. Such children (e.g. older, with behaviour problems, with health care needs or members of sibling groups), are now often successfully placed for adoption; most often with ongoing professional and financial support.

Intercountry

Founding a family by acquiring a child in one jurisdiction by citizens, resident and domiciled in another, who either adopt the child in his or her country or return with the child and initiate adoption proceedings, is a phenomenon that has decreased sharply in recent years for a variety of reasons, including the controls imposed by the Hague Convention. For perhaps 50 years, there had been a steady flow of children from less developed countries into the homes of adoptive couples in western society, particularly from the Philippines, Korea, Russia, China and South America towards Scandinavia and the U.S.[102] There was a clear correlation between intercountry adoption and child care adoption: nations with a high rate of dependency on the former also had low rates of availability via the latter; while social class (intercountry adoption is expensive), racial bias (white Caucasian prospective adopters tended to look towards Russia, Romania and Eastern Europe rather than to Africa for children), a resistance to openness (post-adoption contact with birth family members was for some an unwanted extra) and a preference for babies, all played a part in making intercountry adoption an attractive route for founding a family. However, the effects of Hague Convention constraints, coupled with the growth in surrogacy and in the reluctance of developing nations to participate in

101 See, UN Committee on the Rights of the Child, 2016, *op cit* at para 52.

102 See, for example, the account of 20 years of such experience in Dalen, M. and Saetersdal, B., 'Transracial Adoption in Norway', *Adoption & Fostering*, Vol. 2, No. 4 (1987). Also, Ngabonziza, D., 'Inter-country Adoption in Whose Best Interests', *Adoption & Fostering*, Vol. 2, No. 1 (1988).

what some interpret as a form of 'trafficking', have combined to drastically reduce the numbers of children now available.

Foster care

By the early decades of the 21st century, most children entering national public care systems were being placed with foster parents, rather than in institutional care, in keeping with research findings from psychologists and others clearly indicating that family life was more conducive to the psycho-social developmental needs of children than institutions. The same approach was successfully extended to many children with a disability.

The common law jurisdictions

Whereas previously, it could have been anticipated that children with a degree of physical or learning impairment would have remained in residential care, this is no longer necessarily the case. The new focus on providing family life for children, who might otherwise be retained in institutional care, has been due to the influence of equality and non-discrimination legislation: in all countries, the authorities have been pushed to extend equal opportunities for the promotion of welfare interests, through permanent family care, to children with more complex needs. However, adoption and foster care offer alternative forms of family life – in terms of permanence, security and parity of esteem if not in terms of quality – access to which is wholly dependent upon the respective legal constraints imposed by domestic child care legislation. Such constraints favour the use of foster care or kinship care rather than adoption placements in Ireland, Canada, New Zealand and most of Australia (see, also, Chapter 10).

The civil law jurisdictions

France and Germany differ from their common law counterparts in that they both rely heavily on residential care – rather than on adoption or foster care – to accommodate children admitted to their public care systems.

Surrogacy

Surrogacy has been judicially defined as 'an arrangement whereby a woman (the "surrogate mother") agrees to conceive and bear a child, which she intends to another or others (the "commissioning couple" or the "commissioning husband" and "commissioning wife") upon the child's birth'.[103] This method for founding a family may proceed either on a commercial basis or on an altruistic basis. In the latter case, any payment is restricted to the reimbursement of medical and other expenses. Most nations permit the latter but not the former.

103 *Lowe & Barry and Anor* (2011) FamCA 625 at para 5.

Among the problems associated with surrogacy is that the information the child receives will be entirely at parental discretion with resulting crucial implications for the development of his or her identity and cultural affiliation: due to the anonymity surrounding the use of genetic material, a child may never know their true genetic origins. More immediately, as has been pointed out, there may be questions as to the child's parentage and nationality:[104]

Often, commissioning parents may not be recorded on the birth certificate of the surrogate child. This can create difficulties in obtaining passports and travel documents for the child to enable him or her to accompany the commissioning parent's home. If parentage and nationality cannot be established, there is the potential that the child may be left 'marooned, stateless and parentless'.[105]

Commercial surrogacy has increased exponentially over recent years and, although subject to widely different domestic regulatory regimes, will very probably continue to grow, in part due to its attractions for same-sex couples (see, further, Chapter 6).

Founding families and family life in an Indigenous context

There was a commonality in the colonialists' impact upon the lives of Indigenous people – whether intentional or not – that resulted in similar problems for their communities, their family life and the welfare of their children. This includes inter-generational trauma resulting from systematic assimilation policies, community dislocation and cultural disruption. As a consequence, the contemporary governments of the CANZUS nations have been faced with the challenge of how to adapt national institutions to address and redress Indigenous family and community issues. Primarily, they have all had to consider the gross and consistent over-representation of Indigenous children in their national child welfare and youth justice systems: adjusting the family law system so that it functions with equity and proportionality while at the same time taking the necessary measures to keep the children concerned connected to their families, their communities and their cultural identity (see, also, Chapter 8).

The legal framework

The CANZUS nations have ratified the UN CROC, excepting the U.S., become signatory nations to the UN DRIP and have signed and ratified most other major international treaties, conventions and protocols, including the International Covenant on Civil and Political Rights (ICCPR) 1966, the International Covenant on Economic, Social and Cultural Rights (ICESCR) 1966 and the International

104 See, Pascoe, C.J., 'Issues of Forced Adoption and International Commercial Surrogacy, Federal Court of Australia, Melbourne' (2 October 2013), at: www.law.monash.edu.au/about-us/events/chie-judge-pascoe-dpeech-notes.pdf

105 See, *Re X & Y (Foreign Surrogacy)* (2009) Fam 71 at 76C.

Convention on the Elimination of all forms of Racial Discrimination (ICERD) 1965. However, while this international framework of rights applies with equal force to Indigenous as it does to non-Indigenous citizens, in practice, generations of cultural dissonance and the experience of social marginalisation has left the former unable to fully avail of these protective provisions. As a consequence of earlier experiences, any form of state intervention – even if benign and services oriented – may be viewed as a threat to the presevation of family unity, carrying with it connotations of previous violations to the cultural integrity of their community, and is, therefore, liable to be avoided (see, further, Chapter 8).

Founding families and family life

Traditionally, and currently – if to a lesser degree – Indigenous people regard the concept of a 'nuclear family unit' is anathema: their critical organisational construct is the tribe, an extended kinship organisation comprised of 'bands' and extended kinship groups. There are cultural Euro-centric misconceptions regarding the understanding of 'family' in an Indigenous context which differs from its counterpart in the developed world by being extended, to include blood relations – living in close proximity – such as grandparents, cousins, uncles and aunts; to be complex, in particular by sharing child rearing responsibilities which seldom fall exclusively upon birth parents; and by being mobile, with no fixed concept of 'home' but moving between geographic and kith and kin boundaries. Indeed, kinship is the bond that connects a band or tribe and differentiates it from all others. It is not uncommon for a child to be given by the parents, usually to relatives or even to non-relatives within the tribe, to be raised by them, but the child remains aware of who his or her birth parents are and may well be in frequent contact with them. These kinship caregivers often have greater rights and responsibilities in relation to the child than the genetic parents.

Family planning

From 16 years of age, a child who is denied the permission of their parent or other guardian to undertake, for example, medical treatment, an operation, dental procedure, blood transfusion, commit to marriage or a civil union, may take such decisions themselves or refer the matter to the court or other authority. The fact that a younger female could legally access contraceptives and consent, or refuse consent, to an abortion can give rise to issues.

Cultural identity

For Indigenous individuals and communities, their culture shapes their identity – as it does for many if not all ethnic groups – and explains why it is viewed as being of fundamental importance. Cultural identity has survived to a varying degree and with varying levels of official recognition and respect, among the Indigenous communities of the CANZUS nations. It is based on the assumption that children are best raised within their own cultural context, with and by their own people, and only then can an out-of-home placement be compliant with an Indigenous child's welfare interests or rights. It allows tribal elders to take an active leadership role in family group discussions and requires professional workers to observe – or at least not to ignore – cultural preferences and custom.

Out-of-home placements

Following lengthy and exhaustive official enquiries into historical state sanctioned abusive residential school and enforced adoption policies that sought to eradicate Indigenous culture, there is now a shared awareness of the need to demonstrate respect for cultural identity.[106] This is emphasised in UN CROC, articles 30 and 31, which declare the right of a child from a minority group to practise their culture.

The legal systems of the CANZUS nations make a distinction in their treatment of Indigenous and non-Indigenous children premised on identity concerns: about the justification for separating an Indigenous child from his or her cultural connections and for imposing constraints on the opportunity to be raised within their culture of birth. They have all adopted similar approaches when choosing permanency options for Indigenous children[107] which are variations of the Australian Child Placement Principle. This states that when an Indigenous child needs an alternative to parental care, then every precaution must be taken to enhance and preserve the child's connection to family and community and to sustain their sense of identity and culture.[108] The preferred placement is – in the following order of priority – within the child's extended family or within the child's Indigenous community or, failing that, with other Indigenous people.[109]

Adoption: the law and its effects

To a large extent, the Indigenous experience of family law has functioned separately and in parallel with the statutory law, only conforming when necessary to

106 See, further, O'Halloran, K., *Children, the Law and the Welfare Principle: Perspectives from North America*, and *Children, the Law and the Welfare Principle: Perspectives from Australia and New Zealand*, Routledge, 2023.

107 In the U.S., the Indian Child Welfare Act 1978 specifies that decisions should be made so that Native American (Indian) children can remain within their communities, and it gives the tribal authority exclusive jurisdiction over children on reservations controlled by the tribe. However, in contrast, the Multiethnic Placement Act 1994 forbids states to use race and ethnicity of non-Indigenous Americans to deny an adoption placement.

108 See, for example, Burton, J., et al., 'The Aboriginal and Torres Strait Islander Child Placement Principle: A Guide to Support Implementation', the Secretariat of National Aboriginal and Islander Child Care (2018), at: https://www.aihw.gov.au/reports/child-protection/atsicpp-indicators/contents/background

109 For an insightful account from the perspective of an Indigenous foster parent and lawyer, see McGlade, H., 'My Journey into Child Protection and Aboriginal Family Led Decision Making', *Australian Feminist Law Journal* (2020), pp. 1–18.

comply with official registration requirements. In all CANZUS nations, there have been systemic failings in the efforts made to marry Indigenous cultural custom and practice with statutory law.

Customary adoption

This is the placement of a child for adoption within the extended family group: bloodlines are of fundamental importance to Indigenous communities as is the family history and the particular cultural heritage of the tribe; only in exceptional circumstances is the child placed with 'strangers' or non-relatives as the lack of a blood-tie is perceived as compromising the child's lineage and to that extent would be contrary to their welfare interests and bring shame on the birth family and the tribe as a whole. Customary adoption was and is organised to ensure that the blood-ties of the children involved are respected and maintained.

Statutory adoption

Because the blood-link is so important to Indigenous communities, legal relationships should not hide or terminate blood relationships nor obscure cultural identity. However, in all CANZUS nations, the number of Indigenous children entering the public care system – and possibly becoming available for adoption – far exceeds the number of prospective Indigenous adopters. For many Indigenous children, there is no possibility of an Indigenous placement, so they must be diverted into the statutory process and be placed with approved foster parents or adopters. For reasons of defraying public costs and for promoting the welfare interests of children within 'families for life', the need to use non-Indigenous adopters is a forced choice if permanency placements are to be found for children failed by parental care. This has become a very divisive public policy issue in the CANZUS nations, one that resonates with historical trauma.

Family life

The annual rate of orders used to remove Indigenous children – particularly babies – into the public care system has been the subject of official enquiries (e.g. an internal practice review by *Oranga Tamariki*[110] and a subsequent Māori enquiry, *Time for Change*).[111] In New Zealand, for example, a 2020 report by the Children's Commissioner found that Māori children were five times more likely to be taken into

110 The findings of the internal review were published on 5 November, 2019, citing conclusive evidence of systemic failure by *Oranga Tamariki* in the case of the Hawke's Bay uplift, at: www.orangatamariki.govt.nz/assets/Uploads/News/2019/Practice- Review/Practice-Review.pdfwww.orangatamariki.govt.nz/assets/Uploads/News/2019/Practice-Review/Practice-Review.pdf

111 *Ko Te Wā Whakawhiti, It's Time For Change: a Māori Inquiry into Oranga Tamariki* – Summary Report (2020), at: https://whanauora.nz/wp-content/uploads/2021/06/EXECUTIVE-SUMMARY-REPORT.pdf

care than other children, while the Human Rights Commissioner commented on what was termed 'systemic racism', a perception that mirrors criticisms made of Canadian child welfare agencies and is evidenced by similar facts.[112] In both countries, as in other CANZUS nations, there are good grounds for considering that a cultural clash is playing a part: Caucasian child welfare staff do not seem to always respect Indigenous practices such as allowing extended family members and others to share child care responsibilities with birth parents, avoidance of routine health checks and reliance on traditional medicines, inconsistent school attendance and preference for the teaching of tribal elders, etc.

However, it must also be noted that in all probability, there may also be a correlation between the high admissions of Indigenous children to the care system and the abnormally high levels of domestic violence in their communities.

Welfare interests

It is well documented that Indigenous children experience disproportionate disadvantage across a range of domains, including health and education.[113] This results in the high rates of neglect that have become so characteristic of many Indigenous communities, including a considerably higher infant mortality rate, greater exposure to domestic violence, lower life expectancy, poorer rate of educational achievement and a higher burden of disease. Also, a particular and long-standing issue for child protection in an Indigenous context is the prevalence of child sexual abuse. While this subject has attracted some academic research, it has eluded intervention by the authorities to address its causes and effects.[114]

It would appear that as regards Indigenous children, the welfare principle is severely constrained. It fails to have much effect on consensual state intervention which may be viewed at best as unsuccessful in the provision of sufficient, relevant and accessible family supportive services. It also fails to have much effect on coercive state intervention as evidenced by the consistently disproportionate admission of Indigenous children to the public care and juvenile justice systems.[115]

Conclusion

State retreat from family affairs is as pronounced in the earlier jurisdictions as elsewhere in the developed world. This has, perhaps, become most apparent from

112 See, further, at: www.theguardian.com/world/2021/jan/22/new-zealand-child-welfare-head-resigns-amid-furore-over-maori-baby-separations-oranga-tamariki

113 See, for example, the Steering Committee for the Review of Government Services Provision, *Overcoming Indigenous Disadvantage: Key Indicators 2016*, Productivity Commission, Canberra, 2016.

114 See, McGlade, H., *Our Greatest Challenge*, Aboriginal Studies Press, 2012.

115 See, further, O'Halloran, K., *Children, the Law and the Welfare Principle: Perspectives from North America*, Routledge, 2023, at chapter 8 and *Children, the Law and the Welfare Principle: Perspectives from Australia & New Zealand*, Routledge, 2023, at chapters 9 and 10.

the media attention given to medical issues. These countries have followed others in recently transferring crucial decision-making responsibility from the public to the private realm, for example, as regards the right to medical assistance to end one's own life, as also with the right to avoid such assistance in relation to gender transitioning – both in law now being largely matters of private choice. A creeping ambivalence is also emerging in relation to other medical issues. Commercial surrogacy, IVF, gene editing, access to certain contraceptives and certainly to abortion are all up for debate as to whether they might fall more in the realm of public or private business. They also necessarily impact upon children, their welfare and, indeed, their very existence.

In recent years, the state has stepped aside from benchmarks which for countless generations determined that marriage was a union characterised by monogamy, heterosexuality and mutual lifelong commitment. In the common law and civil law jurisdictions presently being considered, as in others, the introduction of changes, such as 'no-fault' divorce, recognition of cohabiting partnerships, same-sex marriage and the extension of the rights to adopt and foster to same-sex couples, have irrevocably altered the legal definition and cultural significance of those twin traditional social constructs 'marriage' and 'family'.

The focus of the law is now as likely to be on household and parenting arrangements as on 'family'.

7 Adoption

Introduction

Not only is there no legal right to found a family by means of adoption[1] but also, there have been a number of judicial reminders that the purpose of adoption is to provide a child with a family, not a family with a child. As expressed nearly half a century ago, 'providing homes for children who need them is its primary purpose'.[2]

This chapter, like the others in Parts II and III, begins by identifying and explaining the core concepts and principles before outlining the relevant framework of international law. It then examines international caselaw – primarily that generated by the ECtHR – to determine the main characteristics of the relationship between adoption law and the welfare interests/rights of the child. It then conducts a comparative jurisdictional evaluation to ascertain the extent to which each jurisdiction embodies these characteristics and benchmarks the jurisdictions against relevant articles of the UN CROC.

Concepts, constructs, principles and the law

Insofar as it is amenable to a conceptual interpretation, adoption addresses the act of the adopter. It is the voluntary acceptance of the responsibility to protect, nurture and promote the development of the child of another – at least until that child attains adulthood – that lies at the heart of adoption.

Concepts and principles

From the outset, the statutory process for a 'full' adoption was viewed and treated as essentially a matter of private family law – in fact, the most private of all family proceedings. Its primary characteristics were as follows: confidentiality, guarantees

1 See, *X v. Belgium and The Netherlands,* Application No. 6482/147 (1975) 7 DR 75. The absence of such a right was also considered in *Pini and Others v. Romania* (2004) EHRR 275.

2 See, Houghton Committee, *Report of the Departmental Committee on the Adoption of Children* (Cmnd 5107), HMSO, London, 1972.

DOI: 10.4324/9781003269595-11

of anonymity were given to adopters and to the birth parent/s, the court used serial numbers to hide the identity of children and there was a lack of access to agency files, etc.; permanency, this most absolute of family court orders retained its binding effect on all involved at least until the child concerned reached maturity; and exclusivity, all parental rights and duties of birth parents were extinguished, a full complement of parental responsibilities were vested in the adopters, achieving a quick, clean and absolute break between the child and birth family which permitted no form of ongoing intrusion into the affairs of the new family. In most countries, his cloak of secrecy was steadily lifted in the late 20th century, particularly as regards facilitating an adoptee's right of access to personal identity information.

Consent

For most of the history of adoption, it has in the main been a consensual process, resting on the freely given consent of the birth parent/s or on the absence of any need for it due to the child being orphaned or abandoned. During that period, the role of the child was one of silent acquiescence.

Consensual adoption

UN CROC, Article 21, states that 'competent authorities' must ensure that 'if required, the persons concerned have given their informed consent to the adoption on the basis of such counselling as may be necessary'. Consequently, in consensual adoptions, the law has focused on the evidence necessary to establish the existence of a free and fully informed consent – the fact, its form and the circumstances in which it was given.

Non-consensual adoption

In recent years, the non-consensual proportion of annual applications has slowly grown, mainly in the U.S. and the UK, driven by a 'permanency planning' policy based on the belief that children entering the public child care system need the security of a permanent family if they are to avoid drift in the system and serial foster care placements. Instead, in order to be given the opportunity to form the emotional attachments necessary for their psycho-social development, the rights of their parents are judicially removed and the children are 'freed' for adoption. This increase in child care adoptions has brought with it controversy as to the proper balance to be struck between the grounds on which a birth parent may withhold consent and the welfare interests of their child.

Welfare interests of the child

Adoption legislation in the jurisdictions being considered has probably always required that every application be subject to the 'welfare test', meaning that the order if made would be at least compatible with the child's welfare interests which could comprise 'material and financial prospects, education, general surroundings, happiness, stability of home and the like'.[3] Traditionally, the comparative material advantages[4] available in the home of adopting parents would have been judged insufficient justification in itself for severing a child's links with his or her birth parents. So also, reasons such as 'legitimation',[5] immigration[6] or simply to change a child's name[7] have similarly been held to be insufficient. In recent years, the courts have in general become more insistent that the term be interpreted in relation to the particular circumstances of the child concerned, that it be given a greater weighting relative to other factors and that it can be predicted to be beneficial for the foreseeable future.

Paramountcy

Article 21 of UN CROC declares that States Parties that 'recognize and/or permit the system of adoption shall ensure that the best interests of the child shall be the paramount consideration'. This has been held to establish that the best interests of the child are to be the paramount consideration in all matters related to adoption.[8] Therefore, where – as in *Hendricks v. The Netherlands*[9] – there is a conflict between the rights and interests of the child and those of a parent which can only be resolved to the disadvantage of one of them, the interests of the child must prevail. In *Yousef v. The Netherlands*,[10] the ECtHR for the first time used the phrase 'paramountcy of welfare' when comparing the interests of a child with those of the parent.[11]

> The Court reiterates that in judicial decisions where the rights under Article 8 of parents and those of a child are at stake, the child's rights must be the paramount consideration. If any balancing of interests is necessary, the interests of the child must prevail.

In neither France nor Germany is paramountcy established in the national law as the governing principle. In both, the 'simple' form of adoption is widely used, though in Germany, this is no longer permitted in respect of children. This has several characteristics which militate against the process being governed by the

3 See, *Re B* (1971) 1 QB 437, per Davies L J at p. 443.
4 See, *Re D (No. 2)* (1959) 1 QB 229.
5 See, for example, *CD Petitioners* (1963) SLT (Sh Crt) 7.
6 See, for example, *In re A (An Infant)* (1963) 1 WLR 34. Also, see, *In re H (A Minor: Non-Patrial)* (1982) Fam Law 121, where an adoption order was granted in respect of an immigrant child despite contrary advice from the Secretary of State.
7 See, for example, *In re D (Minors)* (1973) Fam 209.
8 Also established by Article 24 of the African Charter on the Rights and Welfare of the Child and Article 4 of the European Convention on the Adoption of Children (Revised).
9 (1982) 5 EHRR 223. See also *Kroon v. The Netherlands* (1994) Series A No. 297–C, 19 EHRR 263, where the court commented that it was a principle of good law to hold that the interests of the child were paramount.
10 (2003) 1 FLR 210.
11 Ibid at para 73. Also, see: *R and H v. United Kingdom* (2012) 54 EHRR 2 (2011) 2 FLR 1236.

paramountcy principle, including the probability that most placements will be made directly by a birth parent or by an intermediary acting on their behalf, either of whom may be open to undue influence; the absence of any objective professional assessment of the needs of a child relative to the coping capacity and related resources of the adopters; and the lack of any provision for post-adoption assessment of whether the placement has proven to be compatible with the child's best interests.[12]

Openness

In sharp contrast to traditional practice – which featured anonymity, secrecy and associated taboos – the probability of an adopted child retaining some degree of contact with his or her birth family has greatly increased in recent years, though less so in Germany. The principle of 'openness' is now standard practice in almost all jurisdictions – ranging from an exchange of letters to face-to-face engagement – and extends to facilitating post-adoption access to identifying information. It most probably originated in customary adoption as practiced throughout the Indigenous communities in the CANZUS nations. However, although transparency and information disclosure are embedded in Australian statute law, this is not the case in New Zealand, while the issue of 'sealed files' has been a perennial problem in the U.S. and is a legacy issue in Ireland, while the maternal anonymity option continues to accompany the relinquishment right of French mothers.

Openness has been greatly facilitated by the relatively recent legal requirement that adoption should accommodate ongoing contact between birth family members and the adoptee, where this is considered conducive to the latter's welfare. A consequence of the broad impact that human rights awareness has had upon adoption, this development has swept away the traditional exclusivity rights of adopters. The former rights of adopters have been undermined by a new judicial attentiveness to principles of 'cultural affirmation' and 'private life', together with respect for the importance of a child's continuity of attachments and of the right to an authentic independent identity.

Constructs

Adoption varies according to its social context. It neither has been nor is confined to children; many countries permit the adoption of adults. In Japan, for instance, its main legal function and use is to establish a fiduciary relationship between adopters and an adult male chosen to continue the business interests of the former, a practice which has resulted in some 'adoptees' entering into serial adoptions for personal profit. Even in its traditional form – to found a family – it need not necessarily

12 However, as Jörg Reinhardt points out, simple adoptions are no longer available for children, and since 2021, all adoption placements must be made by professional staff (note to author, 06.06.2023).

fully create a parent-child legal relationship: a legal distinction between 'full' and 'simple' adoption is maintained in several jurisdictions.

Accouchement sous le secret

Traditionally, a woman's right, under Article 341 of the Civil Code, to give birth anonymously was known as *accouchement sous X* (because the birth mother was recorded on the birth certificate issued in the maternity hospital as 'X' and the child was referred to as '*né sous X*'), but records now refer simply to an 'anonymous delivery' and to the mother as 'X'.[13] The right to anonymity, added to the Civil Code in 1993, has existed in one form or another since 1793 when, under the National Convention of the French Revolution, secret pregnancies and births were protected by law.[14] It is the absence of recognition by the mother of the child (or denial of filiation) to whom she had given birth anonymously that removes the necessity to obtain her consent for the child to be taken into state care.[15]

This right was examined by the ECtHR in the course of its judgment in *Odièvre v. France*.[16] At that time, the court decided in favour of upholding the right of anonymity, despite finding that the concept of anonymous births is relatively rare throughout Europe. In fact, as the court noted, a far greater number of states actually require the names of both mother and father to be registered at birth. In January 2002, this right was modified by the introduction of a law allowing mothers who have a baby in secret to place their name in a sealed envelope. Arguably, in the absence of any further modification, the law still leaves intact the maternal right to choose permanent anonymity. It also, of course, prevents any assertion of paternal legal rights and any discovery of origins information by the adoptee.

The consent to place for adoption a child who is the subject of an '*accouchement sous X*' process is given in effect by the appropriate state authority. Such a placement, by virtue of the provisions of Article 352 of the Civil Code, constitutes a bar not only to the return of the child to the mother but also to any declaration of filiation or recognition.

Full and simple adoptions

'Adoption' in law may be either 'full/plenary' or 'simple': in the former, the legal relationship between the birth parent/s and their child is terminated; in the latter,

13 Article 341–1 of the Civil Code, introduced in 1993, precludes a child born to X from establishing any legal tie to the mother, even if her identity should be discovered. The law has been relaxed somewhat by Statute n° 2009–61 of 16 January 2009. See, also, Art. 325 of the Civil Code. The legal claim is available to the child, where he/she has no legal filiation at all and no de facto parent-child ties. But in practice, this almost never happens for X children since almost all are adopted within their first 10 months. Therefore, the claim is barred due to the establishment of the adoptive filiation link.

14 Statute of 27 June 1904 and Decret-Loi of 2 September 1941. Also, see, Donovan, K., 'Real Mothers for Abandoned Children', *Law & Society Review* (2002), p. 1.

15 See, Article L. 224–4, point (1), of the Social Action and Families Code.

16 (2003) 1 FCR 621. Also, see, *Kearns v. France* Application No. 35991/04, ECHR, 10.01.08.

this relationship is not completely severed.[17] Countries such as the UK, the U.S., Australia and Ireland only give legal recognition to full adoptions, while many others – including France and Germany – also recognise the simple form, though in Germany, children are restricted to the full form. Article 26 of the Hague Convention gives recognition to both forms, and Article 27 empowers a receiving country to convert a simple adoption into a full adoption if the law of that country permits such a conversion and if the appropriate consents are available.

Kafala

This alternative to adoption, widely used in Islamic countries and by Muslims living elsewhere, circumvents the *Quor'an* prohibition[18] on legally mixing bloodlines by facilitating the raising of another's child as the carer's own while providing safeguards to prevent full legal assimilation into the carers' family: the birth parent/s can never be replaced by adopters; the former retain important rights. UNCROC, Article 20(3), expressly refers to adoption and *kafala* as separate institutions; the Hague Convention is, therefore, inapplicable.[19]

Kafala and statutory adoption

The difference between statutory adoption and *kafala* is one which may jeopardise the human rights of those involved, particularly the children, many of whom have been taken into public care due to the concern of authorities about their uncertain legal status and the absence of a parent within the jurisdiction. Not only are some children denied the opportunity of 'full' domestic adoption but some 20 Islamic states also wholly prohibit intercountry adoption. On the other hand, 'the conversion of a *kafala* guardianship arrangement into a domestic adoption, once the child has been brought back to the receiving country, has also been used to circumvent intercountry adoption procedures under the 1993 Hague Convention'.[20]

International law

The relevant European legal framework is comprised of the European Convention on Human Rights (ECHR), the Brussels II bis Regulation, in conjunction with the

17 It might be noted that although the 'plenary' or 'simple' form of adoption has, for many generations, been upheld in countries such as the UK and Ireland as the 'gold standard', it has now become quite contentious. This is due to factors such as the following: adoption becoming more 'open' and adoptees now very often older children, with attachments, rather than babies; the preponderance of step- and kinship adopters; and ECtHR caselaw placing growing importance on personal identity, cultural links and maintaining relationships with birth family members. See, for example, Quellette, F-R., 'The Social Temporalities of Adoption and the Limits of Plenary Adoption', in Briggs, L. and Maure, D. (eds.), *International Adoption*, New York University Press, 2009, at Chapter 3.

18 *Quor'an*, verse 33 and the Sura, verses 4 and 5.

19 See, also, the Brussels II Regulation, 2005.

20 Special Rapporteur report, A/HRC/34/55, *op cit* at para 49.

EU Charter of Fundamental Rights, in particular, Article 24, together with UN CROC. Some have a wide international reach (e.g. the UDHR, ECHR, UN CRC, the Hague Convention and the ICCPR), while others are regional (e.g. the African Charter on the Rights and Welfare of the Child).

United Nations Guidelines for the Alternative Care of Children 2009

These Guidelines were intended to enhance UN CROC implementation 'regarding the protection and well-being of children deprived of parental care or who are at risk of being so' (para 3). They start from the general principle that efforts should primarily be directed towards enabling children to remain in or return to the care of their parents (see, further, Chapter 5).

The European Convention on the Adoption of Children 2008

The provisions introduced by this Convention include the following:

- a requirement that the father's consent be obtained in all cases, even when the child is born out of wedlock;
- a requirement that the child's consent be obtained if the child has sufficient understanding to give it;
- a requirement that adoption be available to heterosexual unmarried couples who have entered into a registered partnership in states which recognise that institution and to single applicants;
- it also leaves states free to extend adoptions to homosexual couples and same-sex couples living together in a stable relationship;
- a requirement that a better balance be struck between adopted children's right to know their identity and the right of the biological parents to remain anonymous; and
- a requirement that the minimum age of an adopter must be between 18 and 30 and the age difference between adopter and child should preferably be at least 16 years.

Intended to enhance UN CROC implementation 'regarding the protection and well-being of children deprived of parental care or who are at risk of being so' (para 3), the Guidelines start from the general principle that efforts should primarily be directed towards enabling children to remain in or return to the care of their parents (see, further, Chapter 5).

The Hague Conference on Private International Law

The increased mobility of families in the latter part of the 20th century was accompanied by ever more cross-jurisdictional disputes concerning matters such as marriage, divorce, child abduction and adoption. In an attempt to substitute international agreement for bilateral negotiations on the rules and procedures for regulating such matters, the Hague Conference on Private International Law held a number of conferences to develop conventions that would state the relevant agreed principles, standards and rules.[21] Eventually, four conventions concerning children were produced, including the Hague Convention on Protection of Children and Co-operation in Respect of Intercountry Adoption 1993.[22] The latter was a response to increased concern regarding trafficking in children, perhaps generated in particular by the international interest in rescuing children from the orphanages of post-Ceausescu Romania (see, further, next section).

Implementation of the earlier Hague Conventions, however, continues to depend upon the voluntary co-operation of signatory states. While the 1993 Convention aimed to raise standards of practice, it cannot be said to have a strictly regulatory function. It stops short of prohibiting non-agency adoptions: prospective adopters remain free to make their own private independent adoption arrangements, though these are not encouraged and are restricted.[23] Its administrative bodies are purely advisory in nature.

The Hague Conference Permanent Bureau

The bureau provides a supervisory function for the Hague Convention. It gives effect to its role by monitoring practice and issuing extensive guidance on ICA issues options.[24] So, for example, in its *Good Practice Guide,* it recognised a need for the stricter accreditation and authorisation of agencies involved in ICA, with special attention to the professional quality and scope of the services they provide and to ensuring that their numbers are not greater than those needed.

The Hague Convention on Protection of Children and Co-operation in Respect of Intercountry Adoption 1993

Of the four Hague Conventions on matters relating to children,[25] this one has the distinction of being truly international due to the near global reach of its

21 See, for example, Dyer, A., 'The Internationalisation of Family Law', *UC Davis Law Review*, Vol. 30 (1997), p. 625.

22 The other two being the Convention on the Civil Aspects of International Child Abduction 1980 and the Convention on Jurisdiction, Applicable Law, Recognition, Enforcement, and Co-operation in Respect of Parental Responsibility and Measures for the Protection of Children 1996.

23 The Report of the Hague's Special Commission on the Practical Operation of the Convention in 2005 recommended that member countries actively discourage direct contacts between prospective adoptive parents and authorities in the child's country of origin until authorised to do so by those authorities.

24 See, the Permanent Bureau, 'The Implementation and Operation of the 1993 Hague International Adoption Convention: A Guide to Good Practice', the Hague, 2008. Also, see publications by the Permanent Bureau in 2012, by the Working Group established to develop a common approach to preventing and addressing illicit practices in intercountry adoption cases and by the Expert Group on the Financial Aspects of Intercountry Adoption.

25 Those being the following: the Convention on the Civil Aspects of International Child Abduction 1980; the Hague Convention on Intercountry Adoption 1993; the Convention on the International Recovery of Child Support and Other Forms of Family Maintenance 2007; and the Convention on Jurisdiction, Applicable Law, Recognition, Enforcement and Co-operation in Respect of Parental Responsibility and Measures for the Protection of Children 1996.

provisions; by 2022, it had been signed by some 103 states.[26] However, it is constrained: implementation of its provisions depends upon the voluntary co-operation of signatory states; there is no regulatory body or governing authority. The Preamble explicitly states that this Convention is to be read in conjunction with the UN Convention on the Rights of the Child (UN CROC).[27] It is underpinned by principles, sometimes explicitly stated sometimes not, that are intended to guide international practice.[28]

The Hague Conference Special Commission

The 85 Member States that now constitute this body meet every five years to review national progress on relevant issues. It has taken steps to improve the operation of the Convention by publishing a guide to implementation and initiating the Intercountry Adoption Technical Assistance Programme (ICATAP) to provide support and training to those new signatory nations, such as Guatemala, that are struggling to meet Convention standards.

The main European grouping of accredited agencies, Euradopt, has also developed ethical guidelines to which its membership commits.[29] ISS and UNICEF are also very relevant.

The United Nations Convention on the Rights of the Child 1989 (UN CROC)

Signed by nearly 200 countries, this Convention has now been ratified by all UN Member States except for the United States.[30] It lists 42 substantive rights that comprehensively address the needs of children – including articles 18, 20, 21 and 35 with direct relevance to adoption – and requires the courts and regulatory bodies to ensure that decisions broadly comply with the general and specific obligations set out in the Convention. While the Convention has no specifically designated means of enforcement, signatory nations are obliged under Article 44 to provide regular reports to the UN Committee on the Rights of the Child detailing the progress made on meeting the terms of the Treaty.[31]

26 See, www.hcch.net/e/status/adoshte.html

27 The Preamble also refers to its links with the 1986 UN Declaration.

28 See, further, O'Halloran, K., *Children, the Law and the Welfare Principle: European Judicial Perspectives,* Routledge, 2024, at Chapter 1.

29 See, further, at: http://portal.euradopt.org/index.php?option=com_content&view=article&id=6&Itemid=15&lang=en

Note the 'Accreditation and Adoption Accredited Agencies: General Principles and Guide to Good Practice', Hague Conference, is available at: www.hcch.net/upload/wop/adop2010_pd02e.pdf

30 The U.S. has signed the Convention but has not yet ratified it. See, O'Connor, D., 'Children's Rights and Youth Justice in the USA', *International Family Law Journal* (2006), p. 183.

31 See, Office of the United Nations High Commissioner for Human Rights, Committee on the Rights of the Child: Monitoring Children's Rights.

Declaration on Social and Legal Principles relating to the Protection and Welfare of Children, with special reference to Foster Placement and Adoption Nationally and Internationally 1986

Articles 13 and 14 of the Declaration state, respectively, that the primary aim of adoption is to provide the child who cannot be cared for by his or her own parents with a permanent family and that in considering possible adoption placements, persons responsible for them should select the most appropriate environment for the child. It also requires that special protection be provided for intercountry adoptions when, as stated in Article 24, 'due regard shall be given to the child's cultural and religious background and interests'.

The International Covenant on Civil and Political Rights 1976 (ICCPR)

This Covenant has become particularly important because of its wide international application and accompanying monitoring process; the Optional Protocol has now been ratified by 170 countries. Some of its provisions replicate, reinforce or extend those of the UDHR and the ECHR. Its relevance for adoption is evident, for example, in the recognition given to the fundamental right to origins information implied in Article 24 and to found a family in Article 23.

The European Convention for the Protection of Human Rights and Fundamental Freedoms 1950 (ECHR)

The difficulty in establishing common benchmarks for adoption law is apparent from even the most cursory analysis of contemporary differences between nations. In many countries, for example, the steady decline in consensual domestic adoption and the unavailability of children from public child care has meant that the adoption of babies is now an almost totally intercountry phenomenon. In France and, more generally, in Europe, the absence of statutory powers to remove all parental rights and totally dispense with the need for parental consent means that the adoption experience is virtually entirely a consensual process. The corollary, of course, is that public child care institutions in those countries have a high investment in family support and long-term foster care services.

In the UK, by way of contrast, the non-consensual use of adoption in relation to children in the public care system has brought with it significant features that are becoming distinguishing characteristics of that nation's adoption experience. So, for example, the children involved are often old enough to have their views taken into consideration, for their consent to be relevant and to have a sense of personal and cultural identity; adopted in sibling groups; suffering from significant health and/or social care problems; committed to ongoing post adoption contact with their birth parents/siblings; and in all probability, will be adopted by persons qualifying for ongoing government funded assistance.

Other

An ever-growing list of international treaties, conventions, protocols, etc., are constantly enlarging the number of bodies and principles that intersect with domestic and intercountry adoption. These include the International Covenant on Economic, Social and Cultural Rights 1966 and the Committee on the Elimination of Discrimination Against Women (CEDAW). The latter, adopted in 1979 by the United Nations General Assembly, refers to the interests of children being paramount in relation to the common responsibility of men and women for their children's upbringing and development (Article 5[b]) as well as in regard to States Parties' ensuring the same rights and responsibilities between men and women as parents in matters relating to their children and in matters of guardianship, wardship, trusteeship and adoption of children (Article 16 [1][d] and [f]). The Committee reviews and makes recommendations on national reports submitted by the States Parties within one year of ratification or accession and thereafter every four years.

Also important are the following: the Convention on the Civil Aspects of International Child Abduction; the Convention on Jurisdiction, Applicable Law, Recognition, Enforcement and Cooperation in Respect of Parental Responsibility and Measures for the Protection of Children; the Charter of Fundamental Rights of the European Union 2000; and the European Convention on the Exercise of Children's Rights 1996. The Declaration on the Rights of Indigenous People 2006 makes specific reference to the special features of adoption in an Indigenous cultural context.

Adoption: established international legal standards

As with earlier chapters and those that follow, a comparative jurisdictional analysis is best facilitated by first benchmarking jurisdictional characteristics against rulings of the ECtHR, drawn from its consideration of cases arising in all 46 Council of Europe member countries[32] and with universal application to all. In particular, Article 8 of the ECHR, as developed by the rulings of the ECtHR and reinforced by its references to UN CROC, has become the primary international provision with relevance for family law in general, including adoption. Other ECHR provisions – such as Articles 6, 13 and 14 are also very relevant and are supplemented by various international instruments (see, also, Chapter 6).

These provide a baseline for identifying and broadly considering relative national differences in this legal function as it relates to the welfare interests and rights of children across Europe. This overview of established international standards paves the way for the more focused comparative analysis which then follows in relation to the six common law and two civil law jurisdictions.

Entitlement to a fair and public hearing within a reasonable time by an independent and impartial tribunal established by law

Article 6 of the ECHR is concerned with such matters as due process, e.g. where Italian authorities had prevented an adoption application in respect of a child placed in the applicants care by the authorities;[33] delay, e.g. where a parent complained of

32 Russia, the 47th member, having been expelled following its invasion of Ukraine.

33 *Moretti and Benedetti v. Italy*, Application No. 16318/07, 2010.

the 'deplorable delay' of almost 2 years in court proceedings concerning her contact application in relation to her child in local authority care;[34] legal representation, e.g. as when the Irish State had failed to either make proceedings accessible, to simplify them or to provide legal aid for the applicant who had been left to represent herself;[35] and as regards parental involvement in decision-making processes when, for example, 'the decision-making process that led to the placement of children in institutions for their adoption, which was not conducted fairly, saw the lack of effective involvement of the applicant'.[36]

Equality and non-discrimination

Article 14 of the ECHR prohibits discrimination. In *Topčić-Rosenberg v. Croatia*,[37] for example, the ECtHR found a state welfare benefit system to be discriminatory as it operated to the disadvantage of adopters of older children. In *Frette v. France*,[38] which concerned a homosexual man who had been discouraged from proceeding with an adoption application once he had disclosed his sexual orientation, the court found that there had not been a breach of Article 14. The ECtHR found that a state was entitled to draw distinctions between homosexuals and others in the adoption process and held that a ban on adoption by lesbian or gay individuals did not violate Article 14, though such a rationale would no longer seem tenable. More recently, in *A.H. and Others v. Russia*,[39] the ECtHR ruled that Russia's ban on the adoption of children by Americans was discriminatory after investigating the appeals of the 22 American parents who had already started the adoption process in Russia but could not complete because of the ban.[40]

Consents

Adoption is fundamentally a consensual process which requires the consent of both birth parents unless this cannot be obtained due to death, their whereabouts being unknown or to one or both not having parental responsibility or to the removal of all parental rights and responsibilities by court order.

Consent of child

As of 2018, a child's consent to their adoption was required from the age of 12 in only 11 of the then 47 Member States of the EU. While no reference to the necessity for such consent is mentioned in the ECHR, it is a requirement under the

34 *H v. United Kingdom* (1988) 10 EHRR 95.
35 *Airey v. Ireland* (1979) 2 EHRR 305.
36 *Case Soares de Melo v. Portugal,* Application No. 72850/14 (2017), at para 123.
37 (2013) ECHR 1131.
38 Application No. 3651/97.
39 Application Nos. 6033/13, 8927/13, 10549/13 and others (2017).
40 Ibid, at para 427.

European Convention on the Adoption of Children (revised) 2009: Article 5(1)(b) requires that adoption should not be granted by the competent authority without 'the consent of the child considered by law as having sufficient understanding'; while Article 6 adds that a child deemed to have insufficient understanding shall 'as far as possible, be consulted and his or her views and wishes shall be taken into account having regard to his or her degree of maturity'.

So, for example, in *Pini and Others v. Romania,*[41] the ECtHR had an opportunity to consider a child's rights to consent/object to their adoption. This case concerned two Romanian children who had been judicially declared to have been abandoned at the age of 3 and 7 and had been in institutional care for nine years when they were made the subjects of adoption orders issued in favour of two Italian couples. The children chose not to accompany their adopters and instead issued proceedings to have the adoption orders revoked on the grounds that they did not know their adoptive parents and did not wish to leave Romania. The ECtHR took the view that adoption meant 'giving a family to a child and not the child to a family' and noted:

> it was the expressed desire of the girls to remain where they were, and that 'their interests lay in not having imposed upon them against their will new emotional relations with people with whom they had no biological ties and whom they perceived as strangers.[42]

The children's interest meant that their opinions had to be taken into account once they had the necessary maturity to express them, which Romanian law deemed them to possess at the age of 10. The Court found that the Romanian authorities could legitimately and reasonably have considered that the applicants' right to create ties with the adopted children could not take priority over the children's interest, notwithstanding the applicants' legitimate aspirations to found a family.

Welfare interests

While the ECHR does not specifically reference this matter, it is stated to be of paramount importance by Article 21 of UN CROC, and both the Hague Convention and the EU Charter of Fundamental Rights are applicable.[43]

Family life

The right to family life requires the state to provide family-based care, whenever possible, for a child in out-of-home care and to have due regard to the child's

41 Ibid. The aforementioned account is taken from the press release issued by the Registrar of the European Court of Human Rights on 22.6.2004 and available at www.echr.coe.int/Eng/Press/2004/June/ChamberjudgmentPini&Bertini220604.htm.

42 See, further, at: http://hudoc.echr.coe.int/sites/eng-press/pages/search.aspx#{"display":["1"],"dmdocnumber":["801296"]}

43 Also, see UN CRC (2013), General Comment No. 14 on the right of the child to have his/her best interests taken as a primary consideration (Art. 3, para 1), CRC/C/GC/14, 29 May 2013.

cultural background when doing so. Accordingly, state care is now provided on a culturally sensitive basis, and transracial adoption placements are arranged only after due consideration has been given to the issues involved.

Definition of 'family'

This is accommodated by the ECtHR in its interpretation of Article 8 which guarantees the right to respect for family life. Its definition of 'family' is not restricted to one based on marriage: it includes unmarried couples, non-marital children and lesbian or homosexual relationships[44] and the children placed in such families for purposes of foster care and adoption. In *Lebbink v. The Netherlands,*[45] the ECtHR accepted that cohabitation was not an essential ingredient of 'family life'. The presumption underpinning this Article is that the entitlement of parent and child to the mutual enjoyment of each other's company constitutes a fundamental element of family life and should be protected against arbitrary action by public authorities. This approach has been upheld by the Court in cases such as *K A v. Finland*[46] and *Kutzner v. Germany*[47] in both of which it was made clear that the essential object of Article 8 of the Convention is to protect the right to respect for family life.

Article 8 does not recognise any legal right to found a family by way of adoption,[48] as this procedure is intended primarily to benefit the child rather than the adopters. It does, however, require respect for a person's private and family life and their home and correspondence, and the ECtHR has found that 'private life incorporates not only the right to respect for decisions to become and not to become a parent'[49] (though how this recognition aligns with the Court's resistance to recognising a right to abortion is a moot point). For example, *Mennesson and Others v. France* and *Labassee v. France*[50] concerned the refusal to grant legal recognition in France to parent-child relationships that had been legally established in the U.S. between children born as a result of surrogacy. In both cases, the ECtHR held that while there had been no violation of Article 8 in respect of the applicants' right to 'family life', there had been such a violation concerning the children's right to respect for their 'private life'. Also, in child care cases, as most graphically illustrated in the many instances where new-born babies were removed from the care of their hospitalised mothers, such removals often presage a placement for adoption.[51] The ECtHR has warned that draconian intervention of this nature can

44 *Keegan v. Ireland*, Application No. 16969/90 (1994) Series A No. 290, 18 EHRR 342, at para 44.

45 Application No. 35582/99, ECtHR, 01.06.2004.

46 (2003) 1 FCR 201.

47 (2003) 1 FCR 249.

48 *E.B. v. France*, Application No. 43546/02 (2008).

49 See, *Parrillo v. Italy*, Application No. 46470/11 (2015), at para 153.

50 Application Nos. 65192/11 and 65941/11 (2014). Also, see: *Foulon and Bouvet v. France*, Application Nos. 9063/14 and 10410/14 (2016); *Laborie v. France*, Application No. 44024/13 (2017); and *D. and Others v. Belgium*, Application No. 29176/13 (2014).

51 See, for example, *P, C and S v. UK.*, Application No. 56547/00 (2002). See, also, the similar case of *Venema v. The Netherlands* Application No. 35137/1977 (2002).

be a disproportionate response to the level of risk presented by the mother and may breach the latter's rights under Article 8.

Parent and child

The primary responsibility for the upbringing of a child rests with the parent/s, but the state is required to render such assistance to parents and legal guardians as may be necessary to facilitate the upbringing and development of their children.

In successive cases, the ECtHR has examined the parent-child relationship and the responsibilities of the state in relation to it. The Court has found that the mutual enjoyment by parent and child of each other's company constitutes a fundamental element of family life[52] (see, also, Chapter 6). That nexus is one which, as the ECtHR has recognised, gives the parent a 'right to personal development through their relationship with the child'.[53] So, for example, in *D.B. and Others v. Switzerland,*[54] a Swiss same-sex couple, who had acquired a child by way of a surrogacy arrangement in the U.S., complained that while the Swiss authorities had recognised the parent-child relationship between the genetic father (the second applicant) and the child, they had refused to recognise the parent-child relationship of the first applicant. Consequently, the applicants had been left for many years with no possibility of securing a definitive recognition of their parent child relationship. The ECtHR held that there had been a violation of Article 8 in respect of the child but not in in respect of the first applicant and the genetic father (see, also, Chapter 9).

Adoption and families

The ECtHR has found family life to exist in many different forms.

Foster parent, or relative, and child

The ECtHR has determined that the foster care of a child for the first 19 months of her life was sufficient to fulfill the definition of 'family life' and so allow the foster parents to proceed with their proposed adoption.[55] Similarly, a close caring relationship between grandparents and a child has sufficed for an adoption.[56]

52 See, *W., B. and R. v. the United Kingdom*, 8 July 1987, Series A No. 121; *Olsson v. Sweden (no. 1)*, 24 March 1988, Series A No. 130; *Eriksson v. Sweden*, 22 June 1989, Series A No. 156; *Margareta and Roger Andersson v. Sweden*, 25 February 1992, Series A No. 226-A; *McMichael v. the United Kingdom*, 24 February 1995, Series A No. 307-B; *Johansen v. Norway*, 7 August 1996, *Reports* 1996-III; *Bronda v. Italy*, 9 June 1998, *Reports* 1998-IV; and *Buscemi v. Italy*, Application No. 29569/95, ECHR 1999-VI.

53 *Paradiso and Campanelli v. Italy,* Application No. 25358/12 (2017, at para 198.

54 Application Nos. 58817/15 and 58252/15 (2022).

55 *Moretti and Benedetti v. Italy,* Application No. 16318/07 (2010).

56 *Marckx v. Belgium* (1979) Series A No. 31, 2 EHRR 330, at para 31.

Step-adoptions

Step-parent applicants have constituted a very large proportion of all adoptions internationally. This form of adoption has been generally viewed as compliant with the welfare test given: the established relationships and motivation of all parties; the fact that one will have a biological link with the child; and the continuity – in most cases – of the latter's home environment. Indeed, the presumption of welfare compatibility was demonstrated in *Eski v. Austria*[57] when the ECtHR ruled that a step-adoption could proceed despite objections from the birth father who had maintained irregular contact with the 8-year-old child following a family breakdown six years earlier. Even though the adoption of a minor severs parental ties, it can still be compatible with Article 8[58] (see, also, Chapter 9).

Intercountry adoptions

The primary instrument in the international framework of laws governing ICA is provided by the Hague Convention on Protection of Children and Co-operation in Respect of Intercountry Adoption 1993 (as amended in 2008). UN CROC and the ECHR are both also crucially important. Also relevant are the United Nations Declaration on Social and Legal Principles relating to the Protection and Welfare of Children with Special Reference to Foster Placement and Adoption Nationally and Internationally and the Convention on Protection of Children and Co-operation in Respect of Intercountry Adoption.

For prospective adopters, attempting to found a family by way of intercountry adoption, this can be fraught with many different obstacles, including politics.[59] For the children concerned, it may also be problematic, as their welfare interests will be compromised by adjustments being made to their name, nationality, culture and family relations. Articles 8, 9 and 11 of the ECHR and Article 27 of the ICCPR specifically recognise the right of minorities to maintain their own culture, language and religion. It is reinforced by Article 20(3) which states that due regard shall be paid to the desirability of continuity in a child's upbringing and to the child's ethnic, religious, cultural and linguistic background. Arguably, this right conflicts with the global practice of intercountry adoption and does so with greater potential for cultural disruption when the child is adopted from a non-Hague compliant country.

Adoption and the public service dimension

While the public service dimension to adoption most usually refers to the adoption of children from the public care system, there are several other relevant aspects of public intrusion into this essentially private family law proceeding.

57 Application No. 21949/03 (2007).

58 See, also, *Emonet and Others v. Switzerland*, Application No. 39051/03 (2007).

59 *A.H. and Others v. Russia*, Application Nos. 6033/13, 8927/13, *et al.* (2017).

Post-adoption contact

Traditionally, contact and adoption have been viewed as mutually exclusive, but this is generally no longer the case (German law being an exception), as current child care practice has moved away from the 'clean-break' approach that was so characteristic of earlier adoptions. Contemporary practice now strongly favours post-adoption contact with any members of the birth family with whom the adoptee has had a meaningful relationship. As most domestic adoptions are now in respect of older children, there is a corresponding stronger likelihood that they will have formed such relationships and accordingly that their continuation will be seen by all parties as a necessary component of the child's future welfare.

One consequence of the recognition given to a child's right to an identity is the accommodation now provided for post-adoption contact between the child and his or her birth family. In *Pedersen,*[60] the ECtHR emphasised that post-adoption contact in itself is not enough; the child must be given an opportunity to develop a 'meaningful relationship' with their biological parents. Moreover, post-adoption contact rights are not confined to birth parents and child. In *Bogonosovy v. Russia,*[61] for example, a grandfather wished to maintain ties with his granddaughter after her adoption by another family, and the ECtHR held that the domestic authorities' failure to examine that possibility had violated his Article 8 rights.

Access to origins information

The ECtHR has explored the extent of a right to information about matters which have a bearing on an individual's sense of personal identity within the general right to privacy and to family life provided by Article 8 and acknowledged in UN CROC, Article 7. This right to access at least basic origins information is also provided for in the European Convention on the Exercise of Children's Rights, Article 3. It emphasises the importance of ensuring that an adopted child is never in any doubt as to the identity of birth parents and members of their family of origin, with whom contact is maintained. It offers an assurance that the child will be reminded of their particular background, heritage, etc., and, in general, will be provided with all information necessary to form an authentic identity and maintain a sense of belonging to their family, culture and community of origin.

So, for example, where a plaintiff who had spent his childhood in care sought to challenge the refusal of social services to give him access to the confidential records they held on him, the ECtHR stopped short of finding a general right of access to information about family ties or personal background but instead found that compliance with respect for private life requires the state to put in place an independent system which adjudicates on disputes regarding access to confidential

60 *Pedersen et al v. Norway*, Application No. 39710/15 (2020).
61 Application No. 38201/16 (2019).

data.[62] Again, in *Godelli v. Italy*,[63] the ECtHR held that the applicant's Article 8 rights had been violated by Italian legislation which, in cases where the mother had opted not to disclose her identity, did not allow her adopted child to access non-identifying information about his or her origins.

Post-adoption reviews

It can be safely assumed that – in accordance with Article 25 of UN CROC – all developed nations have regulatory requirements providing for periodic reviews of foster care, residential care and adoption placements made from domestic public child welfare system. It is considerably less certain that ongoing reviews would be conducted in respect of private adoption placements, though an initial check would be made on notification of such a placement. Ongoing periodic reviews are a requirement in respect of many intercountry adoption placements, but the failure to meet this requirement has long been a cause of complaint from authorities in placing countries, particularly from Russia as evidenced in the case of *A.H. and Others v. Russia*:[64]

> according to information from the Ministry of Education and Science, over the course of the past three years adoptive parents from the United States had failed to provide reports about the wellbeing of 653 children adopted from Russia in 1,136 instances

Given the number of disrupted intercountry adoptions and the suffering of the children involved, there can be little doubt that domestic state-authorised periodic reviews are necessary – perhaps particularly – in 'private' adoptions.

Adoption: contemporary social role and jurisdictional comparisons

Arguably, of all areas of family law, the social role of adoption in particular is shaped by its cultural context: politics determines the extent to which its varying legal functions are distributed across the public-private sectors of family law.[65] In the light of the standards identified earlier as established by many decades of ECtHR rulings on cases that have arisen across all 46 CoE Member States, this section holds a much narrower focus on the distinctive characteristics that differentiate the law as it currently applies to adoption in the selected six common law and two civil law jurisdictions. It does so by benchmarking jurisdictional characteristics against common UN CROC reference points.

62 *Gaskin v. United Kingdom* (1990) 12 EHRR 36.

63 Application No. 33783/09, 2012.

64 Application Nos. 6033/13, 8927/13, 10549/13 and others (2017) at para 394.

65 See, for example, O'Halloran, K., *The Politics of Adoption: International Perspectives on Law, Policy & Practice* (4th ed.), Springer, The Netherlands, 2015.

Social role of adoption

Family breakdown is a shared characteristic of contemporary society in all developed nations: as the annual rates of divorce and separation increase,[66] so also does the frequency with which step-parents turn to adoption as an expedient legal means of sealing the boundaries of their reformed family unit to the exclusion of now inconvenient relationships; kinship adoption has also experienced a widespread growth in popularity as a means of securing the future care of a child within a familiar framework of relatives where transparency and ease of access to birth family members facilitates the development of an authentic personal and cultural identity. Arguably, intercountry adoption also plays a distinctive social role: the freedom to choose to adopt a healthy, voluntarily relinquished baby or orphan from an overseas source necessarily subtracts from the adoption opportunities available for very many disadvantaged children in the domestic public care systems of developed nations and for those in developing countries who are older or have health or social care needs and are left in state institutional care. Abortion is, of course, another variable, together with the availability of more effective contraception, resulting in a rapid decline in the number of children relinquished for adoption: an inverse correlation that has been maintained in recent decades in all developed nations. Simultaneously, improvements in fertility treatment (AID, GIFT, etc.), including donor embryo implantation, is reducing the extent to which adoption is the preferred choice for infertile heterosexual couples, while surrogacy arrangements – particularly commercial arrangements contracted overseas – are now increasingly used instead of adoption, or in conjunction with it, by those in same-sex relationships (see, also, Chapter 7).

Poverty

The contemporary social role of adoption in the jurisdictions currently being studied has largely been shaped by the same cluster of variables, of which poverty is particularly significant. A considerable body of research now testifies to both the enduring level of poverty and the strength of the correlation between poverty and family failure.[67] There can be little doubt that there would be fewer children coming into public care and progressing on into adoption if the coping capacity of vulnerable families was reinforced by appropriate and sufficient public services.[68] Similarly, the correlation between poverty and intercountry adoption is undeniable.

66 In fact, the latest data shows that divorce rate in the U.S. is falling but then so, too, is the marriage rate. See, further, at: www.cdc.gov/nchs/fastats/marriage-divorce.htm

67 See, for example, the Poverty Report for 2020/2021 which shows that in the UK – the world's six largest economy – 1 in 5 of the population live below the official poverty line. See, further, at: https://quakersocialaction.org.uk/sharing-our-learning/poverty-uk?gclid=Cj0KCQiAhomtBhDgARIsABcaYynLgdO-l6pUPS1qnya4RlrB-vyvuxJwQ2EGK1oPQoR-czCZxqJpPMcaAoBWEALw_wcB

68 See, Doughty, J., 'Myths and Misunderstanding in Adoption Law and Policy', *Child & Family Law Quarterly*, Vol. 27, No. 4 (2015), pp. 331–353 at p. 336.

When the socio-economic circumstances of 'sending countries' – such as Korea and China – improve, they withdraw or severely restrict their ICA commitment.

In the U.S., poverty or relative poverty has continued to significantly influence adoption numbers as noted by Patricia Strowbridge of Adoption Professionals:[69]

> Take Florida, which has 5,000 to 7,000 adoptions a year. Over 80% of them are private and most of these involve young women. In many cases they simply can't afford to keep their babies because income is so low and welfare is so poor.

The strong correlation between poverty and the relinquishment of babies for adoption is readily understood in the socio-economic context of the U.S.[70] which has the highest teen pregnancy rate in the western world. The recent *Dobbs*[71] decision – overturning *Roe v. Wade*[72] – has radically reduced access to abortion services and can only increase the annual adoption rates as more young women find they cannot afford child care costs. The rates are also likely to increase as the number of admissions to the public care system increase, given the well-established U.S. practice of facilitating child care adoptions (see, further, Chapter 10).

Jurisdictional comparisons

The UN CROC provisions with most relevance for contemporary adoption would seem to be as follows: Article 1, which defines a child as 'every human being below the age of eighteen years'; Article 2, which prohibits all forms of discrimination against children; articles 3 and 21 requiring that 'the best interests of the child shall be the primary consideration' and that adoption shall ensure the best interests of the child is the paramount consideration; Article 8, which establishes personal and private rights, including to a cultural identity; Article 9, which states a child's entitlement not to be separated from their parents and 'the right of the child who is separated from one or both parents to maintain personal relations and direct contact with both parents'; and articles 12, 13 and 14 which establish the rights of a child in relation to – respectively – expressing opinions, representation in court and the right to make informed decisions. The jurisdictional differences, reflecting their respective cultural and political contexts, are very apparent in the following comparative jurisdictional analysis.

69 See, *The Independent Review*, 5th January 2005, as cited by Hilpern, K., in her feature article 'The Daddy of All Game Shows' at p. 3.

70 The Census Bureau reports that in 2020, there were 37.2 million people in poverty and the official poverty rate was 11.4%, up 1.0 percentage point from the previous year, resulting in approximately 3.3 million more in poverty in 2020 than in 2019. See, further, at: www.census.gov/library/publications/2021/demo/p60-273.html

71 *Dobbs v. Jackson Women's Health Organisation*, 597 U.S., 2022.

72 410 U.S. 113.

Welfare interests of the child (Articles 3 and 21)

Welfare interests have been described as consisting of 'material and financial prospects, education, general surroundings, happiness, stability of home and the like'.[73]

Paramountcy

In the UK, legislation not only establishes that the paramountcy principle governs all aspects of adoption – including passporting a child from the child care to the adoption process – but also that the 'paramountcy of welfare' test applies for projected lifetime of the adoptee. In Ireland, Article 42A.4.1(ii) of the Constitution inserts the principle that 'the best interests of the child shall be the paramount consideration' in proceedings relating to the 'safety and welfare of any child'. So although judicial termination of parental rights is less constrained – now that the 31st Amendment has replaced Article 42.5 with Article 42A – it nonetheless remains more so than in the UK and correspondingly more difficult to utilise adoption as a means of giving priority to the welfare interests of children. While the law is technically compliant with this principle in both jurisdictions, it is arguable that it is breached in Ireland by the constraints on accessing origins information. In England and Wales, the positioning of this principle at the point of entry to the process facilitates adoptions from the public care system and differentiates it from the Irish adoption process.

In Canada, while all provincial adoption legislation makes the granting of an adoption order conditional upon this being compatible with the welfare principle, none specify that the principle must be the paramount concern. It is similar in the U.S., where every state has its own adoption legislation, but none make an adoption order conditional upon satisfying the 'paramountcy-of-welfare' test. In France, the *accouchement sous X* practice leaves no room for the paramountcy principle. However, the welfare-checklist approach is increasingly becoming a feature of adoption law in the U.S. as it already is in Germany. The fact that a large proportion of all adoptions in North America are made privately – either by direct parental placement or through an intermediary person or agency acting on behalf of a parent – in itself precludes the possibility of the objective professional analysis necessary to achieve an adoption that satisfies the paramountcy test.

Right of the child to know their culture/identity (Articles 7, 8 and 20[3])

This Article states that 'due regard shall be paid to the desirability of continuity in a child's upbringing and to the child's ethnic, religious, cultural and linguistic background'. It is a powerful legal acknowledgment that an adoptee has a right of access to information – in the form of agency records, the option of contacting birth family, etc. – that could potentially contribute to consolidating their sense

73 See, *Re B* (1971) 1 QB 437, per Davies L J at p. 443.

of identity. Such legal acknowledgment is one that is in effect nullified in France by the *accouchement sous X* practice. It is also given explicit recognition in other international instruments – such as articles 8, 9 and 11 of the ECHR – and Article 27 of the ICCPR, which specifically ecognizes the right of minorities to maintain their own culture, language and religion.

Accessibility

However, although readily available in the UK, origins information is not currently as accessible in Ireland, where the law has never provided a right for adopted persons to have automatic access to their birth certificates, neither has there ever been a legal right to access agency records for information on an adopted child's family of origin nor a reciprocal duty to disclose such information. Related issues often come before the Irish courts as a consequence of state intervention in the way of life of the Traveller community, and there is also evidence that their culture is treated adversely, particularly in schools. In England and Wales, the regulatory body, Ofsted, has found the gender differentiation practices in Muslim faith-based schools to be culturally affirmative but discriminatory. On the other hand, is probably also breached, if not intentionally, in educational settings when Roma children – and others such as Muslims – are assimilated into generalised classroom-learning programmes without regard for cultural sensitivities.

While it goes without saying that the *accouchement sous X* practice in France clearly violates this right, by providing grounds for total exemption, it should be added that the continued – if recently time-limited – anonymity granted to relinquishing mothers in Germany is similarly in violation. In the latter jurisdiction, traditional attitudes towards adoption are even more extensive – not least in the Civil Code, ss 1747 [2]2 and 1758 – which prohibit any disclosure of an adoptive family's name or address. In both jurisdictions, the right of birth parents to veto the disclosure of identifying information equally violate Article 7.[74]

Child's views/consent (Articles 12, 13 and 14)

In adoption proceedings, the statutory law of some jurisdictions explicitly provide for the right of an older child to give or withhold consent to their proposed adoption.

Types of adoption

Whereas in 1960, adoptions were generally almost entirely by 'strangers' of voluntarily relinquished infants, it now consists mainly of step-parent, foster parent

74 See: for Germany, the Federal Constitution, Basic Law, Article 2 and the Civil Code, ss 1747(2) and 1758; for France, Article 326 of the Civil Code and the provisions of Article L. 222–6 of the Social Action and Families Code, as amended by the Act of 22 January 2002.

and intercountry applicants. For many years – in a complete reversal of the underpinning legislative intent – it had been a consistent feature of the Irish adoption process that most adoptions were in favour of birth parents.[75] Ireland has been affected by much the same variables as in the neighbouring jurisdiction but with some crucial differences: abortion in Ireland is available as a public health service but on very restricted terms; assisted reproduction services, while also available, are unregulated, as is the case with surrogacy which results in many prospective parents travelling overseas to negotiate commercial surrogacy arrangements. The children now becoming available for adoption are far fewer in number, older and more likely to be related to one of their adopters than formerly.[76] This is not unlike the experience in New Zealand and Australia. In the latter, known adoptions (where child and adopters have an already established relationship) comprised most of the total in 2020–2021: with adoption by carers, such as foster parents, the most common (49% of all known child adoptions), followed by step-parents (31%),[77] while intercountry adoptions constituted 7.7%. Much the same pattern is evident in New Zealand, where numbers have fallen from the almost 4,000 adopted in 1971 to less than 600 in 1998 and dropping to just 125 by 2020. A central feature of family law in Australia is the emphasis on conciliation and mediation, at times of marital breakdown, in order that the parties should reach agreed arrangements regarding their children before – or instead of – going to court.

The U.S. experience of adoption has been singular in some respects. If there is a defining feature of life in this society, it's the extent to which the law encourages free enterprise and adoption is no exception. Notable characteristics of the adoption process in this jurisdiction include the role of for-profit adoption agencies, the parental freedom to choose an adoption placement for their child, the acceptance of a parental veto on adoptee access of files containing origins information and the involvement of organised religion (e.g. the Baptist church) in recruiting adopters for African children.

Both France and Germany differ, and in much the same way, from their common law counterparts. They would seem to share a culture of respect for the traditional role of birth parents as the natural protectors of their children's welfare interests which is reflected in national laws relating to children and parental status. This is accompanied by a caveat that at times, undue respect for parents and their rights may obstruct a functional investigation into whether they are endangering the welfare interests of their children. Plenary and simple forms of adoption are both available, the latter being reserved in France for circumstances where the applicant is the step-parent or relative of the child and is used to legally consolidate a reformed family unit. Adoption in France was formerly greatly influenced by the

75 The Adoption (Amendment) Act 2017 finally brought about changes to this anomalous situation by permitting a step-parent to adopt without the necessity of being joined by the birth parent.

76 For example, in 2018, of the 72 adoption orders made, 35 were step-adoptions and 30 were in respect of children aged 17, which must raise questions as to the extent to which adoption is a 'service for children'.

77 See, further, at: www.aihw.gov.au/reports/adoptions/adoptions-australia-2020-21/summary

accouchement sous X practice which dispensed with any necessity for 'openness', obviated the possibility of post-adoption contact and negated any right of the adoptee to access origins information. Child care adoptions are a rarity in France (other than by foster parents). The availability of '*sous le secret*' children and wards of the state has declined, which has meant that adoption has, for some time, been largely interfamilial (step-parents or kinship) or intercountry in nature.[78] The latter are diminishing in number, but a higher proportion are being sourced from non-Hague compliant countries. The characteristics of contemporary adoption in Germany are similar to those in France: it is rapidly fading numerically, most adoptees are the step-children of their adopters, it is essentially used to redraw legal boundaries for reforming family units and in so doing, it accommodates both child and adult adoptees. Domestic adoptions predominate with Germany having one of the three highest rates in Europe (accompanied by the UK and Poland),[79] but adoption by non-relatives continues to fall.[80] According to the official statistics, there are about 66% step-adoptions and 3% kinship adoptions per year[81] (see, further, Chapter 9).

Adoption from public care (Article 20[3])

A characteristic that differentiates the jurisdictions is the extent to which adoption has been adapted to serve a public service role. As this is a hybrid form of adoption, transecting the public-private divide in family law, it is not addressed in this book.[82]

In England and Wales, more so than elsewhere in Europe but in keeping with developments in the U.S.,[83] the public child care system contributes significantly to annual adoptions. In the UK, judicial pronouncements in recent years on the relative merits of adoption – for a child within the public care system – as opposed to care in the family of origin, have adversely impacted the annual numbers being adopted from the public care system.[84] This has been accompanied by academic research findings that the public child care system can be beneficial for many children.[85] In the U.S., however, federal and state financial incentives have consistently promoted public care adoption. Despite the effects of judicial ambivalence

78 See, further, Halifax, J., 'Why Are There So Many International Adoptions in France?', at: www.uea.ac.uk/swp/icar2/pdf's/Halifax99.pdf

79 www.europarl.europa.eu/RegData/etudes/BRIE/2016/583860/EPRS_BRI(2016)583860_EN.pdf

80 See, further, at: www.destatis.de/EN/FactsFigures/SocietyState/SocialStatistics/SocialBenefits/PublicChildrenYouthWelfare/Adoptions.html.

81 German Federal Statistic Office, www.destatis.de/DE/Themen/Gesellschaft-Umwelt/Soziales/Adoptionen/Publikationen/_publikationen-adoptionen.html#_8rvxt84xp.

82 See, O'Halloran, K., *Child Welfare & Rights: a Contemporary Family Law Analysis*, Routledge, forthcoming.

83 See, Sargent, S., 'Adoption and Looked after Children: A Comparison of Legal Initiatives in the U.K. and the USA', *Adoption & Fostering*, BAAF, Vol. 27, No. 2 (2003), pp. 44–52.

84 Particularly *Re B-S (Children)* (2013) EWCA Civ 1146, *per* Sir James Munby.

85 See, for example, the report, 'Looked after children and Offending: Reducing Risk and Promoting Resilience', published in 2012 by The Adolescent and Children's Trust (TACT) and the Centre for Research on the Child and Family at the University of East Anglia. This concluded that 'going into

in the UK, adoption in both the UK and the U.S., unlike in New Zealand and Australia, and to a lesser extent, Canada, has changed from being in the main part of private family law to instead being more of a public service. In Ireland, adoption has so far not been viewed by government as a public child care resource. The common law jurisdictions, unlike France and Germany, have never accommodated – or not to the same extent – the adoption of adults or the 'simple' form of adoption. In Germany, very few children exit the public care system by way of adoption: despite the rate of admission being high, relative to other European countries, the respect for parental rights in the provisions of the Constitution and the Civil Code are such as to erect a particularly high threshold to justify non-consensual adoption.

The proportion of children entering the adoption process whose availability has been determined by coercive intervention of the state – and/or who have physical, mental or behavioural issues – has grown to become a particularly distinctive characteristic of the social role of adoption in the UK and the U.S. (see, further, Chapter 10).

Foster parent adoption (Article 20[3])

The local Indigenous community, organisations and Indigenous professionals in adoption agencies are now automatically engaged when the issue of non-parental care for an Indigenous child arises. In theory, the principles of Indigenous child placement, now statutorily embedded in the law of the CANZUS nations, and the welfare interests of the child are wholly synonymous: implementation of the first should guarantee the second. Therefore, the commitment to this principle should have had the net effect of ensuring the availability of a culture specific form of adoption throughout the CANZUS nations. The fact that this has not happened is attributed to a lack of approved Indigenous carers and insufficient support for those who are approved.[86]

Kinship adoption (Article 5)

In practice, like adoption by foster parents, kinship adoption is most often a variant of adoption from the public care system and, like foster care, is facilitated by the Article 5 requirement to engage 'members of the extended family' in negotiations regarding future care arrangements for children.

Step-parent adoption

The extent to which domestic laws facilitate step-parent adoption reflects a corresponding socio-cultural willingness to allow the functions of adoption to become

---

care can prove effective and extremely beneficial in helping a young person deal with prior abuse and can protect against involvement in crime'.

86 See, for example, Arney, F., et al., 'Enhancing the Implementation of the Aboriginal and Torres Strait Islander Child Placement Principle: Policy and Practice Considerations', Canberra, Australian Institute of Family Studies (2015), at: https://www.aihw.gov.au/reports/child-protection/atsicpp-indicators/contents/background.

more focused on repairing family boundaries in the aftermath of family breakdown – whether in the private or public sphere – rather than enabling 'strangers' to provide a home for an unrelated child in need. It may, arguably, indicate a national emphasis on allowing such functions to be aligned more closely to Article 3 than to Article 21.

This, together with adoptions by relatives, in conjunction with the high level of child care adoptions, has resulted in domestic adoption rates in the UK remaining among the highest in Europe[87] and intercountry adoption rates among the lowest.[88] While the proportion of adoptions by step-parents is high in all jurisdictions, in some applicants, they are restricted to the 'simple' form. However, in recent years, this long-established practice of favouring step-parents has gradually become less acceptable. In some jurisdictions – specifically the UK – there have been recent legislative initiatives designed to divert such applicants towards less draconian court orders.[89] In the future, a step-parent married to, or the civil partner of, a birth parent may – in the absence of special circumstances – be directed towards a 'parental responsibility' order or may enter into a parental responsibility agreement, in respect of the latter's child,[90] or may apply for a 'special guardianship' order.[91] This approach is gradually gaining acceptance in other countries, though not in the U.S. In Australia, for example, step-parents constituted 31%[92] of the 208 adoptions in 2021–2022, the lowest number of total annual adoptions on record – a decline of 93% (from 2,731 in 1979–1980) in less than 50 years. This dramatic fall is largely due to the availability of alternative orders coupled with a general acceptance of the principle that adoption is not always the most appropriate order for carers and step-parents. Much the same pattern is evident in New Zealand, where numbers have fallen from the almost 4,000 adopted in 1971 to less than 600 in 1998 and reaching just 125 by 2020. It is probable that the historical dominance of step-parent applications in New Zealand will continue to decrease as the judiciary increasingly lean towards guardianship as being a more appropriate legal framework for such relationships.

Intercountry adoptions (Article 21[b, (c) and (d)])

According to UN CROC, Article 21, ICA may be considered as an alternative means of providing care if the child concerned cannot be placed domestically in a foster or an adoptive family or cannot otherwise be cared for in the child's country of origin. In practice, contemporary ICA is driven more by constant demand-led

87 See, further, Fenton-Glynn, C., 'Adoption Without Consent: Update 2016', at: www.europarl.europa.eu/RegData/etudes/STUD/2016/556940/IPOL_STU(2016)556940_EN.pdf

88 See, Selman, P., 'Global Statistics for Intercountry Adoption: Receiving States and States of Origin 2004–2015' (2016), at: https://assets.hcch.net/docs/3bead31e-6234-44ae-9f4e-2352b190ca21.pdf

89 The Children Act, s 8(1)(a).

90 See, for example, *S (a child), Re (Rev 1)* (2013) EWHC 1295 (Fam) (2013) All ER (D) 76 (Jun).

91 The Children Act 1989, s 14C(1), as inserted by s 115 of the Adoption and Children Act 2002.

92 See, further, at: www.aihw.gov.au/reports/adoptions/adoptions-australia-2020-21/summary

pressures to satisfy the parenting needs of infertile couples in modern western societies than by the needs of children or by domestic resources of developing nations being suddenly overwhelmed by a crisis caused by war, civil unrest or natural disaster. Having grown to become a significant resource for adopters in all eight jurisdictions, it has been in steep decline in recent years as the constraints of the Hague Convention reduce the numbers of available children in the developing nations.

The political reality driving a national policy of sending children overseas remains rooted in poverty: invariably, it is the poor children, whose parents are unavailable or unable to care for them, that are exported by under-resourced state authorities to meet the needs of adopters in other countries. Necessarily, it is also a consequence of failure in the domestic politics of sending countries, further complicated by the political complicity of western nations choosing to facilitate the removal of children rather than resource the care and protection infrastructure in the child's country of origin (in parallel with domestic policy in receiving nations towards failing parental care). Nonetheless, as has been rightly pointed out, 'for most of the homeless children of the world, international adoption represents the only realistic opportunity for permanent families of their own'.[93]

Increasingly, ICA overlaps with surrogacy and can become entangled in child trafficking. The blurring of the line between lawful adoption and unlawful trafficking of children is well documented in countries as diverse as China, Sri Lanka, Guatemala and Uganda. In recent years, there have been a number of cases involving Uganda children fraudulently removed from birth families and placed with U.S.-based adoption agencies who then facilitated their adoption by U.S. citizens.[94] In France, the CRC has expressed concern regarding 'the high number of intercountry adoptions involving countries of origin that are not party to, nor comply with, the safeguards of 1993 Hague Convention on Protection of Children and Co-operation in respect of Intercountry Adoption'.[95] In Germany, the 2021 amendment to the Adoption Intermediation Act has considerably tightened the safeguards for the welfare interests of children entering the adoption process whether by domestic or intercountry routes.

Perhaps, ICA should now be viewed more broadly as just one aspect of the accelerating pace of change that is internationalising the functions of family law: adoption – in common with marriage, divorce, child maintenance and abduction – is now liable to be conducted across the traditional divides of jurisdiction, race and gender.

Differences and discrimination (Articles 2, 8 and 23)

Jurisdictional differences in the 'type' of child adopted can and often does reflect discriminatory attitudes. At a very basic level, the traditional third-party application

93 See, Bartholet, E., 'International Adoption: Current Status and Future Prospects', *ADOPTION*, Vol. 3, No. 1 (Spring 1993), p. 90. Also, see, generally Doek, J.E., van Loon, H. and Vlaardingerbroek, P. (eds), *Children on the Move,* Martinus Nijhoff Publishers, 1996.

94 See, further, at: www.thenation.com/article/archive/those-kids-are-no-longer-yours-ugandas-adoption-market/

95 CRC/C/FRA/CO/5, at para 55.

has always been more often made in respect of children who are young, healthy and mobile than for those who are not. It is the older and – for whatever reason – less attractive child, perhaps with health and/or behavioural needs, who is less likely to be adopted and instead remain in long term care. Racism, consciously or unconsciously, may also play a part: there is statistical evidence, for example, that Irish adopters exercise a preference for Caucasian rather than Afro-Asian children.[96] Such cultural affinity preferences are, of course, conducive to affirming the cultural identity of an overseas adoptee – or at least lessening the dissonance – and may thereby promote his or her welfare. For by far the majority of intercountry adoptions, there is little probability of a cultural match between the child and their adopters. Nor is there much realistic chance of accessing the origins information necessary to satisfy the Article 8 right to an authentic, culturally compliant, personal identity.

Poverty, discrimination and the welfare interests of Indigenous children (Article 2)

The most striking shared characteristic of the Indigenous communities in the CANZUS nations – differentiating them from their non-Indigenous fellow citizens – is the extent to which they are disproportionately affected by poverty. There is strong evidence indicating a direct correlation between that and the over-representation of their children in the child welfare and juvenile justice systems. Arguably, discrimination in the provision of public services has played a role in perpetuating levels of poverty in the Indigenous communities. In Canada, for example, recent research findings have established that these communities have for many years been receiving an inequitable share of federal funding for family support services. Discrimination is also present following family breakdown, as – despite the requirements of statutory placement principles – the shortage of Indigenous foster parents and adopters in all CANZUS nations results in a higher proportion of culturally incompatible placements than that experienced by non-Indigenous children. This represents a clear breach of UN CROC, Article 3(3), which requires States Parties to ensure that 'the institutions, services and facilities responsible for the care or protection of children shall conform with the standards established by competent authorities'.

Public support services

The public service dimension is apparent in relation to an adoptee's right to identity information and in an entitlement to public support services: in relation to children adopted from the public care system, this support may take the form of ongoing

96 See, the Adoption Board, *Annual Report 2006*, Government Publications, Dublin, at p. 43, Table 14, which records that during the period 1991–2006, approximately 65% of all registered foreign adoptions came from Russia, Romania and Eastern Europe.

government funding. Moreover, public support services are to be provided at any time (i.e. both pre- and post-adoption) and for all parties or others involved in any type of adoption.[97] These entitlements distinguish the UK adoption process from those of the U.S., Canada[98] and other jurisdictions.

Post-adoption contact with birth parents and/or significant others (Articles 8 and 9)

Article 9(3) requires States Parties to 'respect the right of the child who is separated from one or both parents to maintain personal relations and direct contact with both parents'. This principle establishes a child 'contact right' which is prone to being compromised in England and Wales by the practice of concurrent placements and subsequent adoption. In that jurisdiction, recourse to a combination of adoption and contact orders accelerated in the wake of the 2002 Act.[99]

It would seem probable that compatibility with Article 9(3) is more likely in the U.S. than in Canada, as practice in the latter is less inclined to accommodate 'openness'.[100] However, given that step-parent adoptions continue to be generally popular and kinship adoptions have now become the preferred option for children in the public child welfare system, there is accordingly a greater probability of an adopted child in all countries retaining post-adoption the relationships that were previously important.

Adoption in an Indigenous context and UN CROC: compliance with international standards

The CANZUS nations – Canada, Australia, New Zealand and the U.S. – include within their borders Indigenous communities, established over the millennia and sustained in accordance with traditional customs, that have survived relatively intact into the 21st century. These communities – the First Nations/Inuit of Canada, the Indigenous People of Australia, the Māori of New Zealand and the Native Americans/Indians of the U.S. – are, to a varying degree, coherent entities founded on rules and traditions governing relations within and between families and applying to the functioning of their social system as a whole. They coexist alongside and in an uneasy relationship with the prevailing culture of modern western society,

97 Following the 2002 Act, the Department of Health issued a consultation paper entitled the Draft Adoption Support Services (Local Authorities) (Transitory and Transitional Provisions) (England) Regulations and Draft Accompanying Guidance, December 2002. See, also, Department of Health, Providing Effective Adoption Support.

98 See, Committee on the Rights of the Child, session 34 (2003) and, for example, the Adoption Information Act 1997 (Nova Scotia).

99 This was due to the requirement in s 46(6) that the court consider the necessity for post-adoption contact arrangements and because of the insertion through the Children and Families Act 2014, s 9, of sections 51A and 51B into the Adoption and Children Act 2002 permitting the making of a contact order at any time, including any time after the granting of an adoption order.

100 See, *CAS of Toronto v. T.L.* (2010) O.J. No. 942.

sharing time, territory and the necessities of life but often very little in the way of values, knowledge and social infrastructure.[101]

International law

The principles of international law, particularly those concerned with fundamental human rights, apply uniformly across nations and equally to all citizens, including children and those in Indigenous communities.[102] However, despite being most obviously in need of their protection, there is little evidence of such provisions being deployed for the benefit of Indigenous people. Of most relevance is the Declaration on the Rights of Indigenous People 2006 and its specific reference to the special features of customary adoption, which operates in tandem with national statutory laws, and continues to be practised in accordance with Indigenous cultural tradition.

The Indigeous communities share a common history of having experienced adoption as a colonial strategy to expedite their assimilation: an adjunct to mid-19th century policies of residential schooling, enforced adoption was then part of a deliberate strategy to absorb Indigenous children into mainstream Caucasian society. Although the policy largely failed, it did cause systemic harm to the tribal way of life, cultural disruption and inter-generational trauma, all of which have been the subject of much academic study.[103] As a non-consensual process, the statutory form of adoption is still often imposed on Indigenous communities. This tends to occur in circumstances where Indigenous parenting is judged to infringe standards required by the public child welfare law of modern western society. At its most extreme, it can take the form of a discriminatory policy to use non-consensual adoption, perhaps in conjunction with institutional residential schooling, as a means to enforce the assimilation of Indigenous children into non-Indigenous society. Most usually, it occurs as a consequence of the universal application of national child welfare law that inevitably results in some Indigenous children being drawn into the child care system and then entering the non-consensual adoption process.

101 See, further, UN Dept. of Economic and Social Affairs, *State of the World's Indigenous Peoples: Indigenous Peoples' Access to Health Services*, United Nations, 2016.

102 Including the Hague Convention on Protection of Children and Co-operation in Respect of Inter-country Adoption 1993, the UN Convention on the Rights of the Child 1990, the International Covenant on Civil and Political Rights 1976, the International Covenant on Economic, Social and Cultural Rights 1976, the International Convention on the Elimination of all forms of Racial Discrimination 1969 and the Universal Declaration of Human Rights 1948.

103 See, for example, Nichols, R. L., 'From the Sixties Scoop to Baby Veronica: Transracial Adoption of Indigenous Children in the USA and Canada', in Shackleton, M. (ed.), *International Adoption in North American Literature and Culture: Transnational, Transracial, and Transcultural Narratives*, Palgrave Macmillan, Helsinki, 2017, pp. 3–26; Jacobs, M., *A Generation Removed: The Fostering & Adoption of Indigenous Children in the Postwar World*, University of Nebraska Press, Lincoln, 2014; Swain, S., '"Homes are Sought for these Children": Locating Adoption within the Australian Stolen Generations Narrative', *American Indian Quarterly*, Vol. 37, No. 1–2 (2013), pp. 203–217; and Newman, E., 'History of Transracial Adoption: A New Zealand Perspective', *American Indian Quarterly*, Vol. 37, No. 1–2 (2013), pp. 237–257.

A higher-than-average rate of family breakdown in an Indigenous context leads to disproportionate numbers of Indigenous children needing out-of-home care with foster parents and adopters.

Characteristics of customary adoption

Fundamentally, the primary purpose served by adoption in an Indigenous context is no different from that in modern western nations. In both, adoption is essentially the most extreme means for giving effect to the intention to transfer total care responsibility for a child from the birth parent/s to approved other persons, until such time as the child reaches adulthood. The goals address similar factors such as parental death, absence, relinquishment or abandonment, failed parenting, infertility, the need for an heir and the tidying up of reformed family units. There are, however, significant differences in law, policy and practice.

Consensual

Adoption within Indigenous cultures is almost always a consensual process, governed more by practice than by policy or law, and treated as a transparent and ongoing transaction. As such, it involves the consent not just of the parties – particularly that of the child – but will also usually follow discussions involving the extended family, the tribal leader and other prominent members of their tribe. It will require and receive the support of the community.

Openness

From the perspective of the welfare interests of the child concerned, customary adoption has certain advantages. The complete transparency allows the child to know exactly who their birth parents are and where he or she 'belongs' in the nuclear and extended family network. He or she matures being known and cared for by that network, which brings long-term benefits of mutual loyalty for the child and the community.

Consanguinity

Adoption in this context at least favours transactions that respect and maintain blood-link relationships. In that respect, it differs from the approach now evolving in some non-Indigenous communities – notably in the UK – where prospective adopters with a blood-link to a child are increasingly being diverted to other less draconian orders.

Welfare interests (Articles 3 and 21)

Article 21 of UN CROC establishes that the best interests of the child are to be the paramount consideration in all matters related to adoption,[104] though

104 Also established by Article 24 of the African Charter on the Rights and Welfare of the Child and Article 4 of the European Convention on the Adoption of Children (Revised).

there is no requirement that it can be predicted to be beneficial for the foreseeable future. The significance of the placement principle requirement that any adoption – or other form of placement – be compliant with an Indigenous child's culture may be gauged from its current interpretation by the CANZUS judiciary that it constitutes a crucial component of an Indigenous child's welfare interests.

Cultural identity

The right to a cultural identity – also given explicit recognition under articles 8, 9 and 11 of the ECHR, Article 27 of the ICCPR and Article 12 of UNDRIP – specifically recognises the right of minorities to maintain their own culture, language and religion. It is reinforced by UN CROC, Article 20(3), which states that 'due regard shall be paid to the desirability of continuity in a child's upbringing and to the child's ethnic, religious, cultural and linguistic background'.

This right lies at the heart of the inter-generational trauma that has afflicted the Indigenous communities in all CANZUS nations. The right to a cultural identity that reflects tribal affiliation gives rise to constant issues regarding the placement of Indigenous children in contemporary fostering and adoption services and in. It also, arguably, is a right that fundamentally conflicts with the practice of intercountry adoption.

Differentiating the role of adoption in Indigenous and western society contexts

In Indigenous communities, where the public-private distinction and incidences of status are less relevant – though patriarchy is likely to feature – adoption avoided the degree of preciousness it acquired in western societies. As the concept of 'family' becomes more fluid and indeterminate in those societies, with serial parenting arrangements and expanding public service intervention (benign and coercive) becoming ever more intrusive, so it is losing its insularity, its 'nuclear family' characteristics, and is assuming the more flexible traits associated with Indigenous communities. Hallmarks of secrecy, complete severance with birth family, agency mediation, total assimilation of identity and formal judicial endorsement that until recently have always characterised adoption in western societies are now being increasingly challenged by the characteristics of the Indigenous model. In terms of family norms – as in many other respects – the Indigenous communities of the CANZUS nations have much more in common with each other, including as regards adoption, than they have with their respective host societies.

The role of adoption in an Indigenous context has relevance for the law, policy and practice of modern western societies. It suggests:

- a need to ensure the domestic provision of appropriate preventative and supportive services;
- involvement of birth parent/s, significant relatives, friends and/or community representatives in placement decision-making;

- first preference for long-term foster care, where permanency is required, if this better enables the child to maintain relationships with family/community/culture of origin and revert to them on attaining adulthood;
- second preference for kinship placement, where adoption is necessary, to authenticate identity and maintain a sense of belonging; and
- placement with 'strangers' or non-relatives only in exceptional circumstances, where adoption is necessary, and then to be in geographical proximity to the child's birth family, in keeping with parental wishes in relation to contact and accompanied by appropriate arrangements to safeguard the child's cultural identity.

Conclusion

The role of adoption in contemporary western society reflects the nature of changes in the related cultural context. From its historical role in fairly closed societies with their well-defined boundaries, structured roles and ordered social relationships, adoption has now adapted its functions in relation to the needs of nuclear impermanent family units within a more fluid cosmopolitan society. Modern forms of adoption very much reflect the characteristic pressures on contemporary family life in western society: it has become more 'open' with post-adoption contact between adoptee and family of origin the new norm; it accommodates a greater variety of children and adopters than formerly; is often concluded despite opposition from birth parents; is very often little more than an expedient legal procedure for securing family relationships – step and kinship – between parties who are well known to each other; is now international, multiracial and facilitated by commercial agencies; is frequently government funded; and is arguably more responsive to the needs of adopters than of children.

However, a sense of perspective is needed. Far fewer adoption orders are now made than at any time in the history of this statutory process. While all other family law proceedings continue to generate ever more litigation, adoption continues its steady decline. This is partly due to changed social values which no longer stigmatise unmarried mothers, leading to a reduction in voluntarily relinquished babies; a sharp drop in the number of available children as a consequence of legalised abortion and the availability of more effective contraception; increased access to improved fertility treatment (AID, GIFT, etc.); and the exponential increase in commercial surrogacy which offers the added value of a possible genetic link between the commissioning couple, or one of them, and the child.

8 Family breakdown and parenting arrangements

Introduction

Family breakdown may occur due to unforeseen extraneous circumstances such as the death or incapacity of one or both parents through illness, accident or by other means but is more likely to result from irretrievable relationship issues between the parents. Whatever the cause, the consequences will include changes in the care arrangements for any children involved. In a small minority of cases, matters affecting the welfare interests of the children may come before the court in proceedings for divorce, nullity or judicial separation, though are more likely to present at a later stage when disputes arise. Whenever such issues require judicial determination, then the principle of the welfare interests of the child will have a vital role to play. The court orders and proceedings available, together with the weighting then given to that principle – as something to be taken into account, treated as a primary consideration or as of paramount importance – will have a crucial bearing on parenting arrangements, other aspects of parental responsibility and on the future wellbeing of the child or children.

This chapter is structured similarly to its predecessors in this part. It begins with an outline summary of the relevant concepts, principles and provisions of international law. It then establishes the benchmark standards in such law that underpin the relationship between the principle of the welfare interests of the child and family breakdown: identifying the characteristic issues and analysing the related caselaw from the ECtHR and other bodies. Against that background of established international standards, the chapter then conducts a comparative evaluation of similarities and differences in the way in which the eight jurisdictions treat the welfare interests of the child in the aftermath of family breakdown.

Concepts, principles and the law

By the closing decades of the 20th century, the law in most developed nations had moved away from an essentially fault based approach for sanctioning the decisions of spouses to terminate their marital relationship. Instead, for both marital and non-marital couples, this was replaced by a simple finding of irretrievable breakdown, an equitable distribution of family assets and for assurances that the welfare interests of any children involved would be protected.

DOI: 10.4324/9781003269595-12

Concepts and social constructs

For many centuries, the family – particularly the marital family – provided the primary legal frame of reference for examining the welfare interests of children and never more so than at times of family breakdown. However, this social construct has changed greatly in recent decades with the result that, as the ECtHR has explained, 'family life within the meaning of Article 8 includes at least the ties between near relatives, for instance, those between grandparents and grandchildren, since such relatives may play a considerable part in family life'.[1] This change has been due to factors such as the following: the longevity of grandparents; the rising proportion of parents who have remained unmarried or who have been married more than once; the marriages in which the gender of one spouse, or perhaps both, is not the same as it was at birth; and the broadening of marriage to accommodate same-sex couples. It should also be borne in mind that the western concept of the 'nuclear family unit' never had much credence in Indigenous communities, where 'family' continues to be based on complex networks of blood relatives.

Family

The traditional legal model of the family – founded on the monogamous marriage for life of a heterosexual couple and including the children born of their marriage – is no longer the ubiquitous norm it once was. In most developed nations, the law now extends beyond the boundaries of the traditional model to validate a range of relationship frameworks for accommodating the welfare interests and rights of children, whether or not they were born to those now parenting them. The form a contemporary family takes is not without consequences should breakdown occur.

Unmarried couples

Heterosexual unmarried couples, living together as husband and wife with children born to them, have for many years been recognised in law as constituting a family.[2] As the ECtHR has pointed out:[3]

> the notion of 'the family' . . . is not confined solely to marriage based relationships and may encompass other *de facto* 'family' where the parties are living together outside of marriage. A child born out of such a relationship is *ipso iure* part of that 'family' unit from the moment of his birth and by the very fact of it.

The time when a cohabiting unmarried couple had no reciprocal rights and duties towards each other and the father had few or no responsibilities to any children of their family has long gone.

1 *Marckx v. Belgium* (1979) Series A No. 31, 2 EHRR 330, at para 31.
2 *W.J. & D.P.*, Application No.12513/86 (1987).
3 *Keegan v. Ireland*, Application No. 16969/90 (1994) Series A No. 290, 18 EHRR 342, at para 44.

Same-sex couples

Extending the legal definition of 'family' to accommodate same-sex couples living in a stable *de facto* partnership has been a relatively recent development. *Bonnaud and Lecoq v. France*,[4] for example, concerned an application for joint exercise of parental responsibility made by two women living as a couple, each of whom had a child born as a result of medically assisted reproduction. The ECtHR found that all four constituted a family unit from 2006 to 2012. This process of accommodation was very largely due to the contribution made by the Court of Justice of the European Union (CJEU) and the European Court of Human Rights (ECtHR) through their application of contemporary equality principles to traditional legal definitions of 'marriage'. Incrementally, as the law conferred legal status on same-sex civil unions, registered partnerships and, ultimately, marriage, recognition was extended to same-sex families in a series of cases in which the Court affirmed, on equality grounds, a parity of legal status between family units led by heterosexual and same-sex couples. In *Kozak v. Poland*,[5] for example, which concerned succession rights to a tenancy, the Court referred to the same-sex couple as being in a '*de facto* marital cohabitation'.[6] In *Schalk and Kopf v. Austria,*[7] the Court took the view that 'a cohabiting same-sex couple living in a stable *de facto* partnership, falls within the notion of "family life", just as the relationship of a different-sex couple in the same situation would'. In the U.S., *Obergefell v. Hodges*[8] established similar recognition for same-sex relationships across all states. However, it was not until well into the second decade of the 21st century that most common law nations introduced legislation legalising same-sex marriage: Canada doing so as early as 2005, England and Wales following in 2014 and Australia in 2017.

Trans gender couples

Not until 2002 and the case of *Christine Goodwin* v. *The United Kingdom*[9] did the ECtHR consider that there had been major social changes in the institution of marriage as well as dramatic changes in medicine and science in the field of transsexuality, and therefore, biological factors could not any longer be determinative of capacity to marry and found a family. So, for example, the applicant in *Hämäläinen v. Finland*[10] was born a male and married a woman in

4 Application No. 6190/11 (2018).

5 *Kozak* v. *Poland*, Application No. 13102/02 (2010).

6 See, also, *Taddeucci and McCall* v. *Italy*, Application No. 51362/09 (2016).

7 Application No. 30141/04 (2010).
Application Nos. 18766/11 and 36030/11 (2015).

8 135 S. Ct. 2584 (2015).

9 Application No. 28957/95 (2002).

10 Application No. 37359/09 (2014).

1996. The couple had a child in 2002. In 2009, the applicant underwent gender reassignment surgery. However, although she changed her first name, she could not have her gender identity number changed to a female one unless her wife consented to the transformation of their marriage into a civil partnership or the couple divorced. Both the applicant and her spouse wished to remain married but considered that a civil partnership did not provide the same security as marriage for them and their child. At the outset of their deliberations, regarding the applicant's right to have her gender identity number changed from male to female, the Court noted that while there was no European consensus on allowing same-sex marriages, parental responsibility in Finland was based on the fact of parenthood, irrespective of sex or form of partnership, and therefore, a change in the legal status of their relationship would have no implications for the applicant's family life.

The more recently determined cases of *A.H. and Others v. Germany*[11] and *O.H. and G.H. v. Germany*[12] concerned the birth certificate registration of children whose parents had undergone gender transition. The ECtHR noted the German authorities finding that motherhood and fatherhood, as legal categories, were not interchangeable. The authorities had been called upon to weigh up a number of private and public interests against several competing rights: first, the rights of transgender parents and their partners; next, the fundamental rights and interests of the respective children, namely, their right to know their origins, their interest in a stable legal attachment to their parents and the right to receive care and education from both parents (*O.H. and G.H.*); and lastly, the public interest, which lay in the coherence of the legal system and the accuracy and completeness of civil registration records. Given the lack of consensus among European states as to how to indicate in the civil registration records concerning a child that one of the persons having parental status was transgender – a fact reflecting that gender change combined with parenthood raised sensitive ethical issues – the Court took the view that states should be afforded a wide margin of appreciation as regards how they dealt with the matter.

Principles

The introduction of principles such as 'parental responsibility' and 'paramountcy', alongside a fixed menu of child custody and access orders, often with equal application to private and to public family law proceedings, was a development that began impacting family law in the western developed nations in the latter decades of the 20th century. These crosscutting principles, together with judicially approved or legislatively defined indicators for 'child welfare', have contributed greatly to promoting judicial consistency in decisions relating to children and to the overall coherence of family law.

11 Application No. 7246/20 (2023).
12 Application Nos. 53568/18 and 54741/18 (2023).

Parental responsibility

By the turn of the century, the concepts of 'parental rights' and 'parental duties' – which for centuries had constituted the most basic constructs of family law – were beginning to be replaced in some developed nations by the composite term 'parental responsibility'. This is best understood as comprising all the rights, duties, powers, responsibilities and authority that by law a parent of a child has in relation to that child and their property. The change signalled a profound difference of approach from a proprietal frame of reference to one which implied that parental use of authority was valid only if employed for the benefit of the child, thereby allowing it to play a more consistent role in both public and private family law.

Bromley suggests that this composite term comprises at least 16 separate areas of responsibility, including the following: providing a home; having contact; determining and providing for education; determining religion; discipline; consent to treatment, marriage, adoption, emigration and change of surname; vetoing the issue of a passport; taking the child outside the jurisdiction; administering property; protection and maintenance; representing the child in legal proceedings; burial or cremation; and appointing a guardian for the child.[13] More than one person may bear such responsibility in respect of the same child at the same time.

Paramountcy

This principle, together with attachment theory[14] and 'permanency planning',[15] suggested that once the court had confirmed irretrievable breakdown in the parental relationship, then it should secure the future parental care arrangement most conducive to optimising a child's potential for emotional, psychological and physical growth (see, further, next section and at Chapter 6).

Consanguinity

The extent to which the 'blood-tie' constitutes a significant component of a child's welfare in a contest between a birth parent and others has often been a contentious issue in the context of disputed care arrangements following family breakdown. As Baroness Hale once pithily expressed it: the birth mother could not be viewed as being on the same footing in relation to two children as the other 'parent' because she was 'both their biological and their psychological parent . . . in the overall welfare judgment that must count for something in the vast majority

13 Bromley, P.M. and Lowe, N.V., *Bromley's Family Law* (8th ed.), Butterworths, London, 1992, p. 301.

14 See, Bowlby, J., *Attachment and Loss*, Hogarth Press, London, 1973.

15 See, for example, McCafferty, P., Duffy, J. and Hayes, D., 'Permanency Decisions in Child Welfare: A Qualitative Study', *The British Journal of Social Work*, Vol. 51, No. 6 (September 2021), pp. 2134–2154.

of cases'.[16] It's an argument with particular potency when applied in an Indigenous context.[17]

Proportionality

The principle of proportionality[18] requires a fair balance to be struck between the general interests of the community and protection of the individual's fundamental rights.[19] Any intervention of the state in the parent-child relationship should be proportionate to the legitimate aim of protecting family life. The ECtHR looks at the interference complained of in the light of the case as a whole to determine whether the alleged interference is 'prescribed by law' and was (i) for a legitimate aim which is important enough to justify interfering with a fundamental right, (ii) rationally connected to achieving that aim, (iii) no more than reasonably necessary to achieve it, and (iv) in the light of this, striking a fair balance between the rights of the individual and the interests of the community.[20]

Some two decades ago, this principle and its significance was explained with brevity and lucidity in an English case:

> every application involves a court balancing the rights of the participants to the application (including the children who are the subject of it) and arriving at a result which is in the interest of those children . . . and proportionate to the legitimate aim being pursued.[21]

More recently, the Supreme Court in that country, when allowing an appeal against orders made in relation to three children the care plans for whom centred on removal from their mother and placement into separate long-term foster homes, justified its decision with the explanation:

> the judge does not state why the emotional damage that each of the very different subject children would suffer under a care plan which separated them from their mother, from their stepfather and no less importantly from their

16 *Re G (Children)* (2006) UKHL 43 (2006) FLR 629, per Baroness Hale at para 44.

17 See, further, O'Halloran, K., *Children, the Law and the Welfare Principle: Perspectives from North America*, Routledge 2023, at Chapter 8, and *Children, the Law and the Welfare Principle: Perspectives from Australia & New Zealand*, Routledge, 2023, at chapters 9 and 10.

18 See, further, Möller, K., 'Proportionality: Challenging the Critics', *International Journal of Constitutional Law*, Vol. 10, No. 3 (2012), pp. 709–731, at: https://doi.org/10.1093/icon/mos024

19 See: *Olson v. Sweden (No. 1)* (1988) 11 EHRR 299; *Sporrong v. Sweden* (1982) 5 EHRR 35 at para 69; *Tsirlis and Kouloumpas v. Greece* (1997) 25 EHRR 198 at para 116; *Razgar v. Secretary of State for Home Department* (2004) UKHL 27 at para 20; and see, *Kozac v. Poland* (2010) ECHR 280 (2010) 51 EHRR 16.

20 See: *Huang v. Secretary of State for the Home Department* (2007) 2 AC 167, para 19; *R (Quila) v. Secretary of State for the Home Department* (2012) 1 AC 621, para 45; and *Bank Mellat v. HM Treasury (No. 2)* (2013) UKSC 39 (2013) 3 WLR 179, 222, para 20.

21 *Re H (Contact Order)* (2002) 1 FLR 22 per Wall LJ at para 37. See also comments of Hale LJ in *Re C & B (Care Order: Future Harm)* (2001) 1 FLR 611, at paras 33–34 and 620–621 and in *Re O. (Supervision Order)* (2001) 1 FLR 923 at paras 24–28.

siblings, was proportionate to and necessitated by the identified risk of sexual harm[22] (see, also, Chapter 6).

Subsidiarity

The principle of subsidiarity is predicated on an understanding that the exercise of authority will be exercised at the lowest level necessary to achieve commonly agreed objectives and that entities exercising that authority will be guaranteed functional independence at that level. It is a principle providing for state intervention at the minimal level compatible with maintaining the primary responsibility of parents to care for the welfare interests of their children. This is clearly a governing determinant of relevant law and policy in both countries. This deference to parental status, a key shared feature of their family law, probably impedes any prioritising of the welfare principle.

International law

The main components of the relevant international legal framework are the Universal Declaration of Human Rights (UDHR), the European Convention on Human Rights (ECHR), the UN Convention on the Rights of the Child (UN CROC), the Hague Convention and the International Covenant on Civil and Political Rights (ICCPR).

The European Convention on Human Rights (ECHR)

For several decades, the ECtHR has been examining cases concerning the parent-child relationship drawn from the 47 (more recently, 46) countries that constitute the Council of Europe. The outcome is a solid foundation of law and principles providing the basis for responding to evolving issues affecting that relationship.

Article 8

This, the most developed article relating to family matters, states that 'everyone has the right to respect for his private and family life, his home and his correspondence' and that there should not be any interference with this right by a public authority 'except such as is in accordance with the law and is necessary in a democratic society'. However, as the ECtHR established in *E.B. v. France*,[23] Article 8 of the ECHR does not in itself confer a right to found a family nor to do so by way of adoption; the existence of 'family life' is a precondition for the operation of Article 8.[24]

22 *Re H-W (Children) (No. 2)* (2022) UKSC 17.
23 Application No. 43546/02 (2008).
24 Ibid, at p. 18.

Article 12

Article 12 builds upon Article 16 of the Universal Declaration of Human Rights (UDHR), both of which provide for the right of men and women of a marriageable age to marry and to found a family in accordance with their national law. Article 16 is specifically made conditional upon the free and full consent of the spouses who are thereafter – for the duration of their marriage and at time of dissolution – entitled to equal rights.

The UN Convention on the Rights of the Child (UN CROC)

UN CROC, as of 2023, has been ratified by 196 countries (excluding the U.S.) which provides an extensive global platform of acceptance for its stated rights of the child. While it has no legal mechanism for enforcing its provisions, many countries have incorporated the Convention into domestic law, and most importantly, the ECtHR references UN CROC principles in its determinations, thereby giving judicial notice of their recognition as part of international law (see, further, at Chapter 2).

Article 3

Often considered to be the most important provision, this Article merely states that 'the welfare of the child should be a primary consideration'.

Other

Also relevant are the following: the International Covenant on Economic, Social and Cultural Rights (ICESCR); the UN Convention on the Elimination of all forms of Discrimination Against Women (CEDAW) with its Optional Protocol; the Convention on the Rights of Persons with Disabilities (CRPD); and the United Nations Declaration on Social and Legal Principles relating to the Protection and Welfare of Children with Special Reference to Foster Placement and Adoption Nationally and Internationally (see, further, Chapter 8).

Family breakdown proceedings: established international legal standards

Family breakdown – following on from parental death, abandonment or irretrievable relationship difficulties – gives rise to by far the majority of issues regarding future child care arrangements. It almost always occurs in a private family law context characterised chiefly by parent/s or guardians being preoccupied with retrieving what they can from the wreckage of their family life while children are left anxiously dependent upon parental decisions. It can also have a public law dimension as when – whether as cause or effect – the breakdown may result in children coming into the public care system. This may then lead onto their non-consensual adoption. The private adoptions of children in public care being one procedure that crosscuts both sectors of family law can be construed as 'hybrid proceedings' and is, therefore, not addressed in this book.[25]

Where parents are seeking divorce, annulment or judicial separation depending on the legal form of their family – international law requires that as a prerequisite for the issue of a decree/dissolution – they draw up and submit to the court a welfare-compliant 'parenting plan' setting out the proposed care arrangements for any children of their family. Probably in most cases, the parties agree to settle their affairs and part amicably – if only because it is much cheaper than engaging in protracted disputes. Unless the parties make future child care arrangements a contested issue, then most usually, the arrangements avoid professional and/or judicial scrutiny and instead will be routinely endorsed if they appear to be compliant with the child's welfare interests. When disputes do arise – whether in the context of divorce proceedings or later – then the parties will become subject to such control as may be imposed by the court. The extent of that control will be very much conditioned by the degree of discretion available to the judge, which in turn will be dependent upon whether or not the paramountcy principle has a role to play.

Arguably, paternity proceedings might also now be classified under the rubric of 'family breakdown'. Traditionally, paternity laws were formulated and used to establish the identity of a father so that he could be held to account – publicly and privately – for ongoing maintenance responsibilities in respect of his child. However, this is no longer exclusively the case. Given the growing proportion of composite families in which a 'child of the family' is not genetically linked to both – or even to one – of the parents, the contemporary role of paternity proceedings is now often closely associated with family breakdown.[26] Certainly, however constituted, it is the family – and the particular parent-child dynamics – that will be the focus of the court's attention, and it is here that the ECtHR has established some basic standards.

The parent-child relationship and ECtHR rulings

In the context of family breakdown – as in all matters concerning a child's upbringing – it is clear that the law requires the latter's best interests to be given a priority weighting. However, as there is no mention of 'paramount' in Article 3 of UN CROC nor, of course, in the ECHR, there has been a good deal of uncertainty as to in precisely what circumstances that weighting should be 'paramount'. The ECtHR has added to the uncertainty created by inconsistencies in domestic law through pronouncements such as 'the Court recalls that a fair balance must be struck between the interests of the child and those of the parent'[27] and that in doing

25 See, O'Halloran, K., *Child Welfare & Rights: A Contemporary Family Law Analysis*, Routledge, forthcoming.

26 See, further, O'Halloran, K., *Children, the Law and the Welfare Principle: European Judicial Perspectives*, Routledge, 2024, at Chapter 6.

27 *Olsson v. Sweden* judgment (no. 2) of 27 November 1992, Series A No. 250, at para 90.

so, particular importance must be attached 'to the best interests of the child, which, depending on their nature and seriousness, may override those of the parent'.[28] These standards – 'best interests', 'primary consideration' and 'paramount' – clearly imply a differential treatment or weighting for their common subject 'the welfare interests of the child', but there has been a marked lack of clarity as to how, when and why this is to happen.[29]

The parent-child bond

The mutuality of the bond between birth parents and child (or unmarried mother and child) has always been upheld as a cornerstone of family law: the symbiotic relationship being considered to be a crucial component of the child's welfare interests; the younger the child, the more crucial to their interests. As the ECtHR noted more than two decades ago, 'the exercise of parental rights and the mutual enjoyment by parent and child of each other's company constitute fundamental elements of family life', even if the relationship between the parents has broken down.[30] In *Zander*,[31] it found that what constitutes the welfare of the child is always of crucial importance in such cases: a fair balance must be struck between the interests of the child and those of the parent and that in doing so, particular importance must be attached to the best interests of the child which, depending on their nature and seriousness, may override those of the parent – an analysis, it has to be said, that is a good deal more qualified than a simple reference to the paramountcy principle. It noted that in particular, the parent cannot be permitted to take such measures as would harm the child's health and development.[32]

Family life

When faced with conflicting parental custody claims, the court will closely examine the quality of family life that a child had enjoyed prior to the breakdown and assess which parent – or other carer – had contributed most to promoting the child's welfare during that period and would be best placed to continue doing so in the future. The ECtHR has taken the view that when making such an assessment, it must take into account differences in legal and cultural context and their influence on national interpretations of what constitutes good parenting. This is most likely to occur as a consequence of the prevailing national differences in the law governing same-sex relationships and LGBT matters more generally: many countries continue the traditional legal prohibition; in others, there are political initiatives to

28 *B. v. The UK*, Application No. 9840/82 (1987), at para 60. See, also, *E.P. v. Italy*, Application No. 31127/96 (1999), at para 62.

29 See, further, O'Halloran, K., *Children, the Law and the Welfare Principle: European Judicial Perspectives*, Routledge, 2024, at Chapter 6.

30 *R. v. the United Kingdom*, Application No. 10496/83 (1988).

31 *Zander v. the Netherlands*, *op cit*.

32 Citing *Elsholz v. Germany* [GC], Application No. 25735/94 (2000), at paras 48–50.

overturn, amend or narrowly define national legislation that had seemed to establish equality in respect of such matters. Jurisdictional differences have been apparent, for example, in relation to surrogacy as illustrated in *Mennesson v. France*,[95] *Labassée v. France*[96] and *Valdís Fjölnisdóttir and Others v. Iceland*.[97] In the latter case, all things considered, the Court took the view that the state had acted within its margin of appreciation in denying registration in order to protect its ban on surrogacy and that the applicant's right to family life had not been violated. Despite there being little factual difference between the earlier cases, the rights of the child to respect for their family life has more readily found protection where there is a genetic link between a commissioning 'parent' and child.

Contact: a child's right

As the ECtHR noted more than two decades ago, 'the UN Convention on the Rights of Children (Article 9.3) sees a relationship of a child with his parents as a right, not merely an interest'.[33] In fact, the right of the child to maintain contact with both parents is also expressly cited within the CoE Convention on Contact concerning Children 2003[34] and has been emphasised by the ECtHR for at least the past 40 years.[35] In *Luzi v. Italy*,[36] for example, the mother left her partner after four months of cohabitation and went with their baby daughter to live with her parents. For the next eight years, the father had only sporadic contact with the child due to opposition from the mother, despite constant social services involvement and several judicial orders. Eventually, the father complained to the ECtHR which found that the domestic courts had not taken the requisite action to ensure proper contact between the father and his child. However, the contact right is subject to the caveat that this is compatible with the child's welfare. The Court has found in a number of cases – such as *Levin v. Sweden*[37] – that the prohibition of contact by the authorities is justified if it is 'proportionate to the legitimate aim pursued [the best interests of the children] and within the margin of the domestic authorities'.[38]

Contact rights are not confined to the parent-child relationship. The CJEU has ruled that such rights can extend to grandparents and children following the dissolution of the parents' marriage.[39] While the ECtHR has recognised the mutual contact rights of siblings separated by their parent's custody order.[40]

33 *Zander v. the Netherlands*, *op cit* at para 10.

34 Article 4 (1) states that 'a child and his or her parents shall have the right to obtain and maintain regular contact with each other'. Also, see Article 6 of the CoE Convention on the Exercise of Children's Rights 1996.

35 See, *Hendriks-Netherlands*, Application No. 8427/78 (1982), where it was stated that there needs to be strong reasons to deny access rights.

36 Application No. 48322/17 (2019).

37 Application No.35141/06 (2012), at paras 57 and 69.

38 *A.I. v. Italy*, Application No. 70896/17 (2021).

39 *Neli Valcheva v. Georgios Babanarakis*, C-335/17 (2018).

40 *Mustafa and Armağan Akin v. Turkey*, Application No. 4694/03 (2010).

Denial of access

Unilateral opposition from one parent to the child's contact with the other is insufficient justification for separating a child from that parent.[41] As the HRC have advised:[42]

> It seems essential, barring exceptional circumstances, that these criteria should include the maintenance of personal relations and direct and regular contact between the child and both parents. The unilateral opposition of one of the parents, cannot, in the opinion of the Committee, be considered an exceptional circumstance.

Conflicting interests

Forty years have now passed since the ECtHR first established that in any context where there is conflict between the rights and interests of the child and those of a parent which can only be resolved to the detriment of one of them, as in,[43] then the interests of the child must prevail. More recently, in circumstances where the parties have made future child care arrangements a contested issue, the ECtHR would seem concerned to dispel any uncertainty as to the relative importance of parental rights and the welfare interests of their child. In *Yousef v. The Netherlands*,[44] for example, the Court stated unequivocally:[45]

> the Court reiterates that in judicial decisions where the rights under Article 8 of parents and those of a child are at stake, the child's rights must be the paramount consideration. If any balancing of interests is necessary, the interests of the child must prevail.

Later, for the avoidance of all doubt, the ECtHR emphasised:[46]

> the essential principle according to which, whenever the situation of a child is in issue, the best interests of that child are paramount.[47]

This assertion of the paramountcy principle – instead of 'primary consideration', etc. – as the grundnorm[48] that must govern decision-making in relation to issues

41 *Hendriks-Netherlands,* Application No. 8427/78 (1982).

42 Human Rights Committee, *Communication No. 201/1985* (views adopted on 27 July 1988, UN Doc. A/43/40, at pp. 230–241).

43 *Hendricks v. The Netherlands* (1982) 5 EHRR 223. Also, see, *Kroon v. The Netherlands* (1994) Series A No. 297 – C, 19 EHRR 263 commented that it was a principle of good law to hold that the interests of the child were paramount.

44 (2003) 1 FLR 210.

45 Ibid, at para 73.

46 See, *Mennesson v. France,* Application No. 65192/11 (2014), at para 81; reiterated in *K. K. and Others v. Denmark,* Application No. 25212/21 (2022), at para 52.

47 Citing, *Wagner and J.M.W.L. v. Luxembourg,* Application No, 76240/01 (2007), at paras 133–34, and *E.B. v. France* [GC], Application No. 43546/02 (2008), at paras 76 and 95.

48 See, Kelsen, H., *The Pure Theory of Law*, The Lawbook Exchange Ltd, 2009.

such as parental custody and access disputes, is of fundamental significance in the context of family breakdown: it places maximum discretion in the hands of the court to control the terms on which parents and children will thereafter relate, even if conditioned somewhat by the ECtHR acknowledgment that state authorities enjoy a wide 'margin of appreciation' in this regard.

Child's views/representation

In a number of cases, the ECtHR has been clear that the child's rights are limited to having their views sought and taken into account. They cannot be determinative, though they do have a right to proper and effective representation in proceedings. Moreover, in 2013, the CRC published guidance on assessing and determining a child's best interests which listed the following seven elements which should be considered: (a) the child's views; (b) the child's identity; (c) preservation of the family environment and maintaining relations; (d) care, protection and safety of the child; (e) situation of vulnerability; (f) the child's right to health; and (g) the child's right to education.[49]

C. v. Finland,[50] for example, concerned parental responsibility for two children aged 12 and 14 following the death of their mother. The children's views regarding arrangements for their future care, which had been sought and assessed by social authorities and experts, firmly indicated a preference for the mother's partner rather than their biological father. The Finnish Supreme Court duly granted parental responsibility to the partner stating that a different decision could not be enforced because of the opposition from children in light of their ages. This decision was criticised by the ECtHR for giving an impression that children of such an age could determine an issue of crucial importance for their future welfare. Again, in *M. and. M. v. Croatia*[51] (concerning parental responsibility for a 13-year-old boy) and in *Blokhin v. Russia*[52] (a child protection case), the ECtHR was critical of the domestic courts for not ensuring effective representation for the children concerned. In the first case, the ECtHR stated that the seriousness and urgency of the situation was not recognised by the domestic courts and noted that the child, who was 9 years old when the proceedings began, had not been given a chance to be heard in the proceedings. It emphasised that that a child's autonomy is exercised through the right to be consulted and heard. In the second, while the child could express her views, she had not been provided the opportunity to be heard. The Court stated that children may need additional procedural safeguards and that their

49 The Committee on the Rights of the Child, General Comment No. 14, Part V, *Implementation: assessing and determining the child's best interests* (2013). See, also, United Nations High Commissioner for Refugees, 'UNHCR Guidelines on Determining the Best Interests of the Child' (2008), at: www.unhcr.org/uk/protection/children/4566b16b2/unhcr-guidelines-determining-best-interests-child.html

50 Application No. 18249/02 (2006).

51 Application No. 10161/13 (2016).

52 Application No. 11175/02 (2007).

rights should be secured in an adapted, age-appropriate setting. In both instances, the ECtHR found a breach of the children's Article 8 rights. The Court found a similar breach of Article 8 in *N. Ts. and others v. Georgia*,[53] which concerned a father's claim for the custody of his three sons who were in the care of his deceased wife's sister. The claim had been granted by the domestic courts, but the decision remained unenforced because the children refused to move in with their father. The domestic court had instructed the authorities to appoint a representative, but the ECtHR did not consider this to constitute adequate and meaningful representation. It criticised especially the lack of regular contact arrangements for the father with his children. The appointed representatives drafted reports and attended court hearings in the appeal stage as an 'interested party', meeting the children only a few times which the ECtHR considered insufficient. It criticised the domestic courts for not considering the possibility of directly involving the oldest child and for not giving reasons to justify not hearing him. The proceedings had begun when the child was about 7 years old and lasted for approximately two years. The ECtHR also drew attention to the *Guidelines on Child-Friendly Justice* published by the Committee on the Rights of the Child.

Proceedings, orders and ECtHR rulings

Court proceedings triggered by family breakdown will – in all developed countries – almost always take the form of applications for divorce, judicial separation or guardianship, to be followed, if not already settled or if disputes later arise, by ancillary applications for custody/access or step-parent adoption. The grounds for the initial proceedings are now no longer exclusively fault based. In addition to provisions in the ECHR and UN CROC, the European Convention on Recognition and Enforcement of Decisions concerning Custody of Children and on Restoration of Custody[54] and the Convention on Contact concerning Children[55] also contribute to establishing the relevant international framework for custody and access rights.

Custody/access proceedings

Whether incorporated within the earlier proceedings or initiated at a later stage, the central issue will remain the same: to identify the parental custody and access arrangements that are compliant with the welfare interests of the child while taking into account the rights of parents and other parties. It has also become fairly standard practice to suggest – and in some countries to require – parental attendance at a family guidance or relationship counselling service as a preliminary to commencing proceedings.

53 Application No. 71776/12 (2016).
54 CETS No. 105 (1980).
55 CETS No. 192 (2003).

Mediation

The Council of Europe (CoE) has issued a *Recommendation on Family Mediation*, which states that recourse to family mediation could:

> improve communication between family members, reduce conflict between parties in dispute, produce amicable settlements, provide continuity of personal contacts between parents and children, and lower the social and economic costs of separation and divorce for the parties themselves and states.[56]

In the *M.H.* case, later, the ECtHR noted that domestic courts may be obliged to attenuate proceedings to allow for such mediation.[57] The Court suggested that this may require the making of interim decisions regarding contact.

Expeditious

From time to time, the ECtHR has ruled that an obligation rests on national courts to conduct proceedings concerning the custody of children with speed and diligence. So, for example, in *Cengiz Kılıç v. Turkey*,[58] the applicant filed for divorce in 2001 and for parental responsibility in respect of his son but not until 2009 did the court grant the divorce, when it awarded parental responsibility to the mother with specified visiting and staying rights to the father. He complained to the ECtHR in particular of shortcomings on the part of the domestic authorities, which had not taken the necessary steps to allow him to maintain relations with his son and had not removed the obstacles to the exercise of his right to contact despite the court decisions in which he had been granted that right. The Court agreed. It concluded, among other matters, that there had been a violation of Article 13 taken in conjunction with Article 6 (1), as the legal system did not afford litigants the opportunity to complain of the excessive length of proceedings.[59] Unduly protracted proceedings was also the issue in *Kuppinger (no. 2) v. Germany*[60] which concerned the father of a son 'born out of wedlock' in 2003 whose mother refused him contact from shortly after the birth. In 2007, he was granted interim contact rights, but all his efforts to ensure contact arrangements, supervised by a court-appointed guardian, failed. Ultimately, in 2014/2015, his contact rights were suspended – on the ground that contact against a child's will would be against the child's welfare. The ECtHR

56 See, Committee of Ministers of the Council of Europe, Recommendation No. R (98) 1 to Member States on family mediation, adopted by the Committee of Ministers on 21 January 1998, at the 616th meeting of the Ministers' Deputies, at: https://rm.coe.int/rec-98-1e-on-family-mediation/1680a3b3ef#:~:text=a.,cases%20covered%20by%20family%20mediation.

57 Citing, *Kacper Nowacowski v. Poland*, Application No. 32407/13 (2017) and *Cengiz Gilic v. Turkey*, Application No. 16192/06 (2011).

58 Application No. 16192/06 (2011).

59 See, also, *Polidario c. Suisse*, Application No. 332169/10 (2013) and *N.V. and C.C. v. Malta*, Application No. 4952/21 (2022).

60 Application No. 62198/11 (2015).

found that the German authorities had failed to take effective steps to execute its decisions and held that there had been a violation of Article 13 in conjunction with Article 8, finding, in particular, that he did not have an effective remedy under German law against the length of proceedings. More recently, *M.H. v. Poland*[61] concerned divorce and custody proceedings brought by a mother in 2011 after her husband had left the family home, taking their child with him. While divorce and contact proceedings were promptly issued, her proceedings for custody was delayed by seven months during which she had no contact with her daughter. The ECtHR found that child custody cases must be heard and resolved expeditiously: there was a positive obligation on the state to take such action as was necessary to secure respect for the private life and relationships of the parties; the requirement to examine and assess the merits of the case on the basis of qualitative and sufficient evidence were important elements of custody that must be respected if the proceedings were to comply with Article 8. The Court recognised that in such matters, domestic authorities enjoyed a margin of appreciation.[62]

Effective enforcement

As illustrated in some of the earlier cases, there can be a serious problem when an intransigent parent with possession of a child resolutely refuses to allow the other parent a lawful right of access to their child. In *R.I. and Others v. Romania*,[63] for example, the mother had been awarded custody of her two children but had been unable to enforce the orders, which left the children with the father. She complained in particular that the authorities had failed to help her and her children enforce the custody orders and act efficiently over the psychological abuse the children had suffered at their father's hands. The ECtHR found that the authorities had been placed in a difficult position, given opposition from the father and from the children themselves – possibly under the father's influence – but considered that they had not acted in a timely or reasonable manner to enforce the custody orders. It held that there had been a violation of Article 8. Again, in the curious case of *Santos Nunes v. Portugal*,[64] the ECtHR found that the four and a half years it had taken the authorities to enforce the custody order granted to the applicant was excessive and constituted a violation of his Article 8 rights.

Guardianship

A guardian – who may be a relative, foster parent or government agency – is authorised to 'step into the shoes' of a dead or missing parent or parents and to act towards a child as a good parent would. It has been described as 'one of the most

61 Application No. 73247/14 (2022).
62 Citing, *Fernandez Martinez v. Spain*, Application No. 56030/07 (2014). See, also, *Leonov v. Russia*, Application No. 77180/11 (2018).
63 Application No. 57077/16 (2018).
64 Application No. 61173/08 (2012).

important features of a protection system for children who are deprived of their family environment and cannot have their interests represented by their parents'.[65] As a component of national care and protection systems, guardianship safeguards a child's best interests, provides him or her with legal representation and, more generally, promotes the wellbeing of children, when parents are unable, unwilling or precluded from doing so, in line with Article 20 of the UN CROC and Article 24 of the Charter.

Types of guardianship

This ancient proceeding for transferring or acquiring parental responsibility had, until recently, been quietly fading in significance, reserved in the main as a private law mechanism for addressing circumstances where children or adults lacking competency were left without someone to safeguard their personal welfare, property and general affairs. One outcome of national family law reviews was a revival of guardianship, not just as a private proceeding but also as having a potential role in public family law.

Guardianship systems vary from one country to another but share common features and encounter common challenges. Regardless of the type of guardianship system and the national child protection system within which it operates, there are six fundamental principles, derived from international standards that they should all share: non-discrimination, independence and impartiality, quality, accountability, sustainability and child participation.[66]

Parental responsibility orders and similar

Family law has, over the course of recent decades, been reviewed and amended by most developed nations. In part, this has been prompted by the shared perception that it was no longer accurate or appropriate to continue with the traditional legal framing of the parent-child relationship in terms of the former's rights and duties and to the latter's subjective dependency. Instead, there has been an international trend to substitute the concept of parental responsibilities for rights and duties and to reframe that nexus of relationships to give greater weighting to a child's welfare interests/rights by adjusting the roles of guardianship, wardship and step-parent adoptions.

Family breakdown: contemporary jurisdictional comparisons

Family instability is a well-established aspect of contemporary social life and one that places the welfare of children at particular risk. Family breakdown, followed

65 See, EU Agency for Fundamental Human Rights, *Guardianship Systems for Children Deprived of Parental Care in the EU*, at: https://fra.europa.eu/sites/default/files/fra_uploads/fra-2018-guardianship-systems-in-the-eu-summary_en.pdf

66 Ibid, at pp. 9, 10.

by a reshuffling of its component parts with inevitable adjustments to home and parenting relationships, must be at least unsettling for the children involved. For many, it will entail broken attachments, loss of trust and disruption to relationships as to other former reference points and bring feelings of insecurity and uncertainty regarding their future. For some, it will also bring anxiety and depression due to misplaced guilt at having been the cause of the breakdown. With annual divorce rates continuing to climb – currently reaching approximately 42% in the UK[67] – there can be little doubt that family breakdown makes a significant adverse impact on very many children in the developed nations. The fact and consequences of such an impact will, however, in most cases, escape the attention of the court, as by far, the majority of family breakdowns are settled without dispute and the welfare interests of the children concerned will be left to the parties to resolve.

As with previous jurisdictional comparison chapters, this section identifies and considers the characteristic indicators differentiating the jurisdictions, then benchmarks them against the international norms established – primarily by the ECtHR – as identified earlier.

Family breakdown: principles, proceedings and court orders

In theory, the right of a couple to divorce, annul their marriage or separate if unmarried is conditional upon their first satisfying the Court that suitable care arrangements have been made to safeguard the welfare interests of any child of the family. In practice, where there is no legal dispute, the Court will be satisfied by an 'on-the-papers' scrutiny of testimonies submitted by the parties' legal representatives. Decrees for divorce or judicial separation may be accompanied by ancillary or alternative orders for custody, access/contact, guardianship maintenance, etc. They may also be followed by step-adoptions as the nuclear family is legally reconfigured.

The paramountcy principle

In *Y.C. v. The UK,*[68] the ECtHR advised that this principle meant the following:

> first, it is in the child's best interests that his ties with his family be maintained except in cases where the family has proved particularly unfit; and second, it is in the child's best interests to ensure his development in a safe and secure environment.

Recognition and application of this principle is at best uneven across the six common law and two civil law jurisdictions.

In the UK, before the Divorce, Dissolution and Separation Act 2020, the rule making divorce, nullity and judicial separation conditional upon satisfying the

67 See, ONS data at: www.ons.gov.uk/peoplepopulationandcommunity/birthsdeathsandmarriages/families/bulletins/familiesandhouseholds/2020

68 (2012) 55 EHRR 967, at para 134.

welfare test was applied with some rigour in contested proceedings but was not judicially examined in the majority of divorce proceedings which were by mutual consent. Since 2022, following the introduction of the 2020 Act and the replacement of the fault-based grounds with the simple 'irretrievable breakdown' declaration, the welfare interests of all dependent children are now cursorily affirmed, unless the court is put on notice of issues likely to compromise those interests. It is unlikely that this change will detract from the UN CRC opinion that 'the right of the child to have his or her best interests taken as a primary consideration is still not reflected in all legislative and policy matters and judicial decisions affecting children'.[69] Matrimonial proceedings being 'family proceedings' the welfare checklist applies. The court is required to be satisfied as to the following: the ascertainable wishes and feelings of the child concerned; the child's physical, emotional and educational needs; the likely effect on the child if circumstances change as a result of the court's decision; the child's age, sex, backgrounds and any other characteristics which will be relevant to the court's decision; any harm the child has suffered or maybe at risk of suffering; the capability of the child's parents (or any other person the courts find relevant) at meeting the child's needs; and the powers available to the court in the given proceedings.[70] In Ireland, following the 2015 constitutional amendment, Article 42A.4.1(ii) now declares the principle that 'the best interests of the child shall be the paramount consideration' in application to public law proceedings relating to the 'safety and welfare of any child' and private law proceedings 'concerning the adoption, guardianship or custody of, or access to, any child'. This provision now serves to counterbalance those that, until 2015, had traditionally given constitutional primacy to parental rights and to the *locus standi* of 'the family'. The fact that it does so across both public and private sectors of family law places Ireland – in theory – at the forefront of child protection in the civil and common law jurisdictions currently being studied.[71]

In a dispute between two 'fit' parents in the U.S., 'the trial court must apply the "best interest of the child" standard to determine custody and visitation questions'.[72] Despite the presumptive rule that a fit parent has a right to custody of their child, when there is a contest between two equally entitled parents, the rule must give way to the best-interests principle which will determine the child's place of residence and visitation rights for the non-custodial parent and possibly for such others as grandparents. There is no federal requirement that the paramountcy principle should have any bearing on such proceedings nor is there any reference to a welfare checklist. In Canada, recent changes introduced to the Divorce Act 1985 is a degree of specificity in relation to interpreting 'the best interests' of a child under s 16(1) which lists of 11 specific factors but does not mention the paramountcy

69 See, the UN Committee on the Rights of the Child, *Concluding Observations: United Kingdom of Great Britain and Northern Ireland*, United Nations, 2016, para 25.

70 The Children Act 1989, s 1(3).

71 See, further, Aspell, J., 'Children's Best Interests? A Constitutional Question', *Trinity College Law Review* (2018), at: https://trinitycollegelawreview.org/childrens-best-interests/#_ftnref21

72 *Routten v. Routten*, 843 SE 2d, 159 (2020), at 159.

principle nor does it otherwise add any additional weighting to those interests. The SCC seemed to consider, in *Williams v. Hillier et al.*,[73] that the welfare principle was of doubtful relevance in this context when it came to the conclusion that a step-adoption was not subject to the paramountcy principle.

In Australia, the Family Court has taken judicial notice of the fact and importance of the paramountcy principle in domestic family law drawing attention to the breadth of judicial discretion available in relation to parenting orders and the specification of parenting arrangements when it advised that 'as the best interests of the child are the paramount consideration, the court may consider making such orders whenever it would be in the best interests of the child to do so after affording procedural fairness to the parties'.[74] In New Zealand – as in Ireland – a striking feature of modern family law as it impacts children is the pervasive statutory embedding of the paramountcy principle across both public and private sectors of that law.

The absence of the paramountcy principle in the family law of France and Germany is illustrated by the tolerance extended to the wishes for anonymity when requested by birth mothers and adopters/adoptees respectively, despite the consequences for the child's right to the information necessary to form an authentic identity.

Presumption of parental right to custody

Articles 18 and 19 of UN CROC, supported by Article 5, would appear to have the strongest bearing on this presumption which essentially suggests that the traditional status – rights and duties – of birth parents provides the best care framework for ensuring the welfare of their child. The right is reinforced by the following: Article 18 which requires states to assist parents and legal guardians in the upbringing and development of their children; by Article 18(2) which requires the development of appropriate services; and by Article 19(2) which adds that such services should include 'effective procedures for the establishment of social programmes to provide necessary support for the child and for those who have the care of the child'.

Birth parent and child

In England and Wales, this presumptive right is established by s 38(6) of the 1989 Act: as amended by s 11 of the Children and Families Act 2014 which inserted s 1(2A) to create a presumption that the involvement of a birth parent in the life of the child would further that child's welfare. In Ireland, the presumption is subsumed within the 'natural and imprescriptible rights' of Article 42.5 of the Constitution. In both jurisdictions, there are statutory provisions placing a duty upon the authorities to provide parental support services – specified in England and Wales more so than in Ireland – which gives rise to a reciprocal right to receive such services. As

73 (1980) 2 SCR 368.
74 Ibid, at para 65.

child welfare is not easily separated from parental welfare – the younger the child the stronger that assumption – there is a sense in which the parental right could be viewed as a proxy child right as the services are intended for the latter's benefit (e.g. cash grants for necessities, child day care vouchers).

However, the presumptive right is open to challenge. In 2015, the English courts[75] considered and dismissed the appellant birth mother's claim that 'the significance of the blood-tie cannot be denied'[76], and with it, the implication that residual traces of 'family life' as defined in Article 8 of the ECHR survived an adoption order. In contrast, a long-standing and singular feature of the law relating to children in Ireland is the considerable weighting attached to the blood-link as a judicial determinant of the welfare test when making decisions regarding arrangements for a child's custody or upbringing. In *N. v. HSE*,[77] as in *J. McD. v. P.L. and B.M.*,[78] the court stressed the importance of blood or genetic links between a parent and child and intimated, at the very least, that these relationships or links were of paramount importance in deciding parenthood.[79] In the latter case, it was stated that 'the blood-link, as a matter of almost universal experience, exerts a powerful influence on people'.[80] In the U.S., unlike the UK,[81] there is a presumptive right that a child be cared for by their birth parents. This right, constitutionally protected and well established,[82] requires a fit parent to exercise their right – and duty – by taking custody and responsibility for their child. In the context of a parental custody dispute, the best interests principle – rather than paramountcy – will be applied to identify the one most able to protect and promote those interests.[83] The Canadian approach[84] would seem to take this a step further: it sidesteps any presumptive parental right and firmly and objectively applies the welfare test to determine which parent – or grandparent – is best placed to further a child's future welfare.[85]

75 *Seddon v. Oldham MBC* (2015) EWHC 2609 (Fam).

76 Ibid, per Jackson J at para 55. Subsequently endorsed in *Re W (A child)* (2016) EWCA Civ 793, *per* Lindblom LJ at para 71 and in *Re H (A Child)* (2015) EWCA Civ 1284, *per* McFarlane LJ at paras 89–94.

These judicial views must be taken as overturning those of Baroness Hale who, in *Re G (Children)* (2006) UKHL 43 (2006) FLR 629, asserted that a birth mother could not be viewed as being on the same footing in relation to the two children as the other 'parent' because she was 'both their biological and their psychological parent . . . in the overall welfare judgment that must count for something in the vast majority of cases', at para 44.

77 (2006) 1 I.R. 374.

78 (2008) 1 IR 417.

79 See, also, *Roche v. Roche* (2010) 2 I.R. 321, when the Supreme Court considered whether a frozen embryo could constitute an 'unborn' within the meaning of Article 40.3.3.

80 Ibid, at para 81.

81 See, *Re W (A Child)* (2016) EWCA Civ 793.

82 See, for example, *Troxel v. Granville*, 530 U.S. 57 (2000).

83 *Routten v. Routten, op cit* at 159.

84 The Divorce Act 1985, as amended in 2019 with effect from 2021, does not concern itself with parental rights but unequivocally makes the best interests of the child the only consideration in determining custody arrangements nationwide.

85 See, *B.J.T. v. J.D.*, 2022 SCC 24.

If there is a presumption, it is one that favours awarding custody to the 'primary caregiver'. In New Zealand, while it is well established that the child's parents and guardians should have primary responsibility for the child's upbringing, this is subject to the statutory requirement that the paramount consideration is the welfare and best interests of the child.[86] Again, in Australia, the only relevant presumption is that it is in the best interests of the child for he or she to have a continuing relationship with both parents[87] and the judiciary have a wide discretion to specify the parenting arrangements so as to ensure 'the best interests of the child are the paramount consideration, the court may consider making such orders whenever it would be in the best interests of the child to do so after affording procedural fairness to the parties'.[88]

In the civil law countries – France and Germany – there has always been a legal emphasis on maintaining the parent-child bond. In France, it remains the case that technically, parental rights weigh heavier than the welfare interests of the child – as illustrated most graphically in the practice of '*accouchement sous le secret*' which continues the established right of a mother to absolutely and irrevocably relinquish all parental rights.[89] Also, and again supporting the traditional parental rights principle, there have been cases where the claims of a non-custodial but genetically linked parent have been found to be more closely aligned with a child's welfare interests than those of the person bearing actual day-to-day care responsibilities of a parent.[90] Germany – more like France than the UK – places a high premium on maintaining the legal integrity of birth families, an approach which is embedded in the Civil Code. This is evident, for example, in the investment of resources to return a child in care back to their family of origin and in the reluctance to resort to non-consensual adoption.

Contact rights

In almost all parental disputes following family breakdown, as in adoption, there is now some form of ongoing contact between the child and their birth parents and/or with other members of the family of origin, but parental contact rights will always be conditional upon their exercise being compatible with the child's welfare.

In the UK, the court has wide powers – whether in the context of proceedings for divorce, separation or dissolution – to make such orders as it deems appropriate (under ss 22–24 of the 1973 Act and under equivalent provisions in the 2004 Act) as determined by the welfare test applied in accordance with the 'welfare checklist'.[91] The Children and Families Act 2014, s 11, introduced the concept of continued parental involvement into the 1989 Act (s 1[2A]) requiring the court,

86 The Care of Children Act 2004, s 4.
87 See, the Family Law Act 1975, s 61DA.
88 *Goode & Goode* (2006) FamCA 1346, at para 65.
89 *Odièvre v. France* (2003) 1 FCR 621.
90 *Mandet v. France,* Application No. 30955/12 (2016).
91 The Children Act 1989, s 1(3).

when considering a parental application regarding a child's living and contact arrangements, to presume (unless the contrary is shown) that involvement of the applicant parent in the life of the child will further his or her welfare. The order may accommodate contact arrangements between the child and wider family members such as grandparents and siblings. In Ireland, an 'access order' may be granted in recognition of the right of a child to maintain contact with someone, usually a parent but sometimes a grandparent[92] or other person with whom the child does not reside but with whom they have a meaningful relationship. The capacity to grant such an order is governed by Article 42A.4.1(ii) of the Constitution which declares that 'the best interests of the child shall be the paramount consideration ... in proceedings concerning the adoption, guardianship or custody of, or access to, any child'. The fact that the paramountcy principle is constitutionally protected and framed to govern such a wide spread of specified matters concerning a child is a recent and singular characteristic of Irish child care law. Again, what constitutes the welfare interests of a particular child is to be determined in accordance with a statutory checklist.[93]

In the U.S., in issues regarding parental custody or contact disputes 'the trial court must apply the "best interest of the child" standard to determine custody and visitation questions'.[94] There is no equivalent to the menu of function-specific private family orders available in the UK, such as child arrangements orders, 'prohibited steps', etc. Similarly in Canada, where the federal Divorce Act 1985, as revised in 1986 and last amended in 2019, makes the best interests of the child the only consideration in determining custody and contact arrangements nationwide. Amendments, which took effect in 2021, state that when doing so, a court must (under s 16[1]) apply only the 'best-interests' test and be guided (under s 16[3]) by a list of 11 specific factors that include the child's views and preferences, any court action or order relevant to the child's safety and wellbeing and any history of family violence. It makes no mention of the paramountcy principle nor does it otherwise add any additional weighting to their welfare interests.

In Australia, the now very dated Family Law Act 1975 continues to have federal application in respect of family matters, focusing on the rights of children and on parental responsibilities. The Family Law Amendment (Shared Parental Responsibility) Act 2006 placed a sharper focus on the rights of children to have a meaningful relationship with both their parents and to be protected from harm, encouraging parents to equally share responsibility for their children after separation, and established a presumption that it is in the best interests of the child for him or her to have a continuing relationship with both parents.[95] As the Family Court of Australia stressed in *Goode & Goode*[96] in relation to parenting orders, 'as the best interests

92 The Guardianship of Infants Act 1964 as amended by the Children Act 1997, s 9.
93 The Children and Family Relationships Act 2015, s 31.
94 *Routten v. Routten*, 843 S.E.2d 154, 159 (2020), at 159.
95 See, the Family Law Act 1975, s 61DA.
96 (2006) FamCA 1346.

of the child are the paramount consideration, the court may consider making such orders whenever it would be in the best interests of the child to do so after affording procedural fairness to the parties'.[97] When making parenting orders, the court must start with the presumption that future parenting is to be an equally shared responsibility. Much the same applies in New Zealand, where the Care of Children Act 2004, s 48, provides the court with powers to make a parenting order (replacing the 'custody order' and 'access order' in 2005) determining day-to-day care and contact arrangements for a child, including shared parenting arrangements. That determination to be made in accordance with the welfare checklist as specified in the Care of Children Act 2004, s 5. The order may specify that one or both parents will have the day-to-day care of a child or one parent will have day-to-day care of the child and the other will have contact or specify the nature and frequency of care and contact and impose conditions on day-to-day care and contact.

The governing principle in France is that both parents must take joint responsibility for determining all issues, bearing in mind that for one parent to prevent the other from exercising his or her right of contact and accommodation constitutes a criminal offence. If parents cannot agree, they must refer the particular issue to the judge who will rule on that matter. In the case of an intractable parental relationship, the judge may determine that it would be in the interest of the child to assign the exercise of parental authority exclusively to one of the two parents. In Germany, the Family Court may make a variety of function specific orders in respect of children (e.g. for maintenance, regarding education, etc.), but most usually, the orders are either for custody or for visitation rights and, again most usually, are not made in the course of divorce proceedings. Contact has long been recognised in German law as a parental right protected under Article 6(2) of the Basic Law, though is best understood as a parental duty. Under s 1626(3) of the Civil Code, it is held to be in the interests of the child to have contact with both parents and under s 1684 the child has a right of contact with a parent who is not holding parental responsibilities. The control function is very evident in the discretionary powers available to the judiciary who – under s 1628 and s 1666 – are free to make such order as is considered appropriate, whether or not an application has been lodged by a party.

Step-parent adoption

By the beginning of the 21st century, the use of such proceedings as an expedient legal means for a birth parent and new partner or spouse to acquire rather than relinquish parental responsibility for the former's child had grown to become the dominant social function of adoption in most developed countries. It may well be that the widespread judicial acceptance of this social function owed a good deal to the presumption favouring care by a birth parent: in the absence of protest from the other birth parent, there may have seemed to be no good reason why this

97 Ibid, at para 65.

arrangement would not be in the best interests of the child or children concerned. Since then, there has been something of a pushback against the appropriateness of using adoption to achieve objectives that could be achieved without having recourse to such a draconian order, but this change in approach has not been universal; much depends on the availability of appropriate alternatives and on the views of the judiciary.

Since 2005 in England and Wales,[98] a step-parent married to, or the civil partner of, a birth parent may opt to apply for alternative orders – such as a 'parental responsibility' order – instead of adoption or may be required by the court to do so. In Ireland, by the latter part of the 20th century, adoption had changed from being a means of regulating the non-kinship placements of voluntarily relinquished illegitimate babies and become more a means of sanctioning the private family arrangements of birth parents, almost always mothers, in respect of their own children. The Adoption (Amendment) Act 2017 introduced a provision enabling step-parents to become sole adopters without the necessity to do so jointly with the birth parent. In 2021, of the 101 orders granted (the highest number in seven years), 65 were to step-parents.[99]

In the U.S., adoption of a child by the spouse of the child's birth parent has been the most common form of adoption and the one attracting minimum professional or judicial scrutiny. By far, the largest proportion of all children adopted annually are simply the subjects of a process intended to legally consolidate their position within newly configured family arrangements.[100] In recent years, this would seem to have eased. While it has been estimated that more than 50% of U.S. children currently live with a step-parent,[101] in 2018, only 35% of all children adopted went to relatives, including step-parents. In Canada, national statistics show that in 2016, some 1 in 10 children were living in a step family.[102] A United Nations 2009 report has drawn attention to 'the sizeable numbers of adoptions by step-parent or other relatives, ranging between 300 and 600 annually' in Canada.

In Australia, while adoptions by step-parents and other relatives are reported to have peaked in the late 20th century,[103] they nevertheless accounted for 42% of all 'known' adoptions in 2020–2021. Unlike the U.S., for example – but in keeping with the UK – a general legislative presumption now prevails against adoption for step-parents and in favour of alternatives such as parenting orders, with applicants

98 The Children Act, s 8(1)(a).

99 See, Adoption Authority of Ireland, at: https://aai.gov.ie/en/

100 See, for example, Kreider, R.M., 'Adopted Children and Stepchildren: 2000' (U.S. Census Bureau, Census 2000 Special Reports, August 2003). The full Report is available at: www.census.gov/prod/2003pubs/censr-6.pdf

101 See, the Step Family Foundation, at: www.stepfamily.org

102 See, further, at: https://www12.statcan.gc.ca/census-recensement/2016/as-sa/98-200-x/2016006/98-200-x2016006-eng.cfm

103 See, Turner, J.N., 'Adoption or Anti-Adoption? Time for a National Review of Australian Law', *James Cook University Law Review*, Vol. 2 (1995), p. 43 for evidence that applications from step-parents and relatives, during the 1970s and early 1980s, dominated adoption proceedings in Australia.

being usually required to show special circumstances and convince the court that none of the alternative orders available would be more appropriate.[104] Under the Family Law Amendment Act 2006, an adoption order will not be made in favour of a step-parent unless the Family Court considers that in the particular circumstances, this would be in the best interests of the child concerned. In New Zealand, it is probable that step-parent applications will now decrease proportionately – as well as numerically – as the judiciary increasingly lean towards guardianship as being a more appropriate legal framework for such relationships. Step-parents are now encouraged to consider the appropriateness of less radical alternatives to adoption such as parenting orders or guardianship.

Step-adoptions probably occur at much the same rate in France as in the earlier jurisdictions but with one fundamental difference: they are confined to 'simple' or plenary adoptions. France has resisted allowing step-parents to use adoption as a means of usurping the legal standing of a birth parent. This use of adoption as an addendum to divorce, consolidating the reforming of families and constituting a significant generator of domestic adoption proceedings in this as in all modern western nations, has in France been confined to ordinary or 'plenary' adoptions.[105] In Germany, by way of contrast, has a consistently high proportion of adoptions by step-parents (averaging 60%): in 2021, of the 3,843 children adopted, approximately two-thirds were step-adoptions; importantly, 'simple' or plenary adoptions are not permitted in respect of children.

Court orders

The court has wide powers in matrimonial proceedings – whether for divorce, separation or dissolution – to make such orders as it deems appropriate, subject to any child support scheme, for the distribution of such assets, lump sums or periodical payments as may be needed for the maintenance of children. Traditionally, these were custody and access orders, but in some jurisdictions, these have been replaced by parental responsibility or parenting orders. In addition, traditional orders such as for guardianship and wardship have been retained, though, in some cases, repurposed.

Whether married or not, following family breakdown, the parents may either agree future living arrangements and contact times in respect of their children or disagree and apply to the court for a determination. The order granted may direct that the child lives with one or both parents or spends time with a parent or someone named in the order. It may be adjusted by adding such conditions and directions as may be appropriate to meet the particular needs of a child, including specifying

104 See, for example, in Queensland, where s 12(5) of the Adoption of Children Act 1964 (as amended) states that in such circumstances an adoption order shall not be granted unless 'the welfare and interests of the child would be better served by such an order than by an order for guardianship or custody'.

105 See Zachia Belmmoktar, info stat justice n° 175, fév. 2020, *L'adoption de l'enfant du conjoint en 2018*.

indirect contact, and it may accommodate arrangements between the child and wider family members such as grandparents and siblings. In theory, this provides a powerful safety net to ensure that private law proceedings are concluded in a manner compatible with the welfare interests of the children involved. In practice, it is dependent upon information being placed before the court, alerting it to the existence of grounds for concern regarding welfare matters. Even the full formal divorce process provides no guarantee that the court will scrutinise care arrangements for children.

Custody and access

These traditional orders are still in effect in the U.S. and Ireland. A custody order may either appoint both parents as joint custodians with equal rights in relation to parenting decisions and time-sharing arrangements with their child/ren; designate one spouse as the custodial parent, subject to specified visitation conditions for the other; or designate one spouse, or another person, as having exclusive custody and parental rights. It is usually made in cases of judicial separation or divorce, when one parent is granted custody, as well as in paternity or annulment, and may be issued in any situation where there has been a breakdown in the parental care of a child. In Ireland, the Children and Family Relationships Act 2015, s 57, makes provision for relatives or other persons to apply for custody in specified circumstances.

Parental responsibility (PRO)

In England and Wales, this order[106] provides a means whereby an unmarried father, who is unable or unwilling to acquire parental responsibility for his child by making a voluntary agreement with the mother, may be vested with such responsibility by the court or may otherwise acquire it as a consequence of being issued with other orders such as special guardianship or through adoption. Since 2005,[107] a step-parent married to, or the civil partner of, a birth parent may apply for a 'parental responsibility' order or enter into a parental responsibility agreement in respect of the latter's child[108] or may apply for a 'special guardianship' order.[109] These legislative initiatives provide less draconian alternatives to adoption. In effect, they require the court to give precedence to promoting the long-term welfare interests of the child rather than to strengthening the familial role of a step-parent (see, also, Chapter 8).

In Australia, a PRO transfers all duties, powers, responsibilities and authority to which parents are inherently entitled to a nominated third party who might be a relative or foster carer. In New Zealand, the Care of Children Act 2004, s 48, provides

106 Available: in England and Wales under the Children Act 1989, s 4A (as inserted by the Adoption and Children Act 2002).

107 The Children Act, s 8(1)(a).

108 See, for example, *S (a child), Re (Rev 1)* (2013) EWHC 1295 (Fam) (2013) All ER (D) 76 (Jun).

109 The Children Act 1989, s 14C(1), as inserted by s 115 of the Adoption and Children Act 2002.

the court with powers to make a parenting order (replacing the 'custody order' and 'access order' in 2005) determining day-to-day care and contact arrangements for a child, parenting order, which included contact and shared parenting arrangements.

In France, the concept of parental responsibility – which replaced the traditional legal terms 'custody' and 'joint custody' in 1987 – is now firmly embedded in French family law and is accompanied by a legal presumption that this responsibility is jointly shared by both parents until their child attains 18 years of age.[110] In Germany, the Family Court most usually issues orders either for custody or for visitation rights. These tend to be made not in the course of divorce proceedings but later or instead of such proceedings. What is conspicuously missing from the legal landscape in both countries is any equivalent to the range of issue-specific court orders that tend to characterise family law disputes in most common law jurisdictions nor are there 'welfare checklists' – to guide the judiciary and other regulators when making decisions regarding contested parental care arrangements or on other matters affecting the welfare interests of a child.[111]

Guardianship

This is one of the oldest legal procedures associated with substitute parental care and the protection of children. It is perhaps most likely to be utilised in a context where the family breakdown has been due to parental death or incapacity.

In England and Wales, guardianship orders are occasionally issued by Family Proceedings Courts, where no alternative is appropriate. In contemporary practice, guardianship has become either an implied component of the responsibilities of a parent or someone in *loco parentis* to a child, is incorporated into orders such as a child arrangement order or takes the form of a 'special guardianship order'. As with all measures governed by the 1989 Act, when determining whether to make a guardianship order, s 1(1) requires that 'the child's welfare shall be the court's paramount consideration'. In Ireland, the contemporary role of guardianship in a private family law context allows those such as an unmarried father, step-parent, civil partner, a cohabitee or a grandparent to be vested with parental rights and duties. However, recent changes to the law have extended it – if only marginally – into the public sector by broadening the pool of potential guardians to include anyone, such as a foster parent, who has borne direct care responsibilities for a child.

In the U.S., in small minority cases where family breakdown has resulted in proceedings for divorce, nullity or judicial separation – usually where the parents have been convicted of abusing their children – the court may terminate parental responsibility and instead issue a guardianship order or orders in respect of the children involved. In Canada, a guardianship appointment is most usually obtained by

110 Except for fast-tracked proceedings (Article 481–1 of the *Code de procédure civile)* for which the time limit is 15 days.

111 Paradoxical, really, given that the civil code characteristically 'codifies' judicial application of the law while the common law equally characteristically does so in a discretionary manner.

application to the court or by a child's parent making a testamentary appointment in respect of their child to take effect after their death but subject to that appointment being confirmed by the court.

In Australia, a guardianship order will vest full parental responsibility for that child in a designated guardian – probably a relative or the child's long-term carer – with effect until the subject reaches 18 years of age. Increasingly, such orders are being made in favour of foster carers as an alternative to an adoption order, in circumstances where discharge to the birth family is judged to be unsafe. A guardianship order may be made by a Children's Court in the context of both public and private family law proceedings – that is, the court may find that such an order, in favour of a responsible relative, would be an appropriate response to a child appearing before it on care and protection grounds and there is no realistic possibility of restoring the parent-child relationship. Australian courts have a well-established practice of preferring the less interventionist order of guardianship to the finality of adoption where circumstances permit. NZ vests in the appointed legal guardian the same responsibilities as a parent, including determination of place of residence, decisions about health care, religion, schools, culture and language, etc.

In any jurisdiction, once appointed, a guardian undertakes full decision-making responsibility for the child and is vested with responsibility for parenting time and may determine any contact arrangements in favour of third parties.

Special guardianship

This order, available in England and Wales[112] and New Zealand, provides for a named person to be appointed as the 'special guardian' of a child and may be made by a judge on his or her own motion. The legislative intent is that the order should be used to safeguard the welfare interests of a child in circumstance where an adoption order would be too draconian. It allows courts to appoint foster parents and step-parents as 'special guardians', where the child concerned has already formed a sense of identity and/or strong attachments to members of their birth family but where adoption is seen as inappropriate.

Such an order is considered appropriate: where older children do not wish to be legally separated from their birth families; where a child is being cared for on a permanent basis by members of the child's wider family; where a child is from a particular ethnic or religious community and cultural difficulties make an adoption order less likely to be honoured; and where an unaccompanied asylum-seeking child needs a secure, permanent home but maintains strong attachments to a family abroad.[113] In NZ, it allows the innate guardianship rights of birth parents to be restricted, relative to the rights of a special guardian, in the child's best interests. This is the order: specifies the access rights of existing guardians; allows the

112 The Children Act 1989, s 14C(I), as inserted by s 115 of the Adoption and Children Act 2002.

113 See, *Re S (Special Guardianship Order)* (2007) EWCA Civ 54. See, also, *Re M-J* (2007) EWCA Civ 56.

ongoing role played by all guardians to be specified based on what is best for the child; and requires the court to specify which guardianship rights will be shared between the special and existing guardians and which rights (if any) will be held exclusively by the special guardian. This will only be made if the needs of a child cannot be met under parenting and guardianship orders. Although theoretically a private family law order, special guardianship is most often used as a mechanism for transferring responsibility for a child from *Oranga Tamariki* to a private applicant. In most cases, all guardianship rights will be shared by the special guardians and existing guardians who are usually the parents. The court may consider giving specific guardianship rights exclusively to a special guardian if alternative methods cannot resolve any guardianship issues.

Wardship

Like guardianship, this ancient common law order now has a restricted application. McLachlin CJ's observation in *Manitoba* that the statutory provisions 'ousts the common law regarding mature minors'[114] and blocks the possibility of recourse to wardship is generally true for all the common law jurisdictions. In all, wardship offers the judiciary a default option when other statutory proceedings in either the public or private sectors of family law are not available or are inappropriate and the welfare interests of a child require urgent protection.[115] Essentially, the use of wardship is confined to situations of urgency, where only the *parens patriae* powers of the High Court are sufficient to direct intervention on behalf of a child.

Conclusion

The consequences of the earlier noted scale of state retreat from the traditional legal requirements for family dissolution are unsettling for family law in general and for the welfare interests of children in particular. This has become very evident in relation to the law governing arrangements to be made for the care of any children involved in family breakdown. As long as the parties reach agreement on parenting arrangements before applying to the court for legal dissolution of their relationship – by divorce, separation or annulment – then that matter is legally treated as private. As it has been redefined as a matter in which there is no longer a public interest, the Court will do no more than satisfy itself that an agreement has been made and that there is nothing obviously untoward in it. Knowing that, and wishing to expedite the legal termination of their relationship, avoid protracted proceedings and any accompanying exposure to enquiries and to additional costs, the parties in by far the majority of cases present at court with no issues regarding the future care arrangements for their children. In all the earlier jurisdictions, such agreed care arrangements allow by far the majority of parents to avoid judicial

114 *A.C. v. Manitoba (Director of Child and Family Services)*, 2009, *op cit*, at para 126.
115 *Hawthorne v. Cox* (2008) NZFLR 1.

scrutiny of their children's welfare interests at precisely the point in their family life when those interests are most vulnerable.

This is an unfortunate if natural consequence of the increased volume of family breakdown cases: it functions as a filtering mechanism to target only disclosed legal problems; any other approach would risk allowing the family courts to be overwhelmed with child welfare assessments. The result is that judicial scrutiny of child welfare in a family breakdown context is now very restricted – confined to proceedings where the parties are contesting child care arrangements – leaving to parental discretion the determination of the welfare interests of by far the majority of all children affected by family breakdown.

Part IV

Coherence – balancing welfare interests and rights

9 Themes

Comparative jurisdictional analysis; common law and civil law differences

Introduction

In this, the final chapter in the penultimate book of the series, the objective is to identify jurisdictional differences in the law relating to the welfare interests/rights of children in the six common law and two civil countries that have been the subjects of enquiry and to consider whether or not they may be symptomatic of inherent differences between the two legal traditions. The chapter follows the template adopted by its predecessors. Firstly, by way of background, it identifies the main policy parameters and briefly sketches the more essential principles. It then considers the jurisdictional differences in a public family law context: the grounds for consensual and coercive state intervention in family affairs, the welfare and justice systems and the topical problems associated with unaccompanied migrant minors and trafficking. This is followed by a parallel consideration of jurisdictional differences in a private family law context: focusing on matters such as adoption and parenting arrangements in the aftermath of family breakdown. Finally, it notes the main areas of contention in the emerging hybrid sector of family law such as parental abduction of children and adoption from state care.

Jurisdictional differences in children's welfare interests and rights in a policy and principles context

In the late 20th century, as traditional family structures and accompanying social mores ceded ground under pressure from the myriad challenges of modern society, resulting in an unprecedented volume of family law cases coming before the courts bringing with them a disparate range of attendant parenting disputes, the state began its staged withdrawal from intervention in families where child protection was not a presenting issue. This trend has profoundly disrupted the accepted division between public and private family law which had remained intact for centuries. Continuing today, it has proven to be a trend capable of generating a growing middle ground of hybrid proceedings – neither

DOI: 10.4324/9781003269595-14

wholly public nor private – which now threaten the overall coherence of family law.[1]

Policy and principles

In the eight jurisdictions studied – as in many others – child abuse and the need for related government policies emerged in the early 1960s generated by academic studies on the 'battered child syndrome'[2] and by developmental psychology research.[3] Since then, in keeping with trends throughout the developed nations, the statistical data available show increased numbers of children being removed from parental care and entering the public child welfare system.

Policy

The single most important and widespread policy change informing the law relating to children in the early part of the last half of the 20th century was probably the shift from a behavioural psychology approach that linked behaviour to the conditioning effects of the immediate environment to one which was based more on pure psychology and viewed the individual as responsible for his or her behaviour. It was a change reflected in the move away from interpreting a child's deeds as indicative of needs and led to the consequent separation of welfare and justice considerations when assessing his or her behaviour. The founding of juvenile justice courts dated from this policy change. France, however, managed to sustain a more holistic amalgamation of both approaches in the role of the *juge des enfant* in which both were functioned in tandem.

The prevention/protection balance

By the latter decades of the 20th century, consensual preventative state intervention to assist vulnerable families had become an established, if weakly resourced, public service in all eight jurisdictions. In tandem with preventative initiatives, governments were refining and broadening the child protection grounds for state intervention in family affairs. However, there were some jurisdictional differences: state intervention in New Zealand on child welfare grounds made no functional

1 See, O'Halloran, K., *Child Welfare & Rights: A Contemporary Family Law Analysis*, Routledge, forthcoming, 2025.

2 See, for example, Kempe, C.H., Silverman, F.N., Steele, B.F., Droegemueller, W. and Silver, H.K., 'The Battered Child Syndrome', *Journal of the American Medical Association,* Vol. 181 (1962), pp. 105–112.

3 See, for example, Bettelheim, B., *Love Is Not Enough*, Free Press, 1950, Bowlby, J., *Attachment and Loss*, Pimlico, New York, Basic Books, 1968, Goldstein, J., Freud, A. and Solnit, A.H., *Beyond the Best Interests of the Child,* Collier Macmillan, 1973, Piaget, J. and Inhelder, B., *The Psychology of the Child,* Routledge & Kegan Paul, London, 1969 and Rutter, M., *Maternal Deprivation Reassessed,* Penguin, 1972.

distinction between the latter's needs and deeds, so facilities for children – whether abandoned, neglected, abused or offenders – was provided in facilities such as orphanages and child welfare homes; in sharp contrast, Australia, like Ireland, relied on a patchwork of care homes, orphanages and industrial schools provided variously by religious organisations and government departments.

The welfare/justice balance

In the common law jurisdictions, the gravitational pull of these two reference points for responding to the criminal behaviour of children had, by the beginning of the 21st century, strengthened in favour of justice. Welfare interests were certainly not a determining criterion – nor even much more than a marginal factor – for the courts when considering disposal options following the conviction of children for criminal offences. Welfare had become an add-on consideration, along with others, to be taken into account for children found guilty of criminal conduct.

By then, there was a common jurisdictional emphasis in juvenile justice on safeguarding the public, blended with a mix of training and rehabilitation measures that have ever since represented the balance struck between welfare and justice considerations. A differentiating jurisdictional characteristic had, however, begun to acquire salience in the U.S., as the 'due process' clause in the Constitution was applied to ensure that processes and outcomes of juvenile justice conformed to constitutionally protected standards. Arguably, juvenile court proceedings in the U.S. have since become more adversarial in nature – requiring all the normal components and safeguards of an adult trial and tending to transfer juveniles into the adult criminal justice system while also adopting a similarly punitive approach when it comes to disposal options. Australia, with its notable emphasis on due process and defendant advocacy, etc., would seem to be leaning towards the established U.S. approach to criminal justice.

Principles

The same handful of crucial principles have had a varying degree of influence on the evolving law relating to children, their welfare interests and rights over the past few decades and across both the common law and civil law developed nations.

Parental rights principle

Vestiges of the traditional model of the family – a unit centred around parental rights, entitled to state support if called upon to provide it but, otherwise, its integrity to be respected and state intrusion restricted – still persist in the family law of many countries. In Australia, New Zealand and Ireland but less so in England and Wales, there is a relatively strong presumption favouring birth parents – all other factors being equal – as best placed to safeguard the welfare of their child. France and Germany are also characterised by a strong policy of state support for the family, but if, as Eglin claims, the role of the judge in France 'makes the French system close to a defence of the birth family and parents' rights ideology', this would constitute a singular feature of the French child protection system and one that differentiates it from its German counterpart.[4]

Parental rights and corporal punishment

The law in Canada, the U.S. and in England[5] permits a parent to use corporal punishment to chastise their child, subject to the condition that the degree of physical force is 'reasonable'. In Ireland, this right was specifically repealed in 2015. It is also legal throughout Australia but not in New Zealand. It is prohibited in Germany and was finally banned in France in 2019.[6]

The parental responsibility principle

This principle suggests that such responsibilities are exclusively an attribute of parenthood which may be temporarily met by other persons or bodies but can never be wholly shed by a 'parent' to whom, by definition, they must continue to attach.

In England and Wales, the 1989 Act unequivocally established 'parental responsibility' as a key legal construct in family law, thereby consigning the concepts of 'parental rights' and 'parental duties' to history. In Ireland, despite Article 42A, there remains some room for ambiguity as to the standing of this principle relative to the entrenched constitutional protection for the marital family unit. In the U.S., the concept if not the term is a cornerstone of family law as is the corollary of parental accountability.

The law in both France and Germany continues to bear vestiges of the traditional respect given to parental rights, in neither has this been wholly eclipsed by the concept of parental responsibilities. In France, the perpetuation of the '*accouchement sous X*' practice, allowing for an absolute and permanent renunciation of all parental rights and responsibilities, is indicative of state reluctance to radically intervene in matters integral to parental status. State deference towards parental status is most clearly visible in the lack of policy and legislative initiatives to facilitate the non-consensual adoption of children, failed and abused by their parents, who must by default remain in long-term state care (see, further, next section).

The paramountcy principle

This principle was first introduced to the law relating to children through the feudal concept of wardship as developed in England and Wales. The *parens patriae*

4 Eglin, M., 'Judicial Child Protection in France and England: A Comparative Approach' (June 2001), at: www.afmif.fr/Judicial-child-protection-in.html

5 Also permitted in Northern Ireland but not in Scotland or Wales.

6 Amending the Civil Code, Article 371–1, to provide that: *'Parental authority is exercised without any physical or psychological violence'*.

jurisdiction of wardship transferred with colonialism to the common law nations where it would seem to have put in place a basic legal platform for the state's relationship with children – as protector of their welfare – and in all such countries it continues to play a residual role. In none, however, could the hallmark of wardship – the principle that the welfare of the child must be treated as of paramount importance in matters relating to their upbringing – be said to have evolved to become the guiding light for ensuring the consistent prioritising of welfare considerations in the contemporary law, policy and practice relating to children. That was left to the judiciary in England and Wales.

In the latter half of the 20th century, the English judiciary developed the use of wardship and extended its application from a private family law context to public law, specifically to serve as a default mechanism to bridge gaps in the statutory law of child care and protection, until constrained by the 1989 Act which prohibited its use in any circumstances where statutory provisions were available. The paramountcy principle has since migrated from wardship to consolidate child care and adoption legislation and is now established as the governing benchmark in all related decisions taken in a public family law context. Paramountcy is a very recent newcomer to Irish law, having been restrained by the constitutional primacy given to the marital family. Not until 2015, when Article 42A amended the Constitution, did this principle become relevant in relation to public family law as regards the 'safety and welfare of any child' and to private, 'concerning the adoption, guardianship or custody of, or access to, any child'. It seems reasonably clear that in both the U.S. and Canada, this principle has a doubtful legal status and functionality – certainly less so than in the UK. In both, the laws regulating child welfare–related matters are devolved to states and provinces, resulting in a disparate range of weightings being given to the welfare principle in different contexts, depriving it of any possibility of acquiring a consistent, comprehensive and nationally defined role. Statute law in Australia applies the paramountcy principle comprehensively to matters affecting the welfare of a child, less so in New Zealand.[7]

In neither France nor Germany is there an unequivocal statement in any area of law to the effect that the welfare interests of the child must be treated as of paramount importance in determining any particular issue. Though in both, judicial notice has been taken of the fact that Article 3 of UN CROC applies to domestic law. It seems probable that in both countries, the paramountcy principle would conflict with traditional presumptions – constitutionally protected in Germany – favouring family unity, parental status and maintenance of the parent-child bond (which is not unlike the constitutional guarantees that have traditionally constrained family law in Ireland and have yet to be tested in the light of Article 42A).

7 In Australia, the Family Law Act 1975, s s 60CA, governing applications for parenting orders and the Care of Children Act 2004, s 4, which specifies that the welfare and best interests of a child must be the first and paramount consideration; and in New Zealand, the *Oranga Tamariki* Act 1989, s 4A, in respect of any matter affecting 'the well-being and best interests of the child or young person'.

Paramountcy and child's consent

Any interpretation of 'paramountcy' would be deficient if it failed to accommodate the right of the child concerned to contribute to a decision-making process affecting his or her welfare interests, establish when and why a child may independently determine such decisions and define the grounds for differentiating between the two. While both France and Germany have no difficulty in acknowledging the first, neither has any firm rules governing the identification of the few instances when the second might be possible nor do they have any clear rules regarding the third.

The fact that in France, the adoption of a child aged 13 or older is wholly conditional upon the consent of that child does give meaningful effect to the principle, but it remains unrepresentative of the legal weighting generally given to a child's views in French family law proceedings. Indeed, continuation of the '*accouchement sous X*' practice would seem a total refutation of the principle. In Germany, the anomalous right of a young child – even if younger than 7 years of age – to require the authorities to take him or her into state care is open to a capricious rather than paramount interpretation of welfare interests. Arguably, the weighting given to parental status in both Germany's Civil Code and the Constitution would nullify efforts to give legal precedence to the paramountcy principle.

In neither England and Wales nor in Ireland is the consent of a child necessary for their adoption.

The consanguinity principle

In Ireland, a consistent feature of the law relating to children has been the considerable weighting attached to the blood-link as a judicial determinant of the welfare test when making decisions regarding arrangements for a child's custody or upbringing. This long-standing characteristic has been repeatedly reaffirmed in Ireland, while in England and Wales, since the ruling in *Re G (Children)*,[8] it would seem probable that the judiciary now regard the blood-tie as no more than one factor among the many which must be considered when making such decisions, all of which are subordinate to the paramountcy principle. Judicial reticence to endorse the 'blood-link' as a persuasive factor when considering custody disputes is obvious in both Canada and the U.S.

In the CANZUS nations, as kinship grows to become the preferred placement option in an Indigenous and non-Indigenous context, so consanguinity is becoming an established norm in foster care and adoption practice. In neither France nor Germany does this principle have any obvious legal traction.

Indigenous communities

For the Indigenous people in the CANZUS nations, consanguinity – or bloodlines – is a matter of central importance. This is specifically given effect in the

8 (2006) UKHL 43 (2006) FLR 629.

'placement principle'. However, caselaw in these countries is clear that there is no legal presumption in favour of consanguinity: it cannot take precedence over the paramountcy principle.[9]

The proportionality principle

The 'principle of proportionality', as the ECtHR declared 40 years ago, means that any state interference must correspond to a pressing social need, and be proportionate to the legitimate aim pursued, if it is to be 'necessary in a democratic society'.[10] This principle is central to Article 8 of the ECHR and owes much to many ECtHR rulings. While firmly part of UK child care jurisprudence, it is noticeably absent from equivalent USSC rulings but does, however, attract a good deal of judicial attention in Canada. While the principle is prominent in the law relating to children in France and Germany – and both have been equally subject to ECtHR rulings on the matter – it would seem to have a more structured presence in German law. This may well be a consequence of Germany's mid-20th century history of involvement with fascism and the resulting emphasis given to the principle in the Constitution.

In the CANZUS nations, the national statistics disclose a wholly disproportionate weighting of Indigenous children being admitted to the child welfare system and to the juvenile justice system and a similar adverse weighting in relation to those Indigenous children who are reared in poverty, who leave school without qualifications and who do not enter third level education or professional careers.[11]

Jurisdictional differences in children's welfare interests and rights in a public family law context

In all six common law countries and in the two from the civil law tradition, public family law has been under considerable stress for the past few decades due partly to the increasing numbers of families disadvantaged by rising levels of poverty and the decreasing capacity of governments to fund ameliorative public services. In addition to the growing numbers of children being admitted to public welfare and justice systems, governments have been further stretched by the arrival of tens of thousands of unaccompanied migrant minors.

Consensual state intervention

The availability of voluntary admissions to state care has always been indicative of state support for vulnerable families in Ireland, where most children in state care

9 See: New Zealand, *K v. G* (2005) 3 NZLR 104 (HC), and *B (CA204/97) v. The Department of Social Welfare* (1998) 16 FRNZ 522 (HC); and Australia, *Rice v. Miller* (1993) FLC 92–807 at 85, 106.

10 *The Sunday Times v. United Kingdom*, Application No. 6538/74 (1979).

11 See, further, O'Halloran, K., *Children, the Law and the Welfare Principle: Perspectives from North America*, Routledge, 2023, at Chapter 4 and *Children, the Law and the Welfare Principle: Perspectives from Australia and New Zealand*, Routledge, 2023, at chapters 9 and 10.

are admitted with the voluntary agreement of their parents. Similarly in France and Germany, where there is a strong policy of state support for the family, including voluntary admissions to state care for purposes of short-term parental respite. Maintaining the parent-child relationship has been and continues to be a prominent feature of the policy governing state intervention in the family affairs of those countries. Whether intervention is on a consensual or coercive basis, the state objective as constitutionally stated is to restore parental ability to provide a safe home for their children. In England and Wales, the same offer of support, on the same terms, is often regarded with suspicion by such families who fear that a voluntary admission could lead to non-consensual adoption.

In the U.S., the Trump Administration presided over a sea change in federal policy aimed at bolstering preventative and consensual state intervention to assist vulnerable families through legislative initiatives such as the Family First Preventative Servies Act 2018 which has enhanced state funding for preventative services. In Canada, the 2015 UNICEF report ranking that country 17th out of 29 developed nations in terms of response to disadvantaged children prompted a new government awareness of the need to channel extra funding towards vulnerable families, which the Children's Aid Societies and Public Health Agency of Canada have been doing in recent years. In Australia, the CRC in 2012 criticised government prevention policies and urged it to 'take measures to strengthen the current programmes of family support, inter alia, by targeting the most vulnerable families in order to reduce the number of children in out of home care'.[12] This resulted in 'The National Framework for Protecting Australia's Children', which, judging from the increased admissions of children into public child welfare and justice systems, has not been very effective. In New Zealand, the record of government failure to address the chronic problems facing its children – including perhaps the highest global rates of teen suicides and of family violence – remains very poor.

Prevention

The best gauge of the success of a nation's preventative child care policies is the crude but telling statistics of the children it fails and who must then be admitted to state care. Applying that measure, the consistent over-representation of Indigenous children in the child care and juvenile justice systems of the CANZUS nations clearly demonstrates a failure of state consensual preventative intervention on their behalf. Indeed, the scale of Canada's failure is not just greater than that of the U.S. It's greater than most developed countries and not dissimilar to that of New Zealand. In both the U.S. and Canada, the drive to protect children by removing them from abusing or neglectful parental care would seem to be considerably stronger than in the UK and on a par with the rising rates of removal in Australia.

In Ireland, the relationship between state and family was constitutionally consolidated on the basis that the former would protect and support the latter;

12 CRC/c/AUS/CO/4, *Concluding Observations: Australia*, 2012, at para 19.

although the latter was presumed to be a marital unit. In England and Wales, there is a long-standing statutory requirement that every local authority shall take reasonable steps to identify the extent to which there are children in need within its area and make available statutorily specified services to their families. In Ireland, the Child Care Act 1991, as amended, requires the provision of such services as may be appropriate to assist parents and avoid the need for state care. The equivalent duty in England and Wales, under the Children Act 1989, explicitly states the preventative responsibilities of local authorities and specifies the services that should be made available, but in practice, the obligation to do so is mostly interpreted as being discretionary. The preventative provisions of the 1989 Act, reinforced by the Children and Social Work Act 2017 and those of the Care Act 2014, have no Irish equivalent. In both the latter statutes, the legislative intent was to require local authorities to focus on assessing the needs of children and young persons, especially those being discharged from care, to consider how such needs impact their wellbeing and to specify the intended outcomes of their intervention.

Specific support services

The relevant legislation in both Ireland and England and Wales specifies some services – voluntary care admission, accommodation for adolescents and day care for pre-school children – the provision of which is mandatory and others which are discretionary.

In the U.S., the Trump Administration introduced new laws and resources – such as the Title IV-E Prevention Services initiative – intended to support families and children in need and reduce the level of foster care admissions. These measures also had the effect of increasing federal control over state provision for families in need. In Canada, criticism regarding the relatively low levels of equivalent preventative service provision from international bodies such as the UN CRC have also resulted in federal initiatives to address the long-running service shortfall to the children in greatest need. In New Zealand, there are statutory provisions placing specific duties on the authorities to provide support services to vulnerable families, while in Australia, it falls to the legislatures of each state and territory to assign preventative duties to the appropriate local government agencies.

The law in both France and Germany requires service provision appropriate to prevent vulnerable families failing to provide adequately for the care and protection of their children – which is their prerogative right and duty.[13] Such state investment in support services is high in both France and Germany but would seem more so in France. This perception is reinforced by the fact that the French judiciary have discretionary authority to order the relevant authorities to provide family support services, which must constitute a distinctive jurisdictional characteristic.[14]

13 See: for France, the Civil Code, Articles 371–2; and for Germany, the Basic Law, Article 6(2).
14 Civil Code, Article 375.

The state in both France and Germany is to respect and support parents in the upbringing of their children.

Children with a disability

Such children and their families are in particular need of services, and in all jurisdictions, there are statutory requirements mandating provision, but in Ireland, service access is variable and often provided by voluntary organisations.

Coercive state intervention; the welfare system

Within the broad boundaries of family law, the most basic contemporary indicator of the welfare interests of the child lies in the statutory grounds for child abuse and neglect, while evidence of state-inflicted historical abuse can be found in the many official reports testifying to the fact that hundreds of thousands of children suffered as a direct result of government policy in the CANZUS nations and as a consequence of the English government policy of transporting children to those nations. Presently, however, New Zealand has the distinguishing jurisdictional characteristic of having some of the highest rates of domestic violence, child abuse and teenage suicides in the developed world.

Protection

Whether due to insufficient resource investment, inability to cope with the scale of family breakdown or resistance to consensual state intervention, the numbers of children committed to state care and remaining there until they 'age out' has been increasing rapidly for some decades.

Threshold for state coercive intervention

This threshold may, at first sight, seem much the same in all jurisdictions. In fact, however, the Irish threshold is higher: there must be compelling reasons why the child cannot remain within parental care, and he or she must require care or protection which they are otherwise unlikely to receive. In Ireland, the equivalent to the specification of 'welfare', as set out in the checklist in s 1 of the 1989 Act, is to be found in s 31 of the Children and Family Relationships Act 2015. The threshold for removing children from parental care would also seem high in France and Germany, relative to the UK, for example, but more so in Germany, where children can only be removed from parental care if there is no other option. In this context, France has carved out a middle ground: the *service d'adaptation progressive en milieu naturel* allows a child to return home on condition that parents accept and fully participate in an intensive programme designed to improve parenting skills. This expensive and invasive programme will involve teams of professionals working in the family home and in specialist units which parents must attend. It may last years, but it maintains the child in their home, in parental care and in their community, able to continue school attendance and local friendships. It would seem to be a distinctive jurisdictional characteristic.

Parental chastisement

A good deal of child abuse occurs in the family home, so an effective protection strategy would need to address that issue. One way of doing so is to make it a matter of law and public policy that parental violence is not legally permissible. Many states have legislated to protect children in their home environment. Both France and Germany now prohibit the physical chastisement of a child by a parent or anyone else, as do Ireland and New Zealand. However, parental chastisement remains legal in England, throughout Australia and in both Canada and the U.S., subject to the condition that the degree of physical force is 'reasonable'.

Mandatory reporting

The reporting of actual or suspected child abuse or neglect is a statutory requirement throughout the U.S. and Canada but not in England. It is also mandatory in Australia, except for New South Wales and Victoria, but not in New Zealand. The reporting of actual or suspected harm to a child, while mandatory in France, is restricted to knowledge of a 'crime' and in Germany, where it is also mandatory but restricted to those who work with children. There is good reason to believe that official deference to family privacy – compounded by an unwillingness to pry into and be suspected of reporting on a neighbour's affairs – is inhibiting the ability of German authorities to detect and effect early intervention in such cases.

'Safe havens'

Though illegal in Germany, such facilities are tolerated. They are prohibited in the UK[15] and Ireland but are legally permissible in France and in as many as nine other European countries. In the U.S., they are legal and available in all states, but in Canada, only very recently have one or two appeared and their legal standing is uncertain.

Welfare checklist

There is no statutory 'welfare checklist' in the law relating to children in either France or Germany nor is there such a federal statutorily specified 'welfare checklist' in the U.S. There is such a list in England, Wales and Ireland, and a Canadian federal statute specifies welfare indicators.

15 See, the Offences Against the Persons Act 1861, s 27, which makes it a criminal offence to abandon a baby.

Abuse or neglect

The indisputable evidence of the scale and breadth of state failure to protect children in New Zealand would seem to be a distinguishing jurisdictional characteristic.[16] In Canada and the U.S, neglect rather than abuse provides the main grounds relied upon for the issue of court orders transferring care responsibility from parents to the state which is significant, as it raises the possibility that levels of poverty rather than parental conduct is the primary cause of children being removed from their family homes; however, in both jurisdictions, it is probable that the relevant statistics would show a disproportionate weighting towards Indigenous children.

The CRC has expressed deep concern about levels of domestic violence against children in France and the lack of relevant data collection systems.[17]

Abandonment

The availability of safe places where babies may be safely and anonymously abandoned is a contentious issue and one on which there is no consistency among the developed nations.[18] The use of 'baby hatches' for that purpose is prohibited, for example, in the UK[19] but is legally permissible in France, is toleratated in Germany and is legal in as many as nine other European countries. In France, their availability is part of a long-standing and distinctive policy of facilitating the anonymous maternal relinquishment of infants. Baby hatches are available in all states in the U.S., but only very recently have one or two appeared in Canada and their legal standing is uncertain. Their use is condemned by the UN CRC as contravening a child's right, under Article 7 of UN CROC, to be known and cared for by their parents.[20]

16 See, for example, the OECD report that rates of child abuse and neglect are high in New Zealand relative to other developed nations, Gilbert, R., et al., 'Child Maltreatment: Variation in Trends and Policies in Six Developed Countries', *Lancet* (2011), at: https://scholar.google.com/scholar_lookup?hl=en&publication_year=2011&author=R+Gilbert&author=J+Fluke&author=M+O%27Donnell&author=A+Gonzalez-Izquierdo&author=M+Brownell&author=P+Gulliver&title=Child+maltreatment%3A+variation+in+trends+and+policies+in+six+developed+countries); the UNICEF report that this country has one of the worst rates of child abuse in the developed world (of the 41 developed countries included in the 2020 Unicef Innocenti Report Card, New Zealand ranks 35th overall for child wellbeing); and the Youth Health and Wellbeing chart, which ranks this country as having the highest rate of teen suicides in the developed world (at: www.newstalkzb.co.nz/on-air/kerre-woodham-mornings/audio/nathan-wallis-new-zealand-ranks-bottom-of-developed-countries-on-youth-mortality-rates).

17 CRC/C/FRA/CO/5, at paras 27, 42 and 43.

18 See, further, at: www.theguardian.com/world/2012/jun/10/unitednations-europe-news

19 See, the Offences Against the Persons Act 1861, s 27, which makes it a criminal offence to abandon a baby.

20 See, United Nations Committee on the Rights of the Child, *Concluding Observations: Czech Republic* (4 August 2011), CRC/C/CZE/CO/3–4, [50].

Promotion

This added-value adjunct to 'prevention' and 'support' is difficult to pin down in terms of its functionality and its defining characteristics as a legal term, let alone the difficulties involved in isolating and measuring its effectiveness. While it indicates an intervention that results in an improvement that would otherwise not occur, determining cause and effect can be problematic. For example, 'permanency planning' and 'family group conferences' are often praised as being initiatives that promote the welfare interests of children, but perhaps they are just new ways of naming old practices and whether or not they are genuinely new. It remains as difficult as it has always been to attribute positive outcomes solely to that practice when so many other factors are inevitably in play: disaggregating a promotional initiative from all other elements present in any intervention and crediting it with having made the difference is a questionable exercise.

Control: in state care

In all jurisdictions, children are either admitted to state care with parental consent or are committed without it by judicial order. They are then placed either with family members in 'kinship care', in foster care, in an adoption placement or in residential care. In the common law jurisdictions, retention in foster care, under the authority of a care order, is now the accepted basis for ensuring a safe family life environment for children in the public care system.

The Canadian child care population would appear to be significantly higher, proportionately, than that of the U.S. In both countries, Indigenous children are grossly over-represented as is the case in Australia and New Zealand. The trends for admission to state care differ markedly between Australia and New Zealand: in Australia, the number of children in out-of-home care rose by 7% between June 2017 and June 2020;[21] in New Zealand, 2009/2010 to 2018/2019, the total number entering state care had decreased by 33.6%.[22] Even allowing for a lack of synchronicity in the timeframes, the degree of disparity is difficult to comprehend, especially in light of New Zealand's alarming record of domestic violence, child abuse, teen suicide, etc.

Residential care placements

|Once the mainstay of statutory child care systems, the use of such placements has greatly diminished due in large part to the reputational damage inflicted by the number of official reports associating such care with a high incidence of child abuse. This was particularly the case in Ireland, Canada, New Zealand and

21 See, further, at: www.aihw.gov.au/reports/child-protection/child-protection-australia-2019-20/summary

22 See, *Oranga Tamariki*, 'Analysis of the Decrease in the Numbers of Children Entering Care' (June 2021), at: www.orangatamariki.govt.nz/assets/Uploads/About-us/Research/Latest-research/Entries-into-care/Analysis-of-the-decrease-in-the-number-of-children-entering-care.pdf

Australia, where institutional care was most often in facilities owned and staffed by religious organisations, and in the CANZUS nations, where the assimilation policy saw generations of Indigenous children being removed from their families of origin to residential schools and taught to abandon their Indigenous culture in favour of westernised cultural norms. This failed experiment in eugenics caused intergenerational trauma but also had the incidental effect of undermining the legitimacy of state residential facilities as a form of contemporary provision for children in the public care system.

In the latter half of the 20th century, Ireland, England, Wales, Australia and New Zealand radically reduced their reliance on residential facilities in preference for foster care. This was in sharp contrast with policy and practice in France and Germany, where reliance on institutions in preference to foster families – particularly in Germany – for a large proportion of children in state care is unusual for such developed nations, is out-of-step with well-established research findings[23] and has attracted adverse comment from the CRC directed towards both countries.[24] It is a sufficiently notable jurisdictional difference to constitute a theme warranting further examination.[25]

Secure accommodation

The use of secure accommodation represents the most acute form of state intervention to protect the welfare interests of children (whether that of the locked-up child or that of other children at risk of harm from that child) in a care and protection context. Safeguarding their welfare interests requires the provision of secure residential facilities. While all jurisdictions rely to some degree on such provision, the scale of usage is greatest in the U.S.

Foster parent placements

Foster care continues to be viewed as being most conducive to promoting a child's welfare interests because it enables him or her to retain links with their parents, facilitated by contact arrangements, which best ensure that he or she maintain an authentic sense of identity and of belonging to their family and community of origin. In New Zealand, foster care and kinship care were initially virtually synonymous, as it led the way in terms of involving the extended family to lend support in circumstances of parental failure: Māori traditional practice of prioritising family/community care for children in need rather than relying on state intervention is a strong and singular characteristic of this jurisdiction. In both New Zealand and Australia, the preference has been to favour family-based care wherever possible.

23 See, for example, Bowlby, J., *Attachment and Loss*, Basic Books, New York, 1969.

24 See, for France, at: CRC/C/FRA/CO/5, at paras 53 and 54. For Germany, see further at: CRC/C/DEU/CO/5–6, at para 27(c).

25 See, further, O'Halloran, K., *Child Welfare & Rights: A Contemporary Family Law Analysis*, Routledge, forthcoming, 2025.

Fostering services in the U.S. – as with adoption – are largely privatised, adding a for-profit dimension to the public care system in that country. All six common law jurisdictions rely heavily on foster parent placements, whereas the two civil law – while certainly using such placements – do so to a markedly lesser extent.

In France and Germany, a relatively high proportion of out-of-home placements are consistently made in favour of residential facilities which may correlate with both a strong state deference to parental status/family unity and to the, at best, marginal relevance of the paramountcy principle. The practice, if not the law, in both countries would seem equivocal as regards whether the objective is restoration of parental status/family unity or protecting the right of the child to have their developmental needs safely and appropriately catered for.

Kinship placements

Kinship placements are an attractive state option because they provide for minimal disruption to a child's sense of belonging within the family, class, culture and locality of their birth. It is a policy that often leads to adoption with many children being legally returned through that process to their kinship networks.

Ireland, England and Wales rely heavily on kinship placements for children admitted by care order to the public care system. This policy, reinforced by the use of guardianship orders, has been positively developed for some years by public child care agencies in the U.S. and Canada. In Australia, as of 2021, the vast majority (91%) of the 46,200 children in out-of-home care were in home-based provision, mostly with relative or kinship carers (54%) or in foster care (36%).[26] At the same time, in New Zealand, there were 5,239 children and young people in care and protection custody of whom 88% were living with family/whānau or with a caregiver of the same ethnicity.[27] The proportion of children – taken into care under the authority of care and protection orders – that are placed with relatives/kin is a striking feature of both countries. A distinctive feature of child welfare in New Zealand is the contribution it has made to international child care professional practice by developing and sharing not only kinship placements for children but also such innovative forms of family intervention as a focus on 'openness' and transparency in adoption and the use of family group conferences.

An interesting point of difference between France and Germany is their respective use of kinship placements: while this is a strong feature of child care policy in Germany, there is comparatively little reliance on the extended family for such purposes in France. While in Germany, the majority of children in foster care are placed with a relative (60% in 2005). This is true for only a small minority in

26 Note that in 2018–19, all states and territories adopted a standardised national system for defining for out-of-home care and for related data collection.

27 See, further, at: www.orangatamariki.govt.nz/assets/Uploads/About-us/Performance-and-monitoring/Quarterly-report/September-2021/Oranga-Tamariki-Quarterly-Performance-Report-as-at-September-2021.pdf

France (7% in 2007). This is unusual, given the use of kinship in all the common law countries, and constitutes an interesting aspect of jurisdictional difference.

Control: exiting state care

For some time, there has been a distinct jurisdictional difference in the response to the ECtHR statement of principle that 'everything must be done to preserve personal relations and, where appropriate, to "rebuild" the family. It is not enough to show that a child could be placed in a more beneficial environment for his upbringing'.[28]

Rehabilitation

The principle that the state should do all it can to maintain relationships between a child in its care and that child's birth family, and work towards their reunification, is in practice probably more violated than upheld. Foster care, intended to be a temporary solution, has instead become the ultimate destination for tens of thousands of children in care – the vast majority of whom will not be reunited during childhood with their birth families, most being shuttled through a series of foster homes, some being adopted by their foster parents.

In Australia, New Zealand and Ireland, the preferred policy has been to work towards family reunification[29] rather than impose the permanent severance effects of non-consensual adoption. In New Zealand, statutory provisions explicitly require the authorities to maintain relationships between a child in state care and his or her birth family and to work towards reunification.[30] However, in Australia during the last few years, there have been indications that in some states, this policy may now be changing to one of promoting adoption.

In France and Germany, the Civil Codes require the authorities to prioritise the safe rehabilitation of a child in state care to their family of origin.[31] In France, this is reinforced by statutes that necessitate planning for family reunification, wherever feasible, for every child taken into state care, and in practice, there is considerable investment in 'the ideology of maintaining the parent – infant relationship at all costs'.[32] While in Germany, there is no explicit equivalent legal obligation, the Constitutional Court has stated that the proportionality principle requires that every possible attempt be made to reunite families, but in practice, almost all children remain in state care.[33] Rehabilitation would seem to be largely aspirational: in Germany, it has been estimated that family reunification is achieved for no more than 4%–5% of the child care population; in France, judging from the CRC

28 *YC v. the United Kingdom* at para 35.
29 Note, however, that there is no nationally agreed definition of what constitutes 'family reunification'.
30 *Oranga Tamariki* Act 1989, s 13(2)(h).
31 For France, see Civil Code, Article 3750–2. For Germany, see the Civil Code, s 1673 et seq.
32 See, Berger, M., *The Failure of Child Protection Services*, Dunod, Paris, 2003.
33 See BVerfG, 13.07.2022, 1 BvR 580/22 and 15.11.2022, 1 BvR 1667/22.

recommendation to the authorities that they should 'facilitate the rehabilitation and social reintegration of children', the rate of successful rehabilitation is no better.[34]

Non-consensual adoption

Current UK judicial guidance[35] diverges from ECtHR benchmark cases,[36] and from practice in most other common law and civil law jurisdictions, but is in keeping with practice in the U.S. in that it has firmly established a policy preference for adoption rather than long-term foster care. This policy is facilitated by legislative provisions aligning the grounds for care orders and adoption orders, by the practice of concurrent placements, by the use of freeing and placement orders and by significant government financial grants. In Ireland and Canada, while there is no corresponding established policy, a few children do currently exit public care by way of adoption, those that do tend to be adolescents being adopted by their long-term foster parents (see, further, next section).

Coercive state intervention; the justice system

While in all jurisdictions there is a general duty to take into account the welfare of children, their justice systems are generally focused primarily on protecting the public, promoting accountability and preventing re-offending.

The French system is singularly different. The dual civil-criminal jurisdiction administered by the *juge des enfant* represents an approach long since abandoned elsewhere in favour of keeping a legal focus on welfare interests quite separate from that on criminal activity. The Civil Code directive that the *juge des enfants* should 'always strive to obtain family's consent to the measure envisaged' highlights the importance given to considerations of welfare rather than justice and is indicative of underlying state deference to family integrity.

Age of criminal responsibility

According to the CRC, the age at which a child will be held criminally liable for their actions is set too low. It recommends that this should be fixed at not less than 14 years. In fact, in most jurisdictions, it is a good deal lower: 7 years of age in some U.S. states; 10 in England and Wales, Australia and New Zealand; and 12 in Ireland and Canada. The age of criminal responsibility is an aspect of the law relating to children which differentiates France from Germany. While children in the latter – aged 13 years of age or younger – cannot be held criminally liable and cannot be prosecuted as adults if younger than 18, in France, a child aged 10 may be tried in a criminal court and from the age of 13, will be treated in law as an adult

34 CRC/C/FRA/CO/5, at para 54.

35 See, *Seddon v. Oldham MBC* (2015) EWHC 2609 (Fam) and *Re W (A Child)* (2016) EWCA Civ 793.

36 *YC v. the United Kingdom* at para 35.

and as such is eligible for a prison sentence. In France, the age of criminal responsibility is somewhat nebulous, as it is determined in accordance with a child's 'capacity for discernment' which can be below 10 years of age but is otherwise presumed to be at age 13. In Germany, youth offenders will be treated as juveniles until they reach 21 years of age.

Prevention

All jurisdictions have developed a range of diversionary programmes designed to keep youths from becoming involved in the formal justice system and to discourage those who have been involved from recidivism. New Zealand, with its particularly high rates of recidivism, would appear to have been less successful than others.

Children in court

The extent to which a child is authorised to participate in proceedings affecting their welfare interests – to have legal or other representation, to give consent to validate decisions taken relating to those interests – and whether their participation is age dependent are matters that determine whether or not he or she is being treated as the subject of or as a party to those proceedings. It is probable that judicial willingness to allow child participation in proceedings would be strongest in the U.S. In New Zealand, since the turn of the century, the statutory law[37] has required that a child's views should be brought before the court,[38] which, of course, does not necessarily that he or she, rather than their legal representative, will be permitted to do so in person. There is no similarly worded concession in Australian law.

Given that the changes to the court system, and the role of the child within it, transect both public and private family law, further consideration of such matters has been deferred to the next book.

Special children's courts

Such courts are those designated to hear proceedings concerning allegations of child criminality: the Youth Justice court in England and Wales, the Children's Court in both Australia and Ireland and the Youth Court in New Zealand and Australia. In France, the singular defining characteristic of juvenile justice that differentiates it from its German counterpart – and from that of other countries such as the UK – is that it is presided over by a judge who manages the criminal and civil proceedings as part of a unified system.

37 *Oranga Tamariki* Act 1989, s 11, and the Care of Children Act 2004, s 6(2).

38 Now, in New Zealand, under the Family Court (Supporting Children in Court) Legislation Act 2021, s 59(g), a child 'must' be given reasonable opportunities to participate in decisions.

Representation

Clearly, if children are to have access to justice, they need legal representation. Only then can they get the information needed to understand and effectively engage in proceedings, be informed about all aspects of the process and be advised as to options and decisions to be taken and their consequences.

In neither the Youth Justice court in England and Wales nor the Children's Court in Ireland is there any guarantee that legal aid and representation by a solicitor will be provided, and both require the child to be accompanied in court by their parents. Representation is not guaranteed in either the U.S. or in Canada, particularly in private family law proceedings, but is more likely in the U.S., where 'due process' case precedents are rigorously applied. In New Zealand, representation for a child is normally required in all proceedings commenced under the Care of Children Act 2004, and in addition, in all care and protection proceedings, *Oranga Tamariki* is required to submit a 'home background' report. In comparison, the corresponding requirements under the Australian 1975 Act appear to be a good deal more permissive.

In France, the *juges des enfants* conducts informal hearings in his office with the child concerned, their parents and the victim, together with the social worker and such other professionals who may be relevant in attendance. The judge arrives at a conclusion as acceptable as possible to all parties and thereafter in effect manages the local team of ASE staff, psychologists, etc., to ensure that agreed objectives are efficiently pursued. In Germany, the system centres around an orthodox juvenile court criminal proceedings, but these are conducted in a child-friendly manner, every child supported by a guardian *ad litem*.

Role of the welfare principle

The role of this principle is largely evidenced by the extent of the diversionary alternatives available to the authorities instead of a court appearance. In Australia and New Zealand, the role played by the principle in the juvenile justice system is evident in the fewer children entering that system.[39] It is notable that whereas in Australia, the juvenile justice system operates on the basis that the welfare interest of the child is the matter of paramount importance, in New Zealand, the principle – being confined to determining issues of guardianship and care – does not override justice considerations. In both countries, the positive role of the welfare principle is evident in the high proportion of offenders channeled towards community rather than detention options; and its negative role is apparent in its weak preventative function which allows a high proportion of children to transfer

39 See: for Australia, Australian Bureau of Statistics, *Recorded Crime – Offenders, 2019–202;* for New Zealand, Ministry of Social Development, 'Child and Youth Offending Patterns – Research Reports', at: www.msd.govt.nz/about-msd-and-our-work/publications-resources/research/child-and-youth-offending-patterns/index.html

from the care system to the justice system and fails to prevent the consistent over-representation of Indigenous and Māori children in that transfer.[40]

In the U.S., the welfare principle is ostensibly central to the primary objective of the juvenile justice system, which is stated to be the rehabilitation of offenders. In Canada, while there is no legislative mention of the principle, its influence can be seen in the role of the Youth Justice Committees and in the more respectful treatment of offenders in court. In both, the primary functions of the court would seem to be the protection of the public by holding youths accountable for their criminal behaviour. In both Australia and New Zealand, the Children's Court, or Youth Court, processes a relatively small volume of offenders and favours welfare-oriented disposals rather than criminal convictions wherever possible. A notable differentiating jurisdictional characteristic is that serious criminal activity would seem to be comparatively rare – unlike, for example, the numbers of children in the U.S. involved in gun crimes and those involved in knife crimes in the UK. Children convicted for fatal offences against the person are much less common in Australia and New Zealand.

In both France and Germany, the influence of the welfare principle can be seen mostly in the fact that community measures are imposed far more frequently than custodial sentences. A significant jurisdictional difference lies in the respective age parameters, allowing German youths to avail of juvenile rather than adult proceedings together with the associated sentencing tariff. In Germany, a notable feature is the low recourse to custodial sentencing: it has been estimated that the incarceration rate in Germany is nine times less than the U.S. (76 per 100,000 vs. 693 per 100,000).[41] Both countries have been warned by the CRC to be attentive to the needs of children who are victims or witnesses of violence.[42]

Family Group Conferences

Pioneered in New Zealand, as a model for engaging the family and wider community in the process of determining how to respond to the offender and his or her offence, the conference has a decidedly restorative justice function: its effect is to leverage welfare interests into disposal options for youth offenders while also requiring the offender to account directly to their victim and to hear the response from that person and from the wider community. It is a model now adopted by the authorities in many developed nations.

40 See, further, for Australia at: the Australian Institute of Health and Welfare, 'Youth Justice in Australia 2020–21', at: www.aihw.gov.au/reports/youth-justice/youth-justice-in-australia-2020-21/contents/summary for New Zealand, at:www.1news.co.nz/2022/08/24/startling-link-revealed-between-state-care-and-prison/

41 See, *The Crime Report* (2018), at: https://thecrimereport.org/2018/04/10/in-germany-its-hard-to-find-a-young-adult-in-prison/

42 For France and Germany, see, CRC/C/FRA/CO/5, paras 83–6 and CRC/C/DEU/CO/5–6, at para 23(c), respectively.

Indigenous children and the justice system

All CANZUS nations share the same inter-generational experience, whereby the Indigenous children are consistently grossly over-represented in the criminal justice system having, very often, transferred from the child welfare system where they were similarly over-represented.

Unaccompanied migrant minors and trafficking

The phenomenon of children travelling long distances without parents – who may be dead or missing – crossing borders, usually with unrelated adult migrants, until eventually arriving in western Europe or the U.S., where they are detained, is no longer unusual. Unquestionably, the challenge of addressing the welfare interests of such children is considerable, but there would appear to be little in the way of significant jurisdictional difference in the approach taken. While efforts are made to locate birth family members, protect the children from possible traffickers and process their applications for residency permits, the children are most usually assessed by relevant professionals, medically examined, then placed in foster homes or hostels and enrolled in local schools.

The CRC has been critical both of French non-compliance with the Asylum Procedures Directive, Article 25(6), which explicitly requires a host nation to have regard for the welfare interests of the child,[43] and with Germany regarding its treatment of unaccompanied child migrants and has recommended that the latter takes all the necessary measures to improve the situation of children seeking asylum and child migrants.[44]

Detention overseas

Australia has, for many years, been embroiled in controversy over its treatment of 'illegal' migrants, including unaccompanied minors. International criticism has focused on the fact that Australia's system of detention outside its jurisdiction fails to ensure that the best interests of a child are a primary consideration and that children detained for long periods of time are at high risk of serious mental harm.[45] It would seem probable that the UK, unlike Ireland and the civil law countries – France and Germany – will adopt much the same policy.

Trafficking

The unaccompanied migrant minors phenomenon overlaps with, and may often be used as a source for, the worsening social issue of 'child trafficking' which is defined in the Palermo Protocol 2000 as recruiting, transporting, harbouring or

43 CRC/C/FRA/CO/5, at para 73.

44 CRC/C/DEU/CO/3–4.

45 See, further, CRC/c/AUS/CO/4, *Concluding Observations: Australia*, 2012, at para 80(b).

receiving a child for the purposes of exploitation, such as sexual exploitation or forced labour. While the crime of trafficking is most usually associated with the purposes of the sex and labour trades, it is particularly pernicious due to its close involvement with such other forms of organised crime as migrant smuggling, drug trafficking, extortion, money laundering and document fraud, etc. The European Commission estimates that 1 in every 4 persons trafficked is a child.[46] There is little in the way of statistical data to gauge national trends in the rates and purposes of trafficking nor any hard evidence to differentiate between countries in terms of their response to the welfare interests of the children involved.

Jurisdictional differences in children's welfare interests and rights in a private family law context

Traditionally, the law has presumed that the welfare interests of children were subsumed within, and appropriately represented by, the rights of their parents; not until that authority had been displaced, or good reason shown for such displacement, would the welfare interests of their child warrant separate consideration. More recently, this equation has been reversed: child welfare and parental rights are now readily seen in legal terms as separate and distinct, with the rights of parents only exercisable subject to the welfare of their children not being unduly infringed.

Founding a family and family life

In all modern developed nations, families have changed: parents are no longer necessarily heterosexual, let alone married; families are often comprised of parents and children who are not necessarily genetically related; and overall, the traditional family unit is undergoing fundamental change with profound challenges for the future of family law. The scale of such changes requires commensurate changes to the law if the parties are to be equipped to negotiate the fluid complexities of contemporary family life.

The ECtHR has ruled that Article 8 in itself does not confer a right to 'found a family':[47]'family life' must exist before the protection Article 8 of the ECHR can be applied.[48] Nonetheless, in many, if not all, developed nations, the same wide range of family forms exist, and this most basic of human rights – defended by Article 12 – remains unquestioned (see, further, Chapter 2). Germany differs from France in that the right to found a family is recognised by the Constitutional Court and finds protection under Art. 6 of the Constitution.[49] Both are, however, alike in that they have policies which place a high premium on maintaining the relationships

46 See, further, at: https://home-affairs.ec.europa.eu/policies/internal-security/organised-crime-and-human-trafficking/together-against-trafficking-human-beings_en

47 *E.B. v. France*, Application No. 43546/02 (2008).

48 *V.D. and Others v. Russia*, Application No. 72931/10 (2019).

49 See BVerfG 31, 67 or 36,161; Antoni, in: Hömig/Wolff, Grundgesetz für die Bundesrepublik Deutschland, 12th ed., 2018, p. 131.

conducive to preserving the legal integrity of birth families. In that respect, they differ, arguably, from the UK and the U.S. This shared approach is evident in their equally committed policy – at least in theory – of working towards the return to parental care of children admitted to the public care system and in their reluctance to facilitate the termination of birth family relationships by resorting to the non-consensual adoption of such children.

Reproductive rights, etc.

In recent years, the law has been a good deal more concerned with the beginnings than the endings of family life. The restrictions on access to abortion, the use and misuse of embryos, genetic editing, intercountry adoption and commercial surrogacy are among the issues to founding a family that have attracted regulatory controls.

Reproductive rights, pioneered in the U.S. and subsequently becoming front and centre of that country's 'culture wars', are now a contentious focal point, polarising society in the U.S. in a way without comparison in other common law or civil law countries. Following the U.S. *Dobbs*[50] ruling in 2022 and the consequent prompt introduction of legislation restricting access to abortion in at least 15 states, these wars and the risks for the welfare of some children – sadly unwanted – can only increase and more emphatically distinguish this jurisdiction from others. In Canada, the 'Well Woman' centres developed family planning programmes, including abortion, that have been successfully transferred to many other countries. As in England and Wales, a more objective functionality has prevailed in the equivalent law and social policy relating to family and reproductive matters.

New Zealand has the singular jurisdictional characteristic of having one the highest rates of abortions in the world: a characteristic that, paradoxically, sits uneasily alongside the distinction of a domestic court ruling that a foetus can come within the legal definition of 'child' and, as such, is entitled to protection.[51] In France, Germany and Ireland, the policy towards abortion as a public service is similar, but availability is much more restricted than in others, such as the UK. IVF is similarly available but constrained. Surrogacy remains firmly contrary to public policy in both jurisdictions (see, further, next section).

Access to ART services in Germany is restricted and tightly regulated – most probably a reaction to the inhuman eugenic experimentation that occurred during the Nazi period – whereas, in France, IVF and other reproductive medical services are relatively readily accessed. Germany can also be distinguished from France in terms of abortion law. In Germany, abortion is in fact illegal (except in special circumstances) during the first 12 weeks of pregnancy.[52] In terms of rates of abortion, this is considerably higher in France.[53]

50 *Dobbs v. Jackson Women's Health Organization*, No. 19–1392, 597 U.S. ___ (2022).

51 See, *In the Matter of Baby P (an unborn child)* (1995) NZFLR 577.

52 The Criminal Code, s 218.

53 In 2021, France had an abortion rate of 15.5 per 1,000 women aged 15–49. In Germany, it was 5.4.

Adoption

The traditional role of the state in relation to children voluntarily relinquished for adoption by their parent/s continues in all jurisdictions, even if greatly reduced in scale. Jurisdictional differences in family law have been starkly apparent in adoption: in Ireland, it has always been almost exclusively a consensual process; in England and Wales, a much higher proportion of all adoptions are non-consensual. Also, in all jurisdictions, it has become much less a creature of private family law and developed significant public law characteristics, such as professional involvement, government support services and government assistance with accessing origins information. This has been accentuated by a recent and widespread acceptance of 'openness' which New Zealand is credited with having pioneered and which has since become standard practice in countries such as Australia and the UK but much less so in Canada and Germany. In fact, open adoptions have always been the norm in Indigenous communities, where its origins most probably lie.

Moreover, in the U.S., and to a lesser extent, in Canada, the involvement of for-profit adoption agencies and the parental right to directly place their child for adoption are singular indicators of characteristic differences between those jurisdictions and all others, though this approach is showing signs of spreading. The discretion to permit a commercial component to private placements is a distinctive and long-standing characteristic of the adoption process in North America which, elsewhere, is viewed as contentious.

In France and Germany, public policy has ensured that adoption remains very largely a private family law consensual process, most often used in a step-parent context. It shares the same distinctive jurisdictional characteristics, and these differentiate it from adoption in the common law jurisdictions. In both, this domestic legal process is available in plenary and simple forms in respect of both children and adults (though simple adoption has not been available for children in Germany since 1977).[54] It provides for a degree of maternal anonymity, is used primarily and without constraint by step-parents, does not permit the paramountcy principle to have a role in determining a child's eligibility and is subject to legal restrictions as regards 'openness' and information disclosure. This use of 'simple' adoption as an intermediate legal mechanism for transferring parenting responsibilities – in respect of both children and adults – not unlike guardianship, is a distinctly civil law phenomenon deserving of further attention.[55]

Anonymity

This traditional stereotypical characteristic of adoption when it functioned as a private family law process and which now seems quite archaic remains a feature

54 See, Mignot, J-F., *Child Adoption in Western Europe, 1900–2015*, HAL, 2019, at: https://shs.hal.science/halshs-02008838/document

55 O'Halloran, K., *Child Welfare & Rights: A Contemporary Family Law Analysis,* Routledge, forthcoming, 2025.

in some jurisdictions such as France, Germany, Ireland and the U.S. It also, curiously, is a legal characteristic of the New Zealand adoption process which has done so much to spread, internationally, an awareness of the benefits of 'openness' but which still continues to impose conditions on access to identifying information.

Step-parent adoption

In recent decades, the main use of adoption has been the opposite for which it was initially intended: by a birth mother acting jointly with a child's stepfather to legally acquire rather than to relinquish parental responsibility. By the early years of the 21st century, in both common law and civil law jurisdictions, this had become the single most common reason for lodging an adoption application. However, it has now come to be viewed in some common law jurisdictions as compromising for the welfare interests of a child because it's an extreme means of addressing an increasingly commonplace social issue, it legally terminates the rights of a birth parent and can be used to deny access for that parent and his or her family members and it can distort a child's perception of family relationships. Consequently, legislators in certain jurisdictions including Ireland, England, Wales, and New Zealand – but not North America – have, in recent years, introduced a requirement that the courts give preference to alternative orders, such as guardianship or special guardianship, when considering the appropriateness of step-parent adoption applications. In both France and Germany, adoptions by step-parents are the most common.

Intercountry adoption

As abortion and improved contraceptives became more accessible, so the opportunities for domestic adoption reduced, causing prospective adopters in many developed countries to turn to intercountry (ICA) sources. In all developed nations, the correlation between increased recourse to intercountry adoption and decreased domestic availability of voluntary relinquished adoptable children – particularly babies – was unmistakable. Non-consensual adoption as a public family law process has been balanced by a corresponding low reliance on the private process of intercountry adoption, as illustrated in England and Wales; the opposite being true in Ireland.

Canada and the U.S. have in common the fact that in recent years, they have shared the experience of passing from a high reliance on ICA to a sharp and sustained drop. By the turn of the century, however, all developed countries were experiencing a rapidly shrinking ICA market, as countries they had traditionally relied upon ceased to make children available, while surrogacy and ART have made it increasingly possible to by-pass adoption as a means of creating a family.

Cultural affinity

For an older child a placement which reinforces his or her existing cultural identity must be the most welfare affirming. Therefore, the policy decision in England to rescind the requirement in s 1(5) of the 2002 Act that 'due consideration be given to religious persuasion, racial origin and cultural and linguistic background', would seem to breach the Article 20(3) principle and be potentially contrary to the welfare interests of many children.

Cross cultural adoptions are most contentious in the context of Indigenous communities. In all CANZUS nations, the right of non-Indigenous applicants to adopt Indigenous children is often challenged on the grounds that such an adoption, by virtue of its lack of racial congruity, deprives the child of his or her cultural identity and, therefore, cannot be conducive, in the long-term, to promoting their welfare interests.

Post-adoption contact, information disclosure and state support services

On reaching the age of 18, but not until then, every adopted person in England and Wales has the right to access their original birth certificate and any information held by the relevant adoption agency. This is not the case in many other countries (such as Ireland and the U.S.) where the possibility of information disclosure is compromised by the practice of 'closed' adoption files and (in countries like Canada and Germany) is inhibited by a legislative and judicial approach which is generally not facilitative.

There is considerable jurisdictional difference in the extent of financial support available to adopters. Ireland, England, Wales and other countries provide employment leave and a compensatory financial payment from the date of placement, but there is no Irish equivalent to the level and duration of financial grants and professional support available in England and Wales, where it is accompanied by a full package of specified services. An uncertain level of post-adoption support from public and/or nonprofit organisations is available in both Canada and the U.S.

Family breakdown and parenting arrangements

Family breakdown and reconfiguration are much more common than previously, and whether marital or not, they constitute by far the most common risk to the welfare interests of children. It would seem probable that impermanent family structures and serial parenting arrangements are more likely to result in children with attachment issues, and for some, this will manifest itself in behavioural problems that may well lead them into deviant behaviour and into the public child welfare system. All developed countries have experienced a decline in matrimonial proceedings but an increase in rates of family breakdown, resulting in a steady rise in the number of children becoming the subject of disrupted parenting arrangements. Nonetheless, parental disputes are the exception. Most parents privately agree their future child care arrangements. Domestic violence – obviously strongly associated with family breakdown – is a significant social problem and is particularly acute in New Zealand with a correspondingly greater detrimental effect on the welfare interests of children.

Divorce, judicial separation and nullity

The term 'matrimonial proceedings' is becoming steadily more redundant as the parties in an increasing proportion of court proceedings, involving custody or other arrangements concerning the future care of children, are unmarried, or are not married to each other. In general, the relevant law is characterised mostly by state withdrawal from parental decisions on marital status. In fact, in no area of family law is the general policy of state retreat more evident than in the aftermath of family breakdown. Whether or not the parents are married, the law now leaves it to the parties to sort out their affairs. Only if they choose to go to court to contest some aspect of their previously shared assets and parental responsibilities will the law have anything to say about how the parties resolve their differences.

Consequently, in by far the majority of cases, the arrangements are treated as private matters, not amenable to public probing by the judiciary, unless a routine cursory check by a solicitor for one of the parties should give rise to a cause for concern. Where the care arrangements are being disputed, then the paramountcy principle is applied to determine the outcome. In Ireland, New Zealand and Canada, as in England and Wales, a statutory 'welfare checklist' is applied to determine whether or not – or to what extent – the arrangements comply with child welfare indicators. There is no federal equivalent in the U.S.

In the U.S., as in Canada, there is a statutory requirement that a child's wishes be factored into any determination of his or her best interests in custody decisions, while in Australia and New Zealand, their views would certainly be sought, but in no jurisdiction is there any evidence from the caselaw that their consent is necessary. As elsewhere among the developed nations, the marriage rate in France and Germany is in decline, divorces are increasing and there is a steady growth in the proportion of children who are not living with both birth parents, some sharing home life with others to whom they are not genetically related. Germany differs from France, however, in that its family life is generally more stable which, presumably, increases the probability of more German children growing up in a secure framework of consistent relationships.[56] Unlike the law in other countries such as the UK, the courts in France nor Germany do not have available to them a menu of statutory orders each specifying a particular function that can be explicitly permitted or denied to one or both of the parties.[57] In this respect, Germany differs from France in that it can make specific private family orders such as for custody and contact. While both countries share the common legal characteristic that the child concerned must be able to exercise their right to advise the court as to their views regarding proposed arrangements for their care, in neither country is this right determinative.

56 See, further, at: www.huffingtonpost.co.uk/2012/12/29/uk-family-breakdown-rate-_n_2379845.html?view=print

57 As mentioned elsewhere, the absence of 'a menu of statutory orders' may simply reflect a fundamental difference between the common law – founded on the 'no writ, no remedy' approach – and the more accommodating flexibility of the civil law.

Guardianship

This ancient judicial power for entrusting the welfare and property of a child to an appointed person until the child 'comes of age' – initially the most private of family law orders – has experienced something of a revival in recent years. In all common law jurisdictions, birth parents are normally held to be joint guardians of their birth child and legal processes are available for a birth father to acquire guardianship if not already vested with it. Most usually, this order is a means of vesting parental responsibility for a child in someone other than the child's parents. It continues to have a prominent role in Ireland, though less so in England and Wales.

Wardship

In Canada, as in Australia and New Zealand, wardship would seem to function largely as a public order ascribing a status to certain children in state care and as an emergency backstop private law order when statutory alternatives are insufficient in the circumstances or are not readily available.

Jurisdictional differences in children's welfare interests and rights in a hybrid family law context

Increasingly, the primary trend in family law has been the developing cross-sectoral capacity of the welfare principle, whether the proceedings are public or private in nature. A policy thrust has developed that requires the law to follow the needs of the child. The welfare principle has evolved to become a free-standing legal tool to be developed and applied across both public and private family law. Among the consequences has been the emergence of what may be termed 'hybrid' public-private matters – including adoption from state care, commercial surrogacy, parental child abduction together with poverty and public services – which, as they fall outside the traditional understanding of what constitutes family law, are merely noted in this book.[58]

Locus standi of children

The governments in a growing number of countries now signal the importance they attach to the needs of children as a public policy matter by appointing ministers and establishing advocacy bodies with a specific brief to promote their rights and welfare interests and monitor the appropriateness and effectiveness of related services. These include such officials as the Children's Commissioner in England and Wales, the Ombudsman for Children in Ireland, the Chief Children's Commissioner in New Zealand and the National Commissioner for Children in Australia. In France, the office of *Défenseur des Enfants* is an independence but government-funded

58 See, O'Halloran, K., *Child Welfare & Rights: A Contemporary Family Law Analysis*, Routledge, forthcoming.

body, which functions as a subsidiary of a national human rights agency, is located within it and shares its regional offices. In Germany, while there is no national office, there are mandatory locally based *Ombudsstellen* agencies across Germany.

Child

UN CROC defines a child as someone who is less than 18 years of age. In practice, there is some jurisdictional variation: in New Zealand, a 'child' is defined as such in law until he or she attains 20 years of age.

Consent

In keeping with the traditional legal presumption that responsibility for the welfare interests of a child is a matter that lies within the rights and responsibilities of parents, the latter are generally taken to be vested with the authority to make decisions – certainly medical decisions – on behalf of their child. This approach continues despite a fundamental principle of UN CROC, as elaborated in the General Comments, that an 'adult's judgment of a child's best interests cannot override the obligation to respect all of the child's rights under UN CROC'.[59] In fact, there are very few circumstances in which the consent of the child concerned is a legislative requirement for a decision affecting his or her welfare. It, therefore, seems somewhat anomalous that in adoption proceedings in some Australian states, the consent of a child aged 12 years or more is a prerequisite for their adoption and for a guardianship order.

In England and Wales, the *Gillick* decision[60] has provided legal authority for the rule that a child – less than 16 years of age – with sufficient maturity and discernment to understand an issue and its consequences, is entitled to give or withhold their consent in relation to it. In Ireland, the traditional rule requiring the views to be sought and taken into account prevails: there is neither statutory provision nor caselaw granting a child the right to make legally binding decisions. In the U.S., all states have statutes that in certain circumstances allow or require a minor to give their consent to proposed medical treatment and some in relation to the child's proposed adoption, though there is evidence that the judiciary are reluctant to accept the decision of an under-16-year-old adolescent. In Canada, the courts seem to operate on the principle that the greater the age and maturity of the child, the lesser the scope for parental determination and vice versa. In both Australia and New Zealand, while the law seeks a child's views in relation to matters such as medical treatment,[61] it does not – usually – require their consent until they reach the age

59 Committee on the Rights of the Children, General Comment No. 14 (2013) on the right of the child to have his or her best interests taken as a primary consideration (art. 3, para 1)* CRC/C/GC/14, at para 4.

60 *Gillick v. West Norfolk and Wisbech Area Health Authority* (1986) 1 AC 112 (1985) 3 All ER 402, HL.

61 *Auckland Healthcare Services Ltd v. Liu*, High Court, Auckland, M812/96 (11 July 1996).

of 16. There are some anomalous exceptions: the legislation of some Australian states require the consent of a child aged 12 years to be obtained as a prerequisite for his or her adoption, while in New Zealand, the provision of state respite care is conditional upon the consent of the child concerned, if 12 years of age or more and if the respite is for an extended period. And in Germany, a valid legal consent to sexual relations can be given at age 14.

Representation

For the welfare interests and rights of children to be given full recognition and weighting in the many fora in which decisions affecting them are taken, it is essential that they are represented by relevant professionals with the expertise to mediate on their behalf.

In England and Wales, the child is normally a party in public law proceedings, and therefore, a guardian and, most usually, a solicitor will be appointed but not in the majority of private proceedings which are uncontested unless there are significant issues. In Ireland, there is less probability of a child being granted equivalent representation.

Adoption

In all CANZUS nations, adoption is irredeemably and indelibly tarnished by its history of abusive state use as part of government assimilation policies. This historical misuse of adoption particularly impacted Australia, where the scandals of the 'stolen generations'[62] and the 'white stolen generations'[63] continue to cause mistrust regarding state interventionist policies. The practice of 'forced adoptions' is not unknown in the civil law countries. Germany especially employed it during WWII in relation to children of Aryan genetic appearance in the conquered nations of western Europe.

Contemporary adoption from state care

In the U.S. as in the UK and to a much lesser extent in Canada and parts of Australia, the annual numbers of children non-consensually adopted from state care has been increasing – because more children are entering state care, because it secures permanent family care as the best opportunity for promoting child welfare and because it is cheaper than state care – to become a prioritsed option for the state in respect of children failed by parental care. In France, where parental ties have been regarded as legally inviolable, except in the most extreme circumstances, this

62 See, the Australian Human Rights Commission, 'Bringing Them Home Report' (1997), at: https://humanrights.gov.au/our-work/bringing-them-home-report-1997

63 See, Senate Community Affairs References Committee, *Commonwealth Contribution to Former Forced Adoption Policies and Practices*. Commonwealth of Australia, Canberra, 2012.

form of adoption is problematic. However, as in Germany, where children are in state care following abandonment and anonymous relinquishment or where the courts have removed parental rights/responsibilities then, as parental consent is unavailable or unnecessary, the authorities can proceed to place such children for adoption but rarely do so.

Commercial Surrogacy

Legal uncertainties accompany surrogacy arrangements in many jurisdictions – and are most apparent in commercial arrangements made overseas in respect of children who return to be domiciled in a jurisdiction where such arrangements are prohibited. While this itself is averse to the welfare interests of the children concerned, the fact that they are wanted so much by 'parents' willing to undergo the uncertainty and expense must augur well for their future.

Parental child abduction

This occurs when a child is removed from a parent or person vested with legal custody, without their permission and is invariably accompanied by contention if not trauma regarding the welfare interests of the child concerned. With increasing frequency, as globalisation accelerates the volume and rate of international travel, such abduction involves the legal systems of more than one country. The parties concerned find their actions and legal proceedings governed by the Hague Convention on the Civil Aspects of Child Abduction 1980 which requires the prompt return of any child wrongfully removed from, or wrongfully retained in, a country that is not their country of habitual residence.

Guardianship and wardship

These ancient judicial powers for entrusting the welfare and property of a child to an appointed person until the child 'comes of age' – initially, the most private of family law orders – have now, in the common law jurisdictions, become mediatory instruments in both public and private sectors of that law. They essentially blend a mix of state and parental responsibilities in respect of the welfare of a child and would seem to be increasingly used at the initiative of courts, state authorities and parents. Both are archetypal common law court orders and, to that extent, differentiate the common law and civil law jurisdictions as they relate to the welfare interests of children.

Guardianship

A guardianship order will most often be the outcome of a private application in respect of a child who may be in the public care system, or who may not, but in respect of whom parental care is unavailable. It may also, of course, arise from a parental testamentary appointment.

Special guardianship

This statutory order vests a special guardian with responsibility for day-to-day care of a child until the latter reaches 18 years of age. It is now available in the UK, in New Zealand and in some Australian states, where it is used as a means of transferring parental responsibility from public authorities to private applicants. It is accompanied by an entitlement to apply for welfare benefits and is being viewed by policymakers as having potential to be a less radical substitute for both non-consensual adoption from public care and for step-parent adoptions.

Wardship

Canada, New Zealand and Australia have had a traditional public law role in designating the status of children entering state care for whom a return to safe family care is deemed impossible, and as in the UK, it has also proved to be useful in private law for assigning High Court protection and decision-making in circumstances where urgent state intervention is required and alternative statutory orders are unavailable or inappropriate.

Poverty and public services: education and health, etc.

A child's welfare is clearly not determined solely by whether their interests are recognised and protected by national and international law. The domestic social context, conditioning the daily quality of life for families and children, is most often the direct, all-encompassing and enduring determinant. For the majority of the population, the social context of daily life – health, education, etc. – offers security and opportunities for families and children. For a minority, many aspects of their social context are instead experienced as constraints: poverty and its associated disadvantages induce vulnerability and defensiveness. That minority in particular needs public services and ease of access to them. The extent to which a state provides for equality of opportunity and equity of wealth distribution, thereby raising the floor for the general wellbeing of its citizens and in so doing raising the welfare standards of the nation's children, can neither be overlooked nor be fully taken into account in a study such as this (see, also, Chapter 1). Additionally, the quality and accessibility of state public services will mitigate the deficits of the socially disadvantaged and have a direct bearing on the health and welfare of children. This is most obviously the case in relation to health and education.[64]

Courts and regulatory framework

Both France and Germany are subject to the ECtHR appeal process and to CRC monitoring in respect of children's welfare interests and rights. They both have a similar hierarchy of national courts and ancillary regulatory bodies, commissions,

64 See, further, O'Halloran, K., *Child Welfare & Rights: A Contemporary Family Law Analysis*, Routledge, forthcoming.

etc., but the federated governance structure of Germany means that the federal hierarchy (excluding a constitutional court) is virtually replicated in each of the 16 *Länder*. While they each have Family Courts (*juge aux affaires familiales* and *Familiengericht*, in France and Germany, respectively), France, unlike Germany, has a unified legal system – led by a *jug des enfants* – with a combined civil and criminal jurisdiction dedicated exclusively to the needs and deeds of children and youths. In both countries, a child of any age has the right to directly address the judge on a matter that concerns his or her welfare interests.

The court hearings in both countries strive to be child-friendly. This is most obvious in France, where, in sharp contrast to standard common law practice, the parties and the child are all encouraged to speak directly to the judge without the customary procedural stages and without lawyers, expert witnesses, cross-examination, etc. There, a child has party status in proceedings regarding their welfare – unlike a similar child in Germany – and may, therefore, elect to be legally represented.

In Germany, unlike France, the child subject of proceedings will mostly be supported by a guardian *ad litem* who will elicit their views, ascertain their welfare interests and advocate on their behalf before the judge. Nonetheless, any child has the right to be heard personally by the judge in any family court proceedings.[65] If aged 14 or older, the child may, if they so wish, represent himself or herself in all matters affecting them without the need of a legal representative. Both countries belong to the civil law tradition. The main body of domestic law lies in their respective Civil Codes, and also in both cases, the Codes together with other legislation and regulations shelter under constitutional umbrellas. While amendments to the Civil Codes of both countries have provided a modernised body of law relating to children, it should be noted that the CRC in 2022 found the German Code to be weighted in favour of parents and recommended that the government 'strengthen efforts to incorporate children's rights explicitly into the Basic Law'.[66]

Conclusion

Jurisdictional differences between the ancient common law and civil law cultural traditions are not as clear cut as they once were. By the early years of the 21st century, there were some indications of jurisdictional convergence, and these were probably due to a shared exposure to an array of influences that shaped a common response. Among the more potent of these, as regards family law, were as follows: globalisation, population movement and the resulting increased need to overcome differences in national laws in order to resolve the same agenda of issues such as marital status, custody and contact disputes, etc.; the inexorable demographic trends forcing a contraction in public spending; a rise in the rate of family breakdown, creating an ever-growing pool of vulnerable children; the emergence of a body of academic research – particularly in the field of developmental psychology –

65 See Family Proceedings Act, s 159.
66 CRC/C/DEU/CO/5–6, at para 6.

which greatly enhanced and informed a professional understanding of child welfare related matters; and the steady pressure from international judicial and regulatory bodies – particularly rulings of the ECtHR – encouraging national compliance with principles of international jurisprudence.

This chapter has focused on identifying the main areas of jurisdictional difference in the law as it affects the welfare interests and rights of children. In so doing, it prepares the ground for the final book in this series which considers the significance of such jurisdictional differences, and the growing body of hybrid proceedings that now transect the public and private sectors, for the future of that law.

Conclusion

Jurisdictional differences in the nature and extent to which the law impacts the welfare interests and rights of children in the six common law and two civil law countries currently being considered are many and varied, from incidental to structural. The question is, Do they conform to any particular pattern? A further question might be, Are they illustrative of a substantive difference in the law of the two cultural traditions?

Following on from the overall screening and identification of jurisdictional differences in Chapter 9, this closing section selects and summarises some of the more interesting contrasts that may be indicative of differentiating themes. It does so by following the structure that has framed the chapters in this and previous books while deferring the hybrid public-private proceedings – commercial surrogacy, adoption from the state welfare system and parental child abduction, etc. – for closer examination at a later stage. The next and final book will consider the impact of these emerging hybrid proceedings together with the significance of jurisdictional differences and associated themes for family law coherence.

Family, the law and social context

That family law is shaped by cultural context[1] remains true but to a lesser degree than formerly. It has been impacted by global changes that may prove to be capable of displacing cultural context, including the following: the fact that parents are no longer necessarily heterosexual; families are often comprised of parents and children who are not necessarily genetically related, are more mobile and much less likely to be uniformly influenced by the same set of Christian values; and families are not as settled or as durable as they once were, often mutating into shifting shapes as component parts come and go. Overall, the model of the traditional family unit has undergone fundamental change, requiring the law to adapt accordingly, which is likely to at least dilute the influence of cultural context.

1 A conclusion reflected in the majority ruling of the ECtHR in *A, B and C v. Ireland*, Application No. 25579/05 (2010).

DOI: 10.4324/9781003269595-15

Nonetheless, cultural context continues to be significant factor. How else can we explain facts such as the following: the right of a young German child – even if younger than 7 years of age – to require the authorities to take him or her into state care; France and Germany now prohibit parental chastisement but England does not; the reporting of actual or suspected child abuse or neglect is a statutory requirement throughout the U.S. and Canada but not in England; in some U.S. states, the age of criminal responsibility is 7 years of age but is 15 in the Scandinavian countries; the incarceration rate in Germany is nine times less than the U.S. (76 per 100,000 vs. 693 per 100,000);[2] baby hatches are available in all states in the U.S. but not in the UK; in Australia, the number of children coming into state care in June 2021 was almost double the number in 2000–2011,[3] while in New Zealand, during the period 2009/2010 to 2018/2019, the corresponding number decreased by 33.6%,[4] despite the latter having the world's highest teenage suicide rate, and one of the highest rates of child abuse; Manitoba in 2011 had an admission to care rate ten times that of Western Australia;[5] and then there is the U.S., where, in 2020, the infant mortality rate reached 5.44, making it 51st in the world (significantly higher than in dozens of other developed countries such as Sweden 2.15, Japan 1.82 and Australia 3.14).[6]

In all jurisdictions currently being considered – perhaps most obviously the U.S. and Canada – the wealth disparity between high- and low-income families has reached a level of structural inequality, insufficiently mitigated by public service provision which, on the evidence submitted, clearly exacerbates child welfare issues. An adequate framework of such services is essential if many socially disadvantaged families are to achieve and sustain the standard of 'good-enough parenting'. The fact that in 2020, an international body ranked Canada 30th out of 38 affluent countries for childhood wellbeing, while the findings of a 2022 report revealed a significant level of poor mental health among American children,[7] constitute a damning indictment of public health and social care provision for children in North America. It would seem that the leading socio-economic nations are also leaders in child neglect. In the U.S. as in Canada, and to a lesser extent in the other six jurisdictions, being governed by social determinants, the health and welfare interests of children are very much tied to parental socio-economic status.

2 See, *The Crime Report* (2018), at: https://thecrimereport.org/2018/04/10/in-germany-its-hard-to-find-a-young-adult-in-prison/

3 See, Australian Institute of Health and Welfare at: www.aihw.gov.au/child-protection/

4 See, *Oranga Tamariki*, 'Analysis of the Decrease in the Numbers of Children Entering Care' (June 2021), at: www.orangatamariki.govt.nz/assets/Uploads/About-us/Research/Latest-research/Entries-into-care/Analysis-of-the-decrease-in-the-number-of-children-entering-care.pdf

5 See, Brownell, M.D. and Jutte, D.P., 'Administrative Data Linkage as a Tool for Child Maltreatment Research', *Child Abuse & Neglect*, Vol. 37, No. 2 (2013), pp. 120–124.

6 See, the Centers for Disease Control and Prevention's National Vital Statistics System.

7 See, Lebrun-Harris, L.A., Ghandour, R.M. and Kogan, M.C., 'Five-Year Trends in US Children's Health and Well-being, 2016–2020', *JAMA Pediatrics*, Vol. 176, No. 7 (2022), at: https://jamanetwork.com/journals/jamapediatrics/fullarticle/2789946

Indigenous social context

The fact that most Indigenous children entering the public care system are admitted not because of harm wilfully inflicted – by or to them – but because of neglect due to environmental factors that are amenable to remedial intervention should prompt state authorities to direct intervention towards mitigating the prevailing adverse circumstances. The consistent inter-generational gross over-representation of Indigenous[8] children in their respective public welfare and justice systems would suggest that this is not happening, which further suggests that both their welfare interests and rights are severely compromised relative to non-Indigenous children. The circumstances of such children would seem to represent a distinct theme of jurisdictional difference.

Public family law: civil

Perhaps the most interesting civil aspects of jurisdictional difference in the public family law of the countries considered – insofar as they relate to the welfare interests and rights of children – are preventative state intervention, the use of foster care as opposed to residential care and rehabilitation. These and other aspects may offer indications as to the nature of differences between the common law and civil law traditions.

Prevention

Effective early state preventative service provision is clearly crucial if later coercive state intervention to remove children from harm is to be avoided. Mostly, this is addressed through legislation that requires relevant authorities to provide specified services in accordance with specified entitlement criteria. Other standardised preventative measures – such as mandatory reporting of actual or suspected harm to a child – also play their part.

Civil law jurisdictions

In France and Germany, the principle of subsidiarity requires the state to respect and support parents in the upbringing of their children, which is their prerogative right and duty.[9] In Germany, it is probable that subsidiarity has been embedded in the Constitution in order to counter any possible assumption of centralised control of authority at the highest level. In both countries, this principle can be seen in the laws governing the state-family relationship which requires the

8 See, further, for example, at: www.aihw.gov.au/reports/child-protection/child-protection-australia-2020-21/contents/children-receiving-child-protection-services/aboriginal-and-torres-strait-islander-children-in-the-child-protection-system and also at: www.rnz.co.nz/news/national/393208/oranga-tamariki-stats-increase-in-maori-children-taken

9 See: for France, the Civil Code, Articles 371–2; and for Germany, the Basic Law, Article 6(2).

state to provide such resources as may be necessary to ensure that parents can continue to care. The law requiring the state to support families in need would appear to be more explicit in France, more specific as to the range of appropriate services and – by empowering the *juges des enfants* to direct, and thereafter manage, service provision – has a more authoritarian approach to ensuring effective service delivery.

Common law jurisdictions

There is no exact common law equivalent to the aforementioned, certainly not in Ireland and England and Wales, where a strict separation of authority exists between the judiciary and welfare authorities. It is hard to avoid the conclusion that some of this aspect of jurisdictional difference may be attributable to statutory preventative powers being interpreted as discretionary. This may help to explain some of the earlier very troubling common law statistics, illustrated most starkly in New Zealand's record of having some of the highest rates of domestic violence, child abuse and teenage suicides[10] in the developed world despite also having modern and appropriate preventative legislation.

Protection

As a generalisation, it would seem that while the child care population is growing in the developed countries, they are doing so in accordance with a variation in thresholds for state intervention. There are interesting jurisdictional differences in both child care populations and in the provision of placements.

Common law jurisdictions

According to the Australian Institute of Health and Welfare, the number of children becoming the subjects of care and protection orders and placed in out-of-home care, in June 2021, was almost double the number in 2000–2011[11] and rose again by 7% between 30 June 2017 and 30 June 2020.[12] Increases are recorded in many other countries, including the UK, Ireland and the U.S. Curiously, a reverse trend would seem to be dominant in New Zealand, where in the period 2009/2010 to 2018/2019, the total number entering state care had decreased by 33.6%,[13] and where by 2022, the 4,600 in care represented a considerable fall

10 See, further, at: www.newstalkzb.co.nz/on-air/kerre-woodham-mornings/audio/nathan-wallis-new-zealand-ranks-bottom-of-developed-countries-on-youth-mortality-rates/

11 See, Australian Institute of Health and Welfare at: www.aihw.gov.au/child-protection/

12 See, further, at: www.aihw.gov.au/reports/child-protection/child-protection-australia-2019-20/summary

13 See, *Oranga Tamariki*, 'Analysis of the Decrease in the Numbers of Children Entering Care' (June 2021), at: www.orangatamariki.govt.nz/assets/Uploads/About-us/Research/Latest-research/Entries-into-care/Analysis-of-the-decrease-in-the-number-of-children-entering-care.pdf

from the 5,708 in 2017 and seems a little at odds with the reported higher than average rates of child abuse.[14]

Foster care and kinship care

One telling indicator of jurisdictional difference in the preventative role of the state is the existence of a reciprocal parent-state understanding of that role as a public service. This is demonstrated in Ireland by the fact that most children in state care are admitted with the voluntary agreement of their parents – an unusual and perhaps singular characteristic aspect of jurisdictional difference. In New Zealand, state respite care is conditional upon the consent of the child concerned, if 12 years of age or more.

In all common law nations, the first placement preference for a child admitted or committed to state care is a foster home or with relatives. As of 30 June 2021, the vast majority (91%) of the 46,200 children in out-of-home care in Australia were in home-based provision, mostly with relative or kinship carers (54%), or in foster care (36%).[15] At the same time in New Zealand, there were 5,239 children and young people in care and protection, of whom 88% were living with family/whānau or with a caregiver of the same ethnicity.[16] Fostering services in the U.S – as with adoption – are largely privatised, adding a for-profit dimension to the public care system in that country.

Rehabilitation

In New Zealand, the percentage of children and young people in 'return to home' placements is low (less than 10%)[17] and is decreasing. Over the four year period from June 2014 to June 2018, the percentage of children and young people in return to home placements decreased from 9% to 8.3%.[18] The contrast with neighbouring Australia is striking. In 2020–2021, of the approximately 27,300 Australian children in out-of-home care (excluding those on long-term guardianship or custody orders), nearly 5,400 (20%) were reunified with their families of origin.[19]

14 See, further, at: www.orangatamariki.govt.nz/about-us/performance-and-monitoring/quarterly-report/text-only/

15 Note that in 2018–2019, all states and territories adopted a standardised national system for defining for out-of-home care and for related data collection.

16 See, further, at: www.orangatamariki.govt.nz/assets/Uploads/About-us/Performance-and-monitoring/Quarterly-report/September-2021/Oranga-Tamariki-Quarterly-Performance-Report-as-at-September-2021.pdf

17 'Return to home' meaning return to a biological parent.

18 *Oranga Tamariki*, 'OIA Responses, Statistics on Children in Care, Placement Type and Returns Home' (15 November 2018), https://www.orangatamariki.govt.nz/official-information-act/oia-responses/children/

19 See, further, at: www.aihw.gov.au/reports/child-protection/child-protection-australia-2020-21/contents/permanency-outcomes/how-many-children-exited-out-of-home-care-to-a-permanency-outcome

Civil law jurisdictions

France and Germany have been experiencing much the same increase in children requiring care and protection as the common law countries. In 2021, the Youth Welfare Authorities in Germany reported that child endangerment had reached its second highest level since statistics began to be collected in 2012, while the number of children in need of help also hit a new high. The CRC in its 2022 report stated that it 'remains seriously concerned about the high prevalence of violence against children, including sexual exploitation and online violence'.[20] In France, in 2020, there were almost 40,000 officially recorded cases of child sexual abuse.[21] In 2021, 310,525 children were taken into state care which is much the same as in 2020.[22]

Foster care and kinship care

In both France and Germany, a surprisingly large proportion of the child care population is not accommodated in foster families; certainly, more are in residential care than would be the case in the UK and in many other developed countries. The reliance on institutions in preference to foster families – particularly in Germany – for the majority of children in state care, is curious as it is unusual for such developed nations and is out-of-step with well-established research findings that stress the importance of consistent family life for children.[23] This firm policy of keeping state intervention to the minimal level compatible with maintaining parental responsibility and family unity may well correlate with the well-established relatively low use of foster care. In France, in 2007, an estimated 7% of children in care were placed with family members.[24] In Germany, the preferred foster care placement is with a relative.[25] Of the total German foster care population in 2005, approximately 60% of the children were in kinship placements.[26]

Residential care

The fact that a relatively high proportion of out-of-home placements are consistently made in favour of residential facilities is often explained as a default response

20 Ibid, at para 22.
21 See, Statista Research Department (2022), at: www.statista.com/statistics/1246288/monthly-number-sexual-assaults-minors-reported-france/
22 See, further, *Les chiffres clés en protection de l'enfance,* at: https://onpe.gouv.fr/system/files/publication/fs_chiffres_cles_pe_2021.pdf
23 See, for example, Bowlby, J., *Attachment and Loss*, Basic Books, New York, 1969.
24 See, Thoburn, J., 'Globalisation and Child Welfare: Some Lessons from a Cross-National Study of Children in Out-of-Home Care', University of East Anglia Social Work Monographs (2007), at: www.researchgate.net/publication/265357214_Globalisation_and_Child_Welfare_Some_Lessons_from_a_Cross-National_Study_of_Children_in_Out-of-Home_Care
25 See, Kiraly, M. and Humphreys, C., 'It's about the Whole Family: Family Contact for Children in Kinship Care', *Child & Family Social Work*, Vol. 21 (2016).
26 See, Walter, M. and Blandow, J., 'Foster Care in Germany' (2004), at: www.uni-siegen.de/foster-care-research/network_conferences/1st_conference/files/foster_care_germany_-_kindler.pdf

to a lack of foster parents. However, it seems at least possible that it may correlate with both a strong state deference to parental status[27] and family unity and to the, at best, marginal relevance of the paramountcy principle. It might be speculated that the preference for residential care is at least partially due – like the avoidance of non-consensual adoption – to a legal assumption that return to parental care is the objective, and state authorities, therefore, choose placement options that will not be viewed as compromising that legally required outcome. The practice, if not the law, in both France and Germany would seem equivocal as regards whether the objective is restoration of parental status/family unity or protecting the right of the child to have their developmental needs safely and appropriately catered for, perhaps less equivocal in Germany, where the proportion of children in residential accommodation is rarely less than 60% of its child care population.

Rehabilitation

The rate of successful rehabilitation in the civil law countries is extraordinarily poor. In Germany, it has been estimated that family reunification is achieved for no more than 4%–5% of the child care population. In France, judging from the CRC recommendation to the authorities that they should 'facilitate the rehabilitation and social reintegration of children', it would seem that much the same problems exist there.[28] In both countries, instead of being reunited with their families of origin, or being absorbed into adoptive families, most children remain in state care until discharged when they reach 18 years of age. Again, this is curious.

Rehabilitation of a child in state care with their family of origin is in fact firmly mandated in the laws of France[29] and Germany.[30] The Civil Codes of both countries require the authorities to prioritise the safe rehabilitation of a child in state care to their family of origin.[31] In France, this is reinforced by statutes that require planning for family reunification, wherever feasible, for every child taken into state care, and in practice, there is considerable investment in 'the ideology of maintaining the parent – infant relationship at all costs'.[32] While in Germany, there is no explicit equivalent legal obligation, the Constitutional Court has stated that the proportionality principle requires that every possible attempt be made to reunite families.[33] This is reinforced in France by legal requirements for parent-child contact to be maintained and by judicial rulings to the effect that out-of-home placements must not continue unless justified in accordance with Article 375 of the

27 A theory which finds support in the CRC comment in 2022 when it found the German Code to be unduly weighted in favour of parents and recommended that the government 'strengthen efforts to incorporate children's rights explicitly into the Basic Law', at: CRC/C/DEU/CO/5–6, at para 6.

28 CRC/C/FRA/CO/5, at para 54.

29 The Civil Code, Article 375–2.

30 The Civil Code, s 1684, and Art. 6(2) of the Basic Law.

31 For France, see Civil Code, Article 3750–2. For Germany, see the Civil Code, s 1673 et seq.

32 See, Berger, M., *The Failure of Child Protection Services*, Dunod, Paris, 2003.

33 See BVerfG, 13.07.2022, 1 BvR 580/22 and 15.11.2022, 1 BvR 1667/22.

Code. Similarly in Germany, s 1684 of the Civil Code establishes the right – and indeed the duty – of birth parents to maintain contact with their child. Given the clarity and forcefulness of the legal duty to rehabilitate, the consistent failure to do so requires some explanation.

France and Germany are alike in that they have policies which place a high premium on maintaining the relationships conducive to preserving the legal integrity of birth families. In that respect, they differ, arguably, from the UK and the U.S. This shared approach is evident in their approach to foster care, in their joint reluctance to facilitate the termination of birth family relationships by resorting to the non-consensual adoption of children in state care and in their policy – at least in theory – of working towards the return to parental care of children admitted to the public care system. It may be that underlying this jurisdictional difference is a resistance to using the law to break birth parent–child links: it is preferable to allow a child to remain in the anonymity of state care rather than facilitate a break in that linkage and a transfer of attachments, parenting rights and duties to a third party such as a foster parent.

Control

As the child care population increases, so does the need for specialist facilities to cope with that small proportion of children who have mental health and/or behavioural problems. There does not seem to be any significant jurisdictional difference in the function of these units – though France has been repeatedly criticised for the standard of care it provides – and in all jurisdictions, there is a shortage of such facilities.

Public family law: criminal

The welfare principle plays at best a marginal role in the criminal law as it relates to children. The areas of jurisdictional difference that are most relevant – and have been of most concern to the UN CRC – are the age of criminal responsibility and custodial sentences.

Common law jurisdictions

The jurisdictional variation in matters such as the age of criminal responsibility and use of custodial sentences are again interesting but perhaps not indicative of any significant jurisdictional differences.

Age of criminal responsibility

The age at which a child may be legally criminally liable for their actions would appear to be too low – by UN CRC standards – in many jurisdictions: 10 years of age in England and Wales; 12 in Ireland and Canada; while in the U.S., it is mostly at age 7, though 11 for federal crimes. In both Australia and New Zealand, the age of criminal responsibility is set at 10 years.

Custodial sentences

The CRC has expressed concern regarding the use of restraint measures in custodial facilities in England and Wales. It recommends that the authorities 'abolish all methods of restraint against children for disciplinary purposes in all institutional settings, both residential and non-residential, and ban the use of any technique designed to inflict pain on children'.[34] In Ireland, the use of special care orders to authorise a custodial sentence would seem to be used sparingly and for therapeutic purposes. In the U.S., the probability is that juvenile offenders incur a higher rate of custodial sentences – in which African American youth are over-represented – than in other countries,[35] and the sentencing tariff is also higher.[36] In the CANZUS nations, it is the gross over-representation of Indigenous children in custody that is the single most obvious and shared jurisdictional characteristic.

Civil law jurisdictions

As mentioned earlier (see, Chapter 4) in both civil law jurisdictions, juvenile justice policy continues to emphasise the welfare dimension – with its diversional, educational and restorative justice measures – rather than give priority to the control objective as has steadily become the case in the common law nations. The lower end of the sanctions tariff for juvenile offenders is firmly focused on the educative and disciplinary measures necessary to effect successful social rehabilitation.[37] Additionally, the jurisdictional difference between the two civil law countries would seem to be at least as significant as that which differentiates them from their common law counterparts.

Age of criminal responsibility

In France, there is no specific age at which a child can be held criminally liable for his or her conduct. It is for a judge to determine whether a child has attained a sufficient degree of discernment to be held criminally liable. However, in practice,

34 See, the UN Committee on the Rights of the Child, *Concluding Observations: United Kingdom of Great Britain And Northern Ireland*, United Nations, 2016, at para 39(b).

35 The United States, with only 5% of the world's population, has almost 25% of the world's incarcerated population, representing a nationwide rate of imprisonment of approximately 1 out of every 100 persons. See 'The Solitary Confinement of Youth in New York: A Civil Rights Violation', New York Advisory Committee to the U.S. Commission on Civil Rights, December 2014. See also, 'The Pew Center on the States, One in 100: Behind Bars in America' (2008); International Centre For Prison Studies, World Prison Population List (10th ed., 2011).

36 The severity of possible punishments for juvenile offenders has attracted criticism from both the Special Rapporteur on torture and other cruel, inhumane or degrading treatment or punishment (A/HRC/28/685 March 2015, Human Rights Council, Twenty-eighth session, at para78) and the UN CRC (Children's Rights in Juvenile Justice, General Comment No. 10, UN Doc. CRC/C/GC/10 [April 25, 2007]).

37 See, Jörg-Martin Jehle, *Criminal Justice in Germany* (7th ed.), the Federal Ministry of Justice and Consumer Protection, 2019, p. 41.

from the age of 10, a child may be tried in a criminal court and from the age of 13 will be treated in law as an adult. In Germany, children aged 13 years of age or younger cannot be held criminally liable, and none younger than 18 can be prosecuted as adults.[38]

Custodial sentences

In Germany, a notable feature is the low recourse to custodial sentencing. As mentioned earlier, it has been estimated that the incarceration rate in Germany is nine times less than the U.S. (76 per 100,000 vs. 693 per 100,000).[39] Moreover, in Germany, youth offenders will be treated as juveniles until they reach 21 years of age.

In France, the Civil Code directive that the *juge des enfants* should 'always strive to obtain family's consent to the measure envisaged' highlights the weighting given to considerations of welfare rather than justice and is indicative of underlying state deference to family integrity. In practice, however, this approach is not dissimilar to that adopted in Germany, where the emphasis is also less on accountability and more on the needs of the offending child.

Private family law

The pace of change in this area of family law has introduced considerable instability. Advances in medical science have brought challenges to our understanding of some of the more basic building blocks of family law – such as when childhood begins, the protection of embryos and the distinction between procreation and parenting – and the consequent legal complexities can only increase. However, current complications are due not so much to generating family life as to the rate at which families break down, reform and accommodate serial parenting.

Common law jurisdictions

Much the same widening range of family forms now exist across all jurisdictions currently being studied, but for present purposes, the most interesting areas of jurisdictional difference lie in the laws relating to reproductive rights and adoption.

Reproductive rights etc.

Pioneered in the U.S. and, subsequently, at the heart of that country's 'culture wars', reproductive rights are now nowhere more contested, a fact that promises to be a distinctive jurisdictional characteristic of U.S. family law in the immediate future. Specifically, while the laws governing abortion – a corner stone of family

38 Note – under s 828 of the Civil Code – a child aged 7 or older can be held civilly liable for damage he or she has caused.

39 See, *The Crime Report* (2018), at: https://thecrimereport.org/2018/04/10/in-germany-its-hard-to-find-a-young-adult-in-prison/

planning – have stabilised in recent years in most developed nations, they have suddenly become very unsettled in the U.S.

Adoption

In Canada, as in the U.S. – but unlike many other countries, such as Ireland and the UK – the law permits private adoptions, either direct parental placements or mediated by a registered nonprofit or for-profit adoption agency, operating on a domestic or intercountry basis. The fact that an estimated 40%–50% of annual adoptions are arranged privately is a strong indicator of jurisdictional similarity between Canada and its neighbour. In addition, for many years, in both Canada and the U.S., a large proportion of all adoptions have been by step-parents which is not dissimilar to long-established trends in the UK.

Adoption in an Indigenous context

The Indigenous communities of the CANZUS nations have maintained an interpretation of 'adoption' that was and is the polar opposite of the traditional common law model of 'closed' adoption with its characteristic features: a clean break from the child's birth family; anonymity for the parties concerned; leaving birth parent/s and adoptee to come to terms with lifelong loss; and the adopters usually legally in control of identity information. Instead, the Indigenous model offers what appears to be much more welfare-compliant attributes: complete transparency, not just between the two families but also within the community as a whole; a consequent reduction in the probability of personal identity issues and avoidance of any break in cultural links for the adopted child; if welfare issues become apparent, support from community members will be readily available and the adoption can be promptly terminated if necessary; and it also means that the adoptee may build and maintain his or her attachments to birth family members throughout their childhood.

Arguably, over recent decades, the common law model has absorbed many of the characteristics of its Indigenous counterpart which now further accentuate the jurisdictional differences between the common law and civil law as regards adoption.

Civil law jurisdictions

The law in both France and Germany continues to bear vestiges of the traditional respect given to parental rights, in neither has this been wholly eclipsed by the concept of parental responsibilities. In France, the perpetuation of the '*accouchement sous X*' practice, allowing for an absolute and permanent renunciation of all parental rights and responsibilities, is indicative of state reluctance to radically intervene in matters integral to parental status.

Reproductive rights, etc.

In both France and Germany, as in many other developed nations, this most basic of human rights – to found a family – remains unquestioned (see, further, Chapter 2).

Germany differs from France in that the right to do so is recognised by the Constitutional Court and finds protection under Art. 6 of the Constitution.[40] The laws of both, however, are guarded in relation to the terms on which prospective parents can access relevant services. In contrast, the right not to legalise parenting arrangements, and the right to dissolve arrangements that have been legalised by the acquisition of marital status, are matters that in both counties have been left to the discretion of the parties concerned.

Adoption

In France and Germany, public policy has ensured that adoption remains firmly centred in private family law. It is essentially consensual in nature, caters for simple and plenary adoption orders and for the adoption of both children and adults (in Germany, the adoption of children is restricted to the plenary form). It provides for a degree of maternal anonymity, is used primarily and without constraint by step-parents, does not permit the paramountcy principle to have a role in determining a child's eligibility and is subject to legal restrictions as regards 'openness' and information disclosure. Adoption in both countries share the same distinctive jurisdictional characteristics which differentiate it from adoption in the UK and the U.S. In both France and Germany, adoption is fading in significance: traditional third-party adoptions (by an unrelated 'stranger') are rare; it is now mostly used to shore up step families, though in France – unlike Germany – step-parents are confined to 'simple' adoptions which highlights the jurisdictional importance attached to maintaining the legal integrity of birth family relationships in such circumstances.

It would seem that in France as in Germany, and in both to a greater extent than in their common law counterparts, the law emphasises the duty of the relevant authorities – including the judiciary in France – to work in partnership with parents in formulating a plan for addressing the needs or deeds of their children. It is probable that in both countries the paramountcy principle would conflict with traditional presumptions – constitutionally protected in Germany – favouring family unity, parental status and maintenance of the parent-child bond. Similarly, the relatively weaker reach of the welfare principle would explain its lesser cross-sectoral capacity. There is a low level of legal activity in areas such as adoptions from state care and commercial surrogacy because of the corresponding weaker ability of the principle to prevail over other considerations. In neither France nor Germany is there an unequivocal statement in any area of statute law to the effect that the welfare interests of the child must be treated as of paramount importance in determining any particular issue.[41] This, together with tradi-

40 See BVerfG 31, 67 or 36,161; Antoni, in: Hömig/Wolff, Grundgesetz für die Bundesrepublik Deutschland, 12th ed., 2018, p. 131.

41 France: in 1997, the *Conseil d'Etat* ruled that Article 3(1) of UN CROC – the child's interest must be a paramount consideration – was directly applicable to French law. In 2016, the CRC acknowledged

tional presumptions, may lie at the heart of jurisdictional differences between the common law and civil law as regards the welfare interests and rights of children, with consequent implications for the development of hybrid proceedings, which will be explored in the forthcoming *Child Welfare & Rights: a Contemporary Family Law Analysis*.

---

that the *Cour de cassation* and the *Conseil d'Etat* had jointly agreed on its paramountcy weighting but expressed concern that this was not sufficiently integrated in practice and was not always properly assessed and applied in all government actions and decisions. It clearly conflicts with Article 375–1 of the Civil Code. Germany: the Civil Codes, s 1671(2) and s 1680(2) and s 1682, refer to welfare interests but avoid mention of paramountcy; and there is no unequivocal statement in the Constitution declaring that the welfare interests of the child must be treated as of paramount importance in decisions affecting his or her upbringing.

Selected Bibliography

Books and articles

Arney, F., et al., *Enhancing the Implementation of the Aboriginal and Torres Strait Islander Child Placement Principle: Policy and Practice Considerations*, Australian Institute of Family Studies, Canberra, 2015.

Aspell, J., 'Children's Best Interests? A Constitutional Question', *Trinity College Law Review* (2018), at: https://trinitycollegelawreview.org/childrens-best-interests/#_ftnref21

Bartholet, E., 'International Adoption: Current Status and Future Prospects' *ADOPTION*, Vol. 3, No. 1 (Spring 1993).

Bettelheim, B., *Love Is Not Enough*, Free Press, New York, 1950.

Boatswain-Kyte, A., et al., 'Impacts of Race on Family Reunification Etc', *Child Abuse & Neglect*, Vol. 125 (2022), at: www.sciencedirect.com/science/article/abs/pii/S01452 13422000023

Bowlby, J., *Attachment and Loss*, Hogarth Press, London, 1973.

Boyes-Watson, C., 'The Value of Citizen Participation in Restorative/Community Justice: Lessons from Vermont', *Criminology and Public Policy*, Vol. 3 (2004), pp. 687–692.

Bromley, P.M. and Lowe, N.V., *Bromley's Family Law* (8th ed.), Butterworths, London, 1992.

Brownell, M.D. and Jutte, D.P., 'Administrative Data Linkage as a Tool for Child Maltreatment Research', *Child Abuse & Neglect*, Vol. 37, No. 2 (2013), pp. 120–124.

Calkin, S., *Abortion Pills Go Global*, University of California Press, 2023.

Carter, V., 'Prediction of Placement into Out-of-home Care for American Indian/Alaskan Natives Compared to Non-Indians', *Children and Youth Services Review*, Vol. 31, No. 8 (2009), pp. 840–846.

Choate, P. and Tortorelli, C., 'Attachment Theory: A Barrier for Indigenous Children Involved with Child Protection', *International Journal of Environmental Research and Public Health*, Vol. 19, No. 14 (2022), at: www.ncbi.nlm.nih.gov/pmc/articles/PMC9319150/

Colfer, L. and Coulter, C., 'High Court Oversight of Children's Complex Care Needs' (January 2020), at: https://www.childlawproject.ie/publications/high-court-oversight-of-childrens-complex-care-needs/.

Cotterrell, R., *The Sociology of Law: An Introduction*, Butterworths, London, 1984.

Cunneen, C., 'Youth Justice in Australia', *Oxford Academic* (2014), at: https://academic.oup.com/edited-volume/41333/chapter/352357407

Dalen, M. and Saetersdal, B., 'Transracial Adoption in Norway', *Adoption & Fostering*, Vol. 2, No. 4 (1987). Also Ngabonziza, D., 'Inter-country Adoption in Whose Best Interests', *Adoption & Fostering*, Vol. 2, No. 1 (1988).

Deery, C., 'Male Mothers: the Law's struggle to Capture the Modern Family', *The Oxford University Undergraduate Law Journal*, No. X (2021), at: www.law.ox.ac.uk/sites/default/files/migrated/public_law_3.pdf

DeRose, L., et al., *The Cohabitation Go-round: Cohabitation and Family Instability across the Globe*, Social Trends Institute, New York, 2017.

Doek, J.E., van Loon, H. and Vlaardingerbroek, P. (eds), *Children on the Move*, Martinus Nijhoff Publishers, Leiden, The Netherlands, 1996.

Doughty, J., 'Myths and Misunderstanding in Adoption Law and Policy', *Child & Family Law Quarterly*, Vol. 27, No. 4 (2015), pp. 331–353.

Dumaret, A.-M., 'Adoption and Child Welfare Protection in France', at: https://inserm.hal.science/inserm-00476402/file/inserm-00476402_edited.pdf

Eekelaar, J. and Dingwall, R., *The Reform of Child Care Law: A Practical Guide to the Children Act 1989*, Routledge, Abingdon, Oxon, 1990.

Eglin, M., 'Judicial Child Protection in France and England: A Comparative Approach' (June 2001), at: www.afmif.fr/Judicial-child-protection-in.html

Elsea, K.K., 'The Juvenile Crime Debate: Rehabilitation, Punishment or Prevention', *Kansas Journal of Law & Public Policy*, Vol. 5 (1995–1996), p. 135, at: https://heinonline.org/HOL/LandingPage?handle=hein.journals/kjpp5&div=14&id=&page=

Fallon, B., Lefebvre, R., Trocmé, N., et al., 'Denouncing the Continued Overrepresentation of First Nations Children in Canadian Child Welfare' (2019), at: https://cwrp.ca/sites/default/files/publications/FNCIS-2019%20-%20Denouncing%20the%20Continued%20Overrepresentation%20of%20First%20Nations%20Children%20in%20Canadian%20Child%20Welfare%20-%20Final_1%20%282%29.pdf

Fenton-Glynn, C., 'Adoption Without Consent: Update 2016', at: www.europarl.europa.eu/RegData/etudes/STUD/2016/556940/IPOL_STU(2016)556940_EN.pdf

Finkelstein, A., et al., 'Surrogacy Law and Policy in the U.S.', Columbia Law School (2016), at: https://web.law.columbia.edu/sites/default/files/microsites/gender-sexuality/files/columbia_sexuality_and_gender_law_clinic_-_surrogacy_law_and_policy_report_-_june_2016.pdf

Fortin, J., *Children's Rights and the Developing Law*, Butterworths, Oxford, UK, 1998.

Foster, C. and Plowden, J., *The State Under Stress*, Oxford Union Press, Oxford, 1996.

Galm, B. and Derr, R., *Combating Child Abuse and Neglect: Child Protection in Germany – National Report*, Deutsches Jugendinstitut e.V., 2011, at: www.dji.de/fileadmin/user_upload/bibs/DAPHNEGermanReportLayoutFIN.pdf

Gilbert, R., et al., 'Child Maltreatment: Variation in Trends and Policies in Six Developed Countries', *Lancet* (2011), at: https://scholar.google.com/scholar_lookup?hl=en&publication_year=2011&author=R+Gilbert&author=J+Fluke&author= M+O%27Donnell&author=A+Gonzalez-Izquierdo&author=M+Brownell&author=P+Gulliver&title=Child+maltreatment%3A+variation+in+trends+and+policies+in+six+developed+countries

Goldstein, J., Freud, A. and Solnit, A., *Beyond the Best Interests of the Child*, Free Press, New York, 1973.

Hart, H.L.A., *The Concept of Law* (2nd ed.), Clarendon Law Series, Oxford University Press, Oxford, 1994.

Hilpern, K., 'The Daddy of All Game Shows', *The Independent Review* (5 January 2005).

Jacobs, M., *A Generation Removed: The Fostering & Adoption of Indigenous Children in the Postwar World*, University of Nebraska Press, Lincoln, 2014.

Jehle, J-M., *Criminal Justice in Germany* (7th ed.), the Federal Ministry of Justice and Consumer Protection, Berlin, Germany, 2019.

Kelsen, H., *The Pure Theory of Law*, The Lawbook Exchange Ltd., New Jersey, 2009.

Kilkelly, U., 'Child and Family Law', in Kilkelly (ed.), *ECHR and Irish Law*, Jordans, Bristol, UK, 2004.

Kilkelly, U., 'Protecting Children's Rights under the ECHR: The Role of Positive Obligations', *NILQ,* Vol. 61, No. 3 (2010), pp. 245–261.

Kiraly, M. and Humphreys, C., 'It's about the Whole Family: Family Contact for Children in Kinship Care', *Child & Family Social Work*, Vol. 21 (2016).

Kreider, R.M., 'Adopted Children and Stepchildren: 2000' (U.S. Census Bureau, Census 2000 Special Reports, August 2003). The full Report is available at: www.census.gov/prod/2003pubs/censr-6.pdf

Laycock, D., 'The Broader Case for Affirmative Action: Desegregation, Academic Excellence, and Future Leadership', *Tulane Law Review*, Vol. 78, No. 6 (2021), at: www.tulanelawreview.org/pub/volume78/issue6/the-broader-case-for-affirmative-action

Lebrun-Harris, L.A., Ghandour, R.M. and Kogan, M.C., 'Five-Year Trends in US Children's Health and Well-being, 2016–2020', *JAMA Pediatrics*, Vol. 176, No. 7 (2022), at: https://jamanetwork.com/journals/jamapediatrics/fullarticle/2789946

Lowe, N.V., 'The Allocation of Parental Rights and Responsibilities: The Position in England and Wales', *Family Law Quarterly*, Vol. 39 (2005), pp. 267–268.

Maidment, S., *Child Custody and Divorce*, Croom Helm, Kent, UK, 1985.

Matthews, K.R.W. and Morali, D., 'Can We Do That Here? An Analysis of US Federal and State Policies Guiding Human Embryo and Embryoid Research', *Journal of Law and the Biosciences*, Vol. 9, No. 1 (2022), at: www.ncbi.nlm.nih.gov/pmc/articles/PMC9183789/

McCafferty, P., Duffy, J. and Hayes, D., 'Permanency Decisions in Child Welfare: A Qualitative Study', *The British Journal of Social Work*, Vol. 51, No. 6 (September 2021), pp. 2134–2154.

McGlade, H., *Our Greatest Challenge*, Aboriginal Studies Press, Canberra, ACT, 2012.

McGlade, H., 'My Journey into Child Protection and Aboriginal Family Led Decision Making', *Australian Feminist Law Journal* (2020), pp. 1–18.

Mnookin, R.H., *In the Interest of Children*, W.H. Freeman and Company, New York, 1985.

Möller, K., 'Proportionality: Challenging the Critics', *International Journal of Constitutional Law*, Vol. 10, No. 3 (2012), at: https://doi.org/10.1093/icon/mos024

Morris, A. and Giller, H., *Understanding Juvenile Justice*, Croom Helm, London, 1987.

Murray, S., 'Breaking the Link Between Disability and Child and Whanau Poverty', *Policy Quarterly*, Vol. 14, No. 4 (2018), at: www.victoria.ac.nz/__data/assets/pdf_file/0003/1713621/Murray.pdf

Newman, E., 'History of Transracial Adoption: A New Zealand Perspective', *American Indian Quarterly*, Vol. 37, No. 1–2 (2013), pp. 237–257.

Nichols, R.L., 'From the Sixties Scoop to Baby Veronica: Transracial Adoption of Indigenous Children in the USA and Canada', in Shackleton, M. (ed.), *International Adoption in North American Literature and Culture: Transnational, Transracial, and Transcultural Narratives*, Palgrave Macmillan, Helsinki, 2017.

Norman, J. and Oborne, P., *The Conservative Case for the Human Rights Act*, Liberty (National Council for Civil Liberties), London, 2009, at: https://jessenorman.typepad.com/Churchills_Legacy.pdf

Nowak, M., 'United Nations Global Study on Children Deprived of Liberty' (2019), at: https://omnibook.com/Global-Study-2019.

O'Halloran, K., *The Principle of the Welfare of the Child: A History*, Routledge, 2022; *Children & the Law: Shaping the Modern Welfare Principle in the British Isles*, Routledge, 2022; *Children, the Law and the Welfare Principle: Perspectives from North America*, Routledge, 2023; *Children, the Law and the Welfare Principle: Perspectives from Australia and New Zealand*, Routledge, 2023; *Children, the Law and the Welfare Principle: Civil Law Perspectives from France and Germany*, Routledge, 2024; and *Children, the Law and the Welfare Principle: European Judicial Perspectives*, Routledge, 2024.

Parsons, T., *Structure and Process in Modern Societies*, Kegan Paul, Trench, Trubner & Co. Ltd., London, 1960.

Pascoe, C.J., 'Issues of Forced Adoption and International Commercial Surrogacy', Federal Court of Australia, Melbourne (2 October 2013), at: www.law.monash.edu.au/about-us/events/chie-judge-pascoe-dpeech-notes.pdf

Pew Charitable Trust Report, 'Time for Reform: A Matter of Justice for American Indian and Alaskan Native Children' (2007), at: https://www.pewtrusts.org/en/research-and-analysis/reports/2007/11/19/time-for-reform-a-matter-of-justice-for-american-indian-and-alaskan-native-children

Piaget, J., *The Moral Judgment of the Child*, Basic Books, London, 1932.

Piaget, J., *The Psychology of the Child*, Basic Books, London, 1972.

Prentice, K., Blair, B., & O'Mullan, C., 'Sexual and Family Violence: Overcoming Barriers to Service Access for Aboriginal and Torres Strait Islander Clients', *Australian Social Work*, Vol. 70, No. 2 (2017), pp. 241–252.

Rawls, J., *Justice as Fairness*, Harvard University Press, Cambridge, 2001.

Robertson, J.A., 'Reproductive Technology in Germany and the United States: An Essay in Comparative Law and Bioethics', *Columbia Journal of Transnational Law* (2004), pp. 189–227.

Robcis, C., *The Law of Kinship: Anthropology, Psychoanalysis and the Family in France*, Cornell University Press, 2013.

Rutter, C. and Walker, S., 'Infant Mortality Inequities for Māori in New Zealand: A Tale of Three Policies', *International Journal for Equity in Health*, Vol. 20, No. 10 (2021),

Sargent, S., 'Adoption and Looked After Children: A Comparison of Legal Initiatives in the U.K. and the USA', *Adoption & Fostering*, BAAF, Vol. 27, No. 2 (2003), pp. 44–52.

Schrödter, M., 'German Residential Care: Doing Extremely Well in Doing the Wrong Thing', Conference paper presented at 'The international Social Work & Society Academy', Sofia, Bulgaria (August 2014),

Selman, P., 'Global Statistics for Intercountry Adoption: Receiving States and States of origin 2004–2015' (2016), at: https://assets.hcch.net/docs/3bead31e-6234-44ae-9f4e-2352b190ca21.pdf

Spaander, M.M., 'The European Court of Human Rights and the Emergence of Human Germline Genome Editing – The Right to Life and the Right to (Artificial) Procreation', in Slokenberga, S., Minssen, T. and Nordberg, A. (eds), *Governing, Protecting, and Regulating the Future of Genome Editing*, Brill, 2023.

Swain, S., '"Homes are Sought for these Children": Locating Adoption within the Australian Stolen Generations Narrative', *American Indian Quarterly*, Vol. 37, No. 1–2 (2013), pp. 203–217.

Thoburn, J., 'Globalisation and Child Welfare: Some Lessons from a Cross-national Study of Children in Out-of-home Care', *School of Social Work and Psychosocial Studies*, Vol. 228, University of East Anglia, 2007.

Turner, J.N., 'Adoption or Anti-Adoption? Time for a National Review of Australian Law', *James Cook University Law Review*, Vol. 2 (1995), p. 43.

UNICEF, 'Report Card' (2021), at: www.unicef.org.nz/stories/new-report-card-shows-that-new-zealand-is-failing-its-children

Vreeland, A.B. 'The Criminalization of Child Welfare in New York City: Sparing the Child or Spoiling the Family?', *Fordham Urban Law Journal*, Vol. 27, No. 3 (2000), pp. 1053–1103.

Walker, J., 'Barriers to Engagement', Address to the Justice for Young People Conference, Adelaide, Australia (7 November 2018), at: www.districtcourts.govt.nz/youth-court/publications/barriers-to-engagement-enabling-full-participation-in-the-justice-system-for-young-people/

Walter, M. and Blandow, J., 'Foster Care in Germany' (2004), at: www.uni-siegen.de/foster-care-research/network_conferences/1st_conference/files/foster_care_germany_-_kindler.pdf

Welstead, M., 'Every Child Should Have a Mother', *Fam Law,* Vol. 1099 (2020), p. 1102.

Whittaker, J.K. et al., *Revitalizing Residential Care for Children and Youth: Cross-National Trends and Challenges*, Oxford University Press, 2022.

Willis, M., 'Non-disclosure of violence in Australian Indigenous Communities', in *Trends and Issues in Crime and Criminal Justice*, No. 405, Australian Institute of Criminology, 2011.

Wolf, K., 'Promoting the Positive Development of Foster Children: Establishing Research in Germany', *Adoption & Fostering*, Vol. 36, No. 1 (2012), pp. 40–51, at p. 49.

Wolfson, R., 'Concurrent Planning: A Route to Earlier Permanence for Young Children', *Seen and Heard*, Vol. 23, No. 2 (2012), pp. 46–58.

Young, S., Greer, B. and Church, R., 'Juvenile Delinquency, Welfare, Justice and Therapeutic Interventions: A Global Perspective', *BJPsych Bulletin*, Vol. 41, No. 1 (2017), pp. 21–29.

Reports

Adolescent and Children's Trust (TACT) and the Centre for Research on the Child and Family, University of East Anglia, *Looked after Children and Offending: Reducing Risk and Promoting Resilience*, TACT, Norwich, 2012.

Adoption Authority of Ireland, at: https://aai.gov.ie/en/

Adoption Board, *Annual Report 2006*, Government Publications, Dublin.

Australian Government, Steering Committee for the Review of Government Services Provision, *Overcoming Indigenous Disadvantage: Key Indicators 2016*, Productivity Commission, Canberra, 2016.

Australian Institute of Health and Welfare, at: www.indigenoushpf.gov.au/measures/1-20-infant-child-mortality. Also, at: www.aihw.gov.au/reports/child-protection/child-protection-australia-2020-21/contents/children-receiving-child-protection-services/aboriginal-and-torres-strait-islander-children-in-the-child-protection-system

Brussels Times, The, 'Eight-year-old Child Reportedly Locked Up for Life in Germany' (22 April 2023), at: www.brusselstimes.com/318698/eight-year-old-child-reportedly-locked-up-for-life-in-germany

Burton, J., et al., 'The Aboriginal and Torres Strait Islander Child Placement Principle: A Guide to Support Implementation', The Secretariat of National Aboriginal and Islander Child Care (2018), at: https://www.aihw.gov.au/reports/child-protection/atsicpp-indicators/contents/background.

Canadian Bar Association (Child and Youth Law section), 'Alternative Report to the UN Committee on the Rights of the Child' (2020), at: http://rightsofchildren.ca/wp-content/uploads/2020/03/CBA-Report-for-Review-of-Childrens-Rights-in-Canada.pdf.

Canadian Coalition for the Rights of Children, et al., Press Release (16 May 2022).

ChildPact, 'The Harm of Institutionalisation: Putting Child Protection and Family Care at the Heart of EU External Action' (2017), at: https://codeofgoodpractice.com/wp-content/uploads/2019/05/Lumos-Putting-Child-Protection-and-Family-care-at-the-heart-of-EU-External-Action.pdf

CoE, Committee of Ministers, Recommendation CM/Rec(2005)5 on the Rights of children living in residential institutions (16 March 2005).

CoE, Committee of Ministers, Recommendation CM/Rec(2008)11 on the European Rules for juvenile offenders subject to sanctions or measures (2008).

CoE, Committee of Ministers, *Children and Young People in Care*, Government Publications, Strasbourg, 2009.

CoE, Committee of Ministers, Recommendation CM/Rec(2010)2 on deinstitutionalisation and community living of children with disabilities (3 February 2010).

CoE, Committee of Ministers, Recommendation CM/Rec(2011)12 on Children's rights and social services friendly to children and families (16 November 2011).

CoE, Directive 2013/48/EU on the Right of Access to a Lawyer (2013); and Directive 2016/800/EU on Procedural Safeguards (2016).

CoE, Family Reunification Directive 2003/86/EC on the Right to Family Reunification (2003).

CoE, *Guidelines on Child Friendly Justice*, Government Publications, Strasbourg, 2010.

CRC, *Concluding Observations: Australia*, 2012, CRC/c/AUS/CO/42012.

CRC, *Concluding Observations of the Committee on the Combined Third and Fourth Periodic Reports of Ireland* (2016).

CRC, *Concluding Observations on the Sixth Periodic Report of the United Kingdom of Great Britain and Northern Ireland* (2016), CRC/C/GBR/CO/5

CRC, *General Comment No. 10* (2007) on children's rights in juvenile justice (2007), CRC/C/GC/07

CRC, *General Comment No. 12* (2009) on the right of the child to be heard, (2009), CRC/C/GC/12

CRC, *General Comment No. 13* (2011).

CRC, *General Comment No. 14* (2013) on the right of the child to have his/her best interests taken as a primary consideration, CRC/C/GC/14

CRC, *General Comment No. 24* (2019) on children's rights in the child justice system.

CRC, 'Praise Germany for Prosecuting International Perpetrators of Sexual Abuse against Children', at: www.ohchr.org/en/press-releases/2022/09/experts-committee-rights-child-praise-germany-prosecuting-international

Crown Prosecution Service (England and Wales), at: www.cps.gov.uk/legal-guidance/restorative-justice

Department of Children and Youth Affairs, 'Review and Consultation in Respect of the Potential Introduction of Open or Semi-Open Adoption in Ireland' (2019), at: https://assets.gov.ie/38717/3defc42d3e84425ea00e621d1610f800.pdf

Department of Justice, 'Indigenous Youth Roundtables', at: www.justice.gc.ca/eng/cj-jp/yj-jj/tools-outils/iyr-trja.html#ftnref1

Donovan, K., 'Real Mothers for Abandoned Children', *Law & Society Review* (2002), p. 1.

Eglin, M., 'Judicial Child Protection in France and England: A Comparative Approach' (June 2001), at: www.afmjf.fr/Judicial-child-protection-in.html

EU, *EU Framework of Law for Children's Rights*, European Parliament, Policy Department, Brussels, 2012.

EU, European Parliament and Council of the European Union, Directive 2012/29/EU (2012) (the 'Victim's Rights Directive').

EU, European Parliament and Council of the European Union, Directive 2013/48/EU (2013) on the Right of Access to a Lawyer.

EU, European Parliament and Council of the European Union, Directive 2016/800/EU (2016) on procedural safeguards for children suspected or accused in criminal proceedings, OJ 2016 L 132/1.

EU, *The EU Strategy on the Rights of the Child 2021–2024*, European Commission, 2021.

EU Agency for Fundamental Human Rights, 'Guardianship Systems for Children Deprived of Parental Care in the EU', at: https://fra.europa.eu/sites/default/files/fra_uploads/fra-2018-guardianship-systems-in-the-eu-summary_en.pdf

European Court of Human Rights, 'Guide on Article 8 of the Convention – Right to Respect for Private and Family Life' (2022), at: www.echr.coe.int/documents/d/echr/guide_art_8_eng

European Parliament's Committee on Civil Liberties, Justice and Home Affairs, *EU Framework of Law for Children's Rights*, 2012.

Fair and Just Prosecution Report, 'Lessons Learned from Germany: Promoting Developmentally Appropriate and Rehabilitative Youth and Young Adult Justice' (2022), at: https://fairandjustprosecution.org/wp-content/uploads/2022/06/FJP-Germany-Youth-Justice-Brief.pdf

Fallon, B., Lefebvre, R., Trocmé, N., et al., 'Denouncing the Continued Overrepresentation of First Nations Children in Canadian Child Welfare' (2019), at: https://cwrp.ca/sites/default/files/publications/FNCIS-2019%20-%20Denouncing%20the%20Continued%20Overrepresentation%20of%20First%20Nations%20Children%20in%20Canadian%20Child%20Welfare%20-%20Final_1%20%282%29.pdf

Family-Matters-Report-2022, at: www.familymatters.org.au/wp-content/uploads/2022/11/20221123-Family-Matters-Report-2022-1.pdf

Fenton-Glynn, C., 'Adoption Without Consent: A Report for the PETTI Committee' (2015), at: www.europarl.europa.eu/RegData/etudes/STUD/2015/519236/IPOL_STU(2015)519236_EN.pdf

Galm, B. and Derr, R., *Combating Child Abuse and Neglect: Child Protection in Germany – National Report*, Deutsches Jugendinstitut e.V., 2011, at: www.dji.de/fileadmin/user_upload/bibs/DAPHNEGermanReportLayoutFIN.pdf

Gilbert, R., et al., 'Child Maltreatment: Variation in Trends and Policies in Six Developed Countries', *Lancet* (2011), at: https://scholar.google.com/scholar_lookup?hl=en&publication_year=2011&author=R+Gilbert&author=J+Fluke&author=M+O%27Donnell&author=A+Gonzalez-Izquierdo&author=M+Brownell&author=P+Gulliver&title=Child+maltreatment%3A+variation+in+trends+and+policies+in+six+developed+countries

Global Slavery Index, at: www.walkfree.org/global-slavery-index/2018/findings/country-studies/germany/

Gough, P., et al., 'An Overview of the Child Welfare Systems in Canada', *International Journal of Child Health and Human Development*, Vol. 2, No. 3-Special Issue.

Guardian, The, at: www.theguardian.com/world/2018/mar/08/study-one-in-four-new-zealand-children-reported-welfare-agencies

Guardian, The, at: www.theguardian.com/society/2018/nov/03/england-adoption-rates-falling-as-ivf-improves-says-senior-official

Guardian, The, at: www.theguardian.com/world/2021/jan/22/new-zealand-child-welfare-head-resigns-amid-furore-over-maori-baby-separations-oranga-tamariki

Guardian, The, at: www.theguardian.com/global-development/2021/sep/29/canada-indigenous-children-first-nations-trudeau

Hague, The, *The Report of The Hague's Special Commission on the Practical Operation of the Convention*, The Hague, 2005.

Hague, The, The Permanent Bureau, *The Implementation and Operation of the 1993 Hague International Adoption Convention: A Guide to Good Practice*, The Hague, 2008.

Hartney, C. and Silva, F., 'Justice for Some: Differential Treatment of Youth of Color in the Justice System', National Council on Crime and Delinquency (publishers), 2007, at: https://search.issuelab.org/resource/and-justice-for-some-differential-treatment-of-youth-of-color-in-the-justice-system.html

Houghton Committee, *Report of the Departmental Committee on the Adoption of Children*, (Cmnd 5107), HMSO, London, 1972.

Huffington Post, 'UNICEF Child Well-Being Index: Canada Ranked 17th Out of 29 Wealthy Nations' (10 October 2013), at: www.huffingtonpost.ca/2013/04/10/unicef-child-well-being-canada_n_3050119.html

Human Rights Committee, *Communication No. 201/1985* (views adopted on 27 July 1988, UN Doc. A/43/40, at pp. 230–241).

Inter-American Commission on Human Rights, 'Children and Adolescents in the United States' Adult Criminal Justice System' (2018), p. 9. See, further, at: www.oas.org/en/iachr/reports/pdfs/Children-USA.pdf at p. 61.

International Working Group of the International Association of Youth and Family Judges and Magistrates, 'Guidelines on Children in Contact with the Justice System' (2016), at: https://aimjf.info/wp-content/uploads/2022/09/Guidelines_-_ENG_-_Ratified_17.04.26.pdf.

Joint Oireachtas Committee on Justice and Equality, *Report on Reform of the Family Law System*, 2019.

Jordan's Principle Working Group, 'Without Denial, Delay, or Disruption: Ensuring First Nation Children's Access to Equitable Services through Jordan's Principle' (2015), at: www.afn.ca/uploads/files/jordans_principle-report.pdf

Ko Te Wā Whakawhiti, It's Time For Change: A Māori Inquiry into Oranga Tamariki – Summary Report (2020), at: https://whanauora.nz/wp-content/uploads/2021/06/EXECUTIVE-SUMMARY-REPORT.pdf

Kreider, R.M., 'Adopted Children and Stepchildren: 2000', U.S. Census Bureau, Census 2000 Special Reports (August 2003), at: www.census. gov/prod/2003pubs/censr-6.pdf

Law Council of Australia, 'Minimum age of Criminal Responsibility' (2019), at: www.lawcouncil.asn.au/files/pdf/policy-statement/AMA%20and%20LCA%20Policy%20Statement%20on%20Minimum%20Age%20of%20Criminal%20Responsibility.pdf?21fb2a76-c61f-ea11-9403-005056be13b5

Madden, R., 'Children with Disabilities in Australia', *Australian Institute of Health and Welfare*, AIHW cat. no. DIS 38, Canberra (2004).

Ministry of Social Development, 'Child and Youth Offending Patterns – Research Reports', at p. 4. See further, at: www.msd.govt.nz/about-msd-and-our-work/publications-resources/research/child-and-youth-offending-patterns/index.html

National Center for Juvenile Justice, 'Juvenile Arrest Rates by Offense, Sex, and Race (1980–2011)' (February 2014).

National Inquiry into Missing and Murdered Indigenous Women and Girls, *Reclaiming Power and Place*, Ottawa, 2019.

O'Mahony, C., Burns, K. and Brennan, R., 'Voluntary Care in Ireland Study (2018–21)', at: www.ucc.ie/en/appsoc/resconf/res/voluntarycareinirelandstudy2018-2021/

Ombudsman for Children's Office, 'Molly Two Years On: Have Tusla and the HSE Delivered on Commitments to Children with a Disability in the Care of the State?' (2020), p. 5, at: www.oco.ie/app/uploads/2020/01/Molly-Two-Years-On.pdf.

Poverty Report (2020/21), at: https://quakersocialaction.org.uk/sharing-our-learning/poverty-uk?gclid=Cj0KCQiAhomtBhDgARIsABcaYynLgdO-l6pUPS1qnya4RlrB-vyvuxJwQ2EGK1oPQoR-czCZxqJpPMcaAoBWEALw_wcB

Practice Note: Lawyer for the Child: Code of Conduct (2007).

Quellette, F-R., 'The Social Temporalities of Adoption and the Limits of Plenary Adoption', in Briggs, L. and Maure, D. (eds), *International Adoption*, New York University Press, 2009.

Reddy, J., 'The Youth Justice System in Ireland: A Review (revised)', Research Evidence into Policy, Programmes and Practice (REPPP) Project, University of Limerick (2022), at: www.drugsandalcohol.ie/37979/1/Review_of_Irish_youth_justice-2022.pdf

Roy, A., McGill, B. and Fenn, L., *Children & Young People with Complex Needs in the ACT Youth Justice System*, published by the ACT Children & Young People Commissioner, 2016.

Royal Commission of Inquiry (NZ), 'Care to Custody: Incarceration Rates Research Report' (2022), at: www.abuseincare.org.nz/our-progress/library/v/500/care-to-custody-incarceration-rates-research-report

Scott, D., 'Understanding Child Neglect' (2014), at: https://aifs.gov.au/resources/policy-and-practice-papers/understanding-child-neglect

Senate Community Affairs References Committee, 'Commonwealth Contribution to Former Forced Adoption Policies and Practices', Commonwealth of Australia, Canberra (2012).

Step Family Foundation, at: www.stepfamily.org

Stephen, E., 'Child Protection' (2020), at: https://talkingtroublenz.org/wp-content/uploads/2020/12/Emily-Stephen-SLT-child-protection.pdf

UN, *Rules for the Protection of Juveniles Deprived of their Liberty*, 1990 (Havana Rules).

UN, *Guidelines for the Prevention of Juvenile Delinquency,* 1994 (Riyadh Guidelines).

UN Committee on the Rights of the Child, *Concluding Observations: United Kingdom of Great Britain And Northern Ireland*, United Nations, 2008.

UN Committee on the Rights of the Child, *Concluding Observations: United Kingdom of Great Britain And Northern Ireland*, United Nations, 2016.

UN CRC, *General Comment No. 10* (2007) on Children and juvenile justice.

UN CRC, *General Comment No. 24* (2007) on Children's rights in juvenile justice.

UN Dept. of Economic and Social Affairs, *State of the World's Indigenous Peoples: Indigenous Peoples' Access to Health Services*, United Nations, 2016.

UN Economic and Social Council, Resolution 2005/20, *Guidelines on Justice in Matters Involving Child Victims and Witnesses of Crime*, 22 July 2005.

UN Standard Minimum Rules for the Administration of Juvenile Justice, 1985. See, further, at: www.ohchr.org/en/instruments-mechanisms/instruments/united-nations-standard-minimum-rules-administration-juvenile

United Nations, Committee on the Rights of the Child (CRC) (2009), *General Comment No. 12* (2009) on the right of the child to be heard, CRC/C/GC/12, 1 July 2009.

United Nations, *Guidelines for the Alternative Care of Children*, UN Doc. A/HRC/11/L.13, (2009).

Warrki Jarrinjaku, ACRS Project Team, *Warrki Jarrinjaku Jintangkamanu Purananjaku: Aboriginal Child Rearing and Associated Research*, Department of Family and Community Services, Canberra, 2002.

Wild, R. and Anderson, P., *Little Children Are Sacred, Report of the Northern Territory Board of Inquiry into the Protection of Aboriginal Children from Sexual Abuse*, Board of Inquiry into the Protection of Aboriginal Children from Sexual Abuse, Darwin, NT, 2007.

Index

Made in the USA
Las Vegas, NV
19 September 2026

67c840a5-c0e4-42e7-9f18-fe66d69b4e9aR01